Co-operation and the
Owenite socialist communities
in Britain, 1825–45

R. G. Garnett

Co-operation and the
Owenite socialist communities
in Britain, 1825–45

Manchester University Press

© 1972 Ronald George Garnett

Published by the University of Manchester
at the University Press
316–324 Oxford Road, Manchester M13 9NR
UK ISBN 0 7190 0501 9

Distributed in the USA by
Humanities Press Inc
303 Park Avenue South, New York, N.Y. 10010

Made and printed in Great Britain by
William Clowes & Sons, Limited, London, Beccles and Colchester

Contents

Illustrations	vi
Introduction	vii
Acknowledgements	xi
1 Communitarianism	1
2 Robert Owen and the Owenite contribution to co-operative socialist community experiments, 1820–30	41
3 Orbiston, 1825–27	65
4 Ralahine, 1831–33	100
5 Owenism during the 1830s	130
6 Queenwood, 1839–45	165
7 Aftermath and conclusions	214
Bibliography	241
Index	261

Illustrations

Maps

Orbiston, Lanarkshire   *page* 66

Ralahine, Co. Clare   113

Queenwood, East Tytherley, Hampshire   168

Plates

The site of Orbiston House, now park land adjoining the golf
course   *facing page* 130

Orbiston community pillars, now standing in the Sixth District
Council park: the only relics remaining of the community
house   130

Ralahine castle today   131

Farm buildings and cottages at Ralahine   131

Farm buildings on the Queenwood estate (from a contemporary drawing by W. G. Herdman, by courtesy of the University of London Library)   146

Harmony Hall, as Queenwood College, before the fire of June
1902 (from the *Illustrated London News*, 21 June 1902, by
courtesy)   146

The masters' cottages, now converted into a house, the home of
J. Fawcett, Esq., of Queenwood farm, Broughton, Hampshire   147

The former chapel (on the right) and laundry room, now farm
cottages at Queenwood farm, in 1971.   147

Introduction

The subject matter of this study falls within the broad framework of Owenite socialism and the genesis of the co-operative movement in Britain.

It is possible to study Owenism from at least four approaches: first, a tracing of the historical antecedents of Owenite and early socialist thought; second, an organisational study of the institutions of the Owenites; third, an interpretation of the influence of Robert Owen on his followers; fourth, an appraisal of communitarian thought and experiments. There is considerable overlap between these approaches and a need to relate each of them to other strands of the working class movement.

An investigation and an appraisal of communitarian thought and experiments receive most emphasis in this book because of the lack of any adequate historical attention to communitarianism in the setting of early nineteenth-century Britain, despite the relevance of the subject. Moreover, this approach promises to widen our knowledge of working class aspirations, beliefs and organisational experience, as it encompasses certain neglected aspects of social and industrial change: analysing the impact of industrialisation in terms of Owenite socialist reaction should contribute a new dimension to our understanding of maturing capitalism.

Robert Owen's influence was so diffuse that there are immediate problems of delineation, but it would seem appropriate to deal primarily with the dissemination of his ideas within the identifiable circle of his followers. Owenism sought to remodel the whole of society; hence any worthwhile assessment of its activities must, on balance, veer towards sociology rather than attempt a survey of chiliastic doctrine. Specific reference will be made to the social influence and the relationships of Owenism to other aspects of the working class movement only in so far as they contained elements of social reform programmes involving community projects. A detailed investigation of the relationships of Owenism to all other sections of the working class and other reform movements must remain as a suitable topic for further study.

The present work seeks to place Robert Owen in clearer perspective by examining how and to what extent his precepts were implemented, and, more particularly, to analyse the connections between Owen, the Owenites and the early co-operators, an exercise which in turn will help to determine the true origins of the co-operative movement.

Community experiments were the main continuing interest and activity of the Owenites and the present study is the first full-scale critical assessment of the Owenite communities in Britain on a comparative basis. A further outcome of this approach should be a deeper appreciation of the Owenites, who have been too much overlooked in all previous authoritative works on the history of the working class movement. The strength of the Owenites lay not in their numbers, which were far exceeded by the members of friendly societies, Chartists and trade unionists, but in their intense social questioning. Their contribution, as with Owen himself, was not in the consistency of their social remedies but in the dissemination of their ideas and in their demonstration that drastic reform of society need not call for politically revolutionary methods. Perhaps the most apposite lesson modern society can learn from the Owenites will be derived through a study of their communal experience of dealing with the perennial problem of reconciling individual incentive and participation with efficient decision-making in the democratic process.

Historical treatment of the growth of the co-operative movement is at best uneven, at worst parochial and apologetic; too many writers have identified co-operation with the consumer movement and have adumbrated Rochdale *ad nauseam*. The co-operative movement has suffered from the outpouring of too many publications from within the movement which remain largely unread.[1] More specifically, there have been no worthwhile studies of co-operation before the Rochdale Pioneers, except as oblique references in general histories of socialism and the working class movement, as introductory chapters in textbooks on co-operation, or in biographies of Robert Owen.

1 R. G. Garnett, 'Records of Early Co-operation', *Local Historian*, vol 9, No. 4, 1970.

The nature and contribution of Owenite ideology and the experience of the community experiments have also suffered from being classified by Marx and Engels as Utopian–socialist, and, as such, Owenism has been scorned as having no awareness of historical development or political realism. The stigma of Communist disparagement should not, however, diminish the importance of the Owenite movement, as Marx and Engels were not in as strong a position as we are to appreciate the extent of Owenite influence.

Lastly, this study speculates on latter-day influences of communitarian experience on social ideas and planning. The period 1825–45 covers the main subject matter: Orbiston community was established in 1825, and the last Owenite settlement at Queenwood broke up in 1845, bringing about the disruption of the Rational Society and so ending any further concerted Owenite activity. But 1825 to 1845 is also appropriate on other grounds—by the mid-nineteenth century industrialism had so matured that working class institutions, and to a lesser extent working class attitudes, were compelled to come to terms with the economic realities of capitalism, once working men eschewed the revolutionary alternative. Before 1850 it was possible at least to visualise the Owenite alternative; after 1850 the vindication of Owenite questions and remedies could only be through their percolation into other minds and measures. Early Victorian England had much social optimism, despite the uncovering of many social problems. Emancipating slaves or providing cheap lodging houses, public baths and libraries was thought to be within the competence of middle class good works. The age was distinctly amateur in its approach, especially when dealing with matters of social reform: Owenism differs only in the implicit comprehensiveness of its proposals. After 1850 society came more predominantly under the influence and control of specialists and professionals. Social inquisitiveness remained, but it uncovered such extensive problems that no one could fully contemplate, let alone devise, such sweeping remedies as would be needed to overlap (say) sectors of employment, health, housing and education within an urban environment. It is possible, however, to discern the Owenite contribution to many of the disparate reform measures from the latter half of the nineteenth century for providing improved living conditions and welfare. Owenism could not have survived beyond 1850, but even if it had, it would have been persecuted by the Establishment because of its collectivist implications, whereas during 1825–45 one could hazard that Owenism, if it had avoided anti-religious propaganda, would have received an even easier passage than it did in practice, as it was largely thought of as an exercise in working class self-help to provide poor law colonies under the benevolent guidance of Mr Owen of New Lanark.

Acknowledgements

The present work, which is a revised version of a thesis accepted for the degree of Doctor of Philosophy of London University, aims to provide a survey and an interpretation of the content and form of Owenism, seen, as it were, on the ground. It is written from a historian's viewpoint and any commentary on our present-day concern about 'community' should be read as the observations of a mid-twentieth century layman, a creature of his times.

I have received encouragement over the years from a wide circle of historians. Foremost, I owe a warm debt of gratitude to Dr W. H. Chaloner of the University of Manchester, who read the manuscript and suggested several welcome modifications. Professor W. H. G. Armytage has always been available when advice was needed and I have, at times, been sustained by his vitality and dedication to learning. Other scholars have helped me with source-references, supervised my submissions, or have launched me into print: Professor T. C. Barker, H. L. Beales, Professor J. F. C. Harrison, Professor A. H. John, Dr R. K. P. Pankhurst, Professor S. Pollard, R. B. Rose and J. Salt. My colleague Dr R. S. Fitton willingly accepted the chore of checking proofs.

In ransacking the Co-operative Union Library in Manchester and the Goldsmiths' Library of the University of London the late Mr Desmond Flanagan and Miss Margaret Canney gave me their friendship as well as their professionalism.

For Orbiston community I acknowledge assistance from the public libraries of Motherwell and Hamilton and the Mitchell Library in Glasgow. Lord Hamilton of Dalzell and the Reverend A. Bolton of Orbiston Manse gave me sight of valuable documents, provided background material and arranged personal introductions. In Ireland I was warmly received and had the benefit of advice and material from T. P. O'Neill, Deputy Keeper at the National Library of Ireland, and from staff at the Irish Public Records Office, Irish State Papers Office, Irish Land Registry, Royal Irish Academy and local libraries at Limerick and Ennis. Brigadier J. O. E.

Vandeleur and Lieutenant-Colonel G. A. M. Vandeleur of London, and T. Vandeleur of Tenerife, Canary Islands, provided me with family details by correspondence, and the Reverend W. Vandeleur of Dun Laoghaire gave me an illuminating interview. Of the many people I met and was in correspondence with in Ireland, I wish to mention Cormac Halpin of Newmarket-on-Fergus, who gave me first-hand knowledge of the recent history of the Ralahine estate, J. B. MacClancy of Ennis, Desmond Ryan, James Gorman, Seamus Heron of Dublin, G. F. Gleeson of Clare Castle and Bulmer Hobson of Galway.

In England I used the following libraries and repositories and thank their staffs for the cordiality shown in dealing with my re-quests: the Co-operative Reference Library, the Charity Organisa-tion Society, the Bishopsgate Institute, University College, London, the British Museum Newspaper Library at Colindale, the Public Record Office, Somerset House, Manchester Public Reference Library, Hampshire Record Office and Winchester Public Library. Interesting information was freely given by Major Sir H. J. Avigdor Goldsmid of Tonbridge, Captain J. Dalgety of Lockerley Hall, Romsey, the Reverend N. Powell of Broughton, J. B. Chapman of Winchester, G. Bricknell of Andover, and Mrs Robey of Kings Somborne. Mr J. Fawcett of Queenwood Farm kindly consented to allow me to publish a photograph of his home. The records of Shirley parish church, Croydon, provided information on William Pare. Mr G. Petre of the Geography Department of Hendon College drew the maps of the communities from my amateur sketch-plans.

I found newspaper appeals most responsive, and wish to thank the editors of the *Glasgow Herald, Irish Times* and *Hampshire Chronicle* for printing my requests, also the many newspaper readers who wrote to me and provided an insight into the influence of Owenism on established local communities and traditions.

Finally I am grateful to my students, academic colleagues, and people from all walks of life, who have borne with me and have often contested and modified my views on Robert Owen and his influence. My wife and family would now welcome a change of subject and hope this volume closes the chapter!

Communities are made up of groups of individuals with certain commonly held beliefs, aspirations and modes of behaviour; but a community, except as an abstraction, cannot long remain undifferentiated. Individual deviations have to be accommodated in much the same way although not to the same extent as in open society. The success of a community may depend on there being a sufficient plasticity to allow the community to survive through transmutation. Many communities soon lose their corporate identity as a result of these internal transmutations; other communities, particularly those of religious orders, survive—their regimens are simple, they often proscribe familial relationships, and their occupational role-playing is subordinated to their religious observations. In effect, their systems have no power-head; final authority lies outside the community. But there are also transmutations which percolate from outside the community.

The real meaning of any human activity can be found only when it is defined in terms of adjustment, and in every case of adjustment we are faced with the more or less powerful conflict between the impulses of the individual or group towards self-assertion and attainment, and the inhibiting conformity of society: hence the valuable contribution a study of community can make to our understanding of the widespread social changes brought about through industrialisation in nineteenth-century Britain.

R.G.G.

I

Communitarianism

We have had the Savage, the Pastoral, the Commercial, and historians will yet write of the Communitarian age.[1]

I

From the late eighteenth century to the mid-nineteenth century England moved from being a predominantly agricultural society into becoming the first industrial nation. Despite conflicting interpretations of the characteristics of the industrial revolution, there is general agreement that the process of change brought with it a vast social upheaval and the varied reaction to industrialisation which is the concern of this study.

It is commonly held that the outstanding features of this transition were an unprecedented growth in population and industrial output, associated with a shift in balance between town and country. Indeed, increasing urbanisation was seen as the most obvious consequence of industrialisation:[2] but this factor must be kept in perspective—half the population still lived in rural areas as late as 1851, and industrialisation had not penetrated all sectors, let alone caused wholesale redundancy for the many domestic workers and artisans who remained associated with certain processes in precisely those industries, such as textiles, which were regarded as highly mechanised.

The geographical concentration of industry during the first half of the nineteenth century has also been exaggerated by many writers: New Lanark and the Strutt mills at Belper and Milford, the two largest cotton undertakings in 1816, were by no means typical. In 1786 'a stranger approaching the town [Manchester] only saw one high chimney, which was Mr Arkwright's mill', and even as late as the post-Napoleonic war years the evidence given to the Commons Select Committee on Children, of 1816, confirmed that the industrial landscape included many small workshops, converted cottages and mills clustered along the banks of streams, quite apart from the fact that many industrial premises housed a number of separate undertakings.[3]

This view had been expressed just over a quarter of a century earlier by Viscount Torrington, who wrote in his diary:

> Arrived at —— Bridge upon the river [Calder], around which are numberless coalpits, for the whole country seems to be a bed of coal; crossing a common, we pass'd by the village of Accrington, where they are building rows of houses, as every vale swarms with cotton mills; some not bigger than cottages—for any little stream, by the means of a reservoir, will supply them (Cotton mills have chosen the Old Abbey situations; in the abbies [*sic*] there was religion, and decency; in the cotton mills, blasphemy and immorality...)[4]

Many contemporary surveys of the manufacturing districts did not specify with sufficient clarity for modern readers that the typical industrial scene was not one of heavy urbanisation—rather, it was made up of a network of industrial villages, sometimes served by a larger manufacturing and commercial centre in a town, but not commonly so. A number of these industrial villages were new and had been created by manufacturers, especially textile mill owners.

Peter Gaskell, one of the more objective of contemporary observers, writing during the 1830s,[5] noted the industrial diffusion within the Manchester area and also the paternalist nature of most of the larger enterprises:

> An inspection of Belper, Cromford, Hyde, Duckenfield, Stayley Bridge, the villages and hamlets around Oldham, Bolton, Manchester, Stockport, Preston, Glasgow etc. etc., will show many magnificent factories surrounded by ranges of cottages, often exhibiting signs of comfort and cleanliness highly honourable to the proprietor and the occupants. Those cottages are generally the property of the mill owner, and the occupants are universally his dependents.
>
> This dependence is in many cases of the most absolute kind; no power ever enjoyed by the feudal lord was so operative. It is true that the life of the dependent no longer lies at the mercy of his superior: what may be termed his social existence is however at his disposal. Around many mills a fixed population has arisen, which is as much a part and parcel of the property of the master as his machinery. The rapid improvement in this last has put an end to the necessity for new labourers, and thus little colonies are formed under the absolute government of the employer.[6]

The new industrialism thus called for the establishment of some factories on virgin soil, such as the community at New Lanark. It was not, however, the distinctive appearance or scale of operations at New Lanark that drew so many notable visitors, who could equally well have inspected the Arkwright or Strutt textile mills: what attracted them were the communal arrangements, and particularly the educational provisions. The admirers of New Lanark were from many walks of life but noticeably did not include many fellow manufacturers, who as a class remained sceptical of Owen's achievements. We shall argue later that Robert Owen was too ready to translate his experience of the cotton industry, gained largely during his quarter of a century at New Lanark, into generalisations about the national economy, and the social system at New Lanark as applicable to the nation as a whole.

Owen pointed out the harmful consequences which followed from the organisation of society on principles of the profit motive. The results in human terms were leading to a destruction of the traditional character of a settled population and transmuting people into a new type of worker, 'infinitely more degraded and miserable', and having to rely on factory employment. The newly emergent working class not only felt deprived of their livelihoods by machines, but also felt that machine production reduced their status (since too many factory masters treated their hands in the same way as their machines), sapped their initiative and weakened their sense of community. New Lanark showed Owen that wages were only one of many factors; natural and home environment, quality and price of goods and services, stability of employment and security of tenure were just as embracing: 'Whatever wage they received the mass of them must be wretched.'[7] What was apparently an economic problem was essentially a social one. The factory system was wreaking havoc with social relationships.

The new urban environment brought to the fore just as many social and moral problems of discipline and control as did the factory work-situation. Town life was more precarious and anonymous than traditional rural relationships. Urban dwellers had to rely more heavily on the market economy, as it was not possible to supplement earnings by home-grown food. The wage packet was the sole source of income, and cash was needed for all expenditure transactions. Many commentators dwelt on the lack of disciplined spending by the urban working class (both men and women) and the enticement to squander money on drink and riotous living. A further historical explanation of the growing problems of town life could attribute as much to working class patterns of *expenditure* as to low earnings and to an inability of the market mechanism to provide the basic requirements of working class housing and sanitation.

Perhaps this increasing dominance of cash transactions and the market economy also meant that many political radicals became preoccupied with theories of what constituted a just reward to labour and investigations into unequal exchanges and the wastes of distribution.

Reaction to the social problems of industrialisation were mainly of two kinds: first, an isolation of any one of a number of dislocating factors as the outstanding evil, which was then often seen in a confused light as the cause rather than a symptom—the attacks on the poor laws and the corn laws are examples of this type of reaction; secondly, comprehensive panaceas and blueprints which were drawn up to solve a whole range of social evils. Most of these suggested remedies involved resettlement and job provision in the first instance for the poor, and were visualised in a rural setting: Owen's ideal society was of this kind. But even within the general community solution there were many competing alternatives and models, and it should be noted that the community ideal itself was only one form of reaction to industrialism. What was lacking was any consistent ambition or power to control the social consequences of the forces of industrialism. The two controls (and virtues) for an industrialising society which were constantly preached at the working class—hard work and self-help—were scarcely resented by the workers. In a period when the State was hardly concerned with industrial development or social welfare, self-help was also generally acceptable to the Establishment, as it would not increase the government sector, nor add to the burden of taxes or cause any redistribution of income. Moreover, the workers had themselves devised institutions embodying the idea of thrift—which could through mutuality bring dividends as well as social security. It must be conceded, however, that industrial development *per se* might produce resources which could be applied to improve social conditions, but the uneven pace and intensity of such development made it difficult to devise any generalised system of control.

Although Owen argued that the root cause of poverty lay primarily in an economic system founded on 'error' and could be cured only by radical change of the institutions of society, his early appeals were largely couched in terms of self-help and philanthropy, as he did not contemplate calling on the State for resources—he was a man of his time in believing that taxation was already too onerous for the State to be made responsible for providing for additional welfare services.

Faced with the task of devising means for integrating the growing industrial population, some commentators and polemists preferred to arrest or reverse the process of industrialisation and thus preserve the traditional features and loyalties of a predominantly rural society, with a stable balance between agriculture and industry. In this category can be included a host of disparate conservationists, varying from supporters of the corn laws and others who had no love for the cotton lords to pamphleteers who continued to write in the post-Napoleonic war years about natural rights in typically eighteenth-century terms—even Lord Sidmouth, the persecutor of trade unionists, sought remedies for the abuses of industrialism and showed some sympathy for Owen's parallelograms.

Few of the apologists of industrialism could offer anything more than prescriptions from classical economics and disparaging comments on working class morality in towns and factories. Andrew Ure epitomises and exonerates those employers who evaded any moral responsibility for the conduct of their industrial enterprises and he saw the factory system as 'the great minister of civilisation to the terraqueous globe.'[8] The most perfect mechanisation he could visualise would be that which would wholly dispense with manual labour. Charles Babbage, in his pioneer manual for managers on the most efficient use of machinery,[9] argued that a consequence of increasing mechanisation was that agriculture would involve a decreasing proportion of the occupied population.

With more acuity than the foregoing apologists, Gaskell saw the growing poor law problem as merely evidence of the attendant evil of industrialism:

> It is not poverty alone—for the family of the mill labourer earn what is sufficient to supply all their wants; it is not factory labour, considered *per se*; it is not the lack of education, in the common acceptation of the word:—no; it has arisen from the separation of families, the breaking up of households, the disruption of all those ties which link man's heart to the better portion of his nature,—viz his instincts and social affections. It is these which render him a respectable and praiseworthy member of society, both in his domestic relations, and in his capacity of a citizen.[10]

Therefore the 'best preserving power' was to be found 'in the balance of interest between the commercial economy of manufac-

tures and the social well-being of the employers and employed.'
Gaskell also realised that the root of immiseration was to be found
in the weakening of working class bonds of community and that
even those who were receiving higher wages felt deprived of
security, status and identity.

In effect the inventions of the industrial revolution, according to
Owen, 'created an aggregate of wealth, and placed it in the hands
of a few, who, by its aid, continue to absorb the wealth produced
by the industry of the many'[11]—but Owen recognised that the in-
corporation of the machine as a boon to the common people was
possible only in a new society in which man would become master
of the machine.

Luddism, the most violent form of industrial nihilism, was at
the other extreme to Owen's views, but Luddism was not new:
it was a typical response of a peasantry to changing methods of
production which would endanger traditional patterns of livelihood.[12] But in one sense, Owen's plans needed Luddite industrial
redundancy to be prevalent as a precondition for success—the dismissal of workers through the installation of more mechanised production methods would cause the value of labour to fall, and this
eroded value could be restored only by creating employment opportunities on the land. Moreover, this policy would tend to correct the
'error' of 'separating the worker from his food'.[31] Owen was never
wholly consistent when dealing with the labour theory of value.

. Two main changes, eradication of false beliefs concerning the
formation of character, and control of unbridled competition, were
required. Owen wanted to humanise the work situation and limit
the claims of the owner of capital and the entrepreneur, but did not
wish to dispense with either. He could not rely on the workers
themselves because they had suffered too severely from adverse circumstances; he insisted on the *collective* application of his theory
of character formation—individuals would not be moulded to one
helpless pattern in his communities: the qualities acquired would
be generalised—reason, charity, intelligence. The economic life of
society would have to be reorganised to deal with the real problems, which were essentially moral and political. •

Most of Owen's ideas and aspirations can be amply illustrated
elsewhere—the sense of mutuality in the friendly society, the crafts-
man's belief in the labour theory of value, the artisan's distrust of
the middleman, the philanthropic activities of a wide circle of

landed gentry and middle class reformers. It was not until Owen attacked religion, from 1817 onwards, that he was resented: his general criticism of industrial society had been received without rancour—the manufacturing interests also met criticism from many others quarters—but to denounce religion was seen as an attempt to undermine the nation.

John Minter Morgan,[14] who was as concerned as Owen about the moral consequences of indiscriminate industrialisation, was the first writer to support Owen's 1817 plan whilst rejecting his hostility to religion. Robert Southey[15] also wrote in sympathy with Owenism, and its attack on individualism and competition, but the poet had a romantic vision of the past and visualised the perfect society as a mystical fusion of Church and State. William Hazlitt was more critical of Owen:

> Miracles never cease, to be sure, but they are not to be had wholesale, or *to order*. Mr Owen, who is another of those proprietors and patentees of reform, has lately got an American savage with him, whom he carries about in great triumph and complacency, as an antithesis to his *New View of Society* and as winding up his reasoning to what is wanted, an epigrammic point. Does the benevolent visionary of the Lanark cotton-mills really think this *natural man* will act as a foil to his *artificial man*?[16]

Other commentators apart from Owen dwelt on the demoralising influences of a factory regimen and town life on the labouring population. As Sir Archibald Alison, Sheriff of Glasgow, said in 1840, 'The man who can combine manufacturing skill with isolated labour and country residence would do a great service.' But this attitude was basically backward-looking:

> The great difficulty in the management of the poor is in great cities. It is there that vice has spread her temptations, and pleasure, her seductions, and folly, her allurements ... It is to these great marts of human corruption that the base and profligate resort from the simplicity of country life ...[17]

It was the new industrialism that condensed vague aspirations for social justice into forms of socialist doctrine. Charles Hall in 1805 saw the main problem as one of inequality.[18] He estimated that one-fifth of the population received seven-eighths, whilst the other four-fifths received merely one-eighth, of the national income. The solution would be to restore land to the nation under public ownership and to settle on small farms the surplus labour competing for industrial employment.

Hall corresponded with Thomas Spence, who also believed that common possession of the land was the foundation of every other institution. 'The land with all its appurtenances is the natural common or estate of the inhabitants.'[19] The Spencean philanthropists could see that their views implied expropriation of landowners: despite the fact that they looked back to a form of agrarian socialism, they had more awareness than Owen of the nature of political and class power.

From 1817 William Cobbett became the self-appointed champion of the labouring classes, the same year in which Owen announced his plans for social transformation to the world at large. The Sussex farmer yearned for an England of sunny acres and thriving crops, and although Owen and Cobbett made common protest against the social injustice suffered by labour, their remedies were opposed: Cobbett abhorred Owen's 'parallelograms of paupers' because they implied patronage and servility. This was a typical response of political radicals to Owen's proposals. Cobbett simply defied industrialism because it took away freedom, property and thrift. His solution, which he saw as a valid economic proposition to counteract the social ills of the day, was to provide labourers with cottages:

> The laws, the economy, or management, of a State may be such as to render it impossible for the labourer, however skilful and industrious, to maintain his family in health and decency; and such has, for many years past, been the management of affairs of this once truly great and happy land.[20]

There were, of course, other miscreants and economic disasters apart from industrialism which had led to the decay of old England —parasitic fundholders and pensioners, paper money and onerous taxation:

> It is also true that a very large part, and the greater part, of landlords are on the point of utter ruin; but have they been ruined by the 6 millions, or by the 52 millions? Have they been ruined by the poor rates; or by the expenses of the standing army in peacetime; by the pensions, sinecures, grants and allowances... and by the 30 millions a year paid to the usurers...?[21]

Cobbett was widely read. Samuel Bamford maintained that his 'Twopenny Trash' was to be found on nearly every cottage hearth in the manufacturing districts. Riddance of abuses was readily understood by radical readers, but Cobbett did not see a new system so much as insist on a restitution of rights. He typified more than any other publicist the politics of righteous indignation:

> I think of Cobbett as a man who, at a wretched time in the history of the English people, put hope into their hearts, not by telling lies or painting fancy pictures, either of this world or the next, but by good solid cursing that never degenerated into a whine or a mere vapouring of despair.[22]

Another writer who supported home colonies was William Allen, the sometime Quaker partner of Owen at New Lanark. His pamphlet *Colonies at Home or Means of Rendering the Industrious Independent of Parish Relief* was published in 1828 but has no reference to Allen's opinion of New Lanark. Allen supported combined agricultural with manufacturing labour, which, he argued, would tend to greater security and happiness. He deplored the tendency of paying part of the agricultural wages bill out of the proceeds of the poor rates, and he criticised those farmers who would not allow their labourers to keep livestock because they feared the labourer would be tempted to steal food for his pig.[23] The remedy would be to provide the worker with a cottage and holding of some one and a quarter acres in which he could plant corn, potatoes and root crops with supplementary income from poultry and pigs, 'to be deposited in the savings' bank'. Such arrangements could be extended to manufacturing workers and in their case cottage holdings should be situated within two miles of the place of work. This provision would insulate the factory hand from unemployment during periods of slack trade. A further advantage of the home colonies idea was that it was sponsored as a preferable alternative to wholesale emigration. Home colonies would also enable the labourer to acquire a respectable status, hence there would be fewer 'improvident marriages'.[24]

Owen would have none of this. He thought of home colonies as misdirected palliatives which would divert energies away from a thoroughgoing appraisal of the need to pay a just reward to labour and create a set of balanced relationships between agriculture and industry. Under the cottage system, separate dwellings would be more expensive than communal accommodation, and Owen asserted that the cottage system would require half as much land again compared with his plan; but the main evil was that the cottage labourer would remain 'individualised' and the children would become 'stupid, ignorant and brutally selfish'. In a word, the beneficial communal influences on character-building would be lacking, and to emphasise his point Owen argued that in communities one would have the best of both worlds:

> The new villages would combine within them all the advantages of the largest town, without one of its innumerable evils and inconveniences; and with all the benefits of the country, without any of the numerous disadvantages that secluded residences now present.[25]

What happens, he queried, when death strikes at a member of a family under the cottage system? More often than not the family is broken up, whereas in a community the survivors would be upheld because '. . . around them on all sides, as far as the eye can reach, or imagination extend, thousands on thousands, in strict, intimate, and close union, are ready and willing to offer their aid and consolation'.[26]

James Deacon Hume,[27] who wrote *Letters on the Corn Laws and on the Rights of the Working Classes* in 1835 under the pseudonym 'H.B.T.' was a further example of a reformer who pinpointed a single factor—in his case, market imperfection—as the main cause of social and economic distress. He saw protection for the landed interests as the root of the problem. Hume thought the Owenite National Regenerationists were justified in their claim to obtain 'the right to fruits of their labour' but he argued that this situation could be conditional as it was 'a right which no man can be said to enjoy, unless he be at liberty to make the most advantageous exchange he can of the product of his own labour for that of the labour of others'.[28] Obviously, Hume is here proposing free trade, not equitable labour exchanges. He also moved away from the artificiality of the closed economy, which was a tacit assumption in Owenite and most early socialist thought (except in Owen's rhetorical appeals to the world at large). Economic distress can occur, argued Hume, as a consequence of manufacturers having 'to seek foreign markets as sellers of the goods they produce, while they are prevented by artificial causes, from going into that market as buyers of the goods they want'.

Hume then becomes a doctrinaire classical economist when he equates Smith's 'invisible hand' with the Owenite solution: 'There is nothing in Mr Owen's scheme of society which is not of the very essence of society, in its national form.' Owen proposed full beneficial employment, but 'the people of this country would spontaneously fall into the very division of employments which would produce this consequence, if they were left to themselves'.[29] More pertinently he points out that 'We have long since passed that point up to which the prosperity of a country is based on its land'.[30]

The rigours of the poor law, argued Hume, should not distract attention from the injustice shown in the preferential support the landed interests received at the cost of the rest of the community. Agricultural protection could also have Malthusian consequences— a surplus rural population would find it difficult to secure employment in industry if bread prices remained high through protection. On the other hand, should inflated food prices be used as a means for controlling population growth, there would be no justification in subsidising the farming community to the extent of the impost.[31]

Owenism was not backward-looking; in reality its appeal caught the imagination far more than the nostalgia of Cobbett because it was sufficiently eclectic to gather

> artisans with their dreams of short-circuiting the market economy: the skilled workers with their thrust towards general unionism: the philanthropic gentry, with their desire for a rational, planned society: the poor with their dream of land or of Zion: the weavers, with their hopes of self-employment: and all of these with their image of an equitable brotherly community, in which mutual aid would replace aggression and competition.[32]

Although Owenism was not retrogressive, neither was it wholly new—a sense of community was ingrained, and Owenite co-operation drew on the experience of older forms of association such as friendly societies and trade clubs, each with their fellowship rites. The friendly society was prevalent in many trades in the late eighteenth century and was a unifying influence on working class culture. Mutuality and self-help were combined in the day-to-day experience of safeguarding funds, the conduct of meetings and arbitration of claims. Many social reform measures, apart from co-operation, were built on this foundation of working class consciousness. Eden estimated that 648,000 people were members of friendly societies in 1801,[33] and the poor law returns of 1803 gave a figure of 704,000 members, which by 1815 had grown to 925,000 —nearly 8½ per cent of the population. At that time virtually all friendly societies were local organisations with strong communal ties, but by the mid-nineteenth century the large affiliated orders were predominant: the Manchester Unity of Oddfellows alone

could claim a membership roll of 250,000 in 1848, a figure which
far exceeded the number of trade unionists and co-operators combined.[34]

II

Robert Owen has become so closely identified with community experiments and early co-operation in Britain that the impulsion is
to investigate more fully the actual extent of his involvement as an
active participator rather than as a progenitor in those community
experiments in Britain which are usually referred to as 'Owenite'—
Orbiston, Ralahine and Queenwood.

Owen is difficult to contain. Although he was the subject of a
number of mainly adverse biographies soon after his death, there
have been very few substantial studies since Podmore's monu-
mental volumes, written over sixty years ago.[35]

Much of the study that follows is an analysis of the nature and
effectiveness of Owen's influence on the Owenite movement, from
which it will be argued that there are grounds for a reappraisal of
his impact, a reassessment of widely held views on the character
of the man himself, and the place of Owenite thought and practice
in the working class movement and in the wider context of maturing industrialism.

Most studies of Owen have been oblique because the writers concerned are generally dealing with social reform or some aspect of
the working class movement rather than with Owen and his followers. Hence he appears (rightly) in many histories of trade
unionism, co-operation and education; but apart from Podmore
there has been no full study of his influence on the immediate circle
of Owenites in Britain, nor of their main preoccupation—community
experiments. Perhaps this imbalance is due to his very pervasiveness:
his views and contributions to social thought would have remodelled
class structure, and the Victorians, concerned as they were with
debating the proper role of government in collectivist social reform,
were compelled to treat Owen as ogre, crank or prophet.[36] His views
acted as a catalyst for others. This lack of definition is understand-
able because he was dealing with those eternal questions concerning
the relationships between society and the individual which give rise
to moral and religious as well as political, economic and social issues.
A reassessment of Owen is now timely because social questions,

although posed in a slightly different form, are again a major pre-occupation—we are becoming deeply concerned with problems of identity, participation and cohesion in modern society, and although we have at our disposal more refined methods of social investigation and explanation, yet we are perhaps no nearer applying convincing social remedies within our complex social structure than Owen was in his nineteenth-century environment.

Owen wanted fervently to reform society, and economic considerations were subordinate to his concepts of education, psychology and social ethics. If the characteristics of an ideology include over-simplification of issues, emotional appeals, an identifying jargon and a non-scientific approach, then Owenism was an ideology. The imponderable is whether Owenism could have achieved any more than it did with the primitive methods of social analysis available during the early nineteenth century.

A glossary of Owenite terms shows the above emphasis: 'New View of Society', 'New Moral World', 'Universal Community'... Economic considerations could be easily met on Owen's assumptions —that initial capital for transforming society would be readily forthcoming from rich sympathisers, that the implementation of a labour theory of value would create full employment, and that the productivity of machine production and spade cultivation would provide for improving living standards. Owen had his own scale of priorities: society would be rejuvenated and purified within communities. As A. E. Bestor has commented, 'On secondary matters, Owen never felt it necessary to commit himself, permanently or explicitly ... Inconsistencies in economic details were a natural consequence of his pragmatic approach.'[37] But Bestor dispenses too readily with Owen's cavalier attitude to economics. Owen does not discount economic factors because he thinks they are unimportant; rather, he implies that economic behaviour and institutions are a reflection of social *mores* and it would be futile to change economic organisation without transforming society. Owen was often inconsistent in economic thought, but he was even more ambivalent in his views on class structure. In the last resort, he felt he could not rely on the working classes because they lacked organisational experience. He despaired of their 'democratic' elements and regarded workers almost as anarchists: his reliance was on the solidarity of the middle classes. His adoption of the labour theory of value was never wholly convincing in practice except as a cure for maldistribution. Profits were always in the forefront of his mind.

Before 1821 Owen hesitated to disarrange society[38] because he was calling for support from the middle classes to weld workers and middle class organisers together. This new class would reform the world by combining the best characteristics of workers and the middling ranks of society. There was, he argued, a real identity of interest—pursuit of happiness—but it was obscured through the inequalities of maldistribution. Robert Owen should be claimed by the managerial class.

We should try first to appreciate the range of Owen's interests and thought before we pinpoint any further weaknesses. Certainly he changed his formulae and bewildered his disciples, but his many changes of mind were on economic logistics—on the cost, clientele and optimum size of communities; on the basic issues, which were social rather than economic or political, he was consistent throughout his long life. He never wavered on the conditioning influence of environment and education, or on the optimism that industrialization could better serve society.

Owen's was a temperamental weakness; he was psychologically incapable of consistent leadership. G. D. H. Cole[39] has said that he could lead but could not follow. The truth is surely that Owen could neither lead nor follow. He was an isolate, but one who somehow managed to infuse his disciples with dedicated allegiance. Yet whenever Owen led his followers to a point where a policy decision had to be made, he could never follow through its practical implications.

Because Owen and Owenism largely eschewed direct political action, the Owenites felt no impulsion to criticise other radical reform movements: Owenism was more concerned with drawing up its own doctrine and programmes. On the other hand, it was not treated with the same forbearance by rival groups. Scathing attacks were made on Owen by the Established Church in response to his initial onslaught on organised religion, which had alienated much potential support for him from all classes of society:[40] 'I am compelled to believe that all the religions of the world are so many geographical insanities.'[41] This bitterness towards established religion also helps to explain much of his apparent inconsistency. It was necessary for him to eliminate any obstacle to social regeneration: he therefore had to deny original sin and had to believe that culpability for human misery must stem from ignorance, not wickedness. It followed that man was not capable of making himself perfect, and this was plainly an irreligious view of human nature. Owen weakened his argument by pointing out that rivalry between religious sects meant that all religions were false. By the same token, he would have been forced to concede that debate would be puerile in determining correct social reform policies. Perhaps this attitude towards religious controversy explains his single-mindedness and refusal to consider matters of social regeneration except as revealed truths. If human nature is rational, its self-fulfilment must have been warped, and it becomes impossible to explain away these irrational elements except in terms of antagonism of interests. This is Owen's main inconsistency: '. . . if it were really as easy as Owen thought to put the world right, it is the more difficult to explain how the world has got so wrong.'[42]

Even with his irreligion and his rationalism, Owen imparted a temperance to the working class movement through his appeal to the more edifying motives of self- and mutual improvement rather than to class hatred. This lack of knowledge could be rectified only through education on a communal basis. Owen was searching for a diagnosis and a prognosis for society's ills, and his emphasis on the curative powers of education has been strongly vindicated over the course of the century since his death.[43]

There were no bounds, in Owen's view, to the possibilities of social improvement through education:

> On the experience of a life devoted to the subject, I hesitate not to say that the members of any community may by degrees be trained to live *without idleness, without poverty, without crime,* and *without punishment*; for each of these is the effect of error in the various systems prevalent throughout the world. *They are all necessary consequences of ignorance.*[44]

He frequently used the analogy of improved output of mechanised production to ponder whether moral improvement and knowledge could expand at the same progression.

It should, however, be conceded that many members of the working class rejected his political quietism and his anti-clericalism, and responded to more militant calls. But implicit in Owen's thought are strident criticisms of existing society—its acquisitiveness, exploitation, waste and disharmony. Owen saw that the working classes were exploited, but were not sufficiently articulate to generate their own soundly based reform proposals, nor were they powerful enough to insist on the implementation of any such measures—hence his paternalism, which was a perpetuation of the typical attitude of the eighteenth-century Establishment towards the population at large. Addressing members of an Owenite congress, he was reported as saying that governors of communities 'must have undisputed control—subject to removal by Directors and with right of appeal to Congress'. Control was essential:

> ... indeed, of so much importance did he consider it, that in the case of the New Lanark Mills, he had introduced an express clause in the articles of partnership on the subject. It must be remembered that the social communities would be paternal governments carried on upon democratic principles.[45]

Owen needed the working classes as a palimpsest for the ideas which he had developed and operated at New Lanark. He had no reservations that New Lanark was his proven model and material for social regeneration. 'This experiment at New Lanark was the first commencement of practical measures with a view to change the fundamental principle on which society has heretofore been based from the beginning...'[46] He was even prepared to justify the achievement of a higher level of profits at New Lanark than the ten per cent commonly stated.[47]

Despite Owen's asseverations, doubts have been cast on the level of his business ability at New Lanark[48] when its financial success is judged against typical economic conditions in the textile industry during the Napoleonic wars. Moreover, it is difficult to discover the actual extent to which Owen was involved in the day-to-day business operations at the New Lanark mills. He was obviously very active in communal affairs there, and he might well have abandoned New Lanark because he could not infuse a sufficient depth of ethical and social ideas into business; yet the paradox remains that, having deserted business, he was always preaching the merits of businesslike attitudes when dealing with the organisation of social programmes. Indeed, it will be shown that after leaving New Lanark Owen never completed any other practical experiment. The imponderables remain. How far was he original at New Lanark? Would factory legislation have steered any other course without his support? Would trade unionism? Any speculation on these questions would, however, extend this study beyond its terms of reference.

A contemporary biographer of Owen wrote in 1866:

> In the rapture of his schemes he forgot that the population at New Lanark were provided with constant employment and any precedents drawn from the experience of New Lanark could apply only to cases where the persons to be delivered are previously removed from poverty itself...[49]

Owen was not in fact demanding a rejection of the benefits of industrialism. 'Mechanical power cannot in one country be discontinued ... although such an act were possible, it would be a sure sign of barbarism in those who should make the attempt.'[50] He conceded that the stock of machinery could not be destroyed, nor even diminished, without creating more evils than those already experienced. The solution was to decant redundant labour into a spade-orientated agriculture.

Owen was too easily convinced of the merits of the spade versus the plough on the limited demonstration by W. Falla of improved yields of wheat. The merits of spade cultivation are outlined in the 'Report to the County of Lanark':

> Closet theorists and inexperienced persons suppose that to exchange the plough for the spade would be to turn back in the road of improvement,— to give up a superior for an inferior implement of cultivation. Little do they imagine that the introduction of the spade, with the scientific arrangements which it requires, will produce far greater improvements in agriculture than the steam engine has effected in manufactures.[51]

Gluts would be avoided by the ability to switch between agriculture and manufactures. But at the community level there would also be a problem of disposing of produce. If community-produced goods were sold in the open market, there would be risks of price changes; if they were for internal consumption only, the problem of the general disadvantages forced on the community through its limited scale of production would have to be faced. However, a surplus would be created, it was asserted, because each labourer could produce an output of 100 bushels of wheat whereas the cost of individual subsistence for a year was equivalent to only thirty-five bushels. Spade cultivation, it was argued, brought fresh soil to the surface, increased the depth of working, allowed surplus water to leach through the soil, but retained sufficient moisture for plant growth.[52] The spade did not harden the subsoil, as did the trampling of horses or heavy ploughs; the spade was also suitable for use by the small farmer, and during the greater part of winter. But it was not held that the spade could be the universal provider.[53] It was not applicable to every kind of soil, 'or that a

proportionably advantageous return would accrue by cultivation of
1,000 acres of land by the spade, they only assert, that under the
best arrangements of plough, and spade culture, the latter will
produce a greater net produce'.[54] Mechanisation was a technique,
and techniques were neither good nor bad except in their consequences. Owen could welcome the machine, but could criticise the
organisation of industry for not distributing the increased productivity of mechanisation on a more equitable basis. He also argued
that machinery had counteracted some of the dire effects of heavy
taxation by reducing the costs of industrial production and thereby
enabling more infertile land to be cultivated through lower maintenance costs of wage labour in terms of goods.[55]

The main blind spot in Owen's views on production was, of
course, in these excessive claims he made on behalf of spade cultivation. 'He would,' David Ricardo asserted, 'dispense with ploughs
and horses[56] in the increase of the productions of the country,
although the expense as to them must be much less when compared with the support of men.'[57] As a basis for his reliance on the
spade, Owen could point merely to statements on experiments
made by others, and this evidence was much more dubious, given
the variations of soil, than were the working arrangements at New
Lanark mills as an example of industrial efficiency—'the subject
of spade husbandry was in an unsettled state, and to found a new
social system upon it argued singular rashness'.[58] Even Falla did
not adduce so many advantages for the spade as Owen:

> the full energies of the land in general will not be brought into action till
> the Spade generally supersedes the Plough; but several centuries may
> probably elapse and of course the population of the country must be
> increased manyfold before that will, or can be the case.[59]

Perhaps the real explanation is that Owen was seeking justification
for the spade as a means of employing surplus industrial workers
and in providing sustenance for an increasing population. In the
same vein, communities and spade cultivation were supported in
the first instance by the landed classes to help cure widespread
social distress after the Napoleonic wars, but perhaps also to postpone the nemesis of 'that stationary and melancholy state, to which,
from the desperation of natural and necessary causes, every country
is gradually approaching'.[60]

Spade cultivation had many supporters apart from Owenites:

there was a universal desire for tenancy on the land among 'mechanics and artisans of manufacturing towns and villages as well as among the inhabitants of rural districts', and a Parliamentary select committee in 1843 favoured spade cultivation in Owenite terms as a means and an end, because it 'increased the produce and enlarged the general stock of labour to be expended on the soil'.[61]

The genesis of Owen's communitarian ideas was naturally conditioned by his experience at New Lanark, but he also used the word 'community' to describe previous social arrangements at New Lanark under David Dale.[62] The crux of Owen's message to humanity was to be found in its messianism: only he had seen the truth through somehow cutting the knot of environment which remained tied for all others. He changed the metaphors to express this transcendental experience, but the first announcement of his liberation merits quoting in full as it gives an insight into all his subsequent thought and action. Owen was trying desperately to communicate a message only he himself could understand and interpret: 'Causes, over which I could have no control, removed in my early days the bandage which covered my mental sight.' Owen claimed he had discovered blindness in others, but not from any personal merits of his own:

> No! The causes which fashioned me in the womb—the circumstances by which I was surrounded from my birth, and over which I had no influence whatever, formed me with far other faculties, habits and sentiments. They gave me a mind that could not rest satisfied without trying every possible expedient to relieve my fellow men from their wretched situation, and formed it of such a texture that obstacles of the most formidable nature served but to increase my ardour, and to fix within me a settled determination, either to overcome them, or to die in the attempt.[63]

Owen, with these views, could disclaim all responsibility for the actions of his followers, and he constantly emphasised that his views were misinterpreted and misapplied in practice:

> Such Communities as I have recommended, have never yet been in existence—have never been attempted—and therefore have never failed...I was directly opposed to Orbiston, because I saw that the arrangements were not according to the circumstances which would ensure success. It is as necessary that individuals should be trained for a Community; as it is necessary they should be trained for any trade; and this can only be done by proper arrangements for the purpose. These are—the due proportion of labour applied to production, distribution, education, and police. There is as certainly a science of society as there is of mathematics...I have sought

far and wide for an individual who understands Society but without success. In the department of production there is no individual who understands it.[64]

His 'Address to the Inhabitants of New Lanark' in 1816 had also included remarks on communities: 'In due time communities shall be formed possessing such characteristics, and be thrown open to those among you, and to individuals of every class and denomination.' So far it is not clear whether Owen was thinking of generalised communities or a wide range of differentiated settlement groups. But from the evidence of his 'Report for the Association for the Relief of the Manufacturing and Labouring Poor' in 1817, he was obviously proposing poor law communities: 'The first Villages of Unity and Mutual Co-operation may each be occupied by those only who have been trained in the same class, sectarian notions, and party feelings...'[65] Owen argued that men would be as industrious in a community of mutual interest as they are when employed for individual gain. This assertion was, of course, question-begging the term 'mutual interest'.

How far were Owen's views on communities influenced by others? In a letter of 1817 he disclaimed any originality for the principles on which his community plans were based:

I have no claim to priority in regard to the combinations of these principles in theory: this belongs as far as I know to John Bellers, who published them, and most ably recommended them to be adopted in practice, in the year 1696.[66]

Owen was also interested in the experience of the early American communities, and he wrote a sketch in 1818 on the Shakers, which he bound together with a reprint of the Bellers' tract.[67] Yet he parts company from John Bellers and the Shakers because he was interested in applying communitarian theory to society as a whole and not for the elect or the impoverished. Contemporaries coupled Owen's plans with those of Thomas Spence, who also thought in universal terms of re-establishing a state of nature with such parochial intervention as would enable the common people to re-possess their land rights under collective ownership in local communes.[68]

Owen's rationalism has much in common with that of William Godwin. But Godwin called for the abolition of all government and for a completely rational social system based on education in moral and social principles, with property rights to be claimed by those who made best social use of their assets. Godwin's thought was nearer to anarchism than Owen's. He was not interested in economic institutions or relationships, and co-operation was anathema to him because it would involve a restriction in the freedom of the individual.[69] The transformation of society, according to Godwin, required nothing more than insight and, once individuals understood their position,

> men must feel their situation and the restraints that shackled them before, vanish like a mere deception. When the true crisis shall come, not a sword will need to be drawn, not a finger to be lifted up. The adversaries will be too few and too feeble to dare to make a stand against the universal sense of mankind.[70]

Since all men suffered from irrational conditions, all mankind would be ready to change them. The language is apocalyptic and very reminiscent of Owen's writings, even to the use of similar metaphors. But Owen's concept of rationalism was incompatible with his determinist views—the essence of rationalism is really the exercise of freedom of choice in a freely reasoning self-in-action.

In the catalectic search for sources in the development of Owen's social thought, one should take into consideration the evidence of his son, Robert Dale Owen:

> When I first remember him he read a good deal; but it was chiefly one or two London dailies, with other periodicals as they came out. He was not, in any true sense of the word, a student...I never found, in his extensive library, a book with a marginal note, or even a pencil mark of his, on a single page. He usually glanced over books, without mastering them; often dismissing them with some curt remark as that 'the radical errors shared by all men make books of comparatively little value'.[71]

Owen took no notes except from Colquhoun.[72]

Although he had offended the Establishment through his denunciation of organised religion at a public meeting in August 1817, he received continuing support for his plans from individuals in high places, such as the Duke of Kent, David Ricardo and Robert Torrens. A committee was set up and recommended the establishment of experimental communities with capital subscribed from joint stock enterprise and for the communities to be organised on a basis of private property. In the 'Report to the County of Lanark' Owen outlined the organisational difficulties of setting up communities, but suggested that they could be surmounted, pointing

out that superintendence of a community would not require anything more than normal commercial flair:

> The principal difficulty will be to set the first community in motion; and
> much care and circumspection will be requisite in bringing each part into
> action at the proper time, and with the guards and checks which a change
> from one set of habits to another renders necessary. Yet the principles
> being understood, a man of fair ordinary capacity would superintend such
> arrangements with more ease than most large commercial or manufactur-
> ing establishments are now conducted.
>   When one establishment shall have been formed, there will be no great
> difficulty in providing superintendencies for many other establishments.[73]

Warming to his theme, he observed that

> In a short time the ease with which these associations will proceed in all
> their operations will be such as to render the business of governing a mere
> recreation; and as the parties who govern will in a few years again become
> the governed, they must always be conscious that at a future period they
> will experience the good or evil effects of the measures of their adminis-
> tration.[74]

In the 'Report to the County of Lanark' Owen anticipates a wide
range of communities to be set up by public authorities and private
benefactors along the lines of his earlier proposals for poor law
colonies, but the 'Report' adds independent middle class communities to the programme:

> The peculiar mode of governing these estates will depend on the parties
> who form them.
>   Those formed by landowners and capitalists, public companies, parishes,
> or counties will be under the direction of the individuals whom these
> powers may appoint to superintend them, and will, of course, be subject
> to the rules and regulations laid down by their founders.
>   Those formed by the middle and working classes, upon a complete
> reciprocity of interests, should be governed by themselves...[74]

Owen maintained that communities should be based on a mixed
economy of agriculture and industry, but, given his assessment of
the optimum membership size of 1,200, it would have been difficult
to incorporate large-scale methods of production. (The American
communities could survive on a pattern of small-scale production
because of their comparative isolation, but in Britain Owen was
assuming the whole economy would be transformed into a network
of communities.)

One has to conclude that Owen's character and his behaviour
concerning the communities remain largely inexplicable. G. J.

Holyoake was probably nearest the truth when he said, 'He never took Lord Brougham's advice "to pick his men". He never acted on the maxim that the working class are as jealous of each other as the upper classes are of them. All that he did as a manufacturer, he omitted to do as a founder of communities.'[85] Owen acted as if money had already been dispensed with, especially as far as communities were concerned. He believed that proper management was all that was necessary to organise the availability of resources and to distribute the real surplus created by labour. He never really emancipated himself from the idea of poor law colonies: his later plans for rural retreats for the middle classes, although on a smaller scale and not as necessary socially, were not far removed from his first views—eventually he despaired of fusing the classes and felt that the new moral world would be ushered in by a newly constituted working class in the next generation who would hardly be distinguishable from the contemporary middle class.

Only during the years from the mid-1820s was Owen directly challenging the established order of society with his views on property and equality.[76] Bestor dates this second phase, from the mid-1820s to the mid-1830s, in terms of the emphasis shown in Owen's writings, but as far as Owen's contribution to communitarianism is concerned the main period lies more distinctly between 1835 and 1840. It was during these five years that he set up a series of communitarian societies to propagate his views. The most critical year is 1840, when Owenism was sufficiently impressive to become the subject of a debate in the House of Commons. Paradoxically, Owen's irreligion had begun to diminish before 1840—the Owenite missionaries had been instructed to avoid religious controversy in their propaganda and to restrict their message to one of communitarianism. The year 1840 is also important because it marks Owen's turning away from any active participation in the community experiment at Queenwood. Thenceforth he became an embarrassment to his followers and began a long descent into obscurantism. During the early 1840s he reverted to his earlier views on social stratification. He gave up hope of converting the working classes as he conceded that ingrained environmental constraints were too strong to be overcome except through the education of a new generation. He also appealed for rich backers, and in this period, when his views were becoming more nebulous and the community at Queenwood more precarious, he was eminently more successful in raising funds than at any previous time when his proposals at least had the merit of being untried and therefore could be regarded as potentially sound investment propositions or charitable endeavours.

III

Owenism became sufficiently impressive in its impact and allegiance largely to equate with utopian community experiments in Britain during the second quarter of the nineteenth century. This poses certain queries. Why did these communal experiments find roots during this particular period rather than before or since? Why should such social aspirations coalesce into movements only at certain times and in certain forms such as Owenism in 1825–45? Why did Owenism have a wider and more lasting appeal than the individual call to conversion of millenarian cults such as the Southcottians?[77] Answering that Owenism was infinitely more sensible and practical is partly begging the question—fanaticism will always appeal more to those with fanatical tendencies. It seems obvious that the Owenite appeal had a more lasting impact because it promulgated a social programme and an institutional framework, whereas the millenarians were content with personal salvation: there are, of course, exceptions such as the Shakers and Mormons.[78]

After 1840 there was a confusing proliferation of terms with varying connotations on the general theme of socialism.[79] The word 'communitarian' and its associated 'communitarianism' came into use to identify both the ideology of those who planned communities and actual community experiments themselves: 'communitarianism' denoted a system of organisation based on small co-operative land settlements, with the 'communitarian' either an advocate of the community ideal or a member of such a community experiment.[80]

'Communitarian' and its lesser used alternative 'communionalist' had a short life and passed into oblivion after the collapse of the last of the Owenite communities at Queenwood in 1845. Although the word did not exist before 1840, it is possible, with some discretion of definition, to use 'communitarian' to encompass the whole range of aspirations and community experiments during the period 1820–45, of which the contributions from Owenite socialists and co-operators were, at least in Britain, sufficiently outstanding to be almost synonymous with the idea of community.

'Communism' was reserved during the 1840s largely to describe militant revolutionism. Engels later referred to the period: 'Thus, in 1847, Socialism was a middle-class movement, Communism a working-class movement.'[81]

A modern revival of the word 'communitarian' would supersede the looser term 'utopian socialism' with its disparaging overtones and would enable 'pure' communism to describe systems based on complete community of possessions. In fact, most 'communistic' experiments have been communitarian in form, and this feature has been more significant than compliance with the theory of property in common—a theory generally vague and incompletely applied.[82]

This study is restricted to an assessment of the Owenite contribution to communitarianism and does not seek to provide a systematic exposition of apocalyptic doctrine and its place in the history of socialist thought; rather, it is concerned with the linkage of ideology with participation and experimentation. The justification for this approach is that the Owenite solution aimed to remodel the social structure and social relationships *in toto* and is therefore more interesting in sociological terms[83] than is the case with most of the writings of the Ricardian socialists, or of many of the millenarian sects whose followers were bound to remain as select brotherhoods: indeed, part of their self-identification and conviction as sects lay in their strict adherence to ritualistic practices and in their deviant social behaviour, which required the rest of unleavened society to remain redemptive rather than redeemed.

An appreciation of communitarian ideas and experiments in Britain during the second quarter of the nineteenth century provides a clue to understanding the social ferment brought about by maturing capitalism and industrialism. Communitarianism was a response to industrialism but it was by no means the only response. It must be contrasted with revolutionism,[84] and the more British experience of political emancipation and gradualism. Its roots stretch back to utopian thought over many centuries, but particularly to the seventeenth and eighteenth centuries, when the idea of social regeneration began to mingle with the millenarianism of such cults as Shakers, Huttites and Moravians. It drew its inspiration from French political and rationalist theorists, English transcendentalists such as William Godwin, Samuel Taylor Coleridge, Robert Southey, and radical thinkers such as Thomas Paine. In a sense, the communitarians were practising utopians who assumed

their utopias into existence. The benefits of community were to be
so self-evident that the world would follow by emulation—for the
community idea was the law of nature re-established. Providence
was good; property was theft; institutions of government were
evil. The communitarians used the same language as the evan-
gelicals who were seeking to cure the evils of the old unredeemed
world rather than build a new.

The basis of communitarian thought was equality—economic
rather than political—in that the labourer had a right to the full
value of the product of his labour. It was believed that communities
would create their own perfect markets, in sharp contrast to the
imperfectly competitive conditions prevailing outside, where 'the
more employers and distributors . . . the less business is there for
each; and the less business they have, the greater profit do they
require to support them'.[85] It was co-operation in place of competition because competition bred inequality, and it was apolitical because it ignored the State and the Establishment, or rather treated
them as neutral.[86] This attitude remained a characteristic of Owenism throughout the period: in 1840 a branch society of the Owenite
socialists stated:

> The plans of the Socialists will be carried on under entire obedience to the
> laws of the State . . . The Socialists take no part in the agitation for political
> changes, as they are convinced that permanent prosperity and happiness
> can be gradually secured for every human being under any form of
> government which recognises the principle of toleration.[87]

This was immature, but the communitarians were in the main-
stream of nineteenth-century political thought with regard to the
proper function of the State—that the best government was that
which governed least. Moreover, it was conceded that communities
were experiments within capitalist society—William Thompson,
the Irish Owenite socialist, wrote of the difficulties of achieving
social equality through the communitarian solution of social conviction and emulation:

> Meantime, as I cannot cause these measures preparatory to a system of real
> freedom of exertion to be immediately adopted, whether that exertion
> take the form of really free competition, which, I believe, would necessarily
> end in voluntary co-operation or otherwise: as I can do no more than
> endeavour to persuade my neighbour and all whom I can reach, of their
> utility or tendency to promote the general happiness, I must be satisfied
> with attempting to carry into effect, on a small scale, for and with a few
> able and willing, in their several stations, and as an example to all, that

system of united exertion which will accomplish for the few who voluntarily engage in it, the greater part of those advantages which the same
system, if universally and voluntarily adopted, would produce for all. If
we have neither the wealth, nor the power, nor the means of persuasion,
to induce all around us to give their exertions a new direction, particularly
if we have not the means of providing for the ignorant and the poor
around us, or of enabling them rather to provide for themselves, shall it
be called selfishness in us to endeavour to make ourselves, and as many as
will join us, happy, as far as our means will extend, by our united exertions, taking from none, removing ourselves from being a burden on any,
anxious to acquire the means of assisting all?[88]

Capitalism could follow if it wished, and in the interim demonstration of the communal good life there would be no expropriation
of property, merely a reorganisation of production and distribution
so that the benefits of division of labour would not be wasted
through maldistribution of income.[89] Indeed, Robert Owen counted
on the financial support of capitalists to usher in the millennium.

The communitarians were never wholly consistent in their economic thought and policy, but if pressed they would argue that radical
changes in society were the critical aims of their programmes, and
economic reorganisation was an ancillary to social transformation.
A manifesto of 1840 includes a section on 'Economic objects' but
the flavour is distinctly social:

to well educate and advantageously employ ALL its members, so as to insure
their health, permanent prosperity, intelligence, union, and happiness:—
to produce and distribute, in the best manner, the best qualities of all kinds
of wealth abundantly for ALL—to govern most beneficially for all—without
force or fraud, and ultimately, without artificial rewards or punishments—
by the removal of the causes which produce evil, and the institution of
those which produce good; and thus to effect peaceable, and by reason alone,
an entire change in the character and condition of mankind.[90]

Although the Owenite creed appeared to change its priorities and
directions unpredictably, yet the language in 1840 is largely the
same as Owen's first proclamation of his views a quarter of a century earlier:

What ideas individuals may attach to the term Millennium I know not;
but I know that society may be formed so as to exist without crime, without poverty, with health greatly improved, with little, if any, misery, and
with intelligence and happiness increased a hundredfold; and no obstacle
whatsoever intervenes at this moment, except ignorance, to prevent such a
state of society from becoming universal.[91]

The mystique for the communities was the land. There is an

overlying assumption that virtue is more at home in the countryside than in the town. All the communitarian experiments were pre-dominantly agricultural,[92] usually with a superstructure of small-scale industrial pursuits[93] which never exceeded the workshop level:

> May day next is to be the last Congress held out of Community; for that day twelve months the first stone is to be laid of the first Community; and the Congress will, on that occasion, assemble on the land—on the land: we have said and it shall be done.[94]

The communities adhered to a system of common property which was not restricted to the land itself:

> The whole land and other property of each and every community ... and the energies of the members and their families located thereon, shall be held for ever as common property, applicable to the objects of the whole Society ...[95]

There was also to be equality of status and effort: 'each class, according to age, being upon an equality of rights and privileges ... equal services required from each, according to age and capacity'.[96]

The communitarians were not alone in the nineteenth century in regarding agriculture and the land in such mystical terms. They saw clearly the benefits of division of labour—except when dealing with the soil—but their scale of industrial production was restricted by practical factors such as lack of capital equipment, trained workers and markets, rather than through ideological shortcomings. Perhaps their over-reliance on spade cultivation was a confused means of solving the Malthusian knot—that surplus mouths, re-settled on the land, would make survival possible, convert the unemployed into producers, help to equate purchasing power with industrial output, and reduce the bottlenecks of distribution.

We must not pay too much attention to the contradictions of the communitarians. Robert Owen was, at times, a firm egalitarian and at other times would classify people in more detail than a census return. Harriet Martineau, in 1834, thought that communitarianism was a most important social issue—'It will never now rest till it has been made a matter of experiment'[97]—and in 1840 Ralph Waldo Emerson wrote to Thomas Carlyle from America: 'We are all a little wild here with numberless projects of social reform. Not a reading man but has a draft of a new community in his waistcoat pocket...'[98] Was Harriet Martineau wrong? Were the communities only appropriate for the backwoods and merely a type of pioneer settlement? Many contemporary commentators thought of them not as escapism but as paths to social progress. They would convert others with their clarity of purpose and the innate social justice of their policies. The small community was an experiment, with all that an experiment implies: it was limited, its environment was controlled, and its forces were manipulated, not necessarily to give a final answer, but to provide evidence on which an eventual answer could be formulated. Nor did they insist on refined material; part of their purpose was to distil out impurity—they set out to overcome ignorance, poverty and vice, and they did not seek to excuse their failure by pointing out that many of the subjects of their experiments were ignorant, poor, vicious.

The community idea was therefore a means of reconciling immediate social reform with non revolutionary methods. Owen, in particular, deplored 'democracy', which he identified with militancy. He could not accept that conflict was the precursor of social change. There would be no class struggle: blame evils on the system and not on individuals. Communitarianism was social evangelism. Even in the tumult of 1832 Owen never saw any possibility of capitalists objecting to being employed by their workers. He pointed out to his followers that the rich were as much creatures of circumstance as any other class. The communities followed no set blueprint. They were liable to fail but they *could* learn from their errors. Their real weakness was that they refused to learn from their weaknesses.

When one lists the comforts to be attained in community one realises how far the working classes during the second quarter of the nineteenth century had improved their station and had raised their hopes for the future. A communitarian in 1832 included in his vision of communal life:

> In Communities we should all live in habitations built with the best science of architecture, and the most comprehensive views of human comfort: there would be museums, laboratories, libraries, places of elegant social and private resort, gardens, groves, fountains, baths, orchards, pleasure grounds, and fields of recreation and pastime, pasture and arable lands, stables and coach houses; there would also be picture galleries, and halls for music; and above all, perfect schools...[99]

It should be noticed how flamboyant these plans had become compared to the envisaged poor law colonies of the immediate post-Napoleonic war years. They are reminiscent of the utopian dreams of Thomas More, but with this difference—that the writers, although somewhat intoxicated with their visions, believed that such communities *could* be established. The inference, surely, for the historian is that the working classes had not only become articulate but that they had unwittingly conceded that capitalism and industrialisation made such visions capable of fruition. But as an emotional rallying cry, communitarianism in Britain was a panacea, a yearning to escape from the inhumanities, insanitary dwellings, trade uncertainty, long hours, lack of status and inequality ascribed to the new industrialism. It was a manifestation of the belief that society should have a conscious meaning:

> Social ideologies of the present day are ... the expression of a deeply felt want, an aspiration after the beautiful and intellectual ... the criticisms of their authors upon present society may be useful in drawing attention of legislators to many errors and abuses, the dust and cobwebs of the past.[100]

Some writers wedded Christianity to community ideas. A Christian community would be pure, because interests would be unified. World brotherhood would be the goal:

> No particular community or country would constitute a home; every country would be the favourite resort of all. They that were born in the sultry climates of the torrid zone, would long to visit more temperate climes; and they that came into being in temperate or polar regions would advance with eager curiosity to the regions of sunshine and everlasting Spring.[101]

The purity of the good social life assumed biological purity, and so vegetarianism, a strict domestic regimen and teetotalism were usually associated with communitarian experiments. Many community dwellers were eccentrics, but there was an innate friendliness in Owenism: as we shall see, even when an experiment failed, there was scarcely any mutual recrimination; fate had merely been unkind, and fresh programmes should be drawn up as soon as circumstances were propitious.

Communitarianism *per se* did not stir up as much antagonism from the Establishment as did the irreligious strands of Owenism or the fears of Chartist outrage and insurrection. One observer discounted the benefits of communitarianism because it did not attune to the human psyche:

> The disposition to live in a community and by that means relinquish the good as well as the evil, the hopes as well as the fears of independence, is never likely to attract a very large number even of the lower classes ... It

would be giving up all the pleasures of hope and ambition, which stirring spirits cannot live without. Besides this, supposing these associations were to succeed splendidly, how long would they last? Nothing is more probable, than that, finding that their common property had become so large they did not know what to do with it, they might come to the resolution of selling it, dividing the spoil, and separating again into independent members of society. Man is a restless and dissatisfied animal; as long as he is hunted by the dread of poverty, he thinks that any plan which offers him a comfortable provision and a tranquil mind comprehends every thing in life; but let him continue in this state so long as to forget what it is to feel or to fear hunger, and will he not begin to think his mode of life insipid, and long for a more adventurous one?[102]

The communitarians believed their plans to be perfect. They did not, however, pay sufficient attention to the devising of means for achieving their ends. They failed to evaluate the opposition; they over-simplified human behaviour; they were too rigid; they deceived themselves that the pursuit of logistic details in planning would ensure the viability of the main features of their social programmes; they were typical Victorians in their social optimism and in ascribing power to knowledge: to know was not only an antecedent to action, it would lead to action.[103] The communitarians were too optimistic of their powers of disseminating knowledge, of conversion and of discernment of social principles and motivation.

To have been successful would have brought rank immobile materialism. The communitarians could not achieve either sufficient isolation from or sufficient integration with the outside economy and still retain their identity as communities. They did not appreciate that social and economic conditions are corollaries of the division of power in a society and that power elites are tardy of approving actions leading to self-extinction.

In the end, the communities would have foundered politically unless some equation of self-government was devised to temper their predominant paternalism decaying into disruptive anarchy. The communities also raised the problem of disillusionment of reformers who see the fruition of their plans spurned by a new generation.

Living in the heyday of the American communities, Emerson commented on the problem of power:

> Philanthropic and religious bodies do not commonly make their executive officers out of Saints. The Communities hitherto founded by Socialists are only possible by installing Judas as steward. The rest of the offices may be filled by good burgesses.

He later added:

> Of the Shaker society it was formerly a sort of proverb in the country, that they always sent the devil to market... It is an esoteric doctrine of society, that a little wickedness is good to make muscle...[104]

Financial support from official sources was rare during the period of Owenite community experiments. Hence communities could be established only if sufficient self-generated capital was forthcoming. There were no precedents for the accumulation of large funds through trade union fees or from any other working class institutions. To a large extent, therefore, Robert Owen was forced to rely on his own resources, strongly augmented by support from rich sympathisers. Funds subscribed from working class members could only supplement these larger donations, and the communities were bound to fail once capital was withheld or withdrawn or the rich sponsors imposed unacceptable restrictions on the use of funds or dictated their own terms on the way the communities were operated.

The community experiments would also have foundered because they were set up before the protection of legal limited liability became generally available. Comprehensive systems of book-keeping did not develop until the growth of limited liability companies and the imposition of an obligation to retain in a business the subscribed capital: hence the necessity for asset valuation and the need to distinguish between an asset and an expense.[105]

Certainly estate accounts had been kept for centuries, at various levels of refinement, but there was a basic distinction between the accountability of communities and that of landed estates: the communities were newly established and had no rent rolls; they also had the impediments of heavy initial outlays on agricultural and residential buildings, farm equipment and labour costs, which would need to be met before a first harvest could be sold.[106]

One should not ignore the distinct and valuable merits of the communities. They had a sense of social progress and criticism; they demonstrated the influence of social institutions on thought and action and they pointed out the contrast between individual and social wellbeing. They saw the human aspects of industrialisation and mechanisation; they laid emphasis on the problems created by economic inequality; they believed in religious toleration and equality between the sexes; they showed the innate difficulties of social cohesion and leadership. The communities failed only as communities. Despite the contradiction of the early co-operative communities working within a capitalist system, they focused attention on social issues, especially on social rights and justice—matters requiring attention if capitalism was to mature peacefully. As with Owen, their importance lay in their influence and in their ventilation of the new social ills brought about by maturing industrialisation. But the community idea became less practicable as industrialism became even more mature, as barriers to social mobility were broken down, and the economic system became more integrated.

The community plans and experiments of the years 1825–45 deeply influenced the labour movement during the late nineteenth century. There is a permanent strain in English radical thought of escapism, enclavism, saintliness, idealism and crankiness. The pools of virtue of the Owenites appear again in the Guild of St George and the Fellowship of the New Life; the Owenite hymns are sung again in the Labour churches and Sunday schools. The appeal of the land was not the land hunger of a peasant society, but throughout the nineteenth century and beyond there was a continuing urge for acres from Chartists, land nationalisers and single taxers, and for rural resettlement[107] and town planning from a wide circle of social reformers.

In the same year that Queenwood community collapsed (1845), home colonies were being supported by the bishops of London and Norwich, by Lord John Manners and Minter Morgan.[108] There had been a continuing coterie of industrial villages from the eighteenth century, but it should be noted that after 1850 such villages were planned more as communities and less as adjuncts to the mill or the factory. By the turn of the nineteenth century, model industrial villages had been established (often by food manufacturers) at Bournville, Earswick, Port Sunlight, Bessbrook, Saltaire, Street and Vickerstown[109] each owing something to the Owenite communities. The plans laid down for Letchworth and Welwyn Garden City were examples of the intermediate stage between the earliest works villages and our present-day new towns.

Given that a reinterpretation of Robert Owen's influence on the Owenites and an appraisal of their institutions and leading personalities is long overdue, this study is directed away from an assessment of the importance of Owen in the history of the working class movement and concentrates more on the organisational effectiveness of the Owenite community experiments; in so doing, a number of misconceptions, including myths perpetuated by Owen himself, will be deflated. This approach should also help to determine the nature and genesis of the early co-operative movement.

The following chapters will investigate how Owenite agitation for social reform developed its programmes and policies to bring about a remodelled society, with an historical justification that this very comprehensiveness makes Owenism interesting and modern when compared with other aspects and institutions of the working class movement during the second quarter of the nineteenth century —most social reform agitation from below was parochial or particularist or organisationally weak, and so, in consequence, gained little respect or support from other than its own working class generators. On each of the above counts, the Owenite movement was more sophisticated and speculative about social structure and ethics than, say, friendly societies, trade unionism or Chartism.

Notes

1 *The Reasoner*, No. 2, 10 June 1846, p. 26.

2 The population of Birmingham, Glasgow, Liverpool, Manchester and Nottingham grew by 132 per cent between 1801 and 1821, whereas for the country as a whole the population increase was only 52 per cent. (C. Babbage, *On the Economy of Machinery and Manufactures*, 1832, p. 6.)

3 House of Commons Select Committee on Children, 1816, p. 117. See also M. M. Edwards, *The Growth of the British Cotton Trade*, 1967, pp. 212–13.

4 *The Torrington Diaries*, ed. C. B. Andrews, 1954 (the entry was for 23 June 1792).

5 P. Gaskell, *Artisans and Machinery: the Moral and Physical Condition of the Manufacturing Population considered with reference to Mechanical Substitutes for Human Labour*, 1836.

6 P. Gaskell, *Artisans and Machinery*, p. 294. The population of Hyde, Duckenfield [*sic*] and Newton districts in 1801 was 3,000; by 1830 it was almost 26,000. (*Ibid.*, p. 299.)

7 R. Owen, 'To the British master manufacturers', 1816, in *A New View of Society and other writings of Robert Owen*, ed. G. D. H. Cole, 1927, p. 145.

8 A. Ure, *Philosophy of Manufactures, or, an Exposition of the Scientific, Moral and Commercial Economy of the Factory System of Great Britain*, 1835, pp. 18–19.

9 C. Babbage, *On the Economy of Machinery and Manufactures*.

10 P. Gaskell, *Artisans and Machinery*, p. 6.

11 'Report to the County of Lanark', 1820, in *A New View of Society and other writings*, p. 258.

12 M. I. Thomis, *The Luddites: Machine Breakers in Regency England*, 1970.

13 'Report to the County of Lanark', p. 266.

14 J. M. Morgan, *The Practicability of Mr Owen's Plan*, 1819.

15 R. Southey, *Sir Thomas More, or, Colloquies on Society*, 1829.

16 W. Hazlitt, 'Jeremy Bentham', in *The Spirit of the Age* (1910 edition), p. 180.

17 A. Alison, *The Principles of Population and their Connection with Human Happiness*, 1840, II, p. 76.

18 C. Hall, *The effect of Civilization on the People in the European States*, 1805.

19 T. Spence, *The Constitution of a Perfect Commonwealth, being the French Constitution of 1793 Amended and rendered entirely conformable to the Whole Rights of Man*, 1798, p. 16. But elsewhere Spence wrote, 'no individual or community can be deprived of the smallest portion of their property, without their consent, except when the public necessity, legally ascertained evidently require it, and upon condition of a just indemnification' (p. 13).

20 W. Cobbett, *Cottage Economy*, 1821, pp. 3–4.

21 W. Cobbett, 'Legacy to Labourers, or, What is the Right which the Lords, Baronets, and Squires have to the Lands of England?' in *Six Letters, Addressed to the Working People of England*, 1834, pp. 13–14.

22 G. D. H. Cole, *Persons and Periods*, 1938, p. 117. Thomas Carlyle was another who fulminated, in the *Edinburgh Review* of June 1829, that it was not an heroic, devotional, philosophical or moral, but a 'Mechanical Age', which upset old relations and widened the gap between rich and poor.

23 W. Allen, *Colonies at Home*, 1828, p. 27.

24 *Ibid.*, p. 42.

25 'Address, City of London Tavern', 21 August 1817, in *A New View of Society and other writings*, p. 214.

26 *Ibid.*, p. 215.

27 *James Deacon Hume* (1774–1842), a free-trader who consolidated the customs laws and was joint secretary to the Board of Trade in 1828. His *Letters on the Corn Laws* were reprinted from a series published in the *Morning Chronicle* to show the fallacies in the dogma of the Society for Promoting National Regeneration. Hume also used the occasion to ventilate his views on free trade.

28 J. D. Hume, *Letters on the Corn Laws*, p. 10.

29 *Ibid.*, p. 14.

30 *Ibid.*, p. 10.

31 Hume's proposed remedy was much less impressive and comprehensive than his attack on agricultural protection. He recommended that more land should be turned over to grazing, with a modified and reduced corn duty to be used as a subsidy for pasture.

32 E. P. Thompson, *The Making of the English Working Class*, 1968 edition, pp. 883–4.

33 F. M. Eden, *Observations on Friendly Societies*, 1801, p. 7.

34 P. H. J. H. Gosden, *The Friendly Societies in England 1815–75*, 1961, pp. 4, 17.

35 F. Podmore, *Life of Robert Owen*, 1906.

36 Cf 'Robert Owen', *Westminster Review*, October 1860, pp. 384–5: 'There is no danger that the theories of Owen will be adopted in practice. They are

such flimsy chains that they can never bind a nation. Long before his death they were demolished and forgotten.'

37 A. E. Bestor, Jnr. *Backwoods Utopias*, 1950.

38 Bestor sees three chronological phases in Owen's thought: before 1821; the mid-1820s to the mid-1830s; and from 1840 on. (*Op. cit.*, p. 78.)

39 G. D. H. Cole, *Life of Robert Owen*, 1930, p. 237.

40 But some observers, Robert Southey included, thought that Owenism, to be successful, required some infusion of religious belief. W. L. Sargant, *Robert Owen and his Social Philosophy*, 1860, p. 428: 'With all Owen's efforts . . . he has not been able in ten years to raise funds for his experiments. Had he connected his scheme with any system of belief, though it had been as visionary as Swedenborgism, as fabulous as Popery, the money would have been forthcoming.'

41 R. D. Owen, *Threading my Way*, 1874, p. 166.

42 *Pioneers of English Education*, ed. A. V. Judges, 1952, p. 72.

43 Henry Brougham was percipient enough in 1819 to foresee that the lasting contribution of Owen's ideas would be to education: 'The system proposed and acted upon by Mr Owen in training infant children, before they were susceptible of what was generally called education, was deserving of the utmost attention. This indeed was the sound part of Mr Owen's plan, and agreeable to the wisest principles.' In more modern parlance, Owen contributed to the idea of extending educational opportunity as a right to every social class, and that education should encourage self-development of the individual for whole life in society. (*Parliamentary Debates*, ser. 1, XLI, pp. 1195–7, 17 December 1819. See also H. Silver, 'Owen's reputation as an Educationist' in *Robert Owen, Prophet of the Poor*, ed. S. Pollard and J. Salt, 1971, pp. 65–83.

44 Second essay, *A New View of Society*, 1813, in *A New View of Society and other writings*, p. 37.

45 *Report of the Third Congress of the Association of All Classes of All Nations and the First Congress of the Universal Community Friendly Society*, Manchester, May 1838.

46 R. Owen, *Life of Robert Owen, written by himself*, I, 1857, p. 61.

47 *Robert Owen's Journal*, III, No. 74, March 1852, p. 172.

48 P. Gorb, 'Robert Owen as a businessman', *Bulletin of the Business Historical Association*, XXV, No. 3, September 1957, pp. 127–48. See also A. J. Robertson, 'Robert Owen, cotton spinner: New Lanark, 1800–25', in *Robert Owen, Prophet of the Poor*, ed. S. Pollard and J. Salt, pp. 145–66, and J. Butt, 'Robert Owen as a businessman', in *Robert Owen, Prince of Cotton Spinners*, ed. J. Butt, 1971, pp. 168–214.

49 F. A. Packard, *Life of Robert Owen*, 1866.

50 R. Owen, *Address, City London Tavern*, 26 July, 1819.

51 'Report to the County of Lanark', in *A New View of Society and other writings*, p. 257.

52 *Lancashire and Yorkshire Co-operator*, No. 1, 3 September 1831, p. 5.

53 See appendix of *A Vindication of Mr Owen's Plan for the Relief of the Distressed Working Classes*, 1820, p. 53, for letter from Falla to Benjamin Wills, London, 16 December 1818, giving information on spade cultivation to

the 'Committee of the Association for Poor' and explaining that after three years' experiment spade cultivation had doubled the average produce of the land, with normal manuring.

54 *Ibid.*, p. 51.

55 R. Torrens, 'Mr Owen's plan for relieving the distress', *Edinburgh Review*, October 1819, p. 468.

56 For an opposing view, see T. R. Edmonds, *Practical Moral and Political Economy*, 1828, p. 52: population returns, which should show the strength of the nation, omit statistics on horses. If one horse power equals five men and there is one horse in England to ten people or two grown men, then the 'effect of the labour of horses is considerably greater than that of man'.

57 *Parliamentary Debates,* ser. 1, XLI, p. 1206, Thursday 16 December 1819.

58 W. L. Sargant, *Robert Owen and his Social Philosophy*, p. 168.

59 Letter from Falla to I. L. Goldsmid, 23 August 1823, in vol. 1 of the letters of I. L. Goldsmid, Mocatta collection, University College, London.

60 R. Torrens, 'Mr Owen's plan for relieving the distress', p. 461. Torrens argued that Owen's plans were barren, as they would not repeal the corn laws, reduce taxes or increase the area of fertile land.

61 *Report of Select Committee on Allotments*, Parliamentary Papers: Committees (3), 1843, VII, 402, quoted in J. Macaskill, 'The treatment of land in English social and political theory, 1840–85', B.Litt. thesis, University of Oxford, 1959, pp. 4, 15.

62 Second essay, *A New View of Society*, in *A New View of Society and other writings*, pp. 30, 35.

63 'Address at New Lanark', 1816, in *A New View of Society and other writings*, p. 108.

64 *Report of the Second Co-operative Congress*, October 1831, p. 14.

65 'Letter to the Public published in London Newspapers, 10 September 1817. Further Development of the Plan for the Relief of the Poor and the Emancipation of Mankind', in *A New View of Society and other writings*, p. 227.

66 R. Owen, *The Life of Robert Owen written by Himself*, IA, p. 76.

67 *A New View of Society: Tracts Relative to this Subject*, 1818.

68 Paper read by Thomas Spence before the Newcastle Philosophical Society in 1775 'On the mode of administering the landed estates of the nation as a joint stock company in parochial partnership by dividing the rent'.

69 W. Godwin, *An Enquiry Concerning Political Justice*, 1793, VIII, ch. VI, p. 844.

70 *Ibid.*, IV, ch. II, p. 223.

71 R. D. Owen, *Threading my Way*, p. 67.

72 P. Colquhoun, *A Treatise on the Wealth, Power and Resources of the British Empire*, 1815.

73 'Report to the County of Lanark', in *A New View of Society and other writings*, 1820, p. 286.

74 *Ibid.*, p. 287.

75 G. J. Holyoake, *Life and Last Days of R. Owen*, 1871, p. 19.

76 With the emphasis on community experiments, it is beyond the terms of reference of this study to trace the contribution of the labour economists to Robert Owen's thought. For nineteenth-century interpretations of the labour

theory of value, see especially: J. Gray, *A Lecture on Human Happiness*, 1825, and *The Social System*, 1831; T. Hodgskin, *Labour Defended against the Claims of Capital*, 1825; J. F. Bray, *Labour's Wrongs and Labour's Remedy*, 1839; A. Menger, *The Right to the Whole Produce of Labour*, 1899; E. Lowenthal, *The Ricardian Socialists*, 1911; M. Beer, *A History of British Socialism*, 1929; G. D. H. Cole, *Socialist Thought: the Forerunners*, 1953. The important contributions of William Thompson to communitarianism and Owenite socialism are set out below, pp. 47–50.

77 An account of Joanna Southcott and her sect is given in E. P. Thompson, *The Making of the English Working Class*, 1968 edition, pp. 420–6, and W. H. G. Armytage, *Heavens Below*, 1961, pp. 68–70.

78 See E. D. Andrews, *The People Called Shakers*, 1963, and W. H. G. Armytage, *Heavens Below*, especially ch. VII, 'Liverpool: gateway to Zion', pp. 259–71. See also W. H. Oliver, 'Owen in 1817: the millennialist movement', in *Robert Owen, Prophet of the Poor*, ed. S. Pollard and J. Salt, pp. 166–88.

79 The term 'communionist' was first used in the *Co-operative Magazine*, November 1827, p. 509: 'The chief question on this point, however, between the modern (or Mill and Malthus) Political Economists, and the Communionists or Socialists, is, whether it is more beneficial that this capital should be individual or in common.' In November 1841 John Goodwyn Barmby set up the Universal Communitarian Association and issued a monthy journal, *The Promethean, or Communitarian Apostle*. See also J. G. Barmby, *The Outlines of Communion Associality and Communitarianism*, 1841. The lasting contribution of Barmby is merely etymological in the history of socialist vocabulary; his practical contributions to social ideas and communitarianism were negligible. For other contemporary uses of the term 'communitarianism', see the Rev. E. Miall, *Nonconformity*, II, 1842, p. 809: 'Your communitarians, or societarians of modern days, who seem intent on fashioning a new moral world by getting rid of all individual feeling.' T. Frost, *Forty Years' Recollections*, 1880, p. 46: 'The Ham Common Communitarians found raw carrots and cold water unendurable when the snow lay thick on the ground.'

80 In this study the term 'millennarianism' will be used to denote apocalyptic cults which may or may not have developed settlement programmes (contrast the Moravian, Shaker and Mormon communities with the Southcottians, who had no plans for community experiments). 'Communitarianism' will be reserved for secular ideology and experiments.

81 Preface to the Manifesto of the Communist Party, 30 January 1888.

82 A. E. Bestor, Jnr., 'The evolution of the socialist vocabulary', *Journal of the History of Ideas*, IX, No. 3, June 1948, p. 293; also *id.*, *Backwoods Utopias*, p. viii.

83 Perhaps it would be more appropriate to see the individual transformation required under the Owen creed as a transcendental experience which did not require any understanding of the process of social change.

84 'Wherever the poor form themselves into successful co-operative communities, these evils must cease; they will no longer quarrel with their masters, for they will have no master to quarrel with; they will need no

assistance from the parish, and they will have no temptation to invade the property of others . . .

'Their influence must be anti-revolutionary; all those concerned in them will have a something at stake; and consequently a motive for preserving the peace and order of society. Besides, the object of these societies is the same as that of the legislature; namely, to take labourers out of the market, and place them in circumstances in which they shall want neither employment nor relief . . .' (undated letter No. 91, William Pare papers, Goldsmiths' Library); see also John Finch, letter ix, *Liverpool Chronicle*, 12 May 1838: 'If we can obtain all our political objects today, they would—*could*—not remove one of the social evils I have enumerated.'

85 A. Combe, *Sphere of Joint Stock Companies*, 1825, p. 23.

86 'We have now before us,' said Robert Owen, 'a plan of improving society which has hitherto been only understood by a few individuals, and can only be understood by those who understand the science of human nature; but this is so simple that a child of eight years of age, well educated, may understand it. I speak this from experience. We are now, I think, in a position to command it from the hands of the Government; and why? because they do not know how to relieve the community from a state of wretchedness and poverty, and we will show them the means of creating a Paradise.' (*Report of the Second Co-operative Congress*, 1831, p. 11.) A decade earlier Owen had stated, 'My aim is therefore to withdraw the germ of all party from society.' ('An address to the inhabitants of New Lanark,' in *A New View of Society and other writings*, p. 106.)

87 *Statement submitted to the Marquis of Normanby relative to the Universal Community Society of Rational Religionists by Branch A1, London*, February 1840, pp. 7, 14.

88 Letter iv (undated) from William Thompson in the William Pare papers, Goldsmiths' Library.

89 As late as 1848 it was argued in the *Westminster Review* (July 1848) that Owen was right in advocating land communities—one-third of the price of food in London comprised cost of carriage and retail profits.

90 *Statement to the Marquis of Normanby*, p. 6.

91 'An address to the inhabitants of New Lanark on opening the Institution for the Formation of Character,' 4 January 1816, in *A New View of Society and other writings*, p. 106.

92 With the exception of George Mudie's urban community in London in 1821–22; see *The Economist*, January 1821–March 1822, *passim*.

93 'Articles would always gain sale outside the communities, for they would be staple articles and of superior quality.' (*Constitution and Rules of the Universal Community Society of Rational Religionists*, 1839, p. 13.)

94 J. Smith in the *New Moral World*, 119, 4 February 1837, p. 113.

95 *Constitution and Rules of the Universal Community Society of Rational Religionists*, p. 38.

96 *Ibid.*, p. 39.

97 H. Martineau, *Society in America*, 1837, 11, pp. 57–8.

98 Quoted in M. Holloway, *Heavens on Earth*, 1951, p. 19.

99 T. Wayland, *National Advancement and Happiness Considered in refer-*

ence to the Equalization of Property and the Formation of Communities,
1832.
100 'Social Utopias,' *Chambers' Papers for the People,* 1850–51, No. 18, p. 32.
See also M. Hennell, *An Outline of the Various Communities which have
been founded on the Principle of Co-operation,* 1844.
101 J. E. Smith, *Lecture on a Christian Community,* 1833, pp. 14–15. See also
H. H. Norton, *Community the only Salvation for Man,* 1838. John Minter
Morgan offered to endow a professorship at King's College, London, provided the college would include co-operative studies in the syllabus. (W.
Anderson Smith, *Shepherd Smith, the Universalist,* 1892, p. 96.) See also
J. Saville, 'J. E. Smith and the Owenite movement, 1833–34', in *Robert Owen,
Prophet of the Poor,* ed. S. Pollard and J. Salt, pp. 115–45.
102 See undated letter No. 91, William Pare papers, Goldsmiths' Library,
quoting from an adverse article on co-operation in the *Quarterly Review.*
103 General surveys of utopian communities are to be found in W. H. G.
Armytage, *Heavens Below,* W. N. Loucks, *Comparative Economic Systems,*
7th edition, 1966, H. W. Laidler, *Social Economic Movements,* 1948. H. F.
Infield, in *Co-operative Communities at Work,* 1947, argues that failures were
rarely economic; more often communities collapsed because of poor selection,
lack of agricultural experience and internal quarrels. For an assessment of
community failure, see ch. 7, pp. 214ff.
104 R. W. Emerson, 'Power', *Collected Essays,* 1908 edition, p. 362.
105 'Cost accountancy represents the influence of the industrial revolution
upon double-entry book-keeping: it is an important element in marking the
expansion of book-keeping (a record) into accountancy (a managerial instrument
of precision).' Depreciation of assets was not accounted for until the development of railways, but an accountant at the time thought that the railway
financial disasters of 1847–48 'did more than anything else to place professional accountancy on a solid and substantial basis'. (A. C. Littleton, *Accounting Evolution to 1900,* 1933, pp. 280, 360.)
106 The difficulties over legal security of funds and property which bedevilled the early co-operatives hastened the overhaul of commercial law
through the lobbying of Christian socialist lawyers—for the ruling classes
were always more sympathetic to co-operators than to trade unionists. Even
so impressive a figure as J. S. Mill could crusade for co-operation. 'Whatever
may be the merits or defects [of communist schemes] they cannot be truly
said to be impracticable.' J. S. Mill, *Principles of Political Economy,* 1883
edition, p. 124.
107 See William Booth's solution to the social problem in H. Begbie, *Life of
William Booth,* 1920, II, p. 360. General Booth visited Germany in 1905 and
wrote to William Bramwell on the problem of the unemployed: 'The spade
is the solution. I maintained it sixteen years ago. I am stronger for it than
ever. Think of the stuff three acres of decent land would produce cultivated
to the uttermost by the sweat of a man's—not a horse's—or a hired labourer's
—but his own brow.'
108 J. M. Morgan, *Letter to the Bishop of London,* 1830, and *The Christian
Commonwealth,* 1845.
109 B. Meakin, *Model Factories and Villages,* 1905, pp. 417–33, *passim.*

2

Robert Owen and the Owenite contribution to co-operative socialist community experiments, 1820–1830

The mass of writings on Robert Owen and the growth of the co-operative movement is matched by a dearth of references to the Owenites. Owen's visions were transmuted to his disciples, many of whom tempered the views of the master with a finer sense of practicability and balance. They were also generally more consistent —notwithstanding constant admonitions to his followers to behave as 'men of business', it was Owen himself who squandered resources, especially in connection with his community experiments. He could organise but was never really a co-operator at heart. This was the function of the Owenites, and the co-operative movement was the creation of the Owenites, not of Owen. The Owenites are usually regarded as his humble disciples, whereas in reality they were far from pale shadows, nor were they dogmatists. Their self-appointed mission was to reinterpret and apply Owen's directives and encyclicals. Evidence of their effective dedication is shown when the Archbishop of Canterbury felt compelled to admit in 1840, 'The misionaries sent forth by the socialists were ... for the most part, active and intelligent and very often educated persons.'[1]

> The first evidence of the use of the term 'Owenite' was in 1821: Polemical discussions upon religion and politics might help to fill your pages to an indefinite extent; but would be liable to draw the Owenites from one thing, in their opinion, needful—the establishment of the system.[2]

But the first evidence of any attempt to integrate Owen's views into a practical experiment[3] was in August 1820 at a meeting at which George Mudie[4] proposed a 'Plan of Association' referred to in the 'Report of a Committee of Journeymen chiefly printers to take into consideration propositions by George Mudie for a system of social arrangements to effect improvement in condition of working classes and of Society at large'.[5] George Mudie was virtually the first Owenite, although he was later to quarrel with many of Owen's views. The journeymen printers aimed to provide better housing, less domestic drudgery, medical attention and a share in communal management 'and *emphatically* we shall have the happiness of *seeing* our children well educated and trained...'[6] The majority of the journeymen were employed in London, but they thought that a farm would be a useful means of occupying the unemployed. A capital sum of £12,000 in denominations of £100 shares was to be subscribed for setting up an urban community for 250 families. If successful, the experiment could be emulated:

> We may remark, that for succeeding Societies in the Metropolis, new erections will not always be required; as, after the great advantages of the Plan have been practically demonstrated, persons now occupying contiguous dwellings, will of course avail themselves of the facility with which they are enabled to associate in their present residences.[7]

The report concluded that a new journal would be published, which George Mudie launched as *The Economist*[8] while he was still editor of *The Sun*.

A meeting of the London printers on 22 January 1821 had suggested the formation of a 'Co-operative and Economical Society'[9] and the following day a constitution was drawn up stating that 'The ultimate object of this Society is to establish a Village of Unity and Mutual Co-operation, combining Agriculture, Manufactures, and Trade, upon the Plan projected by Mr Owen of New Lanark'.[10] The 'Prospectus' in the first issue on 27 January 1821 noted that 'The great majority of the members will however continue at their present employments—each male member paying one guinea weekly to the general fund', for which he would receive board and accommodation for himself and family, sickness benefit and a share in communal property and capital. In the second issue of *The Economist* it was announced: '*Poverty must continue*, while Production is confined within the bounds of Consumption.'[11] The Co-operative and Economic Society went on to report, in the third issue, on the merits of barter as a means of equating wants with supplies,[12] but it was argued that considerable saving in expenditure would be forthcoming in the proposed community, as goods could be bought at wholesale prices. Each member was to contribute towards shares in units of five shillings and 'to facilitate the distribution of goods, and for other social purposes, as many of the members as can conveniently quit their present residences, do live as nearly as possible together, in one or more neighbourhoods'.[13] The members intended to set up a store from which the public were to be allowed to buy goods, but disillusionment soon set in at the lack of progress—a letter from 'A Few Co-operative Economists' pointed out that four strangers who jointly bought a sheep at Smithfield had done more than all the meetings during the course of twenty issues of *The Economist*.[14] The Co-operative Society was at pains to point out that 'The Community was to be no Owenite village, nor a spade paradise, but located in the City itself'.[15]

An early example of what became the acknowledged formula for setting up communities appeared in a letter in June 1821 which suggested that the stages should be ones of retailing and profit accumulation, before eventual investment in Owenite communities, with labour as the standard of valuation and exchange:[16]

> The secret is out. The system is known—has been well explained—and holds out such a train of benefits to the poor, and indeed to all classes, that it can never again be lost sight of.[17]

The object 'is not *community of goods*,—but full, complete, unrestrained co-operation, on the part of all members . . .' This was not meant to lead to holding goods in common:

> A community of goods, therefore, is neither the distinguishing feature of the system, nor the direct object which it is intended to accomplish. On the contrary, it distinctly recognises, and *carefully preserves*, the *right of private property*, and of individual accumulation and possession.[18]

A letter from the 'Owenian, Friendly, or Practical Society of Edinburgh (for which we have not yet fixed on our designation)' requested specimen regulations from the London co-operators. The Edinburgh society had already published 'Minutes of the Congregational Families' showing evidence that they had entered into some form of communal arrangement.[19]

A London builder submitted plans for communal premises, and an attorney, who was also a member of the Co-operative and Economical Society, advised that the co-operative body could come within the provisions of protective legislation for friendly societies.[20] By November 1821 it was reported that 'The Co-operative and Economical Society has taken several houses in Spa Fields, rents to commence Christmas. Two or three families will move in in a few days.'[21] Rents were fixed—room charges were to range between two and four shillings weekly, including taxes and the use of dining room, stores, kitchen. Members decided, however, not to pool their incomes. A scale of weekly expenses was drawn up with maintenance for a man and wife at 14*s* 5*d*; single men would also be obliged to pay 14*s* 5*d*—the same charge as for a married couple—because of the communal value of a wife's industry.[22] Families were duly 'congregated' from 25 December 1821 and instructed that 'each member should appoint, from amongst the congregated members, his own friendly monitor ...' who was to give notice of errors of conduct, temper and language, and to admonish where necessary. In turn, the monitor was to be subject to the admonitions of his own appointer—'these monitors are the *sole* channels through which complaint or admonition can be conveyed'.[23]

Some indication of the range of skills of this small group of London co-operators is given in a notice inviting orders for work in 'carving, gilding, and for boots and shoes, gentlemen's clothes, dressmaking and millinery, umbrellas, hardware (including stoves, kettles, etc), cutlery, transparent landscape window-blinds, and provisions'.[24] For a period *The Economist* had been produced at the community, but printing ceased with issue No. 52 of 9 March 1822. Mudie later asserted that he had lived for two years in association with twenty-one families[25] until the proprietor of *The Sun* compelled him to abandon either the community or his editorship. Mudie thereupon left the community, and the congregated members shortly afterwards dispersed.

There is no evidence that Robert Owen had any direct involvement in the Spa Fields experiment. A quarter of a century later Mudie referred to Owen's apostasy:[26]

> In my *Economist* I had endeavoured to retrieve both you and the co-operative cause from the consequences of some of your errors. Even if I had not differed from some of your tenets as to religion and morals and even if I had not been too practical a man for the waste of time consumed in never-ending metaphysical disquisitions and discussions ... I was, and am, too much of a *politician* not to be aware, that the utmost result of your 'Views and objects' would only be the institution of a sect ... and even that has not yet taken place; while the cause of co-operation, if it has not been entirely ruined, has been retarded by your mischievous efforts.

Mudie then took issue over Owen's reliance on spade cultivation, 'one of your pet "views and objects" ', and he finally rounded on Owen:

> Now, Sire, and believe me that it gives me real and heartfelt pain to speak thus plainly to one whom I once fervently admired, esteemed and loved—I well knew, what indeed you will find, if you enquire, is well known to every man of any intellect, who has ever been closely connected

with you, or who has closely observed your tactics—I well knew that you will act only with blind worshippers.

Mudie thus accused Owen of decrying the Spa Fields experiment, which Mudie felt had been the main cause of the disbandment of the community.

After the disbanding of the Spa Fields experiment Mudie continued to give weekly lectures in London:

> It is by political economy that your system must triumph. The world must be convinced that it will be productive of increased wealth, as well as of increased intelligence. The latter, though the more valuable, is of secondary importance in the estimation of the present generation.[27]

During the summer of 1822 the British and Foreign Philanthropic Society, the only body ever directly associated with Owen for establishing a model community, duly adopted his plan because it 'ensures security for payment of rent, improvement of soil, safe investment can extinguish poor rate without disturbing relations of society, increase production . . .' A resolution was then moved by the Society 'That subscription be forthwith entered into: first for a Parent Establishment at Motherwell in Scotland, which may both serve as a Model, and also effect the training of Teachers to be employed in the formation of succeeding Communities . . .'[28]

In November 1822 William Watson, president of the Edinburgh Practical Society, asked Owen for admittance of his thirty members, chiefly mechanics, to any future Owenite community. 'The idea of living together, in a Community, has been the soul of our Society . . . The New Society excludes no one from its advantages.'[29] Shortly after this request was received, the British and Foreign Philanthropic Society ceased to function. I. L. Goldsmid proposed a resolution that the society should disband, as no meetings had taken place since August 1822[30]—Goldsmid had declined an invitation to subscribe £5,000 to the erstwhile Philanthropic Society, as he was not convinced of the viability of untried communities as sound investment propositions:

> I believe that I may through your means have a chance of doing some good to my fellow creatures, but when you wish me to subscribe £5,000 as a commercial speculation, I must decline being a party to such a measure because to advance money with such an intent it ought to be for objects the success of which are far from problematical but as your society is to be guided by principles which have hitherto had but a very limited influence on the actions of mankind and as many well-disposed persons

are of opinion that they must chiefly rely on the theoretical statements of the benevolent protector I do not think anyone ought to invest such a sum ... if you succeed but in one establishment the multiplication from interested motives will be no difficult task.[31]

What of Owen's contribution to these early debates and experiments on co-operation? He was almost continuously absent in America from 1824 to 1829 and the co-operative movement was generated without him. In fact, the theory of co-operation, and particularly of community organisation, was contributed more by William Thompson, whose book[32] Owen took to America. The early co-operators in Britain found communitarian ideas singularly appropriate for setting an ultimate objective to their consumers' co-operative societies. Owen was later to court the equitable labour exchanges and the labour movement during the early 1830s, but these excursions, at most, were merely asides or variations on the community theme and can be regarded as exploratory paths to community in much the same way as the setting up of retail co-operative societies.

Owen had departed for America in 1824 but he was back in England the following year and gave a lecture on co-operation at the Mechanics' Institute in London in September 1825.[33] A new journal, *The Co-operative Magazine and Monthly Herald*, was issued from January 1826 as a platform for a group of London co-operators who had first met in hired rooms in Burton Street from the end of 1824. Several changes of venue took place during early 1825—to the Crown and Court Rooms in Chancery Lane, and from April a floor was hired in a building in Temple Bar. From November 1825, with an influx of members, meetings were held thenceforth at 36 Red Lion Square.[34] The *Co-operative Magazine* debated plans for community, but the journal did not contemplate 'the formation of any great State into one community';[35] what it looked forward to was a network of communities. 'Owenism' came under fire:

> We do not like the term 'Owenism': it is extremely vague; it defines nothing; it mixes up Mr Owen's character (which fortunately has been found irreproachable) and his private opinions on various subjects, with the new system of social arrangements, in favour of which he has challenged the fullest investigation. *The Co-operative Magazine* does not propose to support 'Owenism', but to call the attention of the public to the principles of mutual co-operation and equal distribution, of which Mr Owen is a very powerful advocate.[36]

Owen was becoming thought of almost as a liability: 'We are not
... the mere blind followers of Owen.'[37] It was then argued more
in support of Owen that 'the system advocated by Mr Owen, and
properly called the Co-operative System, is not founded on the
principle of trade'. Little saving could be derived from engaging in
wholesale and retail transactions—the solution lay in an association
of producers to create their own internal market. Owen's tactics
were defended: he had been circumspect in first appealing to the
upper classes for support. If he had solicited the workers, the upper
classes would have become alarmed and would have thwarted any
extension of co-operation. 'Now, however, we may rest in perfect
confidence that, however indisposed the Legislature may be to
come forward and support the system, no active opposition need be
apprehended from that quarter.'[38]

In 1826 the London Co-operative Society drafted a set of 'Articles
of Agreement for the Formation of a Community within 50 miles
of London on Principles of Mutual Co-operation'.[39] Much of the
language was derived from William Thompson[40] and from John
Gray's *Lecture on Human Happiness*. There would be 'Community
of Property' and 'Equal means of enjoyment', self-government by
majority vote, and 'to women, forming half the human race—freedom from domestic drudgery of cooking, washing, and of heating
apartments, which will be performed on scientific principles on a
large economical scale'. Labour was not to exceed eight hours daily.
There would be a system of mutual instruction, and all community
dwellers were to undertake some tasks in both agriculture and industry: any unhealthy occupations that could not be done by
'machinery, chemical or scientific means, or modified, or by rota,
will be banished'. There would be guardians of public health, and
three classes of shareholders. Those who could subscribe £100 had
a right of immediate admission to the proposed community; £40
shareholders could enter after the first harvest; and £10 holders as
soon as land was purchased, with entitlement to food and shelter
until the produce of their own labour provided a surplus. At the
end of the 'Articles' was appended an Owenite creed on charitable
conduct, knowledge of human nature, methods of production and
distribution, infant education and government, and 'principles of
uniting in one general system the previous five branches'.

It was generally accepted by contemporaries and later historians
that William Thompson of County Cork contributed far more to

the economic theory of co-operation and socialism than Robert Owen.[41] Writing at the turn of the nineteenth century, H. S. Foxwell thought that Owen was 'less important' as an economic theorist 'than many who fought under his flag'.[42] Though socialism was of Owenite origin, 'the ideas we associate with the term today came not so much from Owen as from Thompson and his school'.[43] Thompson went beyond Owen's conception of community and a labour theory of value, and he was more politically conscious than Owen. A just society would not evolve merely from a proliferation of co-operative communities: the acquisition of political power was also necessary, for 'added to knowledge, the Industrious Classes must also acquire power, the whole power of the social machine in their own hands'.[44] The Irish socialist wrote his treatise on the economic theory of co-operation in 1824,[45] and his *vade mecum* of plans for community development in 1830.[46] Between these two dates he published an essay on labour theory of value,[47] and was a regular correspondent to the co-operative journals.

'Community' was defined by Thompson as 'an association of persons in sufficient numbers, and living on a space of land of sufficient extent, to supply by their own exertions all of each other's wants'.[48] Mutual co-operation implied for him a constraint that 'every individual entering a community is willing to direct his or her labour, mental or physical, or as is most frequently the case, both combined, to whatever objects may be deemed by the general voice, most conducive to the general good'.[49]

Some form of division of labour was essential, but communities should not become specialised.[50] A variety of employment opportunities must be provided, even within the basis of agricultural communities:

> Even fifty persons renting or cultivating 200 acres of land (for mere agriculturalist must take four times the quantity of land necessary for their own support in the way of food)... would require stock equivalent to machinery, to the amount of £20 each person for the successful cultivation of the land and rendering its surplus produce saleable, to purchase by exchanges, clothing, furniture, etc. and to pay charges.[51]

Thompson put the main political objection to communities that they would gradually supersede the institutions of society and would interfere with public revenue by directing industry to articles of general consumption rather than luxuries, 'thus evading many of the most productive taxes'.[52] He then contested the validity of the foregoing on grounds of the proper function and purpose of social institutions:

> The whole of the first part of this objection is well founded. If the present institutions, the comforts, the characters, and enjoyments to which they give rise, were such as they ought to be, it would be superfluous to devise new arrangements to evade or improve upon them. It is exactly because these institutions are supposed to be defective, to be irreconcilable with the real improvement and happiness of man that the new arrangements are proposed for adoption.[52]

The Irish socialist was thinking in pre-Marxist terms that the State would wither away because no government could stand against the universal adoption of co-operative communities. As the communities would be crime-free,[54] little taxation would need to be levied for personal or property protection.[55] The basis of a just tax could be a graduated rent on the wealth of each community. He pursued other objections to a system of communities[56]—that they would cause over-population, breed dull uniformity, that they would be founded on 'restraints', and that competition would merely transfer its level from the individual to the individual community. Thompson could not accept the inevitability of such a clash of interests except as a long term contingency which 'might be left to find its cure by means of expedients which the increasing wisdom excited by the new institutions would induce'.[57]

As with Owen, Thompson went into flights of fancy when contemplating the benefits of community. In a letter to the *Co-operative Magazine* on the internal features of a model community, he suggested a square of buildings laid out as a world map on a scale of one inch to ten miles:

> Omitting waste of the Pacific and Southern Oceans ... and trees planted in suitable countries. Of course Ireland should be their potato garden ... The waste lands of Africa and Asia might be used for gymnastic exercises ... The Mediterranean would be large enough for the young people to bathe in. Britain would be signified by an acre of playground.[58]

To Thompson, co-operation afforded the nearest approach to the ideal of the entitlement of the worker to the full value of his labour, although he conceded that it was impossible to allow each person the exact product of his individual contribution. Nevertheless, he saw more clearly than did Owen the full political implications of adhering to a labour theory of value in terms of exploitation.[59] Thompson's argument was weakest where it tried to reconcile the whole produce of a labour theory of distribution with a system of equality. When conflict arose between the produce of labour reward and equality, 'security', which he defined as 'whole produce', would receive priority, and any departure from 'security' should be in favour of equality.[60] Only in a co-operative system could he visualise any resolution of equality with security, as so much inequality was due to the system of exchanges, 'not differences in productivity of different labourers'.[61] Thompson was willing to write off the property already in the hands of the rich because, like Owen, he did not contemplate expropriation by force. In any case, Thompson thought that existing wealth was negligible compared with the vast accretions to be made possible with the improved techniques and efficiency of labour which could be brought about by sponsoring the incentive of reward of whole produce of labour. But he parted company with Owen over the role of political agitation in attaining a transformation of society. As long as the competitive system prevailed, 'the root of inequality' remained, but there was 'some sense in demanding political reform' as a preliminary to a co-operative commonwealth, as it would be advantageous if the making of laws could be the prerogative of the working people.[62]

The *Co-operative Magazine* reported that a small community had taken possession of six acres near Exeter during the summer of 1826. Part of their plans was the erection of 'a boarding house . . . for the reception of ten or twelve genteel families of independent income, which will form a market for the productions of, and be a source of revenue to the community'. Hence those sympathisers who did not wish to enter 'upon an equality in every respect with the co-operative classes' could nevertheless contribute to its success.[63] The Exeter community soon had to disband when a Mr Vesey withdrew his capital; most of the members were taken on at an adjoining farm.[64]

At least one correspondent to the *Co-operative Magazine* felt that the idea of communities should not become associated in the public mind with rural depravity. 'I do not like the terms, villages and villagers, as applied to the establishments of Communities . . .' 'Village' gave the impression of poverty, uncouthness, ignorance and dependence,[65] whereas co-operative communities would mitigate not only the evils of towns but also those of isolated settlements.[66]

What evidence have we of Owen's views on these co-operative

ventures from 1825? He arrived back in London in 1827 with a considerable change in the scale of his plans—even ten or twenty people could now form a community. By the end of 1827 the co-operators themselves were even more insistent on their independence than previously stated:

> Of Mr Owen, we have often said before, and we now say again, that we never considered him either as the author, the infallible high priest or the prophet of the Co-operative or Communional—or as accurately as either, the social . . . system.

Owen was always setting himself up as the author, 'the very Alpha and Omega of the System, when he could bring forward in support of it so many great names . . .'[67] Moreover, co-operators resented 'his religio-phobia, when he could easily prove the Christian religion most expressly commands and most continually inculcates, as the first thing necessary, the practice of our System . . .'[68]

It was Dr William King of Brighton[69] who joined Owenism to the co-operative store. A co-operative society was formed in 1827 at Brighton and by the November of that year it was reported that the members were trading co-operatively with a view to eventually establishing a community: the 200 members 'will hire farm with purchasing clause, locate themselves, and live in community . . .' Self-interest was at the root of public interest and co-operation, 'for if labourers are growing poorer and poorer every day . . . they have the strongest of all motives—self-interest for co-operating together to prevent it . . .'[70] Another co-operative society of eighteen members was formed on 1 January 1828—the Sussex General Co-operative Trading Association—with the aim of wholesale purchasing, accumulation of profits for land, and 'equal distribution of property'. All transactions in the general provisions store were to be on a cash basis. Dividend on purchases was also provided for: 'In order to hold out an encouragement to the members to deal at this, their own store, a drawback of 2½ per cent is allowed upon all sums so expended.'[71] The benefits of mutual trading were compared with community in the first issue of the Brighton *Co-operator*, a journal of distinct literary merit:

> . . . if members choose to remain in a town instead of going into community, they may derive all the advantages from the Society . . . We must go to a shop every day to buy food and necessaries—why then should we not go to our own shop?[72]

E. T. Craig later thought the Brighton *Co-operator* 'was more clear in all its expositions than anything Mr Owen had submitted to the public, and less elaborate than Thompson's work . . .'[73] The aim of co-operation was self-help and improved status, as far as Dr King was concerned. 'Co-operation aims at giving property and character to the working classes . . . The possession of property tends, more than any other cause, to produce respect for the property of others.'[74] And the desire for property, fairly acquired, was anti-revolutionary. 'The revolutionary principle is one of destruction: the co-operative principle is one of accumulation.'[75] Brighton was therefore the first of the early co-operative societies to have community as an eventual object to be attained through the profits of co-operative trading:

> There are some [societies] that mistake the means for the end, and from the success attending trading at their store, regard buying and selling as their main object; forgetting that our motto is 'Labour is the source of wealth . . . trading is only the ladder'.

The true object was 'to form a capital upon which to labour for ourselves and to acquire knowledge and wisdom to direct us in the use of it. We must invest our savings in trade as the readiest means of forming this capital'.[76]

Dr William King, of Brighton, was also the first writer on co-operation to be accepted by the Establishment:

> There is reason to believe that Mr Hill proposed to the Useful Knowledge Society the publication of a Treatise on co-operation by Dr King of Brighton . . . The motion, however, if made, was lost.[77]

The *Co-operative Magazine* announced that by October 1828 applications had been received from groups of supporters at Kingstanley (near Stroudwater), Belper and Birmingham for instructions in starting co-operative societies. The Birmingham Co-operative Society was duly launched in November 1828, and stated that it aimed to support the formation of co-operative societies 'not to relieve the miserable but to abolish the causes of misery . . .' Co-operation would combine the advantages of other self-help institutions—sick clubs, friendly societies[78] and savings banks[79] because:

> The income of EVERY INDIVIDUAL, and consequently of the WHOLE COMMUNITY (except only those persons who have fixed money incomes) IS LIMITED BY COMPETITION. And each obtains the LEAST that his labour, his services, or the use of his property CAN POSSIBLY BE OBTAINED FOR.[80]

William Pare, who was largely instrumental in forming the Birmingham Co-operative Society, corresponded with James Doherty, the trade union leader who had agitated for 'an active union . . . not only workmen of one particular trade, but of all trades, to assist in supporting men in case of a turn out . . .' Pare pointed out the futility of such a policy—labour was subject to the competition of capital, but capitalists could afford to be idle and beat down workers because the worker who refused the wage offered could exist only on a strike fund. 'Don't pay your subscriptions to trade society funds, which are invested and assist capitalists,' said Pare. 'Trade with your subscriptions and get 200 per cent, not 5 per cent.'[81]

The stated aims of the Birmingham society were 'mutual protection against poverty' and 'independence through growth of common capital' by means of weekly subscriptions, trading and manufacturing operations, and community settlement. Each potential member had to be proposed, was debarred from belonging to any other co-operative society, and would have to subscribe 4*d* weekly. Profits were to be added to common capital so that 'Nothing in the way of profits of trade, or any part of the capital, shall even be divided among the members, as Community of Property in Land and Goods is the great object of this Society'.[82] All members were expected to purchase from the society store, where 'they at present retail articles in the Grocery Line . . .' The Birmingham *Address* listed sixteen co-operative societies in operation in other parts of England. Pare, who was undoubtedly the author of the *Address*, later described the occupations of the Birmingham co-operators:

> The following are the principal trades of the members of the first Birmingham Co-operative Society: brassfounders, jewellers, silversmiths, japanners, platers, gilt-toy makers, wire-workers, button-makers, screwdrivers, saddlers, hot-house manufacturers, rule-makers, gun-makers, engravers, wood-turners, book-binders, pocket-book makers, Britannia metal workers, shoe-makers, tailors, millers, bakers, etc.[83]

Pare urged societies not to lose sight of the land:

> I conceive it to be of the greatest importance for the societies to rent and cultivate land; as soon as possible. For the produce of the land there is always a good market in the members of the Society; and its cultivation may often give employment to members in want of work.

He reported that the Birmingham Society had taken over for cultivation several acres outside the town. But initial difficulties were expected in establishing a farming community: one obstacle was the 'loss of income which the associates sustain upon quitting their occupations in old Society, before arrangements have been made in the new establishments for regular employment, or a market found for the surplus produce'. It was estimated, for instance, that 200 families at a weekly maintenance of 20s would require an outlay of £10,400 for the first year before a harvest could be gathered and other running funds needed for farm buildings, stock, and raw materials for manufacturing:

> Any commencement of, or approximation to, the social system, that will secure to the members their present employment and wages, and at the same time hold out inducements to those capitalists who seek only a safe and profitable investment... must have more successful prospects than any previous attempts.[84]

By the early summer of 1829 it was reported that about forty societies had been formed, although at the time of launching the First Birmingham Society there had been only four co-operatives in the entire kingdom.[85] A society in Leicestershire was manufacturing stockings; another at Belper had its own store and killed its own meat.[86] Birmingham First Society claimed over 100 members, and was operating a butcher's shop; in addition a boot and shoe manufactory 'almost constantly employ two of their members'.[87]

A society formed at Liverpool by John Finch during the winter of 1829[88] insisted on plotting an independent course:

> The promoters of the First Liverpool Co-operative Society disclaim all connexion with the views or intentions of other Societies, or with any designs entertained by Mr Owen, or his supporters. They acknowledge them as fellow labourers in the same great and good work.[89]

The Liverpool society also took issue on other matters of the Owenite creed: for instance, the promoters

> would make Christian precepts the very foundation and law of their conduct, and as one of their principal objects is the improvement of a great and important body of the people, they cannot at present perceive that this would be promoted by a separation into distinct communities, instead of mingling with the world, and inducing others by the influence of example to acknowledge the excellent effects of co-operation... A Community of property is not at present among the ultimate objects of the Society...[90]

Other co-operative societies argued that their primary aim was self-employment: the First Preston Society aimed to provide 'capital sufficient to keep all members in constant employment' and wished to diffuse principles of co-operation so as to 'form [a] community of independent labourers'.[91] The Carlisle Co-operating Society of 1829 gave a full account of its objects in a letter to the *Carlisle Journal*:

> to form common capital upon which members may work, to support own poor and sick and provide employment for out-of-work members, to provide education for children, commodities of best quality at fair prices.

There was an embargo on credit transactions, the consumption of liquor at meetings, and engagement in political or religious discussions. The society would 'combine advantages of Friendly Societies, Benefit Clubs, and Savings Banks, with the additional one of mental improvement and the education of children of members'.[92] The society limited its members to fifty and subscriptions to 6*d*, with members obliged to spend at least 5*s* weekly at the co-operative store, otherwise they would be liable to a fine of 3*d*; the penalty for reported trading at other shops was a fine of 6*d*.[93] The Lamberhead Green Co-operative Trading Fund Society wished to establish a school of industry for girls and a day and evening school for boys. But the society also sought to protect its funds by restricting its membership: 'No person can be admitted as member if in general bad health, or who labours under any debility of body, which is likely to disable him from getting his living.'[94]

Some centralisation of effort and propaganda for the early co-operative movement was set in motion through the formation of the Association for Promotion of Co-operative Knowledge in the spring of 1829.[95] The total number of established co-operative bodies reported at the second quarterly meeting of the Association had risen to 125.[96] A co-operative silk handkerchief was to be produced by distressed co-operators of Spitalfields and Bethnal Green. ('We never saw so interesting a nose rubber before—full of satire and intelligence—giving a perfect lesson on political economy . . . the centre piece is a perfect representation of the various classes of Society in Great Britain and Ireland . . .'[97]) Aid was sought for the Spitalfields silk weavers and a bazaar was acquired at Greville Street to dispose of silk goods produced by fourteen weavers. Co-operative societies were reported as manufacturing silk, cotton, worsted stockings, woollen cloths, boots, shoes, silk stuffs, serges, *gros de naples*, galoons, brushes, nails, cutlery, watches, trunks, boxes, pocket books, tambour work, chintzes, ginghams, bobbin net, lace, line, shirtings, waistcoat stuffs, towelling, carpets and cabinet work.[98]

A Manchester and Salford Dressers' and Dyers' Co-operative Society was formed during a trade dispute and lock-out in 1829. The workers, fearing a general turn-out to break up their union and destroy their funds, 'resolved on becoming master dyers', and took over works premises in Pendleton.[99]

By April 1830 individual membership of the APCK was 639, and the number of co-operative societies in existence had doubled to 226. *The Magazine of Useful Knowledge and Co-operative Miscellany* was issued from October 1830, and expressed a wish to publish details of the further progress of co-operation—but the total number of societies in October 1830 could not be given more accurately than between 400 and 500.

Plans were laid for an Irish community at Ross Carbery, in County Cork, which William Thompson published as a 'Prospectus of the Cork Community'. Podmore described the prospectus as 'an authoritative exposition of the economic creed of the Socialists of the period'.[100] Thompson's *Practical Directions*[101] is in effect an elaborate exposition of the Cork prospectus, which was reprinted with an 'Address to the industrious classes of Great Britain' in the *Orbiston Register* and in the *Co-operative Magazine*. The Cork community would eventually cater for 2,000 residents, but Thompson was prepared to launch the project with as few as 200 members. Unlike Owen, he did not believe that the security normally offered by co-operators would be satisfactory to outside investors, and argued that a community could grow to Owenite dimensions only when it had proved itself an efficient producing entity. Thompson wrote to William Pare concerning the conditions of lease for the proposed Irish community, which he saw as an incipient model:

> New communities might be formed every year, or soon, perhaps, every three months, by the co-operation of the trading fund associations, of their individual members, and of such persons of Society at large as may be inclined by the gift or loan of £20 ... to become a resident. The continual repayment of the loans by the members of the first communities would always be supplying new funds for loans to future communities.[102]

Contributors were invited to submit their names to the secretary of the Co-operative Knowledge Association. In such a community it would also be possible, wrote Thompson, to learn a second trade, which was not possible within the competitive system.[103]

Another development during 1830 was the appointment by the Association of the first co-operative missionaries, James Watson and William Pare. James Watson reported, 'In the beginning of 1830 I visited Leeds, Halifax, Dewsbury, Bradford, Huddersfield, Todmorden, Wakefield and other places to advocate the establishment of co-operative associations.'[104] There was also some preoccupation with the business methods of co-operative production and retailing:[105] 'Observe, the management must not be assigned to a few, as in your sick and burial societies. All must take some part, or be preparing to take some part.' Emphasis was laid on book-keeping:

> Another point of vital importance, is an accurate system of accounts. In this all societies are liable at first to be deficient, because no one is aware of the necessity of accounts who has not been concerned in business.[106]

Dr King of Brighton recommended a 'patron' for each co-operative society to preclude litigation to recover loss due to peculation by a member. If all members signed an arbitration bond, the patron could decide questions of individual property claims.[107] As for co-operative storekeepers, the only procedure open to a partner suing a co-partner would be to file a bill in equity in the Court of Chancery. This remedy was costly—£60 would barely cover the expenses of the bill, hence many frauds had taken place owing to the lack of funds for litigation. Thus it was important to choose a suitable shopman, who should cease to remain a member of the co-operative society in order to place him in the situation of a punishable servant of the society, or of the trustees, who could then accept a bond or security for him. But the guarantor must not be a joint guarantor, for an individual guarantor could plead exemption as a joint partner. Hence a guarantor should be an outsider, neither member nor trustee. Co-operative storekeepers should also deal with reputable firms in the form of written orders, which would save the trouble of having to make a personal visit to inspect purchases and thereby save the 'dashing' of 'presents' by the seller as a *'douceur'*—'this practice is universal in all large houses, and obliges the vendor to put on, in addition to the price, a further percentage to meet the present...'[108]

There was also a suggestion in 1830 for a pioneer wholesale co-operative society with each member society buying goods from a central co-operative bazaar. Wholesale and retail prices were to be affixed by the local society selling the goods, with a commission of 2½ per cent chargeable for sales servicing 'and at such times as surplus accrues it will be sent as dividend to the societies'.[109] A group of Manchester co-operators also attempted wholesaling at this time. 'In 1830 we established a Central Store, on the principle of the Wholesale, in St James's, Thomas St., Shudehill. It did not exist more than two or three years...'[110] An example of the fusion between producer co-operation and community ambitions is shown in the 'First Co-operative Manufacturing Community Society' of London, which was mooted to provide constant employment, and, *inter alia*, 'to enquire into the causes of failure of co-operative societies. Members were requested to learn two or more trades to avoid casual employment.'[111]

An interesting personal view on co-operative trading during this early period can be gleaned half a century later from the autobiography of William Lovett,[112] who became a storekeeper for the First London Co-operative Trading Association at Red Lion Square. It was symptomatic of the self-sacrifice of many of these early co-operative workers that Lovett's salary as co-operative storekeeper

> was less than I could earn at my trade. But like many others, I was sanguine that those associations formed the first step towards the social independence of the labouring classes... I was induced to believe that the gradual accumulation of capital by these means would enable the working classes to form themselves into Joint Stock associations of labour, by which (with industry, skill and knowledge) they might ultimately have the trade, manufactures and commerce of the country in their own hands. But I failed to perceive that the great majority of them lacked the self-sacrifices and economy necessary for procuring capital, the discrimination to place the right men in the right position for managing the plodding industry, skill and knowledge necessary for successful management, the moral disposition to labour earnestly for the general good... I had not, however, been in the situation of storekeeper many months before a reduction in my salary took place...[113]

Lovett went on to attribute the failure of many co-operative ventures during the early 1830s mainly to religious differences:

> The question of religion was not productive of much dissension until Mr Owen's return from America, when his 'Sunday Morning Lectures' excited the alarm of the religious portion of his members, and caused great numbers to secede from them.[114]

Although in favour of Owen's ideas on community of property, Lovett thought that the facilities provided by communities would not cure poverty at its root:

> I was one who accepted the grand idea of machinery working for the benefit of all, without considering that those powers and inventions have been chiefly called forth, and industrially and efficiently applied by the stimulus our industrial system has afforded, and that the benefits to the originators and successful workers of them—though large in some instances —have been few and trifling, compared to the benefits which the millions now enjoy for their general application.[115]

A first Co-operative Congress met in 1831[116] and its dominant theme was the establishment of an incipient community. William Thompson would not agree that Owen's grand plans were feasible as capital projects; Owen, in turn, refused to associate himself with any community involving a proposed capital outlay of less than £240,000. The schism between Owen and Thompson widened. Thompson opposed a vote of thanks to Owen at the end of the second congress, and at the third congress he opposed the labour exchange experiments. His remarks against Owen were tetchy: 'he [Thompson] would not despair but that in a short period he would show to the world, an institution that might even please Mr Owen...' Thompson thought the safeguards Owen suggested were too weak—Owen had said a community could offer security of land, building sites and labour (he was still thinking in terms of New Lanark), whereas Thompson initially wanted small-scale communities, and pointed out the efficiency of Ralahine,[117] with its system of committee rule. Owen snapped back. Committees and majorities would never answer, there would be too much confusion: 'He had found by thirty years' experience, that people could not act for themselves in a Community. There must be some conducting head.' Neither Thompson nor William Lovett liked this despotism. Owen continued:

> No one was more opposed to despotism than he was; but such a combination as they had in view could only be effected by the direction of one mind. He would put an end to despotism and would give to every child, when it was born, his full share in the government of the world. He would wish perfect equality.

Thompson thereupon asked Owen 'if he had taken care to give to the world, after his own death, the valuable knowledge he possessed?'[118] Lovett later described the general feeling of Congress delegates who

> instead of waiting for the grand plan of Mr Owen retired for dinner. When we came back our friend Owen told us very solemnly, in the course of a long speech, that if we were resolved to go into a community upon Mr Thompson's plan we must make up our minds to *dissolve our present marriage arrangements, and to go into it as single men and women*. This was like the bursting of a bomb-shell in the midst of us. (I may add that the reporter of our proceedings, Mr William Carpenter, thought it wise not to embody this discussion in our printed report.)[119]

By the end of the 1820s there were at least four strands emerging within the loosely defined early co-operative movement—Owenite communitarian theorists, Owenite co-operators who thought of community as a long term prospect, co-operative traders with some hesitancy about using resources for communities, and trade-club producer co-operators with leanings towards radical political agitation. There were, of course, individuals who supported all the above programmes, and others who altered their scale of priorities to match the particular trend in social reform activity at the time, and yet others who used any popular platform to canvass support for their own particular social remedies. A labour historian has summarised the situation as follows:

> By the end of the 1820s one variant or another of co-operation and labour economic theory had taken hold of the working class movement. Cobbett offered no coherent theory. Carlile's individualism was repellent... The rationalist propaganda of the previous decade had been effective; but it had also been narrow and negative and had given rise for a more positive moral doctrine which was met by Owen's messianism. Owen's imprecision made it possible for different intellectual tendencies to exist.[120]

Notes

1 Speech of the Archbishop of Canterbury before the House of Lords, 4 February 1840, reprinted in *The Times*, 5 February, 1840.
2 Letter from 'Philo Justitia', *The Economist*, No. 39, 20 October 1821, p. 205.
3 This was not, of course, the first experiment in co-operation. See, for instance, letter from a 'Journeyman Smith' in *The Economist*, No. 11, 7 April 1821, pp. 170–1, giving an account of co-operation between smiths and wheelwrights in the carriage department of Woolwich Arsenal in 1816, where goods were bought in common.
4 In 1812 Mudie had been a member of a discussion group meeting in St Andrew's Chapel, Edinburgh. See G. Mudie, *A Few Particulars respecting the Secret History of the late Forum*, 1812, referred to in W. H. G. Armytage, 'George Mudie, journalist and utopian', *Notes and Queries*, May 1957, p. 214.

5 A copy of the report is in the Howell collection, Bishopsgate Institute, London. The report is dated '13 January 1821 (second edition)'.

6 'Report of Committee of Journeymen,' p. 21.

7 *Ibid.*, p. 26. Henry Hetherington was one of the signatories.

8 *The Economist*, 'A periodical paper explanatory of the New System of Society projected by Robert Owen and of a Plan of Association for improving the condition of the Working Classes during their continuance at their present employment.'

9 *The Economist*, No. 1, 27 January 1821, p. 15.

10 *Ibid.*, No. 29, 20 October 1821, p. 205.

11 *Ibid.*, No. 2, 3 February 1821, p. 32.

12 *Ibid.*, No. 3, 10 February 1821, p. 48.

13 *Ibid.*, No. 15, 5 May 1821, p. 235.

14 *Ibid.*, No. 22, 23 June 1821, pp. 351–2.

15 W. H. G. Armytage, 'George Mudie', p. 215.

16 *The Economist*, No. 23, 30 June 1821, p. 359.

17 *Ibid.*, No. 24, 7 July 1821, letter 'Philo Justitia', p. 376.

18 *Ibid.*, No. 29, 11 August 1821, p. 45.

19 *Ibid.*, No. 47, 15 December 1821, pp. 336–7. The Edinburgh Practical Society then had about seventy members. By March 1822 membership was reported as between 200 and 300.

20 *Ibid.*, No. 40, 27 October 1821, p. 219.

21 *Ibid.*, No. 43, 17 November 1821, p. 265. The houses were at corner of Guildford Street East, Bagnigge Wells Road and Spa Fields.

22 *Ibid.*, No. 45, 1 December 1821, pp. 298–9.

23 *Ibid.*, No. 50, 19 January 1822, p. 379.

24 *Ibid.*, No. 45, 1 December 1821, p. 300.

25 Letter from Mudie to Owen, 25 August 1848, Robert Owen correspondence, No. 1665.

26 Letter from Mudie, 29 August 1848, Robert Owen correspondence, No. 1668.

27 Letter from Mudie, 3 January 1823, Robert Owen correspondence, No. 25. Mudie published the *Advocate of the Working Classes* during 1826–27 in Edinburgh, and was again in London in 1840, where he taught and published *The Grammar of the English Language, truly made Easy and Amusing by the Invention of 300 Moveable Parts of Speech*, 1840.

28 *Proceedings of the first General Meeting of the British Foreign Philanthropic Society, held 1 June 1822*, pp. 4–5, 15. The committee included I. L. Goldsmid, J. Minter Morgan, Sir James Graham, Henry Brougham, A. J. Hamilton, and twenty-nine members of Parliament.

29 Letters of 15 November 1822, Robert Owen correspondence, No. 1a.

30 See letter from E. Cowper, 18 April 1832, Robert Owen correspondence, No. 29, informing Owen that the British Philanthropic Society was about to give up its accommodation for lack of funds, and appealing to Owen for an object to work for. The last subscriptions were paid in January 1823 and the balance in hand at April 1823 was £70.

31 Letter from I. L. Goldsmid, 22 December 1823, Robert Owen correspondence, No. 23.

32 W. Thompson, *An Inquiry into the Principles of the Distribution of Wealth most conducive to Human Happiness applied to the newly proposed System of Voluntary Equality of Wealth*, 1824.

33 Owen's salary at New Lanark ceased from September 1825. See letter from J. Wright of Glasgow, 10 October 1825, saying that a Mr Walker was appointed manager of New Lanark Mills: Robert Owen correspondence, No. 80.

34 *Co-operative Magazine and Monthly Herald*, February 1826, p. 56.

35 *Ibid.*, January 1826, p. 9.

36 *Ibid.*, January 1826, p. 28.

37 *Ibid.*, January 1826, p. 18.

38 *Ibid.*, February 1826, p. 56.

39 *Ibid.*, February 1826, p. 57.

40 For William Thompson, see pp. 75–81 below.

41 R. K. P. Pankhurst, *William Thompson; Britain's Pioneer Socialist Feminist and Co-operator*, 1954.

42 H. S. Foxwell, introduction to A. Menger, *The Right to the Whole Produce of Labour*, 1899, p. lxxxvii.

43 *Ibid.*, p. lxxxiii.

44 W. Thompson, *Labour Rewarded*, 1827, p. 73.

45 W. Thompson, *An Inquiry into the Principles of Distribution of Wealth most Conductive to Human Happiness.*

46 W. Thompson, *Practical Directions for the Speedy Establishment of Communities on the Principles of Mutual Co-operation, United Possessions and Equality of Exertions and of the Means of Enjoyment*, 1830.

47 W. Thompson, *Labour Rewarded.*

48 W. Thompson, *Practical Directions*, pp. 2–3.

49 *Ibid.*, p. 3.

50 *Ibid.*, p. 3.

51 *Ibid.*, p. 182.

52 W. Thompson, *An Inquiry into the Principles of the Distribution of Wealth*, p. 563.

53 *Ibid.*, p. 564.

54 *Ibid.*, pp. 231, 564–6.

55 *Ibid.*, pp. 569–70.

56 *Ibid.*, pp. 491–580, *passim.*

57 *Ibid.*, p. 523.

58 *Co-operative Magazine*, October 1826, pp. 306–8. An acre for Britain was a gross exaggeration on a scale of one inch to ten miles.

59 R. K. P. Pankhurst, 'William Thompson, his life and writings', 1952, p. 105.

60 W. Thompson, *An Inquiry into the Principles of the Distribution of Wealth*, p. 95.

61 W. Thompson, *Labour Rewarded*, p. 12.

62 *Ibid.*, p. 119.

63 *Co-operative Magazine*, July 1826, pp. 226–7.

64 *Ibid.*, January 1827, pp. 22–3.

65 *Ibid.*, July 1826, p. 232.

66 *Ibid.*, pp. 230–1.

67 *Ibid.*, December 1827, p. 533.

68 *Ibid.*, p. 534.

69 For Dr William King and the Brighton co-operators, see *Dr William King and 'The Co-operator', 1828–30*, ed. T. W. Mercer, 1922; also S. Pollard, 'Dr William King of Ipswich: a co-operative pioneer', *Co-operative College Paper*, 1959.

70 *Co-operative Magazine*, January 1828, pp. 3–4.

71 Letter from J.P., Corresponding Secretary, 10 Queen's Place, Brighton, 20 February 1828, in the *Co-operative Magazine*, February 1828, p. 68.

72 *The Co-operator* (Brighton), No. 1, May 1828.

73 *American Socialist*, letter XI, 15 November 1877. For E. T. Craig, see chapter 5 below.

74 *The Co-operator*, March 1830.

75 *Ibid.*, April 1830.

76 Letter from C. Fry, 30 October 1829, William Pare Papers, letter No. 55.

77 R. and F. D. Hill, *The Recorder of Birmingham: a Memoir of Matthew Davenport Hill*, 1878, p. 379.

78 Letter No. 91, William Pare papers. Co-operative societies were superior because of their greater potential growth of funds. Friendly society funds could increase only through adding interest to capital.

79 *Birmingham Co-operative Herald*, No. 1, 1 April 1829, p. 4.

80 *Address at the Opening of the Birmingham Co-operative Society, 17 November 1828*, 'by a member', pp. 12–13.

81 Letter No. 33, William Pare papers.

82 Rule 39, *Address, op. cit.*, p. 32.

83 Letter of William Pare to *Weekly Free Press*, 11 August 1830, in response to an article on labour exchanges by William King (of London). Pare argued that many of the above skills would not be suitable for labour exchange transactions. See pp. 139–42. below.

84 *Co-operative Magazine*, March 1829, p. 65.

85 *Birmingham Co-operative Herald*, No. 1, 1 April 1829.

86 *Ibid.*, 1 June 1829.

87 *Ibid.*, 1 November 1829.

88 W. H. Brown, *Story of Liverpool Co-operative Society Ltd.*, 1929, p. 16.

89 *Rules of the First Liverpool Co-operative Society*, p. 10, Howell collection, Bishopsgate Institute.

90 *Ibid.*

91 *Rules of the First Preston Co-operative Society, instituted Whit Monday 1834*, Howell collection.

92 Letter No. 47, William Pare papers.

93 *Rules of the Carlisle Co-operative Society formed 13 April 1829*, Howell collection. There was also a 'Carlisle Co-operation Association', formed in 1830: *ibid.*

94 *Rules of the Lamberhead Green Trading Fund Society, May 1830*, Howell collection.

95 See *Reports of Proceedings of the Association for the Promotion of Co-operative Knowledge*, Howell collection.

96 Letter No. 110, William Pare papers.

97 *British Co-operator*, April 1830.
98 *Report of the third quarterly meeting of the Association for the Promotion of Co-operative Knowledge*, 7 January 1830.
99 *United Trades' Co-operative Journal*, 27 March 1830.
100 F. Podmore, *Life of Robert Owen*, 1906, p. 403.
101 The chapter headings of *Practical Directions*, include 'Funds', 'Land', 'Numbers', 'Selection', 'Buildings', 'Agriculture', 'Manufacture', 'Moving power', 'Expenditure of funds', 'Preservation of health', 'Education and mental pleasures' and 'Management'.
102 Letter No. 11 from William Thompson, 27 January 1830, listed as letter No. 74, William Pare papers.
103 In the competitive system there was neither time nor means of training for a second skill, nor would fellow workers or employers favour such training. (Letter No. 111, from William Thompson, 6 February 1830, William Pare papers.)
104 W. J. Linton, *James Watson*, 1880, pp. 21–2.
105 *British Co-operator*, April 1830–October 1830, William Lovett collection, Goldsmiths' library.
106 *The Co-operator*, August 1830.
107 *Ibid.*, February 1830.
108 *British Co-operator*, No. 2, May 1830.
109 *Ibid.*, No. 3, June 1830.
110 Letter from Alderman Heywood, November 1887, to E. T. Craig, in *Co-operative News*, 6 August 1887, p. 778.
111 *British Co-operator*, No. 3, June 1830.
112 W. Lovett, *Life and Struggles of William Lovett*, 1876.
113 *Ibid.*, p. 41.
114 *Ibid.*, p. 42.
115 *Ibid.*, p. 44.
116 For the series of Co-operative Congresses during the 1830s, see chapter 5 below.
117 An account of Ralahine community is given in chapter 4 below.
118 *Report of Proceedings of the First Co-operative Congress*, 1831.
119 W. Lovett, *Life and Struggles*, pp. 49–50.
120 E. P. Thompson, *The Making of the English Working Class*, 1968 edition, p. 875.

3
Orbiston, 1825–27

Orbiston is important because it was the first communal experiment on British soil with a view to emancipating the working class
through a transformation of the economic system. It was therefore
an example of communitarianism *par excellence*, and should be
contrasted with the earlier, more limited, experiment of the London
Owenites at Spa Fields. Orbiston was planned to integrate agriculture with industrial production on the assumption that it would
attract funds from sympathetic capitalists, who would receive adequate dividends in the interim period until communal assets were
eventually taken over by the tenants on an amortisation basis out
of expected profits. Attention should also be paid to Orbiston because it was a piece of social engineering; there was no precedent
for its comprehensive provisions for communal living, work and
leisure. The first buildings in Britain specifically designed for
working class habitation—in fact the first buildings to be directly
associated with the working class movement—were at Orbiston.

The preliminaries to the setting up of the community can be explained largely in terms of the leading personalities associated with
the experiments—Robert Owen, A. J. Hamilton, the son of General
Hamilton, a Lanarkshire landowner, and Abram Combe, an Edinburgh tanner.

Owen was disillusioned over the lack of Parliamentary support
for implementing the proposals for communities outlined in his
'Report to the County of Lanark', and he turned to other forms
of sponsorship. His critics were not confined to members of Parliament:

> Mr Owen's villages will always be useful, as so many wholesome asylums
> to which the surplus population of old society, the unfortunate or whim-
> sical, will flee to, in season of embarrassment or of commercial fluctuation;
> but they will by no means transform cities into towns, towns into villages,
> and introduce, no matter how progressively, a new aspect on the affairs
> of the world.[1]

The British and Foreign Philanthropic Society, which included

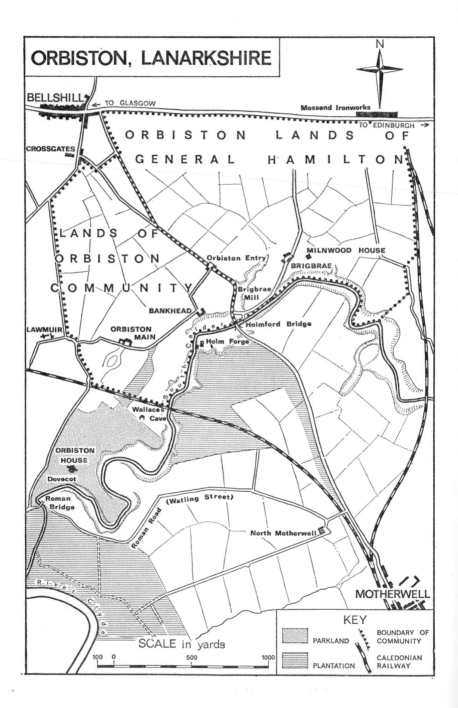

ORBISTON, LANARKSHIRE

N

BELLSHILL
← TO GLASGOW
Mossend Ironworks
TO EDINBURGH →

ORBISTON LANDS OF
GENERAL HAMILTON

CROSSGATES

LANDS OF
ORBISTON
COMMUNITY

Orbiston Entry
MILNWOOD HOUSE
BRIGBRAE

Brigbrae
Mill

BANKHEAD

South Calder

LAWMUIR
ORBISTON
MAIN
Holmford Bridge
Holm Forge

Wallace's
Cave

ORBISTON
HOUSE

Dovecot

Roman
Bridge
Roman Road (Watling Street)

North Motherwell

MOTHERWELL

River Clyde

SCALE in yards
100 0   500   1000

KEY

PARKLAND

PLANTATION

BOUNDARY OF
COMMUNITY

CALEDONIAN
RAILWAY

so many notable names, intended to raise £100,000 for a community experiment, but met once only—in June 1822. Many potential supporters refused to accept Owen's proposal that there should be absolute equality and common property in any forthcoming land colony. There is also evidence by 1822 that Owen was beginning to prevaricate over the earlier proposals for a community at Motherwell. During the autumn of 1822 he departed for Ireland to propagate his views among the Irish landlords and to set up the Hibernian Philanthropic Society on the model of the then moribund British and Foreign Philanthropic Society. He wrote to the president of the Practical Society of Edinburgh:

> I am not in the least surprised at the impatience of you and your friends to commence the practice of the New System... I am perhaps still more so ... My present proceedings in this country will I trust hasten the period materially... I have not for a moment lost sight of Motherwell, Sir, it is my intention to commence there at the earliest practical period. I hope this Spring.[2]

The opportunity was available, for Owen had purchased 660 acres of the Motherwell estate from General John Hamilton for £14,756, but after three years of inactivity Abram Combe and A. J. Hamilton wished to dissociate themselves from Owen's plans for a Motherwell community: they wanted a system of individual reward for labour with economic equality to come later; they also preferred to begin a community on a smaller scale. General Hamilton therefore sold to Abram Combe, as trustee, part of the remaining estate of 291 acres at Orbiston, one mile west of the Motherwell site, for £20,000 by feu disposition on 13 May 1825, on the condition that the Orbiston community would relieve General Hamilton of 'all feu and tiend duties, minister's stipend, cess or land tax, and of all other public burdens'.[3] A letter from Robert Dale Owen of 17 March 1825[4] to A. J. Hamilton had stated:

> In reply to your letter of 13th we now understand that you have purchased from us on behalf of Mr Owen the Lands of Motherwell as acquired by him from your Father at £14,000 seven hundred and fifty six pounds 14/9 and to relieve him of his obligation for payment of the debt affecting the same due to your Father.
> It is further understood that this price is to bear interest at 5% from Whit Sunday 1825 when your entry to the land is to commence and that you are to pay any sums that may be advanced by Mr Owen on account of the lands after that date including the expense of converting them: and to

relieve Mr Owen of his obligation to the servants and others engaged on the lands. In short you just go into Mr Owen's place as regards these lands.

It is therefore apparent that Owen resold the 660 acres at Motherwell back to A. J. Hamilton on behalf of his father, General Hamilton.[5]

William Maclure and Richard Flower from America had visited New Lanark in 1824 and imbued Owen with ideas for establishing his model community in the purer conditions of the New World. Owen responded enthusiastically and went to America at the end of 1824, severing any connection he might have had with the Orbiston community, which he did not visit until 1827,[6] although his wife and daughters remained in residence at Braxfield House in nearby New Lanark. Owen's lack of involvement at Orbiston is an indication of his evanescence, nowhere more marked than in his relationships with the organisers of community experiments.

Abram Combe, the leading organiser of the Orbiston experiment, was born in 1785, and in 1821 helped to establish the Practical Society of Edinburgh, after having visited New Lanark in 1820, where he was deeply impressed by the infant school. The Practical Society opened a co-operative store and claimed a membership of upwards of 500 families.[7] Combe then set up a short-lived community experiment in his Edinburgh tanyard after the demise of the Practical Society, with the leather-workers living in common and sharing profits with Combe. As there appeared to be no prospect of success for Owen's Motherwell project, Combe in 1823 set about planning and writing up his own views on the arrangements for a model social experiment. The famous parable of the national economy as a cistern, which was an ingenious exposition of an income-flow model, was included in his *Metaphorical Sketches*: 'Plenty would be made Guardian of the stop-cock, instead of competition.'[8] The issue of individualism and equality was also raised:

> The time is fast approaching when the value of every Individual will be rated by the tendency of his services to promote the general welfare of Society . . .[9]
> *Quere.* 'Is it possible to make all men equal?' A great proportion of the happiness which one Individual enjoys above another is derived from superior habits and attainments . . . Hence no rational being could entertain equality in this sense.[10]

Combe thought that the conflict between the old system and the new would be resolved within eight or ten years, unaided by the Establishment. Difficulties would resolve themselves after the initial stages—when it began to move the new system would carry all before it: 'No one will have cause to be alarmed, because the change in every instance, will be voluntary. The wealth which individuals possess at present, will not only be secured to them, but its value will be considerably increased.'[11] Combe developed a concept of 'Divine Revelation' as a self-revealed truth which could act as arbiter for all community affairs. Justification for the title of 'Divine Revelation' was disputed in the form of a mock trial: the judge expounded that 'Divine Revelation' was 'Beneficial Truth, Evident, or Demonstrable, or as that which comes directly from God. We use the term in contradistinction to mere human testimony. The one is the source of all good; and the other the origin of at least nine-tenths of our misery.'[12]

A. J. Hamilton, the other leading party concerned with Orbiston, was the son of General Hamilton of Dalzell and Orbiston, and was born in Edinburgh in 1793, 'a year which will be long remembered both by despots and priests'.[13] Hamilton was a peculiar product of the landed classes. Perhaps his social sympathies were first aroused as a junior officer during the Napoleonic wars. He complained that he was dogged by army bureaucracy long after his active service with the Scots Greys had ended—in 1824 he claimed arrears of half-pay due to him as a Waterloo veteran, and the reply from the army bankers stated:

> We regret to acquaint you that your affidavits for last quarter will not pass at the Army Pay Office in consequence of it being upon an old form —we enclose a fresh one which we will thank you to execute and return— and in future to make use of the blank forms also sent herewith.[14]

He had been quartered in the Netherlands during the Waterloo campaign, where he had had the opportunity of observing local methods of cultivation, which relied on heavy manuring, deep working of the soil and strict weeding. His experiences made him a firm advocate of spade cultivation,[15] and he contributed to the *Farmers' Magazine*[16] an account of his own farming methods at Dalzell in Lanarkshire, where he kept cut grass for dairy cows and thus increased natural manuring rather than disposing of his hay harvest.

A. J. Hamilton also queried whether there was a real surplus of production in the nation at large:

> It is the want of consumers that at this moment paralyses the efforts of both the manufacturing and agricultural interests. There is but one way left for us to get out of the scrape, which is by adopting such measures as shall enable the people of our own country to consume a much greater proportion of what they produce.[17]

During 1820 he had attempted to provide relief works for the unemployed of Lanarkshire in digging, trenching and forming an embankment on the river Calder. He also endeavoured to introduce his version of the 'cottage system', which involved letting long leases for building, but he found 'that persons who had been all their lives working within doors, as weavers, had neither clothes nor constitutions adapted to outdoor labour . . . their appetites were so much increased that they ate double their former rations'.[19]

His first meeting with Robert Owen had taken place in 1816. After the unfortunate reception of Owen's 'Report to the County of Lanark' by the Commissioners of Supply in May 1820, discussion of the problem of poverty was renewed at a meeting of nobility, freeholders and justices at the town of Hamilton on 16 November. A. J. Hamilton there proposed to the county justices of the peace that he was prepared to let from 500 to 700 acres 'to facilitate the formation of an establishment on Mr Owen's Plan, which would supersede the necessity of erecting a Bridewell for the County'.[19] The land would be let on long lease at a grain rent to be fixed by assessors, and the county authorities were to advance up to £40,000 for establishing the community, to which delinquents, otherwise sent to bridewells, would be directed. Owen disagreed with Hamilton's views. He thought it better to establish a community for the specific purpose of relieving the involuntary unemployed rather than the improvident and indolent. With some modification, he thought the arrangements for the community could be made applicable to 'middling and higher classes of society; being calculated to increase, in an extraordinary degree, the benefits now derived from any given expenditure'.[20] The specific proposals of A. J. Hamilton were more clearly defined in the prospectus appended to Owen's 'Report to the County of Lanark':

> for relieving public distress, removing discontent, giving permanent and productive employment to poor and working classes—under arrangements which will essentially improve their character and ameliorate their con-

dition, diminish the expenses of production and consumption and create markets co-extensive with production.[21]

Shares were to be issued of £25 each at 5 per cent interest, and as soon as 1,000 shares were subscribed a meeting of proprietors would elect a committee of management which would be matched by a committee of equal number nominated by the community dwellers. Any profit would be distributed equally to shareholders and working members, and when the amount accumulated by workers achieved the level of the subscribed capital, the shares of the proprietors would be redeemed and the workers would then become the sole proprietors. A. J. Hamilton wrote to Owen in December 1820 concerning the terms for letting 600 acres at Motherwell at a rent of 40 per cent of produce, and offered to undertake the general management, 'being assisted by you, and I shall act under the directions of the Committee of Management'. But the doubts expressed by Hamilton over the likelihood of support from the county regarding the Motherwell project were subsequently justified: 'I am perfectly certain the County will do nothing, but I agree with you that we are in their hands at present, and must get clear of them before we can do anything further. After we are clear of the County, it will be mainly a private speculation, the same as the Union Canal.'[22] A. J. Hamilton agreed to subscribe £1,000 and 'if I can I shall subscribe £200 more under fictitious names'. He suggested that Owen should draft a prospectus which should be circulated with each copy of the 'Report'.

Hamilton became a confirmed supporter of Owen after a meeting at Hamilton on 19 April 1821, convened to consider further Owen's 'Report'. The committee appointed by the meeting was to prepare petitions asking Parliament to take into consideration the measures suggested in the 'Report' for providing permanent employment for the poor and working classes. Several professors of law from Glasgow University argued with Owen, but A. J. Hamilton reported that Owen worsted them: 'This second triumph completely determined me to take a fair and full examination of Mr Owen's plans.'[23] There was, however, little response to appeals for capital for the proposed community at Motherwell. The Philanthropic Society outlined new proposals for a community of 500 residents and proposed that 'there shall be attached to the establishment a sufficient extent of *land* to render it essentially *agricultural*'.[24] In effect, the landowners and justices of the county of Lanark had abandoned Owen's scheme after criticism and rejection by the House of Commons on 26 June 1821 of the motion of John Maxwell, MP for Renfrewshire, to appoint a commission to enquire into Owen's plan. There was also strong resentment over Owen's anti-religious outbursts.[25]

A. J. Hamilton accompanied Owen on a visit to the Holkham estate in Norfolk in 1821 and recorded that 'amongst the company present, and who slept in the house were the Dukes of Sussex and Bedford, the Marquis of Tavistock, Lords Albemarle, Crewe, Erskine and Nugent, Sir Francis Burdett, Mr Joseph Hume, and a host of other titled and celebrated men, including my countryman Sir John Sinclair'.[26]

From about this time, Hamilton became deeply interested in phrenology and also attended classes at Edinburgh University in metaphysics and political economy. It was here that he became associated with Abram Combe:

> Acting upon the principles of co-operation we established a Society called the Practical Society and opened a store and a school; and we intended to have other corresponding arrangements. This was done without paying any attention to the truths of *Phrenology*; the consequence was a very religious man who was storekeeper, applied all the funds of the Society to his own use; and thus the association was destroyed.[27]

A. J. Hamilton and Abram Combe eventually decided to establish their version of a community at Orbiston on 18 March 1825 without any assistance from Robert Owen. Abram Combe explained that although the community would be conducted on strict grounds of economy, yet the comfort of the inhabitants would be borne in mind. The community would be secure from all injury:

> On the contrary a similar establishment erected in our immediate neighbourhood will increase the comfort of the inhabitants and the value of both properties at the same time. A third and a fourth will still add to those advantages; and the value of the whole will continue to increase with their number, till the world shall be saturated with wealth.[28]

The prospects were therefore cheering:

> We shall have no enemies, we shall have the powerful aid of Government, as soon as our exertions exhibit their natural tendency to increase the peace and prosperity of the country; and we shall have the friendly aid of the Church as soon as we exhibit the absence of vice and immorality, and the presence of the spirit of True Religion.[29]

The articles of agreement for the joint stock company of proprietors laid down that voting would be according to the value of funds contributed, and the proprietors were proscribed from engaging in any financial speculations. The company of tenants was to be liable for maintenance, insurance and taxes: 'Tenants have a right to conduct their own affairs without interference from Proprietors' (article 11). Combe argued that 'the idea of philanthropy is not here introduced, because it is believed that nothing will ever become extensive but that which yields a good return for capital expended'. The tenants would not *own* the property; therefore they could not be proceeded against by third parties. Each share of £250 included a £100 loan at 3½ per cent on security of the land and a £50 cash loan to tenants, with the remaining £100 to be called up quarterly over two years. No shareholder was entitled to hold more than ten shares, 'to avoid appearance of monopoly'. Proprietors could admit tenants in the first instance at a rate of one family for each share subscribed, but as soon as the company was formed the privilege of admitting members would become the prerogative of the tenants. The trustees were forbidden to spend beyond the sums subscribed, 'it being a fundamental principle of the Company to avoid every species of speculation which could possibly make the individual members liable for more than the sum which they actually subscribe'.[30]

Orbiston was purchased from General Hamilton for £19,995 and the trustees were given power to raise loans upon the security of the land to the extent of the purchase price. To acquire the estate Abram Combe had borrowed £12,000 on bond from the Scottish Union Insurance Company, £3,000 from Archibald Ainslie and £4,995 from General John Hamilton. Abram Combe threw down the gauntlet:

> That if experience shall demonstrate to the satisfaction of the majority of the Proprietors that the New System, introduced and recommended by Mr Owen, has a tendency to produce in aggregate, as much ignorance in the midst of knowledge . . . as much poverty, cruelty, vanity . . . conceit . . . filthiness . . . avarice . . . fraud . . . discord as have invariably attended the existing system . . . then shall the property either be let to the best advantage to individuals acting under the old system, and the proceeds divided . . .[31]

Combe was undoubtedly right in not thinking of New Lanark as a model community:

> New Lanark, however, bears no resemblance to the proposed villages of unity and mutual co-operation. It will be impossible for one of these villages to be a year in existence without *either* convincing the world

of their incalculable utility, *or* proving that the plan is utterly impracticable. One or other of these results must inevitably follow; and be
the result what it may, the sooner it is known the better.[32]

The root evil, according to Combe, was competition, which acted
as injuriously in the system of distribution as it had done beneficially in the system of production. Nor was there any inborn
aversion to labour, as no stimulus could be greater than rewarding
labour in full for its exertions.

Article 1 of the agreement of tenants stated that there would be
'no distinctions except those of Nature and which arise from
superior habits and attainments'. All male and female tenants were
eligible for membership of a committee of management, but executive power was to be held by a single member, 'chosen annually
or oftener and removable'.[33] The labour or personal capital of
members would entitle them to a credit, at the local market rates,
on the community store. Individual members were to have liberty
to labour as little as they pleased—but an individual's demands on
the general store were not to exceed the value of goods or materials
he had brought in. Members were to prepare their own estimates
of hours and valuation of their labour, but these claims were to
be open to inspection. Profits were to be divided equally and
children were to be maintained at the expense of the community,
'to whom their services will belong, till they attain their eighteenth
year'.[34]

Article 10 was crucial: 'Cleanliness, temperance, and the means
of living, be the only further indispensable qualifications for admission.' Tenants should aim to become proprietors,[35] and Combe
expected a speedy conversion of their status with all the advantages
at hand. The manager of the community was not to be forced to
act by majority will; he was to follow his own judgement and to
be replaced only if he lost general confidence.

Credit on the community store would be as good as money, but
some currency would be needed for such incidentals as travelling
expenses.[36] If all were to receive a fair value for their labour no one
could object to a fair division of profit among all members, 'since
this profit arises chiefly from the use of Materials which belong to
other individuals'.[37]

Combe then became somewhat mechanistic in his community
planning; perhaps he accepted too readily the Owenite contention
that if rules were devised to encompass the pettiest detail and

minutest contingency, the overall plan *per se* would be unassailable
and self-justifying: psychologically, the skein of detail was a self-
convincing and reassuring part of the project. Each of the community experiments suffered from this over-specificity. Combe devised
a 1–7 point rating for each of seven human desires: a product of
28 (4 × 7), for instance, would denote that a certain member had a
'medium' character.[38] He saw the object of all government as
happiness and prosperity. Should Orbiston fail, 'it is because a
better mode has not been revealed to their understanding. All that
is requisite, is to convince them, how the general welfare of mankind can be augmented; and they will be less than human beings,
if they resist such conviction.'[39] This was surpassing optimism because it took no cognisance of the possible validity of any alternative mode of behaviour, or of the truism that if you do not expect
opposition you will not fight for your ideas.

The main building of the community was to be sited 500 yards
from the river Calder, and its dimensions were to be 680 ft long,
with two wings extending 63 ft, to house, in all, 200 families, including 400 children: 'It is built with "Broached Ashler", from a
quarry on the ground, distant about 400 yards from the building.
Back front, and ends are all done in the same way. The roof is
blue slate.' There were to be a kitchen, bakehouse, library, drawing
rooms, lecture room, eating rooms, and 'it has been proposed to
fit up these rooms with boxes after the fashion of a Coffee Room'.
Provisions would be brought up from below 'by means of a machine
called an Elevator'[40] and arrangements were put in hand for cutting out all domestic drudgery: 'The clothes, shoes, etc. will be
cleaned by Machinery'.[41] The building operations began on 18 March
1825, the first day of the establishment of the community, and 100
workmen were engaged.[42] A letter was received from the London
Co-operative Society saying that many members wished to join
the Orbiston community and enquiring about various points.
Would the tenants ever become proprietors? Would the liability
for debts be general? Would the passages between the rooms be
very dark? Immediate employment was offered for intending members who had experience as masons, sawyers, joiners, agricultural
workers, shoemakers, tailors, leatherworkers.

The first issue of a journal for the community, the *Orbiston
Register*,[43] was published on 11 October 1825. At a meeting on
16 October, attended by nine out of the sixteen proprietors, it was

reported that 125 shares had been taken up, and over £5,000 spent. 'We do not anticipate much difficulty upon account of capital.' The first applicants to seek admission to Orbiston were mainly weavers from nearby Hamilton, but they also included a principal of a school of industry at Fraserburgh. Combe reported in January 1826 that 'The applicants are chiefly from the middle and working classes.'[44] Official screening for admittance did not take place, however, until March 1826—the first applicant to undergo examination was a 41 year old man with five children.[45] Almost £10,000 had been expended by that date, whereas income received or promised was barely £4,560.

The community soon showed signs of disruptive elements. Already by November 1825 an overseer was dismissed because of conversion of goods, and an ex-resident accused the society of overcharging workmen for their provisions.[46] A Quaker storekeeper at New Lanark declined to sell the *Register*, as he was critical of the phrase 'Divine Revelation'. Combe explained:

> Christ did not say 'Did you follow Calvin or Luther or the Pope?' but 'Did you clothe the naked, feed the hungry, visit the sick and lodge the stranger?' We know that his is true religion, because the practice of it invariably produces agreeable sensations, and these as naturally produce sincere love to God.[47]

A building progress report was given by Combe in January 1826:[48] the left wing was the first section to be completed. The kitchen was not yet floored, but the bakehouse was finished. A large room in the south wing was to be a day room for children. There were fireplaces in all the 120 private rooms: 'The building is all of hewn stone, and though plain, has rather a magnificent appearance.' Grounds on the banks of the Calder was marked off for a first manufactory. (Shares of £250 each had been issued, payable in instalments of £10.)

The qualities sought in applicants were stressed in the March issues of the *Register*: no 'polished gents' would be considered, at least in the first year of the experiment; only those who knew character was formed for and not by the individual would be admitted, and they must be willing to improve themselves and not be disgusted at others:[49] 'We do not wish that any one should be refused admittance to our meeting, upon account of previous bad character.'[50] Although the language is that of Owen, it should be remembered he was not associated in any direct way with Orbiston, in fact he was unaware of the existence of the community until some months after its inception.[51]

At a meeting of proprietors on 18 March 1826 it was decided to hand over the property of Orbiston to the tenants in March 1827, provided they could show adequate signs of success. There was an unexplained interruption of five months in the publication of the *Register* between March and August 1826, when it was stated, 'Regarding those who have come together . . . it is only necessary to say, that they were not selected. We took them as they made application, as long as we had accommodation of any sort.'[52] Most of the members had entered the community to avoid the evils of the old system rather than obtain advantages of the new. Abram Combe's classic remarks on the ultimate redeeming purpose of Orbiston also appear in this August 1826 issue of the *Register*: 'We set out to overcome Ignorance, Poverty and Vice, it would be a poor excuse for failure to urge that the subjects of our experiment were ignorant, poor, vicious.'[53] But it was becoming apparent that the community included increasingly disruptive elements:

> The weather was wet and hazy, and the roads bad; the days listless; and a dog called Basto, of the terrier breed, used to bark in the passage at night. In fact, the New System appeared altogether so inferior to the Old that the wives, disillusioned at the disorder, wanted to march out.[54]

The public rooms were almost deserted, and a proposal that individuals should be allowed to cook for themselves was passed unanimously. Individuals were allowed to fit out their own rooms at an annual rental of £4. Abram Combe felt the community balance sheet should be drawn up more fairly:

> At this time last year, there was not one stone above another of the present building. Now we have a building to the extent of 330 feet in length by 40 feet broad and four storeys high, completed, roofed in, and capable of being fitted up for the comfortable accommodation of about 100 families.[55]

A dancing master and two teachers were engaged, the children being expected to repay with labour the cost of their maintenance. The fare would be plain. 'Children will *prefer* the plainest food if they see nothing to contradict the idea that it is the best for them.'[56] But parents could feed children at their own expense in private.

London co-operators had shown keen interest in Orbiston, and several made the journey to enter the community. 'Mr R arrived here . . . after a tedious voyage in the sailing packet of 17 days, on

his passage from London to Leith.'[57] He brought a letter mention-
ing that a cabinet-maker and wheelwright were also wanting to
come to Orbiston. New members were advised to bring their own
beds, which were expensive to buy locally. A group of co-operators
from the south duly arrived in May 1826, including John Gray,
who left a 'valuable job in a London wholesale and manufacturing
house as traveller' when he journeyed to Orbiston. Gray stayed but
two days, as he found that 'the management of the Orbiston establishment was not in the hands of clear-headed practical, and busi-
ness-like men. The plan of operations was never reduced to any
definite form even on paper.'[58] He also observed an indifferent
attitude on the part of some of the influential members 'as to the
nature of the occupations that are to be carried on in the establishment'.[59] It was no answer to retort that the existing members were
not fitted for trades. The first criterion should be to ascertain 'the
greatest number that can be conveniently accommodated in the
building for whom profitable employment can be found'.[60] The
most suitable trades would be those with strong local market connections, and Gray warned: 'They must not be of any description
which affords but a bad living in the present state of Society as
compared with other kinds of employment.'[61] There was, for instance, insufficient labour at Orbiston for cotton manufacturing;
more suitable crafts for the community would be tailoring and
shoemaking, which required little mechanisation and hence would
entail fewer disadvantages in a small undertaking when competing
with the economies of large-scale enterprise.

A. J. Hamilton received a letter from a James Jennings, a London
co-operator, during the summer of 1826. Jennings stressed the need
for increased vigilance over the admission of members:

> an indiscriminate admission of persons whose means only will entitle them
> to it, is and will be, one of the greatest mischiefs that can befall a Co-opera-
> tive Society. It is a fault in which Thompson has fallen—to succeed in
> such a Society there must be a selection. I trust that you in Scotland will
> not split upon such a rock.[62]

Hamilton continued to concern himself with projects to alleviate
general social distress in Lanarkshire. At a meeting in June 1826
which recommended a public works policy 'a letter from Mr Hamilton of Dalzell was read stating that it would not be convenient
for him to attend the meeting, but praising the temper with which

four operatives had borne their sufferings, and requesting to subscribe £50 for their relief'.[63]

The builders at Orbiston decamped in a body in April 1826, although the building was unfinished, with the consequences that
members themselves were directed to complete the operation. Each
occupational group was to report on the value of hours of work of
its individual labourers. In the pages of the *Register* it was pertinently stated that the chief superiority of the new system was in
its policy of distribution, but 'as yet we had nothing to distribute'.[64]
A resident wrote that 'no good men will co-operate with the herd
that are here . . . I should find no difficulty in making a far better
selection—even in Ireland'. Others agreed with him: the land had
been bought when prices were high, and building operations had
taken place when labour and material were costly. Combe reiterated
that Orbiston was an experiment and the new system must be
demonstrated to be capable of profit to the capitalist before it
could be made general.

A certain William Sheddon joined the community in the early
summer of 1826 during the absence of Abram Combe, who had
been taken ill as a result of arduous labour in trenching. Sheddon
was an ex-student of the Edinburgh School of Arts for Mechanics
and offered to set up a foundry at Orbiston. Alexander Campbell,
a joiner—later to play an important role at Orbiston—also wished
to join the community. An iron company was duly formed, also
an agricultural company, and horticultural, dairying and building
companies were envisaged. Shoemakers, bookbinders and printers
were already in production. A gardener applied for admission: 'His
appearance was rather unfavourable but he had a good phrenological development.'[65] An observer who gave opposing evidence
to that of the resident quoted above noted that most of the residents
were 'hardworking, cool, calculating Scotchmen'—there was no
place for the unskilled or those who could not work in the fields.
He thought that Orbiston would be a good place of residence for
half-pay army officers with small incomes and an ability to rough it.

Despite the fact that the community had to buy butter, milk and
meat outside, members could still live for not much more than one
shilling daily. Their earnings were rated according to the levels
prevailing in old society and ranged between 12s and 30s.[66] It was,
however, becoming apparent by September 1826 that plans for the
community were not as advanced as had been expected. The com-

plement had reached nearly 300 and was divided into squads of
ten to twenty families, each chiefly engaged in one activity—one
group had been erecting the iron foundry. A new system was debated which promised the 'whole produce of labour' with equal
privileges rather than a strict equality of distribution—'if one works
hard and other not, if there is Equal Distribution it is wholly from
the bounty of the hard-working one'.[67]

No community can hope to operate with completely harmonious
relations, but Orbiston was strongly demonstrating that the working class needed to be educated for the responsibilities of industrial
democracy: 'The greatest difficulty is overcoming the aversion
which working people have for managing their own affairs.'[68] It
was reported that there had been thefts of tools from the machinery
and building department—hence three members were instructed to
patrol the community precincts with dogs and firearms.

In October the community advertised its scale and range of
manufacturing and craftwork:

Orbiston, October 1826

Advertisement of articles available of goods in First Style and at Moderate
Prices now available for supply.

Printing and Bookbinding

Handbills, cards of address. Magazines. Books of any style or quantity
bound. Fancy coloured paper for Stationers.

Boot and Shoemaking

In London and Edinburgh style and much cheaper. N.B. superior blacking.

Carving and Gilding

Looking glass and picture frame.

Turning

Lent wheels and reels made and repaired. Wooden basins.

Painting and Glazing

Paper hangings, sign, house painting, mutations of all woods.

Watch and Clocks

Particularly Repeating watches, musical snuff boxes.

Tailoring

Gents' naval and military uniforms and plain clothes, all kinds of common
apparel suitable for working in.

Hairdressing and Perfumer
Wheel Carriage Makers

Barrow, ploughs, cart wheels.

Machinery Makers

Steam engines. Brass and iron castings, apparatus for gas lighting, saws hammered and set. Screw presses.

Upholstery

Mattresses, fringe, etc.

Masons and Joiners

Cabinet and chair making.

Tinsmith

Brazier and tin plate baths.

Weaving

The Community intend, very shortly, to open a Bazaar for Public Inspection.

In General Society it too often occurs, that an opposition of interests prevents some part of an undertaking from having the same superior skill employed in the execution of it that the rest may have, but in this Establishment the united intelligence of the whole body will be always employed either in forwarding their respective occupations or concentrated, when necessary, to any given operation. This superiority can only be found amongst persons united for the mutual benefit of each other.

(Printed at Orbiston Press)

Stephen Fenner, a resident, thought the nub of the problem of equitable distribution was that labour varied in its efficiency, and the weak ought not to expect an equal share with the capable; but at least the weak were entitled to an equal share of increments brought about by scientific improvements in labour organisation and production. With the approval of the proprietors, the tenants met on 2 October 1826 and resolved to take over the community with all its debts and undertook to pay the proprietors 5 per cent on their share capital. The proprietors, in turn, insisted that the tenants should ballot for membership, and as an outcome, Abram Combe was given the office of president, and Alexander Paul that of general secretary, with a number of superintendents of departments—A. Campbell, J. Lambe, E. Simpson and Miss Whitwell.[69] Government would be conducted through these superintendents in

conjunction with representatives to be chosen by the whole communal body, one for every ten residents.

William Thompson, the Irish socialist, wrote at the time that he
would have liked Orbiston community to have printed his *Labour
Rewarded*. He was thinking of drafting a pamphlet on the setting
up of small, inexpensive communities—on this particular matter
Owen had given no advice.[70]

Abram Combe's health was fast declining—'the fee simple of my
life would not *now* sell for four weeks' purchase', he wrote at the
end of 1826.[71] His brother, W. Combe, was appointed executive
vice-president. During the last months of his life and that of
Orbiston itself, Combe was becoming more convinced of the merits
of a policy of equal distribution. The *Co-operative Magazine*
thought that Abram Combe should have insisted on community of
property as a first rule at the inception of Orbiston. Equal distribution it was explained, had not been incorporated at an earlier stage
because of the slow progress of the community towards becoming a
'real community'. 'Community of property' was a more accurate
expression of co-operation than 'equal distribution'—every member
could not consume equally, 'but all should obtain the equal distribution should they want it; and this they would obtain by community of property'.[72] There seemed to be remarkable evidence of
progress and harmony at this late stage in the experiment, and no
indication or hint of impending disruption. In September 1826 it
was advised that the machinery department would shortly provide
lighting for the establishment: 'The necessity for immediately
erecting the gas works, so as to light up every part of the premises
where it may be deemed prudent to do so, has been exceedingly
dwelt upon by the tenants.'[73] Panegyrics continued to be written
on the importance of Orbiston: 'The experiment now in silent progress at Orbiston, if successful, will effect a greater revolution in
human affairs than was produced by either the art of printing or
the mariner's compass.'[74] The community idea was quixotically
patriotic, despite its implied subversion of the economic institutions
of the State. If communities were to suffer attack by a foreign
power '... every community would have its regiment... The men
would be ready to fly to any spot at an instant's notice. The best
roads with iron railways, or vacuum cylinders, would convey them
with incredible rapidity'. Their armoury would include 'cannon,
steam guns, Congreve rockets, air balloons to rain down fire...'[75]

'S. F.' at Orbiston wrote to 'M. M——n' of London on 15 October 1826. He was very optimistic—the buildings at Orbiston were 'solidly useful' rather than splendid as described in the *Co-operative Magazine*. True, the buildings were perhaps too high for 'our London friends' but they were more typical of Scotland. And if there was shortage of capital it was because the co-operative movement was too diffuse in its projects; moreover, only a few London co-operators had thought fit to support Orbiston with capital.[76] The co-operators from the south were reticent over contributing funds because they preferred a community within fifty miles of London. It would have been better, they argued, to have provided mere subsistence at Orbiston in the first place, with a policy of community of property rather than to have launched an expensive building programme.

By the end of 1826 building operations were commenced on the central block, but soon after the laying of the foundations the proprietors found they could provide no further finance for completing the accommodation.

Reports of the progress of the departments were submitted in January 1827. Alexander Campbell taught joinery to the youths. The agricultural department reported forty acres under wheat and a livestock of eleven cows. Abram Combe explained further the distinction between equality of distribution and equality of property in answer to William Thompson: in a system of co-operation profits are shared equally, but land and capital would remain as property in common.[77]

Abram Combe wrote from Edinburgh to A. J. Hamilton in London in February 1827 concerning dissension at Orbiston fostered by a Captain O'Brien. A. Paul, the secretary, had assured Combe of the perseverance of the members' efforts, and that the greatest danger was not discontent but lack of support by investors:

> This has made the burden rest exceedingly heavy on you [A. J. Hamilton] ... The whole community at Orbiston being divided into Departments enables us *to know to a certainty* whether the concern pays or not ... The Blast Furnace has been used and suits, I am told, most admirably.[78]

A lengthy letter from William Combe to A. J. Hamilton in March 1827[79] gave a comprehensive account of the community at that date. Combe valued the foundry and stock at £1,050, 'being £650 above the debts owed by them to the public'. There were about twenty workers associated with the foundry, and the £650 was security for providing these workers with their maintenance. The masons were laying a large drain which ran from the building to a cesspool for the land.

> In the workshops at the water side we have five weavers who had to be furnished with looms etc. three of them are employed in the manufacture of cotton for shirting, trousers, jackets, etc. for the store, the other two work silk handkerchiefs and cloth for hats... Mr Lambe and a Mr Pasce from London who has been with us for some time keep the weavers at work with their own private funds... We also have as many shoemakers as we can keep the store in shoes... The printers who occupy the upper part of the workshops are employed just now by a Dr Anderson in Hamilton with a work entitled 'A Supplement to the House of Hamilton'... The bookbinders have plenty of work from the Old Society, they have just finished twenty-four volumes of Quarto Law Books for Mr Henderson of the British Linen Coy. Office... they have also got a machine for ruling paper which will be a source of profit to them as the paper when ruled for Accounts books is sold at double price. I may mention that the ruling machine and screw press were made by the Community.

The agricultural workers, under a Mr Hutton, were laying out paths and digging trenches; the older boys were widening a road between the laundry and a bridge. William Combe then dwelt on the most pressing problem:

> You tell me to see and supply Hutton with money to buy dung, now I have no means of supplying him except by the Cash Account... We are sadly in want of some money just now and if any delay takes place in getting money from the Bank at Airdrie, the consequences may be very serious, after getting the community to the point of doing for themselves, to be obliged to retrace our steps for want of funds is very unfortunate.

A recent visitor from Dublin had inspected progress at the community with a view to bringing his family over to Orbiston and Combe commented, 'He is in independent circumstances and says his wife (daughter of a Baronet) "is more in love with the New System than himself and most anxious to come to Orbiston".' About £80 in cash per month and a supply of potatoes could cover the basic outgoings; 'if we could pay present debts . . . I think the most of our demands would cease.' But if outstanding bills were not met Combe feared legal action by creditors. For the past three months the only cash income had been £130 from A. J. Hamilton. On the other hand, £2,000 of bills were outstanding for purchases over the previous four months for farm, foundry and food. Combe conceded that there had been some thefts among members, yet there was far less crime at Orbiston than in any equivalent population in society at large. 'All we want to insure success is funds and whatever the result of that may be I would go into the world again more convinced than ever of the soundness of our views.' Combe finished his letter on a poignant note by referring to Miss Whitwell, the schoolmistress, 'offering her services without remuneration to assist us, as we are much in want of friends just now'.

By the early summer of 1827 there were reports of the submission of deceitful labour returns and of further pilfering from the community store. Despite the striving for equality, different scales of diet were operating in the communal mess. Arrangements for common catering appear very economical at the published cost of 4s per head, but despite this, of the 298 members in the community during July 1827, seventy-seven were reported as eating out of mess.

Surprisingly enough, the provision of cultural pursuits became most prominent during these last days of Orbiston—a theatre was opened, and it was reported that reading was the main leisure activity.

Robert Hicks was reported as the first resident to leave Orbiston, selling his community shares at half price. Another ex-member, William Wilson, could not find a purchaser for his £26 9s 9d of stock, which he claimed as a legal debt against the Orbiston Company. By April 1827, although the building operations were not completed, the community offered a wide range of handicrafts:

> Upon the upper flat, the whole length of the wing, twine is spun, which is afterwards taken to the School of Industry, where fourteen children are employed in manufacturing garden and fishing nets... There are three cotton and two silk weavers, and a clever tradesman from Derby is putting up machines upon an improved plan for throwing and winding.

Yarn was bought, woven, and made up into clothes. Cotton shirting was sold to members at 10d per yard and shirts were made up for 3s 6d; 'There are also two looms for manufacturing silk shag for hats.' Each of the seven shoemakers earned from 15s to 18s a week, 'beside the profit devolving to the community'. Cast iron grates, fenders and hollow-ware were manufactured; cartwrights constructed spring carriages. It was estimated that £227 monthly was being spent on food, including meat, ale, flour, groceries, butter, cheese, milk for 144 adults and 140 children.[80] The weekly earnings of 200 adults were 15*s* on average, and left a surplus of £373 (in individual pockets) after meeting the monthly food bill. All this seemed most encouraging. A member wrote in April 1827 to J. Minter Morgan, saying that he found the general appearance of Orbiston much improved. Almost 1,000 trees had been planted since the beginning of the year, the grounds were laid out with pleasure walks and new entrance gates had been erected. The theatre, which held 300, was completed and visitors were invited to the performances without charge. 'We have also a new and commodious store opened on the ground floor, for supplying ourselves and the surrounding countryside with all kinds of provisions and manufactured goods.'[81] Another correspondent compared Orbiston favourably with Robert Owen's New Harmony community in America: a feature of both experiments was the possibility of learning each other's trades, which if it had been prevented could have led to jealousies over differentials in skill and status.[82] Letters of unbounded optimism continued to leave Orbiston during the summer:

> The prospects here appear more gratifying every day. The whole of our crops look exceedingly well, and the more intelligent members think that after the next harvest we shall not stand in much need of aid of the proprietors. The zeal which Mr Hamilton and Mr Combe have evinced, is almost incredible, it borders upon the romantic.[83]

By September 1827 it was reported that the governing power was in the hands of six individuals representing the principal proprietors. Planning went on unabated with little apprehension of any impending disruption:

> A quantity of silk shag, wove in the Community, is now manufacturing into hats at Glasgow for our own store; and it is intended to put two other looms to work, and have a hatter in the Community. It is also in contemplation to erect a brewery and a tan yard.

There were thirty to forty pigs in the sty, 'which is perhaps the most compact one in Scotland'.

A meeting was arranged to choose a librarian and a library committee. The boys in the community were about to be clad 'in a beautiful tartan dress' and the girls 'in a dress equally suitable, purple bombazet'.[84] Nevertheless, during the summer of 1827 there was an increase in the number of members leaving Orbiston (although 'the most part of the people actually quitted in November . . .'). An eye-witness later laid the blame for the impending failure on the lack of training of members and the early preponderance of outside labour employed in building the community.[85] A. J. Hamilton believed that many departing tenants left for America.[86] Soon after Abram Combe's death in August 1827 the Orbiston Company decided to suspend all proceedings and dispose of the property. George Combe,[87] who was the legal agent, took the necessary steps, as the bondholders were pressing for repayment:

> The growing crops and every other moveable article which could be converted into money were sold without reserve; the trustees of the foundry company which held a separate lease for their premises were imprisoned for the payment of the money advanced for the erection of their building and machinery, for which interest only was agreed to be paid . . .[88]

The last issue of the *Orbiston Register* appeared on 19 September 1827.

A. J. Hamilton's failing health allowed him to reside at Orbiston only for a short period after the death of Abram Combe. Nor did Hamilton believe the individual members were sufficiently interested in working for eventual success of the community. He later ascribed the break-up of Orbiston to the mischievous influences on tenants of local relatives and friends, the clergy[89] and 'the bad times of 1826', when the rate of interest, previously $3\frac{1}{2}$ per cent, was raised to 5 per cent. 'This alone added more than £1 per acre to the rental of the land.'[90]

George Combe urged that Orbiston should be exposed for sale in August 1828 for a reserve price of £21,500, but not a single offer of purchase was received.[91] Alexander Paul had been appointed judicial factor by the court of session in June 1828, and he remained at Orbiston to supervise the payment of debts and accounts. He reported the sale of 100 acres of wheat and oats, but he remained dubious about the prospects of the community, even had more favourable circumstances prevailed, funds been more lavish, and Abram Combe survived:

> There was with a majority of those we had with us here such a deficiency as to knowledge as to the very nature of the principles of the system— such a want of principle, and even of common morality, and habit of a contrary tendency so strongly fixed, that it would have baffled the most favourable circumstances that it would have been possible to place them in. Mr George Combe has succeeded in convincing me that from the way that

we have all been brought up and from the difference in our desires and feelings, it will be scarcely possible under any circumstances to find an equal number of individuals to what we had here who could go hand in hand with one another in such an experiment. I agree with you in thinking that an experiment of the kind *must* be commenced on a small scale to make it succeed, that the individuals joining should be known to each other and have full confidence in one another.

Paul agreed with A. J. Hamilton that America was the most fitting environment for such an experiment. The optimistic expectation that America would be unsullied by the vices of old society was a widely held working class conviction. Emigration was also in Paul's mind when he referred to the activities of the Combe brothers and Robert Owen:

> Mr George Combe writes me he had a letter from Mr Wm. from America he is not doing anything, Mr George says he displays the same *want* of energy on the other side of the Atlantic that formed so striking a feature of his character on this ... Mr Owen is expected home daily ... Mrs Owen and family is now residing at Hamilton in a house belonging to John Allen, the Grocer.[92]

Alexander Campbell wrote to Owen in 1828 from Hamilton jail, where he was imprisoned as a debtor for the plant and materials advanced at the Orbiston manufactory,[93] and the letter confirms that Owen had indeed on one occasion visited the Orbiston foundry. Campbell was not disillusioned over his experience, but thought the failure of Orbiston

> will prevent for a long time other capitalists from embarking on like speculations and the *Labouring Class* are the only parties when convinced of the superiority of the system to embark in the undertaking but their want of capital will be a considerable drawback, I think however this may be overcome by union societies raising funds for such purposes as friendly societies and gradually increasing their premises and numbers.[94]

A valuation of Orbiston was drawn up in November 1828[95] at a figure of 19,547 for 234 acres, with the buildings at £4,000. The valuer suggested offering the estate for sale as a whole, but he thought it would bring in a higher price if sold in lots, provided that a purchaser would buy the manufactory and land for business purposes. There were, however, considerable disadvantages in treating the property as an industrial site:

> I am not aware of any sufficient inducement to a man or Company of capital to choose this site for a manufactory—it would be near good roads

and cheap coals and have the advantage of the Calder water—but this water is too light in summer to drive machinery and a steam engine would be necessary—a reservoir might be made near the source of the Calder but the expense of this would exceed any advantage to be gained by it, beyond the use of a steam engine. This distance from a shipping port and land carriage is important in considering this question.

The £4,000 valuation for the buildings was low, but

> The houses and public apartments are not constructed on an approved plan as residences for workmen, and are too extensive unless the manufactory was greatly enlarged and no part of the large building could be made into a manufactory without entirely altering the interior, I am therefore doubtful if so much as £4,000 may be obtained for the building... If the building is not sold for a manufactory, we must sell materials in lots, which would be £1,500 or lower.

The valuer recommended a reserve price at £16,000 including the main building and manufactory at £4,000, but the depressed state of trade had to be taken into account:

> Since the Depression of Trade in 1825 very little has been feued in Edinburgh or Glasgow—other towns and villages are similarly situated—in villages houses are built by tradesmen etc. from savings of industry but since 1825 they have with difficulty supported themselves and instead of building many of them are unable to pay the feu duties of houses already built. In good times feuars borrowed money to erect buildings but this cannot now be done.

But J. A. Smith of London, a creditor of the Orbiston Company for £5,000, would not agree to the scheme for sale by lots when the proposal was circulated to creditors. Under these circumstances, the Scottish Union Insurance Company considered it necessary to seek a judicial sale, as the property was burdened beyond its value.

Creditors took legal possession of Orbiston through an instrument of possession of 21 March 1829. From 4 June 1829 Alexander Paul was appointed as factor of the estate for collection of rents. George Combe wrote in September 1829 that almost all the debts due by Orbiston that were not heritably secured had been paid.

Lawrie, the valuer, had reckoned that a considerable outlay would be required to adapt the main building at Orbiston for manufacturing; he thought a purchaser 'might probably remove them altogether'.[96] The gross value of Orbiston was therefore re-calculated at £15,022, including a mere £2,000 for the buildings. The principal claims lodged were a bond of £12,000 to the Scottish Union Insurance Company,[97] £3,000 to Archibald Ainslie,[98] and

£528 on a cash account bond to the National Bank of Scotland.
The total ranked debt was therefore £15,528, exclusive of arrears
of interest, which at 5 per cent was £775. With an estimated rental,
including buildings of £664, there remained an annual deficiency
of £111, so that 'in either view it is evident that bankruptcy is
established . . .'[99]

The 'Memorial and abstract of ranking and sale' was drawn up
in February 1830 by the Scottish Union Insurance Company against
the Orbiston Company trustees—A. J. Hamilton, Alexander Paul
and William Watson.[100] The upset price was further reduced to
£13,492 and the property was again exposed for sale on 7 July
1830 at Edinburgh. An advertisement later appeared in the *Glasgow
Herald* of 22 November 1830 for the letting of the buildings of the
Orbiston Company: 'This Building, having the command of the
Calder water . . . has been considered well-calculated for a Grain
Mill, or for Steam Bleaching, Paper Making, etc.' Particulars could
be obtained from Alexander Paul, who was still resident at Orbiston. The materials of the main building and dwelling house remained on sale.

George Combe later explained the position regarding the bond
to Mr J. A. Smith:

> The Bond to Mr Smith for £5,000 was not claimed for on the heritable
> estate, and no part of it has been paid. The funds of the Company have
> been used to extinguish small debts due in County and management. All
> the debts known have been paid except Smith and Ainslie. Essentially
> therefore the partners of the Company have these two debts to provide for
> . . . Mr Hamilton was in this country lately, and has arranged matters for
> getting the Orbiston debts included under his Trust. If any security can be
> given to Mr Ainslie for payment of interest in the meantime and ultimate
> payment of capital, he will be disposed not to push matters to extremi-
> ties . . .[101]

Eventually the Orbiston lands were purchased by Mrs Douglas,
an adjacent landowner who, during the life of the community, had
accused the Company and A. J. Hamilton of making encroach-
ments on her land on the banks of the river Calder.[102] Mrs Douglas
finally bought Orbiston for £15,050 at Martinmas 1830, and from
the proceeds the debt to the Scottish Union Insurance Company
was repaid in full, and the debt to Ainslie, the other outstanding
ranking creditor, was partly cleared. 'To complete the havoc,'
wrote Alex Campbell, 'the purchaser of the estate determined that
no vestige of the community should remain, and ordered the build-

ing to be sold for old materials; so that the site where once a happy and prosperous community is now only occupied with a group of trees.'[103]

Why did Orbiston fail? Certainly, insecurity of funds was a salient factor. There was also strong local antagonism, and there was no consensus among the members over the basic issues of individualism versus egalitarianism, either of effort or reward. But present-day sociologists would be surprised, not that Orbiston collapsed, but that it survived for as long as it did, given its crude attempts at social engineering. Orbiston was the first of the Owenite communities: the subsequent experiments at Ralahine and Queenwood learned nothing from the experience at Orbiston. The Scottish community was bedevilled by the demise of its founder-manager, Abram Combe, but his death was the occasion rather than the cause of the collapse of the experiment.

Ultimately, Orbiston failed because it was attempting a radical change in social attitudes and cohesion without any of the preconditioning necessary for converting members from the old society into the new. The newly endowed working class Owenite co-operators—newly endowed with an identity and a social programme—were to be the agents for this conversion, but the dilemma was how to accommodate a radical change of human nature as both a precondition and a resultant. Even if an individual could lift himself up by his bootstraps, it would obviously be a more difficult exercise for a whole social class. Orbiston was significant because it showed the working class as *agents* rather than as objects of social reform, as they had been previously. The financial backers of Orbiston were middle class (apart from A. J. Hamilton) and should be contrasted with the large landowners who had made sympathetic gestures of support for Owen's Motherwell project but were not forthcoming with funds. Co-operation was not only the first important exercise in nineteenth-century self-help; it was also a path from old society to Utopia which allowed its supporters to have their feet astride both worlds. In one sense, co-operation in its communitarian phase was the equivalent of emigration to a new land without radical upheaval from home ties and resettlement in a strange and often hostile environment. The early co-operators did not think of themselves as visionaries or agitators; they were practising socialists, and their blindness was not in seeking unattainable ends but in misjudging the effort that would be required to prepare people for communal living. Ingrained social habits are as hard to break as individual ones. Obviously, the communities were ahead of their time, and a resolution of their problems of social conflict could not be anticipated solely by drawing up paper constitutions. The communitarians learned on the job (Combe was a firm exponent of the value of experience), but in the end the job became too complicated to understand or control with the primitive knowledge of social science at their disposal. In economic terms, the communities had to be either self-sufficient, which was impossible as an enclave in a capitalistic world, or they would have to compete with the outside world in the line of production concerned.

A. J. Hamilton thought that Orbiston failed because 'our enthusiasm . . . by far outran our judgment and induced us to admit, without adequate enquiry as to character, the mere live devotees to our system. This is an error—which must for the future be avoided: Mr Owen has split upon the same rock.'[104] The qualities needed for a successful co-operative community, said A. J. Hamilton, should be: 'Knowledge of more than common kind; a disposition to labour and ability to think as well as labour, forbearance as to the opinions of others, and temper in expressing his own; and in addition to all this, good health . . .'[105] Soon after the collapse of Orbiston, A. J. Hamilton visited Brighton *en route* for Italy during the summer of 1828. 'Here also I found many co-operative friends . . . I visited the store of one of the societies, it was well provided with everything; and precisely on the same plan as that of the Practical Society of Edinburgh.'[106] Owen later referred to A. J. Hamilton soon after his early death in 1834: 'Hamilton was another specimen of as good a beau ideal of moral perfection as this old world can furnish . . . Though reared amongst the aristocracy, he was a man of the people . . .'[107]

John Gray was severely critical of the regimen and management at Orbiston: 'You may *talk* about equal distribution if you please, but, at least for some years to come, you cannot *act* upon it.' *En passant* Gray put forward a strong case for engaging competent managers and for paying them accordingly. The salaries of managers of London concerns were often 'from twice to six or seven times the amount given for the performance of like duties' in other establishments.[108] In the difficult situation prevailing at Orbiston the president ought to have been better remunerated; in practice, Abram Combe was a unique character who gave his unstinted services gratis. John Gray thought that Abram Combe was 'the victim of his own indefatigable industry and enthusiasm . . .' His glaring weakness was an over-emphasis on the powers of experience:

> He had got fast hold of an indefinite something . . . and instead of devoting, as I humbly submit he should have done, years of mental labour to the formation of a well-digested theory, he commenced to work, like a builder without a plan, or like an author without a subject; and he vainly hoped that time and experience would develop that in practice which he appears never to have been aware should have first existed not generally, but definitely and minutely, in theory.[109]

What Gray was accusing Combe of was lack of systematisation. George Mudie also had reservations about Combe's organising ability: 'I forewarned him [Hamilton] that Combe's incapacity for management would speedily ruin the enterprise.'[110]

John Gray was farsighted when he argued that Combe did not see that a practical exercise in social science 'requires to be directed, controlled and regulated upon a proper plan', whereas Combe had admitted all applicants to Orbiston. 'His errors, however, were those of judgement, and of judgement only; for, in sincere, ardent, and disinterested disposition to do good—to benefit his fellow creatures and not this or that man . . . Abram Combe was surpassed by few . . .'[111] A contemporary French commentator thought, *à propos* Abram Combe, 'on pourrait dire qu'il a été le nouveau Saint Paul de la nouvelle divine révélation'.[112]

William Thompson also was critical of the Orbiston experiment. There was so little selection of appropriate tradesmen that 'a person went from London who could do nothing but gild pictures, and make looking glasses'. Thompson referred to the

> shocking mismanagement of the storekeeper, who was in fact the tyrant of the establishment, changing the whole face of affairs by his arbitrary measures, causing the sudden expansion and contraction of the currency, a consequent want of confidence, then a struggle by individuals to get what they could, and ultimately the most complete anarchy and confusion.[113]

Robert Owen argued at the third Co-operative Congress in London 1832 that Orbiston failed because his advice was repudiated: 'That society was not the one-tenth part of a community; it was not formed upon community principles, but in direct opposition to them, and that from beginning to the end.' Alexander Campbell also reminded the delegates at the same congress that they must not go ahead with community experiments until they had the means in full:

> This was the fatal mistake of their Orbiston friends. They were provided with an estate of from £20,000 to £30,000, and they expended from first to last more than £40,000 . . . They were full of enthusiasm and they thought that when they commenced operations, money would flow upon them. But to the ruin of some, and to the serious detriment of the social system, they were disappointed; and Orbiston became the laughing stock of the surrounding country . . .

An Owenite social missionary, J. Farn, visited the site of Orbiston in 1841 and reported an interview with a local resident on the fate of the community:

> *Lady informant.* Money was lost, but Sir, what could you expect when they had people here who could not work, and if they could, had not work for them to do? A good worker could do three times the quantity of work a majority of those who were here could. And thus it was they ate up everything, and ruined the affair.
>
> *Farn.* How was it such an assemblage was brought together?
>
> *Lady.* Mr Combe was a very benevolent man: if any body, no matter what they were, went to him and told their tale of woe, he signed an order for their admission and support, whether they were wanted or not.
>
> *Farn.* What kind of people were admitted?
>
> *Lady.* Oh, we did not like them at first, but we were very sorry when they went away; they were a peaceable kind of people, only they did not pay much respect to the Sabbath, for they used to play music on that day.[114]
>
> If Mr Combe had lived, the company's affairs might perhaps have been rectified, as they had begun to discover their errors, but when he died, all went to rack and ruin; the opposition of Mrs Combe and his brother George, caused Mr Combe much pain; but Mrs Combe thought better of it after her husband's death . . .
>
> *Farn.* What became of buildings?
>
> *Lady.* Lady Douglas, when she purchased the estate, did so with the intention of pulling them down to prevent any public work being near her estate: she has razed them to their foundations; but three underground arches remain.[115]

The Orbiston community building was chalk-marked into sections and sold to the highest bidders. Many houses in Bellshill and Bothwell were built of its dull grey stone. 'Nothing now remains to mark the spot save some subterranean passages, a pond, and an old mill lade,' it was reported in 1888,[116] and in 1892 it was claimed 'the walls of theatre were still standing in the farm of Orbiston

Mains'.[117] Dr Gardiner, a local cleric, had proposed that while the new church at Bothwell was being built his parishioners should meet for divine service in the desolated hall of the Babylonians.[118]

If Orbiston had survived several years longer, it would have benefited from railway development and the sinking of more coal pits.[119] Until the late 1960s two arches which could be seen on the golf course at Orbiston were reputed to be the remnants of ovens of the community, but it may well be that the 'ovens' were the arches of a causeway, previously referred to in the *Orbiston Register*. By 1971 this last visible trace of the community had disappeared. Local hearsay has it that the golf house was built on the original burial ground of the community.[120]

The Babylon coal pit was worked on the site of Orbiston. A local authority housing scheme at Bellshill now covers the area, but the community is commemorated by street names such as Babylon Road, Community Road, Hamilcombe Road, Register Avenue.

Notes

1 *Clydesdale Journal*, 4 May 1821.

2 Letter of 29 December 1822 from Robert Owen in County Cork to Mr Wilson, president of the Practical Society, Infirmary Street, Edinburgh, in the Hamilton collection, Motherwell Public Library.

3 From 1804 the land of Orbiston was liable to contribute towards the stipend of the minister of religion at Bothwell. The public burdens continued to be paid by General Hamilton, and he claimed reimbursement during the life of the Orbiston Company for its proportion. The burdens were calculated as follows: minister's stipend £10 17s 10d; cess average 1826 to 1828 £6 3s 2d; poor rates £5 1s 0½d; school salary £1 19s 7¾d; total £24 3s 4¼d. (Memorial and abstract of the sale of Orbiston, 1830, p. 11.)

4 Hamilton collection.

5 Alex. Cullen's account in *Adventures in Socialism*, 1910 (p. 182), is wrong in assuming that Owen kept this Motherwell land for an indefinite period, and F. Podmore, *Robert Owen* (p. 355 n.), is confused on this issue.

6 For Robert Owen and the New Harmony community, see the bibliography in A. E. Bestor, *Backwoods Utopias*, 1950.

7 A. J. Hamilton, 'The soldier and the citizen of the world' (n.d.), p. 170. For A. J. Hamilton, see pp. 69ff. below.

8 A. Combe, *Metaphorical Sketches of the Old and New Systems*, 1823, p. 182.

9 *Ibid.*, p. 116.

10 *Ibid.*, p. 157.

11 *Ibid.*, p. 167.

12 *The New Court*, No. 1: *The Records of the New Court established by the First Society . . . for the Extinction of Disputes*, 1825, p. 8.

13 A. J. Hamilton, 'The soldier and the citizen of the world', p. 4 (copy in the possession of Lord Hamilton of Dalzell and kindly lent to author). The book is a highly personalised and critical attack on the Establishment, especially on the brutality and indiscipline in the army: Hamilton served in the Peninsular campaign. See, for instance, his views on the Duke of Wellington: 'Dress was one of the things about which the Marquis of Wellington did not tease his army. Everyone dressed just as he liked, and his Lordship shewed the example by wearing a pepper and salt coloured coat, a white neckcloth, and sometimes a round hat. Upon the whole, although no one liked our generalissimo, still no one could say why he did not, as he gave no one cause for offence. His staff never liked him, as he gave perhaps some offence to the married officers by flirting a little too much with their wives' (pp. 19–20).

14 Letter from MacDonald & Campbell, bankers to the army, 6 November 1824.

15 'The soldier and the citizen of the world,' p. 43.

16 See letter of 2 February 1821 'On the state of farming in Lanarkshire', in the *Farmers' Magazine*, March 1821, p. 78; also a letter signed 'Veritatis Amicus, near Hamilton', 22 September 1820, in the *Farmers' Magazine*, November 1820, pp. 416–17.

17 A. J. Hamilton became a self-confessed republican after Peterloo. His father, General Hamilton, sent £50 to the victims of Peterloo. 'This annoyed the Whigs . . .' ('The soldier and the citizen of the world', p. 186.)

18 *Ibid.*, p. 146.

19 'Report to the County of Lanark', in *A New View of Society and other writings*, pp. 65–6. See also *The Economist*, No. 9, 24 March 1821, p. 143. (Vol. II of *The Economist* was dedicated to A. J. Hamilton 'as a mark of heartfelt esteem and gratitude for his services to the cause and for his personal virtues and liberality . . .')

20 'Report to the County of Lanark', p. 66.

21 Prospectus appended to the 'Report to County of Lanark', p. 2.

22 Letter of A. J. Hamilton, 5 December 1820, Robert Owen Correspondence, No. 348.

23 'The soldier and the citizen of the world', p. 148.

24 Prospectus appended to the 'Report to the County of Lanark', p. 46.

25 A. J. Hamilton was also opposed to religion. He wrote that the thirty-nine articles were nonsense. (*Glasgow Chronicle*, 27 December 1823.)

26 'The soldier and the citizen of the world', p. 152.

27 *Ibid.*, p. 170.

28 A. Combe, *The Sphere of Joint Stock Companies, with an Account of the Establishment at Orbiston*, 1825, p. 5.

29. *Ibid.*, pp. 6–7.

30 Articles of agreement of the Orbiston Company, 1825.

31 Articles of agreement of the Orbiston Company. See also A. Combe, *An Address to the Conductors of the Periodical Press upon the Causes of Religious and Political Disputes*, 1823, *passim*.

32 A. Combe, *Observations on the Old and New Views and their effects on the Conduct of Individuals as manifested in the proceedings of the Edinburgh Christian Instructor and Mr Owen*, 1823, p. 15.

33 Article No. 3, Agreement of the tenants of the Orbiston community.
34 Article No. 9, Agreement of the tenants of the Orbiston community.
35 It was suggested that tenants should be absolved from interest payments during the first year; in second year, 4 per cent; 7 per cent to the fifth year, and 7½ per cent thereafter for the remainder of the ninety-nine-year lease. (*The Sphere of Joint Stock Companies*, p. 67.)
36 *Ibid.*, p. 39.
37 *Ibid.*, pp. 42–3.
38 *Ibid.*, pp. 52–3.
39 *Ibid.*, pp. 56–7.
40 *Ibid.*, pp. 66–7.
41 *Ibid.*, p. 65.
42 'Two flower borders, with a broad gravel walk between them, will encircle the building, and the gardens … are beyond this.' (*Co-operative Magazine*, January 1826, p. 19.)
43 *Orbiston Register*. By the second issue of the *Register* the new buildings were already being referred to as 'Babel'.
44 *Co-operative Magazine*, January 1826, p. 20.
45 *Orbiston Register*, No. 14, 16 March 1826, pp. 107–8.
46 *Ibid.*, No. 3, 24 November 1825.
47 *Ibid.*, No. 4, 1 December 1825.
48 *Co-operative Magazine*, January 1826, pp. 17–20.
49 *Orbiston Register*, No. 13, 2 March 1826, p. 101.
50 *Ibid.*, No. 14, 16 March 1826, p. 112.
51 *Ibid.*, No. 9, 12 January 1826, p. 70.
52 *Ibid.*, No. 16, 19 August 1826, p. 121.
53 *Ibid.*, No. 16, 19 August 1826, p. 125.
54 *Ibid.*, No. 16, 19 August 1826, p. 123.
55 *Co-operative Magazine*, April 1826, p. 134.
56 *Ibid.*, May 1826, p. 150.
57 *Ibid.*, May 1826, p. 161.
58 J. Gray, *A Word of Advice to the Orbistonians on the Principles which ought to regulate their present proceedings*, 1826.
59 J. Gray, *The Social System*, 1831, p. 342.
60 *Ibid.*, p. 344.
61 *Ibid.*, p. 346.
62 Letter from J. Jennings, 24 July 1826, Hamilton collection.
63 *Glasgow Herald*, 2 June 1826.
64 *Orbiston Register*, No. 16, 19 August 1826, p. 123.
65 *Ibid.*, No. 16, 19 August 1826, p. 127.
66 Letter of 8 May 1826, in the *Co-operative Magazine*, June 1826, pp. 195–7.
67 *Orbiston Register*, No. 18, 9 September 1826, p. 131.
68 *Ibid.*, No. 18, 9 September 1826, p. 136.
69 *Co-operative Magazine*, December 1826, pp. 388–9.
70 *Orbiston Register*, No. 24, 20 December 1826, p. 184.
71 *Ibid.*, No. 25, 27 December 1826, p. 188.
72 *Co-operative Magazine*, October 1826, p. 340.
73 *Ibid.*, October 1826, p. 328.

74 *Dublin Morning Post,* 4 September 1826, quoted in the *Co-operative Magazine,* October 1826, p. 325.

75 *Co-operative Magazine,* October 1826, p. 324.

76 Ibid., December 1826, pp. 389–91.

77 *Orbiston Register,* No. 27, 31 January 1827, pp. 9–10.

78 Letter from A. Combe to A. J. Hamilton, 19 February 1827, Hamilton collection.

79 Letter from William Combe, Orbiston, to A. J. Hamilton, 4 March 1827, Hamilton collection.

80 *Co-operative Magazine,* April 1827, p. 169.

81 *Ibid.,* June 1827, pp. 246–7.

82 'Remarks on the State of New Harmony' by Junius, *Co-operative Magazine,* August 1827, p. 348.

83 Letter from S. Fenner to C. Griffiths, 14 July 1827, in the *Co-operative Magazine,* August 1827, p. 373.

84 Letter from S. Fenner, 21 September 1827, in the *Co-operative Magazine,* November 1827, p. 499.

85 'Account of Orbiston' by E.S., *New Moral World,* III, No. 132, 6 May 1837, pp. 217–18.

86 A. J. Hamilton, 'The soldier and the citizen of the world', p. 200.

87 For George Combe, writer to the Signet, see G. Combe, *Education: its Principles and Practice,* ed. W. Jolly, 1879, and A. Price, 'George Combe: a pioneer of scientific education', *Educational Review* (University of Birmingham), XII, No. 3, June 1960.

88 *Life and Testimony of Abram Combe,* ed. A. Campbell, 1844, p. 24.

89 There was freedom of religion at Orbiston—a Baptist church service was held at the community. There was also a high rate of church attendance at New Lanark—1,300–1,400 were estimated as churchgoers out of a population of 2,200 in 1823. (Unsigned letter in the Goldsmid letters, Mocatta collection, University College, London.) The places of worship at New Lanark included a Gaelic chapel and an Independent meeting house.

90 A. J. Hamilton, 'The soldier and the citizen of the world', p. 201.

91 The sale of Orbiston was advertised in the *Glasgow Herald,* 7 July 1828. The main building was of four storeys and the manufactory had five floors and 'was commodiously fitted up for workshops'. There were also four farmsteads and three dairies on the site.

92 Letter from Alexander Paul at Orbiston to A. J. Hamilton, Geneva, 17 August 1829, Hamilton collection.

93 *The Life and Testimony of Abram Combe,* p. 12, gives an account of the leasing arrangements for Orbiston foundry.

94 Letter from Alexander Campbell, 3 October 1828, Robert Owen correspondence, No. 85. For other evidence of Owen visiting Orbiston, see letter No. 1148 from Alexander Paul, 25 August, 1848, and letter No. 2713, 8 May 1856, from Alexander Campbell.

95 'Reports as to the contents and estimated rents and value of the lands and estate of Orbiston belonging to the Orbiston Company, from a plan of lands belonging to General Hamilton,' Thomas Lawrie, land valuer, Stockbridge, 22 November 1828, Hamilton collection.

96 Memorial and abstract of the ranking and sale of Orbiston, pp. 14–15.

97 Secured by bond, 6 June 1825, registered in the General Register of Sasines, Edinburgh, 4 July 1825.

98 Registered 4 July 1825. Considerable arrears of interest were due on these debts.

99 Memorial and abstract.

100 *Ibid.*, p. 2.

101 Letter from George Combe to A. J. Hamilton, 9 June 1831, Hamilton collection.

102 See the petition of Mrs Cecilia Douglas of Douglas Park to the sheriff depute of Lanarkshire, 23 December 1826, Hamilton collection.

103 *Life and Testimony of A. Combe*, p. 24.

104 A. J. Hamilton, 'The soldier and the citizen of the world', p. 172.

105 *Ibid.*, p. 172.

106 *Ibid.*, p. 204.

107 *The Crisis*, No. 26, 22 February 1834, pp. 214–15.

108 J. Gray, *The Social System*, p. 348.

109 *Ibid.*, p. 352.

110 Letter from George Mudie to Robert Owen, 25 August 1848, Robert Owen correspondence, No. 1665.

111 J. Gray, *The Social System*, p. 353.

112 J. Rey, *Lettres sur le Système de la co-opération mutuelle*, 1828, pp. 114–15.

113 Report of a talk by William Thompson at Manchester Mechanics' Institute, *Glasgow Herald*, 10 June 1831.

114 Orbiston lived on harmoniously in at least one respect—the Shotts Foundry band, which was established in 1829, acquired its first sheet music and band instruments from the Orbiston community—six clarionets, a bag of flutes, two serpents, two bassoons, two keyed bugles, two French horns, a trumpet, a brass horn, trombone and drum. (*Third Statistical Account of Scotland (Lanarkshire)*), 1960, p. 141.

115 *New Moral World*, x, No. 9, 28 August 1841, p. 67.

116 *Reed's Directory of the Parish of Bothwell*, 1888, p. 12, in Lanark County Library.

117 J. H. Pagan, *Antiquities of Bothwell*, 1892, p. 70.

118 *Ibid.*, p. 71.

119 On a map of 1862 the Clydesdale Junction railway bridge at Orbiston is marked as 'Babylon Bridge'; see A. McPherson, *Handbook of Hamilton, Bothwell*, etc., 1862.

120 The local newspaper, *The Bellshill Speaker*, maintained a link with Orbiston community, as the proprietors, until recently, were members of the Combe family—descendants of Abram Combe. By another remarkable coincidence the firm of architects who built the new Orbiston church was founded by Alex. Cullen, the author of the first account of Orbiston. Alex. Cullen himself served articles with James King of Motherwell; a James King of Motherwell was the contractor for the original Orbiston community building.

4
Ralahine, 1831–33

Ralahine community in County Clare cannot be fully understood
in purely Owenite or communitarian terms; one must also know
something of Irish land history. Of the three leading Owenite communities, Ralahine was the most parochial and the least grandiose
in its settlement plans and architecture; it was also the experiment
with the strongest agricultural basis. As was the case with Orbiston,
there were two leading parties—a landed proprietor sympathetic to
Owenite ideas, John Scott Vandeleur, and a working class Owenite
organiser, E. T. Craig. The Irish community is no less remarkable
because it was the most successful of the early co-operative land
schemes; but its organisation can be explained only in terms of
changing types and methods of land-holding brought about by
Irish population pressure, the new methods of tenure in turn leading to further increases in population. It is also necessary to relate
the levels of employment, remuneration and subsistence at Ralahine to prevailing Irish standards rather than to any English counterpart before any evaluation of the experiment can be attempted.

As early as 1808 an adverse account was given of the landlords
of County Clare:

> I regret to have to remark, that with a few exceptions the gentlemen of this
> county, in common with too many of those in some other counties,
> neither know, nor seem to care much how their cottier tenants live...

The author of this survey then quoted advice he had given in a
previous survey of Dublin to which he now added a footnote: 'I
would not have given this extract, but that the book I allude to
is in the hands of very few, and County of Clare gentlemen are
not much in the habit of reading.'[1] There was little indication of
agrarian disturbances to come. 'In general the people are remark-
ably peaceable, travelling at night being equally safe as in the
day.'[2] A passing reference was made to Ralahine Castle, where on
an ancient chimney-piece there was inscribed in bas-relief 'Fear
God, and remember the poor'.[3]

The critical period for land hunger in Ireland began during the 1820s—the population of Clare, for instance, increased by 25 per cent (from 208,000 to 258,000) between 1821 and 1831, and this growth was almost entirely rural. A system developed of leasing landed property to bailiffs or agents, who contracted to guarantee their lord a certain revenue on condition that his estate was subdivided for a fixed term under their management. During the period 1800–33 no fewer than 114 Parliamentary commissions and sixty select committees investigated the 'state of Ireland' question, but in spite of all this inquiry very little was done in the way of remedial measures. For example, a public works programme instituted in 1831 enabled the raising of loans for land reclamation, but interest was chargeable at 5 per cent and capital had to be repaid within three years of the completion of improvements; moreover, loans were available only to full owners. Hence it is not surprising that the total sum lent between 1832 and 1845 was barely £2,200.[4]

Sufficient encouragement from the government could hardly be expected when it was known Sir Robert Peel had said in 1830 that from his experience of Ireland he never saw any permanent good effected by vote of public money.[5]

In these conditions of 'morcellement', a type of tenure known as 'conacre' became widespread in Ireland during the early nineteenth century:

> The term 'conacre' appears to mean a contract by which the use of a small portion of land is sold for one or more crops, but without creating the relation of landlord and tenant between vendor and vendee, it being rather a licence to occupy than a demise...the vendor manures the ground...whilst the vendee procures seed, plants it, and performs all subsequent labour.[6]

At the time of the Devon Commission on Agriculture in the mid-1840s there were three classes of labourer—unmarried farm servants; cottiers who held small plots at a fixed rent generally payable in labour; and aforementioned 'conacre' labourers with a cabin and small garden whose subsistence was chiefly dependent on potatoes. The usual level of conacre rent ranged from £10 to £40 an acre, and if the crop could not justify the rent payment the labourer had to abandon the land. But even before 1830 many estate owners were changing over to direct cultivation, thus causing many labourers to become landless.[7] The hirer of conacre land was being exposed to the full risk of the year being bad with no remission of conacre rent, which was paid sometimes in cash, frequently in labour, and sometimes partly in cash and partly in labour. 'The result of this barter of land and labour sometimes was that, each being accounted to balance the other, no money changed hands'[8]— so that the conacre system was much the same as the truck system in the payment of manufacturing wages.[9]

An estimate of the wage for agricultural workers in Ireland in 1830 was given as tenpence per day.[10] But Sir George Cornewall Lewis thought that only one third of labourers had the benefit of all-year-round employment:

> If every labourer in Ireland could earn 8*d* per day for 310 days in the year, we should probably never hear of Whiteboys. It is the impossibility of living by wages which throws him upon the land; it is the liability of being driven from the land and the consequences of having no other resource that makes him a Whiteboy.[11]

Barry O'Brien, writing in 1880, summarised the situation:

> We are probably not far wrong in concluding that the average wage of the Irish cottier in the first half of the nineteenth century was from eight pence to ten pence a day, and that there were about 200 working days in the year.[12]

Robert Owen first visited Ireland in 1822 when he stayed as a guest of Lord Cloncurry, but there is scant evidence that he grasped the nature of Irish land problems. Ireland was for Owen the first staging post in his transfer to a community in the New World. Perhaps he thought that the dire economic condition of Ireland, being less involved with industrialism than either England or Scotland, would be more suitable for a social improvement plan based on the provision of adequate agricultural employment. He held a series of public meetings in Dublin in 1823: the first meeting launched into economics, but then drifted into religion before it broke up; subsequent meetings were confined to discussion of Owen's plans.[13] Owen wanted the government to be the agent for his proposed reforms, but the Select Committee on Employment of the poor in Ireland, of 1823, flouted the idea. The Hibernian Philanthropic Society, which Owen set up on the model of the British and Foreign Philanthropic Society to gather funds from private sympathisers in the absence of government support, was just as moribund as the parent Society. The wonder of Owen's reception in Ireland was that he got a hearing at all from Roman Catholics when in his scheme 'there was to be no public worship—no avowed recognition of God, no belief of responsibility to a higher tribunal than man's'.[14] But it was reported that Owen cleared the ground by visiting Maynooth, where he gave his word that he was not interested in the spread of Protestantism in Ireland. 'Hence his subsequent operations in Ireland were never interfered with by the clergy.'[15] There is, however, other evidence that it was Owen's tour of Ireland after the Dublin meetings that brought the final disenchantment:

> In his journey to Limerick and Clare, his principles more plainly unfolded themselves, and then his visit to Ireland caused a feeling of horror and of awe in those whose opinion he would probably wish to conciliate.[16]

Probably Owen visited John Scott Vandeleur during this extensive tour, which included County Clare. The Vandeleur family can trace their ancestry in Ireland back to the early seventeenth century, when 'James Vandelure, a maltster and tanner, of Six Mile Bridge, a Dutch Protestant, deposes that he was robbed of property worth £1,836, part of which consisted of debts due to him'.[17] Giles Vandeleur was one of two surveyors appointed in 1658 to make an inspection of waste lands which were avoiding the payment of Crown quit rents.[18] He subsequently became high sheriff of County Clare in 1664, and in 1680 was living at Ralahine Castle. In 1682 he took a leasehold from Viscount Clare of 732 acres at a rental of £35.[19] The Vandeleurs continued as large landowners in County Clare, and when John Scott Vandeleur,[20] the son of Colonel Boyle Vandeleur, took possession of the estate at Ralahine he found it divided into a number of small farms, except for a portion of home farm where his father had laid out a race course and built extensive stabling. John Scott Vandeleur had another estate of about 700 acres elsewhere in County Clare, but at Ralahine he personally directed operations, although he had to face difficulties in acquiring good labour, especially at harvest time, when there was heavy migration to England. John Scott Vandeleur had frequent talks with Robert Owen during the Dublin meetings and was deeply impressed with Owen's account of New Lanark. The benefits of New Lanark, he thought, could be transposed on to an agricultural basis to achieve higher rents, adequate interest on capital, and also provide benefits for labourers. Ralahine, in many ways, was to become the agricultural equivalent of New Lanark. In fact it was to have more in common with New Lanark than with the other co-operative experiments at Orbiston and Queenwood. It will be shown that Vandeleur became the truest disciple of Owen, the mill manager: both sought and achieved a buoyant level of profits; but Vandeleur turned out to be not quite so autocratic as Owen: at Ralahine profit-sharing was at least contemplated, in contrast to New Lanark.

In 1823 there was widespread famine in Ireland and Vandeleur called a meeting at Ennis to consider Owen's plans. Vandeleur took his responsibilities seriously, as an improving landlord, and one of his first decisions was to remove his small tenants to farms more distant from his residence, until the home farm under his personal supervision increased to 700 acres. He made several improvements by building a number of cottages and providing his labourers with small allotments. He also built a flax mill, a weaving factory and a bleaching house',[21] but the local people were averse to the introduction of manufactures.[22]

The conacre system was becoming common in the district around Ralahine by 1831. James Molony, a local landowner, wrote:

> Much to be wished that system lately adopted in neighbourhood of Newmarket-on-Fergus, of trenching ground for potatoes, whereby the produce is doubled, and the crop divided equally between the Landlord, who furnishes land and manure, and the Workman, who furnishes labour, should be extended throughout the county.[23]

Farm labourers in County Clare were being paid wages at the standard rate of 8*d* per day, but 'there are thousands who would gladly work for a smaller sum of 6*d* if regular employment was secured throughout the year'.[24] It was estimated that there were 80,000 landless labourers in Clare at the time, with a further 80,000 having insufficient land for subsistence out of a total population of a quarter of a million. A pamphleteer, 'Agricola', suggested the establishment of a model farm in the county to demonstrate improved methods of cultivation, and an open invitation was extended to anyone who had reservations about the advantages to be derived from a more careful attention to management:

> If they doubt the efficacy of improved husbandry to better the conditions of the soil and to increase its productiveness to an extent hardly creditable [*sic*], let them visit the domain of that most intelligent Farmer and Gentleman, John Vandeleur Esq. of Ralahine –there they will witness its effects in an eminent degree—there they will see land that was hithertofore considered poor and unproductive yielding crops of every description...

effected by steady and systematic management, under the immediate direction of that talented and enlightened Proprietor.[25]

Insurrection and sabotage became rife in County Clare from 1830, largely concentrating on the land stewards, the hated agents of the absentee landowners. It was reported from the county in the previous year that 'Bodies of peasantry, called O'Connell's Police, set out in pursuit and do much damage to crops.'[26] William Pare later wrote of the period:

> In the County of Clare, in particular, all decent persons of all opinions declared that the County was no longer tolerable as a place of residence. The serving of threatening notices, the levelling of walls, the driving off of cattle, the beating of herdsmen, the compulsory removal of tenants, the levying of contributions in money, the robbery of dwelling houses, the reckless commission of murder were driving the better classes of inhabitants to desert their houses and seek refuge in some other quarter.[27]

The bands of marauding peasants in Clare were known as Terry Alts and Whiteboys.[28] E. T. Craig gave an example of a Terry Alt initiation oath:

> I hereby swear to suffer the right arm to be cut from the left, and the left from the right, and the right to be nailed to the metropolis of Armagh jail door, before ever I'll waylay or betray a brother, or go on a green cloth to swear against him.
>
> I hereby swear never to hear the moans or groans of dying children, but always to wade knee-deep in Orange blood, and to keep down land-jobbers and tithe-jobbers.[29]

Vandeleur, then high sheriff of Clare, offered rewards for information concerning the murder of a land steward in February 1831. The situation was approaching anarchy. 'How shall we describe it?— One sentence. We assert that from one end to the other of this County, the people are in open hostile array against the Government.'[30] In April 1831 a detachment of 17th Lancers left Limerick to be quartered at Six Mile Bridge.[31] By the end of April the violence raging in County Clare reached Ralahine:

> A cold-blooded murder took place near Ralahine, the seat of John Scott Vandeleur...Daniel Hastings, a confidential man in the employment of Mr Vandeleur, had returned home from his employment as a land steward, and was in the act of fastening the door of his house...when he was fired at through a window. The poor man received the bullets in the back of the head, and died instantly...His death cannot be attributed to any other cause than the system now prevailing in this County—one

which wishes to eradicate from the land, not only the gentry but the honest faithful stewards...[32]

In May 1831 a copy of a threatening letter to a land steward was published in the local Press. The letter was signed 'Terry Alts and Mrs Alts, King and Queen of Clare'. The newspaper reported that the land in question was in possession of Terry Alts: 'His herds-man's house is now deserted, his cows driven off, his dairy utensils broken to pieces, and no person dare go look for the cows to have them milked.'[33] In the same month an Insurrection Act was applied to County Clare and a special commission was appointed in June to try offenders at Limerick and Ennis: in all, four were hanged and ten transported. Vandeleur had decided, before the outrages against the land steward, to set up some form of agricultural association, and building operations, which had been commenced in 1830, con-tinued into the spring and summer of 1831. Cottages of two storeys were erected, slated and glazed, and dormitories were built. Vande-leur's plans were opposed by his own land steward, whose murder induced Vandeleur to launch the community experiment earlier than intended.[34] (Vandeleur's family took refuge in nearby Lime-rick, and the Ralahine residence was left in charge of armed police after the murder.)

Early in 1831 Vandeleur had visited England to solicit help, as he foresaw difficulties in the way of implementing improvements as a representative of the landed classes. It was also necessary to work with the material available, his own farm labourers, although he felt they were not well disposed to the proposed measures. Vandeleur first met Craig in a Manchester hotel.[35] Craig wrote of the meeting:

> It was ... the work I had done in Manchester that Mr Vandeleur heard of, through John Finch of Liverpool, that induced him to come to Man-chester, where I had an interview with him at the Talbot Hotel, which existed at the bottom of King Street before the improvements were made.[36]

Craig's imagination was stirred by the desire of Vandeleur to pro-vide improved conditions for his farm workers, and he wrote to Owen about the Irish project:

> Mr J. S. Vandeleur of Ralahine has invited me to Ireland to assist in his arrangements. I shall go there with pleasure, as my whole heart is with the cause. As the success of the experiment will mainly depend upon its

management I should feel a pleasure if you could furnish me with any suggestions, especially respecting the machinery of Infant Schools...

> *Fellow Labourer E. T. Craig,*
> *Corresponding Secretary*
> *to the Manchester Owenian Society.*[37]

The friends of Craig feared for his life, and his grandfather opposed the suggestion of going to Ralahine: 'I should attend to my interests and get on in the world.' Craig would not be deterred, and recounted how 'I left Manchester in company with an agent Mr Vandeleur had sent over to England, and on our arrival at Liverpool, he related the melancholy state of the population at Ralahine.' Later it became clear to Craig that Vandeleur was not being completely altruistic in seeking better conditions for his tenants and labourers; his plans were also meant to safeguard his property, as was elicited by Craig from the evidence of a letter he had sight of from James Molony to Vandeleur on 21 September 1831 in which Molony was seeking Vandeleur's advice on leasing land and relating rents to prices and wages.[38]

Craig could not claim to have any intimate knowledge of agriculture at this time. He never became a farmer; he was an organiser, a manager, and the parallel situation of Craig in 1831 is that of Owen as a young man showing all the qualities of leadership in taking over the Drinkwater mill in Manchester with scant experience but with a will to learn and to organise. For all the garrulity of his reminiscences in old age, Craig must have been a courageous man to have left Manchester for Ralahine during the autumn of 1831 with slight knowledge of Ireland except for newspaper accounts of the turmoil of riot and murder which ravaged its countryside. Within six weeks of his arrival in Ireland four murders had been committed in the immediate area of Ralahine. He must have feared for his life and he was told that an outline grave had been dug to receive his body and he was warned to vary his paths to his lodgings after dark to evade assailants. Although Craig was at pains to stress that in the 'new system' to be drawn up there was no place for a steward, he was treated as a stranger, a landlord's man, and the local labourers held that he was at Ralahine for his own profit.

His first tasks were to superintend the building of a store room and the acquisition of stores. Gaining the confidence of the majority of the English-speaking peasants was difficult, but Craig tried to convince them of the benefit that would come from living together and working in association. His tact and forbearance must have been very great, for not only were the peasants suspicious of the impending reforms, but the comments by members of Vandeleur's family and their house servants were scathing.

Craig reported that he spent some months examining the situation before drawing up a draft constitution. The Ralahine estate of John Scott Vandeleur consisted of 618 acres, of which 268 were cultivated, the rest being pasture, some of it stony or rough, and sixty-three acres of bog, from which peat was dug for fuel. A boundary of the original estate abuts on to the Limerick–Ennis road several miles from Newmarket-on-Fergus. From this road the ruins of Ralahine Castle can still be seen. The Vandeleur residence was pulled down some years ago although the original farm cottages are still standing along the roadside to Newmarket-on-Fergus.

A highly personalised account of Ralahine community was written in book form by E. T. Craig in 1882, but at this interval of time it becomes necessary to investigate whether the account written by Craig when he was seventy-eight years old was consistent with his own earlier supporting evidence and that of several other contemporary observers, including John Finch and William Pare. Their commentaries do not wholly support Craig's interpretation; hence his account must be analysed, especially with regard to the relationship between Ralahine and the Owenite co-operative movement.

The ideology of the Ralahine experiment was Robert Owen's, but the actual planning and direction were the work of Vandeleur and Craig, who were the only persons at Ralahine conversant with Owen's principles. If this shows anything, it indicates that, provided members of a community agree to be governed in the first instance by officials, 'it is not absolutely necessary at the beginning that every member should be thoroughly acquainted with all the principles and duties of our system'.[39] John Finch visited Ralahine, and in the first letter of a series on the community he wrote in sweeping terms for the benefit of an imagined throng of sympathisers and interested parties. The language is that of Owen rather than Craig or Vandeleur:

> To Queen, Ladies of Great Britain and Ireland, Poor Law Commissioners, Parish Authorities, Irish Landlords, Manufacturers and Capitalists, Clubs and Trade Unions, Patriots, Philanthropists, Political Economists, Professors of Religion, Britons of every class, Party or creed . . .[40]

Finch proposed to lay before these readers the means of preventing ignorance, poverty, drunkenness and crime, and superseding the necessity for introducing poor laws into Ireland, without any extra outlay and with the least interference with private property.

The pressing decision of Vandeleur to set up the Ralahine community was based on the alternative of anarchy facing a landowner in County Clare. Conditions at Ralahine when the community was in operation were graphically compared by John Finch with living standards in other parts of western Ireland at the time. Finch describes a typical cabin: 'No bed, no furniture, scarcely any utensil save a cast iron pot, which the potatoes are boiled for the family dinner, and in which afterwards the surplus and refuse are served up to the grunters.'[41] Before assessing the success of Ralahine as a community, it must be appreciated that Ralahine was a first step away from such squalor.

Vandeleur wrote to William Pare in Birmingham on 3 October 1831 stating that he was busy with the preliminary arrangements for setting up the community and:

> would have started previously but disappointed at having some linens misconveyed that were going to England to be exchanged for some Co-operative-made goods, such as blankets, rugs and goods to furnish our store; we cannot, of course, commence without blankets, but we have dwelling houses, dormitories for male and female, and infant school, dining rooms and lecture rooms and though we commenced with only thirty members, yet we have 595 (British) acres of land, highly cultivated, and food enough this year for at least 500 persons.[42]

The intended community was to be managed by a committee of nine members—J. S. Vandeleur, chairman; E. T. Craig, secretary; a treasurer, three members for agriculture, three for trades and manufactures. The store would be stocked with foodstuffs at the follow-prices: beef and mutton $4d$ per lb, pork $3\frac{1}{2}d$, milk $1d$ per quart: 'The wages are low but all the children from $1\frac{1}{2}$ years upwards are to be fed and clothed from the common fund.'

From the above letter it is apparent that the community was launched some time before the historic agreement which was drawn up on 1 November 1831 and then presented to the Ralahine farm labourers. The preamble to the laws of the Ralahine Agricultural and Manufacturing Co-operative Association gave as the objects of the Association the acquisition of common capital, assurance against poverty, sickness and old age, the attainment of a higher standard of living, mental and moral improvement and the education of children. In all, fifty-two members were admitted to the Association, but of these only eighteen could be classed as efficient agricultural labourers.

Support for the experiment was by no means universal: 'Some of the labourers at Ralahine were employed as regular farm servants and received food and lodging and a given sum yearly...they much opposed the scheme. They included relatives of the murdered steward and they thought power at an end...' Craig noted that 'they were large-headed men, at least in the basilar region, and I therefore anticipated some difficulty in their management'. There were also some day labourers whose families lived often seven or more miles away. The conditions of admittance of applicants for membership at Ralahine were drawn up and based on capability for practical work, 'and, what was of still greater moment, his moral and intellectual capacity, phrenologically considered...Each member had a number, as well as every horse and implement'.[43] The new members were introduced and approved by Vandeleur on probation for one week and then balloted for:

> I could now, before the rules are adopted, or the agreement signed, turn out any or every person that I supposed was not cordially inclined to co-operate for the benefit of each and all.[44]

Vandeleur, as proprietor, therefore insisted on a vote.

The rules of the Association laid down that the farm stock, equipment and land were to remain the property of Vandeleur until the society accumulated sufficient funds to pay for them; they would then become the joint property of the members. A committee would control labour tasks and discipline; men labourers would receive 8*d* per day, women 5*d*. There were regulations concerning the education of children, the prohibition of gaming, rights of arbitration, procedure at meetings and for the alteration of rules. After a vote in favour of the constitution a further agreement between landlord and tenants was drawn up on 10 November 1831 relating to the terms of tenancy, profits and rent. Vandeleur drew up this rent agreement, which was the basis of the community, but the initial rules of the Association had been devised wholly by Craig, who thought 'Our constitution was, as far as I could make it, a Pantisocracy, where all governed and all served'.[45] The level of rent payable was not a set sum of money; it was fixed in terms of farm produce. Although the rent was high, and acknowledged to be so by Vandeleur, he pointed out that all profits would belong to the members. If farm output increased through a good season or sound methods, then the members would gain and the landlord would derive benefit through any increased value of his property. Within the terms of the agreement Vandeleur would gain directly from any rise in the market price of produce, as the tenants were required to supply a notional quantity which, at the average price levels ruling in 1830–31,[46] would sell for £900: hence, if prices rose, the tenants still had to supply the same physical corn rent. The total rental of £900 was broken down into £700 for land, and £200 interest on capital stock and implements (machines for thrashing corn and scutching flax were provided). It was argued that as members had no control over market prices, it would have been unfair for them to have to produce more output rent as a result of a fall in prices, but it was firmly expected that prices would tend to rise as a result of more settled farming conditions in the area. The tenants were therefore relieved of anxiety over falling prices and could concentrate on increasing their output. But the rent agreement had some of the elements of conacre—the hirer of a conacre was exposed to the full risk of a bad harvest, and Ralahine tenants likewise would have to bear the brunt of crop failure. In sum, Vandeleur took the risk of falling market prices and the members the risk of bad years. Any surplus was to accrue to wages and the repayment of interest on capital. Ralahine was not a *métayage* system because Vandeleur received rent in kind—under the *métayage* system there was a fixed percentage of actual annual produce in rent, but at Ralahine there were fixed quantities irrespective of actual output or price change. If the rent was not paid, or if stock deteriorated in quality, or cultivation receded, Vandeleur reserved the right to rescind the agreement and take back the land.[47]

The lease was for one year in the first instance and although a longer lease was contemplated it was never actually executed. So long as Vandeleur managed the estate this was of little importance, as he was not interested in ending the experiment.

It was common prudence on Vandeleur's part to retain ownership of stock and premises, the power of expulsion, a veto of members and to agree to pay the labourers no more than the prevailing low level of wages. He was businessman enough to weigh the risk of entrusting such a proportion of his property and income to an impoverished band of labourers and to advance them a bare sufficiency until the first harvest.

The stipulated rent was fully paid during the two years of the life of the community, in addition to investment in more buildings and some land reclamation. Wage differentials above the general level of 8*d* were later paid to artisans and the storekeeper—the low level of wages was a brake on over-consumption, but Vandeleur could not recruit skilled carpenters and smiths without paying them higher wages than common labourers. Apart from these adjustments in wage differentials, there were no amendments to the rules of the Association during the life of the community.

A system of labour notes was introduced, which, in contrast to other Owenite co-operative experiments, worked successfully. Vandeleur advanced food, stores and materials, and each member could draw on the store to the value of his labour notes. Records were kept and the labourers were debited collectively with rent at 25*s* per acre, county rates, and interest on stock and capital advanced by Vandeleur; on the credit side of members' accounts were entries for the value of their labour.

By January 1832 a labour sheet gave the total weekly wage of fifty adults, a third of whom were women, and seventeen children as £10 4*s* 2*d*, with consumption at £4 0*s* 11 ½*d*, leaving £6 3*s* 2*d* for clothing and other expenses. Most of the adults were aged between eighteen and thirty. It should, however, be noted that at this early stage of the experiment the weekly rental of £18 greatly exceeded the book value of the labour output. Nearly half the wages were spent at the community store. Labour notes in fact enabled Vandeleur to support members without having to make cash advances.

The labour notes were issued in denominations of from one week to one-sixteenth of a day 'and are taken by a tailor, shoemaker and hatter in the neighbourhood . . . These labour notes are exchanged at par, when the holders desire to purchase articles not produced in the Society.'[48] In reality, it would have been difficult to have overvalued the labour notes, given the low wages prevailing at Ralahine in terms of the input–output ratio of the community's resources. Craig explained that labour notes were exchanged at the store but, as the quantity and rates of corn rent were fixed, the actual marketable value was immaterial to the members. The Ralahine labourers were

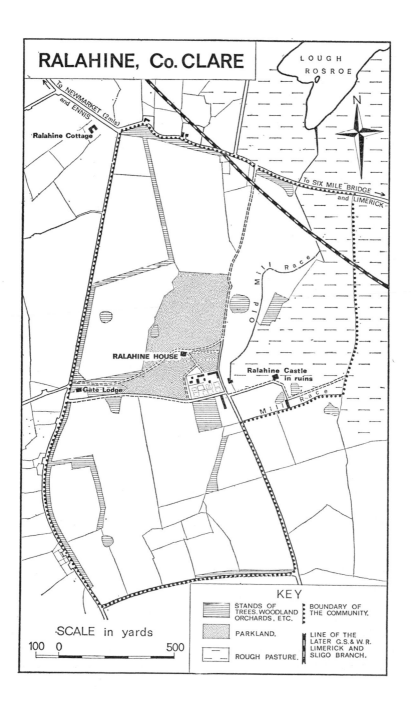

RALAHINE, Co. CLARE

LOUGH ROSROE

To NEWMARKET (2 mls) and ENNIS

Ralahine Cottage

To SIX MILE BRIDGE and LIMERICK

Old Mill Race

RALAHINE HOUSE

Ralahine Castle in ruins

Gate Lodge

Mill Race

KEY

STANDS OF TREES, WOODLAND ORCHARDS, ETC.

BOUNDARY OF THE COMMUNITY.

PARKLAND.

LINE OF THE LATER G.S.& W.R. LIMERICK AND SLIGO BRANCH.

ROUGH PASTURE.

SCALE in yards
100   0   500

proscribed from using their labour notes for procuring drink and tobacco. Indeed, the labour note system was a method of strictly regulating the level of purchasing power. The prices of products were fixed by a committee at an on-cost margin, and books and accounts were open to inspection. Nevertheless, there had to be some currency transactions with the outside world because Ralahine was never wholly self-sufficient; but in these cases Vandeleur acted as sole intermediary—he supplied cash for outside supplies, and all saleable produce from the community passed through his hands— otherwise the labour note system, with its inherent weaknesses of leakage and depreciation when involved in outside exchange trans- actions, would not have worked so smoothly.[40]

Some of the Ralahine labourers lived in small cottages, the remainder in a new communal building, the economies of which 'obviate the necessity of the young labourer marrying merely that he may have someone to cook and bring him his meals'.[50] Obviously, the labour force of sixty to seventy in early 1832 was inadequate to cultivate all the 600 acres. Vandeleur wanted to institute manufac- turing as a supplementary form of indoor winter employment: Terry Alts had thwarted Vandeleur's previous efforts to establish a weaving shed, a flax scutching mill and bleaching works.[51] By 1833 it was reported that wool was being woven by hand into coarse flannel for use in the community, and Craig commented:

> The absence of machinery in this and other departments is a subject that has attracted the attention to its importance in other respects. (The Com- munity had a threshing machine and a sawmill.)[52]

During his short visit to Ralahine William Pare observed that 'shafts were conducted into the mechanical workshops for the purpose of turning lathes; also a scutching mill, for dressing flax'.[52]

Craig gave instruction to the youths and adults. The community library had sixty volumes, 'with an orrery and terrestial globe, a few chemical and other philosophical apparatus'.[53] Religion might have been a problem, but Craig safeguarded the situation by not using the Bible as a school book.[54] Sunday was a general rest day, and the teaching of religion to children was left to parents. The local clergy at Ralahine did not appear to be as antagonistic as those at Orbiston.

The regimen at Ralahine was severe by any standard—a twelve- hour day and a low standard wage. One evening a week was spent auditing accounts, two nights were for dancing and one for lectures.

There were severe membership restrictions: members could marry outsiders, but if an outsider was not voted into community both partners were bound to leave. (Voting for expulsion was on a 75 per cent poll basis.) The infant teacher, who was trained at the model infant school at Dublin, married an outsider but her husband was rejected and hence she was expelled. Over the entire life of the community only two members left of their own accord. During 1833 there were many applicants for admission and by November the nominal roll stood at eighty-one members.[56]

John Finch described the domestic arrangements at Ralahine. The cottages were 'as clean and neat as the average of houses of the best part of the working people of England'.[57] The infant school, which was supported out of common funds, had cribs, beds, slates, books, playground, ropes and swings, and the school was open from 6.00 a.m. to 6.00 p.m. during summer. Craig, apart from teaching the youths and adults, also instructed the older children and followed a curriculum of alternating physical with mental exercises. He argued that drawing should be taught before writing, as he believed that writing was just a more difficult form of drawing. Because he found lecturing to the adults in English difficult, Craig tried a variety of visual aids but had to abandon them.

The total value of produce at Ralahine for 1832 was £1,700, with advances for clothing, food, seed and other items £550. (Finch pointed out that distribution costs were less than £50.) The advances for building materials and furniture took all the proceeds of surplus produce during the period, but it should be noted that standards of living were improving. The eventual aim was to convert labourers into co-partners. In fact, the rent and interest payments received by Vandeleur were much higher than the levels of rental and surplus ruling before the commencement of the community. Nothing was actually divided as profit, but this was offset by land reclamation, and profit distribution was within the members' long term planning. 'They would first purchase machinery for manufacturing, next their agricultural implements and farm stock, then the estate itself . . .'[58]

Adulteration of food was checked, and Pare quoted the dictum of John Bright that 'adulteration is but a form of competition'.[58] Finch compared the standard of nutrition of the Ralahine labourers with those of a typical worker in Liverpool who 'lives on withered vegetables, blue milk, stale and bad water ... sixty shillings per week in the present society would not procure the advantages and comforts that were enjoyed in community at Ralahine for 6s. 6d'.[60] Some credence may be placed in Finch's comparisons when the level of prices at Ralahine are examined: potatoes 2d per stone; milk 1d a quart; pork 2½d a lb.[61] The men at Ralahine each paid 1s weekly for as many potatoes as they could eat; womenfolk paid 6d. The diet was mainly milk and potatoes—the higher-paid wage-earners had tea and coffee and occasionally fresh meat; 'a little pork was taken, but rarely any bread'.[62]

According to John Finch, Vandeleur always acted as president and chairman of all meetings. 'King Vandeleur had a power which we would by no means entrust to the governor of a community ... but he never used it.' Vandeleur intended to maintain his power until the members acquired capital; he could not give them a long lease in the early stages when members were using £3,000 of his capital. All members over 17 years of age had a right to attend the meeting of the general committee which was elected at interval of six months. (The practice at Ralahine was to put the most effective members on sub-committees.)[63] Evidence of the solidarity of the labourers was shown when the 'New Systemites' barred the Ralahine farmyard gate against a party of fox-hunting gentry during the winter of 1832 when Vandeleur was absent. Thus self-interest, given the right incentives, was productive of communal benefit.

There were sensible, conservative arrangements of estate management and cultivation: for instance, members could cut trees provided two were planted in their stead. Limestone and turf were available for mortar, and Vandeleur agreed to defray a portion of the cost of slating and glazing additional cottages. All farm animals were held in common. The precise aims of Vandeleur were to obtain higher rent, secure interest on capital and its punctual payment, safety of property, and security for the advances he made upon the labour of the members. All these aims were realised and the value of his property increased over the period of the experiment.

Attention was drawn to Ralahine during the summer of 1833 by William Pare and Robert Owen, who saw possibilities of using the community as a source of agricultural produce for the Owenite labour exchanges in England. Robert Owen made plans to meet the trustees of William Thompson's estate in County Cork, and also visit 'Mr Vandeleur's infant community, to ascertain in what way it can be made available to promote the Equitable Labour Exchange...'[64] The inference must be drawn that Owen at this stage was more interested in labour exchanges than communities, as he had first visited Lord Wallscourt's estate before arriving at Rala- hine—which is indicative of his casual attitude to the importance of the experiment, although he did compliment Vandeleur on being

> the only gentleman in Ireland who has made experiments on a large scale to try the effect of our principles...Mr Vandeleur is quite pleased with his tenants, and on both sides they confess to be doing much better by these plans of co-operation than they could otherwise do.[65]

Craig returned to Ralahine from England early in August 1833. A reaping machine was delivered and the whole crop of 120 acres of wheat was cut by the end of the month. The reaping machine was invented by a Mr Mann, of Kelso, and a visitor to Ralahine commented, 'The mechanic employed by the Ralahine Society was sent over to Scotland to watch the progress of the work, and to accompany the machine to its destination.'[66] Lord Wallscourt also visited Ralahine at this time for a copy of Owen's Dublin meeting of 1823.

Early in October William Pare journeyed to Ireland in the company of Vandeleur, who was returning to Ralahine after a visit to Eng- land.[67] Pare was eager to investigate the possibility of forming a labour exchange with a view to providing the Birmingham exchange with Irish farm produce in exchange for Birmingham wares.[68] The first meeting convened by Pare was held in Limerick and he was reported in the local Press as having resolved to set up a branch labour exchange in the town.[69] Craig attended the meeting and commented that 'there would be a difficulty in paying rents with notes of the Labour Exchange Bank'.[70] Pare must have been fully aware of Craig's experience of labour notes at Ralahine, but he gave no indication of this foreknowledge in his reply:

> Mr Craig's inquiry was an important one, though not, he thought, a neces- sary one in the commencement. He knew corn dealers who took them in payment of their goods. Lawyers he knew took them as fees, and mid- wives and sextons took them in payment of their offices, (laughter) so that a man could get into this world and get out of it again through the medium of these notes.[71]

A local newspaper proprietor offered, once the exchange was set up, 'to accept notes in payment for newspapers, advertisements, and all descriptions of printing work, as he held these notes to be of such good value, being the representatives of real value deposited at the Exchange'.[72]

As an indication of the continued lack of awareness of the existence of the Ralahine experiment, a local pamphleteer in County Clare referred in 1833 to the Dutch poor law agricultural colonies set up in 1818; the author also referred to Orbiston but queried: 'Having given these interesting extracts from the volume published in 1828 [by a member of the Highland Society of Scotland] I ask why might not such a Benevolent Society be established in Ireland?'[73] The pamphlet was written and published in Limerick.

During these last days of the community the livestock of the estate included cattle, pigs, sheep, horses and poultry. Craig claimed that each year sixteen fat beasts were sent from Ralahine to Liverpool.[74] There were workshops for carpenters, a blacksmith and flax dressers:

> A large weaving factory, and the shell of a flax mill, with a water fall equal to 20 hp, running to waste, but capable of employment after a small outlay of capital.[75]

When John Scott Vandeleur married Emily Molony a fortune of £20,000 passed to him. He became a member of the Kildare Street and other Dublin clubs, and wagered for high stakes. In November 1833, then aged thirty-eight, he gambled away his Ralahine estate and fortune. The course of events was reported in the Dublin Press:

> *Extensive Forgeries*—The branches of the Bank of Ireland and Provincial Bank have been smartly hit, and the Bank of La Touche, in Dublin, is said to have been made instrumental in transferring stock of some amount by fabricated documents proceedings from the same quarter. The first detection, we hear, was made in the Provincial Bank, Mr Vandeleur himself offering a bill for discount, upon which some suspicion arose in the mind of the manager, who referred to the directors, and they concurring, the same was signified to Mr Vandeleur, who continued waiting—when the communication was made to him he affected to be highly indignant and threatened punishment in the course of an hour, but he did not return, and has not since been heard of. A warrant was issued for his arrest and his name published.[76]

Another Dublin newspaper commented on the repercussions of Vandeleur's bankruptcy:

> It is expected that his connections, who are respectable and affluent, will discharge the heavy responsibilities which are incurred otherwise most

summary proceedings will be adopted to expose and punish the transgression. We have received several letters relative to this unfortunate affair; but, as the disclosure may wound private feelings, we must decline publishing them. The banks of Limerick, the banking houses of Dublin and some firms in London, have suffered.[77]

But Vandeleur had absconded and 'Peace officers have been despatched after him to England'.[78] The case against him was brought before the Commissioners of Bankruptcy in Dublin in December, but Vandeleur did not appear; the proof of his debts amounted to £9,360.[79] The original agreement setting up the Ralahine Association was treated as so much waste paper; the members of the community were held to be common labourers, and the Vandeleur family refused to view them as more than tenants at will and took possession of the estate.

The collapse of Ralahine was due to lack of security either of tenure or for improvements:

> With such security, the capital lent by Mr Vandeleur might have been obtained from some other source when it had to be paid back to his creditors. There never was a more striking instance of the folly of basing a commercial undertaking on mere confidence in a good landlord...[80]

Ralahine was regarded at the time and during the subsequent half-century as the most successful of the experiments in agricultural co-operation.[81] 'The importance of Ralahine was not in its ultimate failure, but in its initial success.'[82] Certainly there were improved relations between landlord and labourer, preservation and improvement of cultivation, encouragement of thrift, and an increase in self-respect. Vandeleur received prompt payment of a higher rent and interest on his investment; hence he did not need to run the risk of allowing his Owenite sympathies to run away with his self-interest. Farm machinery was not resented, as well it might have been in a general climate of Luddism, but was seen as an aid to greater efficiency and higher output. James Connolly saw Ralahine as a triumph of Communism, but the mode in which the tenants shared the produce of the land was less relevant than the fact that the amount of produce available increased: 'Ralahine was an Irish point of interrogation erected amidst the wilderness of capitalist thought and feudal practice.'[83]

The prerequisites for the success of Ralahine were, first, a homogeneous local peasantry with everything to gain from co-operative effort and use of capital—significantly, the only failures at Ralahine were overzealous outsiders; second, a proprietor who was a hard bargainer, with personal power of expulsion of members during the first year of community.

Debate over the merits of Ralahine continued in the pages of co-operative journals for many years after the demise of the community: a correspondent in the *Manchester Co-operator* of January 1864 asserted that Orbiston and Ralahine were not true co-operative societies. Craig staunchly maintained in a later issue that Ralahine was a model co-operative:

> Orbiston was a community where all were held equal, and where consumption, recreation and enjoyment far exceeded the powers of production in the essentials of existence. Ralahine was an entire novelty. No similar plan had ever been adopted in this or any other country; for it united the labourer and farmer in one, dealing directly with the landlord and the capitalist.[84]

Individual members had accumulated savings from £1 to £5 by the end of the experiment, when they had been admitted to the community as penniless labourers: Craig redeemed holdings of labour notes out of his own pocket.

At least one Irish commentator argued that the experiment at Ralahine would have spread but for its lack of legal protection: 'Came the fearful famine...all the old landmarks of the community being removed...and co-operation became a thing of the past.'[85] For thirty years after the community's demise no murders were perpetuated in the district around Ralahine. (But in 1849 there were in Ennis workhouse 2,114 paupers fed at a weekly cost of 1s 8½d per head; in Kilrush poor law union—of which C. M. Vandeleur was chairman—there were 5,005 paupers, with 1,014 deaths in a half-year and an average cost of food at 11¼d per head per week.)[86]

Professor Hancock, the Dublin statistician, condemned Ralahine as too artificial, since it could not have survived without Vandeleur, who gave the community a factitious vigour.[87] None of the radical reformist Irish leaders of the early nineteenth century showed any interest in co-operation. The agitation for land reform on a co-operative basis came from Irish landed proprietors—Thompson, Vandeleur, Cloncurry,[88] Wallscourt—not radicals such as Daniel O'Connell; and it is symptomatic that Feargus O'Connor was later to preach land reform in England, not Ireland.

The first account of Ralahine to be published in book form was printed in French in 1853.[89] John Finch and Craig had each written a series of letters to the Press during 1838;[90] Pare and Craig were both destined to write books on Ralahine in their old age. Craig also wrote a series of letters to the journal *American Socialist* in the 1870s in which he included many references to Ralahine.[91] The first official reference to Ralahine was included in the evidence Finch submitted to the Parliamentary Select Committee on Drunkenness in 1834. Finch drew on his observations at Ralahine but did not mention the community by name. He was so impressed by the arrangements and sobriety there that he announced, 'I am determined to devote a considerable portion of my time to a promulgation of them.'[92]

William Pare's account of his visit to Ralahine appeared in 1870, but Craig did not write his own account until 1882.[93] Craig's book received numerous favourable press reviews. *The Spectator* wrote that the subject was:

> One of the most interesting experiments that has ever been tried in Ireland . . . We could wish, however, that he [Craig] had done better justice to a most interesting narrative. It is mixed up in the oddest way with irrelevant matters; Mr Craig's notions on things in general, on Pythagarus [*sic*] and the Greeks, on chest expanders, coloured cubes to register the teacher's silent approval, and the like.[94]

E. T. Craig was an old man when he wrote the book; perhaps it was intended to coincide with the widespread interest in Irish land reform in the 1880s (20,000 copies were printed), but one is left with the imponderables. What would have been the impact of his account of Ralahine had it appeared immediately after the disruption of the community? Would it have been written without the hotchpotch of cure-alls with which he interleaved the final version in the garrulity of his old age? When Horace Plunkett, another Irish landed proprietor with co-operative sympathies, proposed the formation of the Irish Agricultural Organisation Society in 1894 he did not forget Ralahine. He credited Craig as 'the author of the most advanced experiment in the realisation of co-operative ideals', but doubted whether joint ownership of land, except for common grazing, was practicable. 'The ready response, however, of the Irish peasants to Mr Craig's enthusiasm, and the way in which they took up the idea form an interesting study of the Irish character.'[95] Did the importance of Ralahine tend to be overlooked because Craig gave the reading public the impression that he was a crank? General

Booth did not think so: he felt that co-operation was the key to social problems. 'I shall endeavour to start a Co-operative Farm on the principles of Ralahine and base the whole of my Farm Colony on a Co-operative foundation.'[96] Booth also thought, with Craig, that such a venture would create great opportunities for technical education.[97]

A. R. Wallace wrote in 1900 what was probably the last appreciation of Ralahine to be published in England: 'Never perhaps in the history of our country was there a more important social experiment tried, or one that was so completely successful and so thoroughly beneficial.'[98] Since Wallace there have been no other commentaries on Ralahine except as references in the general literature of the history of co-operation or Irish labour history. 'When John Scott Vandeleur gambled at his club, he gambled away not merely his own property but what may well have been a happier destiny for his country.'[99] Vandeleur passed out of history after the collapse of Ralahine. Family hearsay has it that he fled from Ireland to the United States, where he became a locomotive engineer. Playing cards were subsequently forbidden in the Vandeleur household. In 1835 the wife of John Scott Vandeleur left Ralahine for Limerick.[100] The Ralahine residence was offered, 'in the matter of Vandeleur minors', on a seven years' lease in 1842, 'the Dwelling house, offices, and walled garden at Ralahine, with about eight acres of land in prime heart'. Mrs Emily Vandeleur died in 1843 and her son Arthur determined to atone for his father's debts.[101] Arthur's guardian was James Molony, of Kiltanon, and in 1851 the young Vandeleur undertook to repay his father's creditors by borrowing through mortgages on the Ralahine estate.[102] He improved the cottages at Ralahine, although he lived at nearby Kiltanon, where he married Mary Molony in 1856. After serving in the Crimean war he died at Woolwich in 1860, but his wife survived until 1914.[103] The Vandeleur family held on to the ownership of the Ralahine estate and let it to a succession of lessees: Arthur Vandeleur leased out 1,271 acres in all in 1855 in plots of between thirteen and eighty acres.[104] In 1866 William Halpin took possession of Ralahine and made a number of improvements, but Mary Vandeleur would only offer him in 1885 a sixty-year lease at the same rent so long as he held it as demesne land—which meant that at any time he could be given six months' notice to quit. Land judges backed her claim and Halpin had to give up the estate in 1886.[105] In the 1920s the estate was split into holdings of about seventy acres each. Most of these holdings were dairy farms. The original cottages are now outhouses, and the Vandeleur residence was demolished some years ago; only the tower of Ralahine Castle remains as it was in the days of the community.

A century after the disruption of Ralahine, County Clare was selected for a pioneer study by two American anthropologists in 1932.[106] (The investigators used similar techniques to describe a community in the British Isles as previous scholars had done for the South Seas.) There were many customs in County Clare which had remained unchanged since the days of Ralahine. The basis of family kinship was still firmly patriarchal—when the land commissioner employed farmers' sons, it was the father who came to collect the sons' wages. The researchers also found a strong inclination to rural co-operation even without any institutional framework. Farms and kindreds were linked and brought into alliance through marriage:

> This will reinforce the patterns of co-operation, 'friendliness' or 'cooring' which are one of the networks uniting the small farmers of the countryside. Co-operation ... in rural Clare is continuous and intimate. It is the process of matchmaking which to some extent provides the scaffolding ... Between a man and his 'friends' there grows up an elaborate system of reciprocal co-operation ... The man who refuses to help, or for that matter to be helped, is opting out of society and condemning himself to social isolation.[107]

How did Ralahine differ from a typical present-day agricultural co-operative? The main distinction was in the imposition of authority by Vandeleur, the sponsoring capitalist, who provided all the stock and equipment on hire and insisted on maintaining his legal ownership of the land. The community dwellers at Ralahine were in effect licensed residents with a contractual obligation to pay rent in perpetuity. Ralahine was a most successful experiment in communal living and social equality, but it was not a self-generated co-operative, and it is unlikely that the successors of John Scott Vandeleur would have conceded their land entitlement to erstwhile peasants. Seen in terms of co-operation, the most unfavourable interpretation that can be put on Ralahine is to treat it as a variant, albeit in a more efficient and improving form, of agrarian feudalism, with strong incentives for the communal members to increase productivity and maintain discipline. The distinction between governor and governed was too wide for Ralahine to be a true example of co-operative ownership.

Notes

1 H. Dutton, *Statistical Survey of County Clare*, 1808, p. 217.
2 *Ibid.*, p. 271.
3 *Ibid.*, p. 311.
4 R. Barry O'Brien, *The Irish Land Question from 1829 to 1869*, 1880, p. 147.
5 *Ibid.*, p. 39.
6 *Report* of the Devon Commission, 1845, pp. 519–20.
7 The Catholic Emancipation Act of 1829 also provided motives for clearing the landed estates of antagonistic forty-shilling enfranchised freeholders.
8 G. Sigerson, *History of Irish Land Tenures*, 1871, p. 154.
9 Professor W. N. Hancock, 'On *laissez-faire* and the economic resources of Ireland', paper read at British Association meeting, Dublin, 1847.
10 *Report* of the Select Committee on the Poor in Ireland, 1830.
11 Sir G. C. Lewis, *Irish Disturbances*, 1836, p. 313. Sir George Cornewall Lewis was Chancellor of the Exchequer, 1855–58.
12 R. Barry O'Brien, *The Irish Land Question*, p. 19.
13 See *Report of Proceedings of Several Meetings held in Dublin*, 1823. (Meetings were held on 18 March and 12, 19, 24 April 1823.) Also *Letter to the Nobility, Gentry and Clergy of Ireland*, 1 March 1823, and *Letter to the Nobility, Gentry, Professions, Bankers, Merchants and Master Manufacturers of Ireland*, 21 March 1823, National Library of Ireland.
14 W. Urwick, *Biographic Sketches of James Digges La Touche*, 1868, p. 166.
15 J. F. Hogan, 'Early modern socialists, II', *Irish Ecclesiastical Record*, XXVI, 1909, p. 24.
16 W. Urwick, *Biographic Sketches*, pp. 160–1.
17 J. Frost, *History and Topography of the County of Clare*, 1893, p. 355.
18 *Ibid.*, p. 307.
19 *Ibid.*, p. 592.
20 John Scott Vandeleur became a Fellow Commoner at Trinity College, Dublin, and entered Gray's Inn in 1812.
21 J. S. Vandeleur was not unique in seeking development of the textile industry in County Clare: see an advertisement in the *Glasgow Herald*, 12 September 1828, from James Molony, Kiltanon, Co. Clare, inviting investors of sums of £500–£1,000 for a cotton weaving plant. A factory of sixty to eighty looms had been set up in 1826 at Newmarket-on-Fergus: 'The Establishment has been superintended by persons from Manchester, and from fifty to sixty boys have been instructed in the art of weaving.' The object of the proprietor was to establish manufacturing rather than to act as manufacturer. He would be willing to allow use of the looms to investors rent-free for one year: 'Embroidery of muslin has been extensively carried on in Newmarket-on-Fergus.'
22 E. T. Craig, letter No. IV, *Star in the East*, 15 September 1838.
23 'Agricola,' *Considerations for Landed Proprietors, Clare*, 1831, p. 110, Halliday collection, Irish Royal Academy.
24 *Ibid.*, p. 25.
25 *Ibid.*, appendix, 30 December 1831, p. 126.

26 Letter from Chief Constable W. Coffey of Tomgrany, 11 July 1829, *Papers on Clare*, 1829, Irish State Papers Office, Dublin.

27 W. Pare, *Co-operative Agriculture*, 1870, pp. 5–6.

28 For the suggested origin of the term 'Terry Alt', see J. Barrow, *Tour Round Ireland in 1835*, 1836, p. 279; for an alternative explanation, see P. White, *History of Clare*, 1893, p. 344.

29 E. T. Craig, letter No. III on Ralahine, *Star in the East*, 8 September 1838.

30 *Clare Journal*, 14 April 1831.

31 *Ibid.*, 18 April 1831.

32 *Ibid.*, 25 April 1831.

33 *Ibid.*, 23 May 1831.

34 E. T. Craig, letter No. IV, *Star in the East*, 15 September 1838. See also E. T. Craig, *A Remedy for the Pacification of Ireland*, in the Ludlow collection, Goldsmiths' library.

35 'Ralahine: state of the people,' *New Moral World*, No. 113, 24 December 1836, pp. 67–8.

36 E. T. Craig, 'Early history of co-operation', *Co-operative News*, 7 January 1888, p. 16.

37 Letter from E. T. Craig, 69 Hanover Street, Manchester, 1 September 1831, in Robert Owen correspondence, No. 143.

38 E. T. Craig, letter No. V, *Star in the East*, 29 September, 1838.

39 J. Finch, letter No. II, *Liverpool Mercury*, 24 March 1838. John Finch wrote a series of fifteen letters on the subject of 'Ralahine; or human improvement and happiness'. He visited Ralahine during the spring of 1833. The series published in the *Liverpool Mercury* ceased on 18 August 1838, and Finch invited further correspondence, but none was forthcoming.

40 J. Finch, letter No. I, *Liverpool Mercury*, 17 March 1838.

41 Letter No. IV, *Liverpool Mercury*, 7 April 1838.

42 *Lancashire and Yorkshire Co-operator*, No. 4, 15 October 1831.

43 E. T. Craig, letter No. X, *Star in the East*, 8 December 1838.

44 E. T. Craig, *A Remedy for the Pacification of Ireland*, p. 5.

45 *Co-operative News*, 11 December 1875, p. 636.

46 The quantity of each crop rent was fixed on the average produce of Ralahine during the three years before the community and at average prices ruling at Limerick market 1830–31. The rent was payable on six named products: wheat, barley, oats, beef, pork and butter.

47 E. T. Craig, *A Remedy for the Pacification of Ireland*. The produce rent was made up as follows:

	£
6,400 stone of wheat at 1s 6d per stone	480
3,840 stone of barley at 10d per stone	160
480 stone of oats at 10d per stone	20
70 cwt beef at 40s per cwt	140
30 cwt pork at 40s per cwt	60
10 cwt butter at 80s per cwt	40
	900

The rental was derived from the use of the following assets:

	£
Rent on land (622 acres)	700
Interest on £1,500 livestock	90
Interest on buildings	60
Interest on tools	50
	900

48 Craig later used labour notes at Ealing Grove school for paying pupils for gardening work. See letter XI on Ralahine, *Star in the East*, 15 December 1838, for a facsimile of a labour note:

'*Agricultural School Labour Note* (equal to ¼ *d*). *Jan.* Dig and trench the ground. In frosty weather wheel manure to those beds which may want it. Gooseberry, currant and raspberry cuttings may be planted. [Obverse] *Work Ticket* (¼ *d*) "Sloth, like rust, consumes faster than labour wears; while the used spade is always bright".'

49 On the disruption of Ralahine communal savings amounted to £25 and were redeemed in full by Craig.

50 *Lancashire and Yorkshire Co-operator*, March 1832.

51 E. H. Craig, *A Remedy for the Pacifiation of Ireland*, p. 3.

52 *The Crisis*, No. 27, 13 July 1833.

53 W. Pare, *Co-operative Agriculture*, p. 35.

54 *The Crisis*, No. 27, 13 July 1833.

55 John Finch asserted that many English Bibles sent to Ireland were pawned and resold in England at a half to one-third of the price they cost the Bible societies. He knew a bookshop in Manchester which received a box of Bibles regularly from Dublin. (Letter No. XI, *Liverpool Mercury*, 23 June 1838.)

56 Viz. thirty-five adult men, twenty-three women, seven orphans under 17 years of age, sixteen children under 9. E. T. Craig, as secretary, was paid 8*s*, also the storekeeper and carpenter. Labourers were paid 4*s*, women 2*s* 6*d*. Youths and children were supported out of common funds. The salaries of Craig and the storekeeper were partly charged to Vandeleur and partly to communal funds, as their responsibilities were dual.

57 Letter No. VIII, *Liverpool Mercury*, 5 May 1838. Washing and cooking were done centrally: 'They had very convenient apparatus for washing and boiling their potatoes. The potato washing machine was a cylindrical vessel, something like a squirrel cage, placed horizontally on a frame, on which it was turned round with a handle in a trough filled with water till the potatoes were clean. They were then put in a cask with holes in the bottom for the admission of steam. This vessel filled the top of a boiler filled with boiling water upon which it was placed, and they were soon nicely cooked by steam. One man could by these means prepare in two hours sufficient for the whole Society.' (W. Pare, *Co-operative Agriculture*, p. 75.)

58 W. Pare, *Co-operative Agriculture*, pp. 145–6.

59 *Ibid.*, p. 158.

60 J. Finch, letter No. VIII, *Liverpool Mercury*, 28 April 1838. Finch compared the Ralahine labourer earning 4*s* and his wife 2*s* 6*d* with a Liverpool mechanic

earning 30*s* and paying 3*s* rent for a cellar dwelling, 6*s* 3*d* for potatoes, 10*s* for adulterated milk, 1*s* 10*d* for fuel and water, 5*d* dues to a mechanics' institute, benefit society 4¾*d*. The typical expenditure of a Ralahine labourer earning 4*s* was: 1*s* for potatoes, 10*d* for milk, 2*d* for washing, 2*d* sick fund, surplus 1*s* 10*d* for clothing, etc; rent was 6*d* extra, fuel 2*d*.

61 See 'Account of provisions for eighty-one people, week ending 6 October 1833':

	£	s.	d.
446 qts. milk at 1*d*	1	17	2
Potatoes and vegetables	2	13	6
Butter 12*s* 1*d*, pork 19*s* 7½*d*	1	11	8½
Cottage rent 4*s* 3*d*, fuel 9*d*		5	0
Total cost Food and lodging 81	£6	7*s*	4½*d*

This averaged out at less than 1*s* 7*d* each.

62 W. Pare, *Co-operative Agriculture*, p. 75.

63 J. Finch, letter No. xiii, *Liverpool Mercury*, 7 July 1838.

64 *The Crisis*, No. 22, 8 June 1833, p. 170.

65 Letter of R. Owen, *The Crisis*, No. 23, 15 June 1833, p. 178.

66 Letter from 'S', Eden Quay, Dublin, 23 May 1836, *New Moral World*, No. 83, 28 May 1836, p. 243.

67 See letter from William Pare, Dublin, 3 October 1833, to the managers, Birmingham Equitable Labour Exchange: 'Our excellent friend Vandeleur, of the County of Clare, who crossed the Channel with me, is turning his attention to the establishment of a tannery for us, in his peaceful, happy and harmonious community of producers.' (Letter in Co-operative College Library.)

68 W. Pare, *Co-operative Agriculture*, p. 129. See also *Limerick Evening Post*, 5 November 1833.

69 *Limerick Evening Herald*, 17 October 1833. The editorial was most antagonistic to the proposal: 'Equitable Exchange' was an attractive title but it could be a wedge for introducing infidel Owenism.

70 *Clare Journal*, 7 November 1833.

71 *Ibid.*

72 *Ibid.*

73 James Connery, *The Reformer*, 1833, p. 34, at Limerick reference library.

74 *Co-operative News*, 10 February 1877.

75 W. Pare, *Co-operative Agriculture*, p. 35.

76 *Dublin Evening Post*, 21 November 1833; see also *Limerick Evening Herald*, 18 November 1833: 'Bankrupt John Scott Vandeleur'.

77 *Freeman's Journal*, 15 November 1833.

78 *Dublin Evening Post*, 26 November 1833.

79 *Clare Journal*, 12 December 1833.

80 *Phrenological Magazine*, iv, 1833, pp. 15–19.

81 C. W. Stubbs, *The Land and the Labourers: a Record of Facts and Experiments in Cottage Farming and Co-operative Agriculture*, 1884, p. 64. There are references in Stubbs to the Assington Hall, Suffolk, co-operative farm set

up by Gurdon in 1829 (p. 107). James Connolly, *Labour in Irish History*, 1910, gives examples of several small Irish community experiments, including the White Quakers of Dublin (pp. 143–4).

82 G. O'Brien, *Economic History of Ireland from the Union to the Famine*, 1921, p. 120.

83 J. Connolly, *Labour in Irish History*, p. 143.

84 *Manchester Co-operator*, No. 50, April 1864, pp. 155–6.

85 Richard J. Kelly, 'A co-operative farm in Ireland fifty years ago', *The Month*, VII, 1884.

86 *Limerick Chronicle*, 23 January 1849; also P. White, *History of Clare*. In 1848 a M. Molony was found dead in a dyke in County Clare. A quantity of raw potato 'and a small quantity of seaweed found in his person'. (Press cuttings, County Clare, compiled by Theobald Fitz-Walter Butler, National Library of Ireland.

87 Report of a paper by Rev. E. R. Larkin, 'On the results of a scheme by Mr Vandeleur for improving the condition of labourers tried at Ralahine, Co. Clare', *Athenaeum*, 3 July 1847, p. 717. A letter of John Finch to Robert Owen, 27 June 1847, also referred to the Larkin paper, which was read at an Oxford meeting of the British Association. Finch asserted that the paper was 'taken from my account of Mr Vandeleur...' (Robert Owen correspondence, letter No. 1469.)

88 W. J. Fitzpatrick, *Life and Times of Lord Cloncurry*, 1855.

89 L. Goupy, *Quaere et invenies*, 1853, pp. 166–76.

90 *Liverpool Mercury* and *Star in the East*.

91 Letters Nos. 17–46, 'Socialism in England', *American Socialist*, December 1877–January 1878. Craig acted as English agent for the journal.

92 Evidence of John Finch, question No. 3825, *Evidence on Drunkenness Presented to the House of Commons*, ed. J. S. Buckingham, 1834.

93 E. T. Craig, *The Irish Land and Labour Question illustrated in the History of Ralahine and Co-operative Farming*, 1882.

94 *The Spectator*, 24 June 1882, p. 840.

95 H. Plunkett, *Ireland in the New Century*, 1904, p. 184. See also M. Digby, *Horace Plunkett*, 1949.

96 W. Booth, *In Darkest England, and the Way Out*, 1890, p. 231.

97 *Ibid.*, p. 136; also letter from Booth, *Co-operative News*, 27 September 1890, p. 986. Another supporter of combining agriculture with technical education was P. Kropotkin (*Fields Factories and Workshops*, 1898).

98 A. R. Wallace, 'Ralahine and its teachings', in *Studies Scientific and Social*, 1900, chapter XXV, pp. 455–77.

99 A. E. (George Russell), *An Irish Commune*, 1920, p. iii.

100 John Scott Vandeleur married Emily Molony of Kiltanon and had five children, three of whom died of tuberculosis, and the eldest son was drowned. (Evidence of the Rev. W. Vandeleur to the writer.) Mary Diana, daughter of Colonel Boyle Vandeleur, of Ralahine, married in 1827 the Rev. William Vandeleur. She spent her widowhood with Ormsby Vandeleur, who was father of the Rev. W. Vandeleur of Dun Laoghaire.—Rev. William Elder George Ormsby Vandeleur, b. 1875, Canon of Christ Church, Dublin, 1944–

1949, son of Ormsby Vandeleur, b. 1843. (*Burke's Landed Gentry of Ireland*, fourth edition, 1958.)

101 The writer is also indebted to Lt.-Col. G. A. M. Vandeleur and Brigadier J. O. E. Vandeleur for notes on the Vandeleur family.

102 C. M. Marsh, *Life of Arthur Vandeleur*, 1862.

103 Will and schedule of assets of Mary Vandeleur, died 14 June 1914, Irish Public Records Office, T11865.

104 See 'Valuation lists of rateable property', 1855, National Library of Ireland. Also Perambulation book, Tomfinlough, Irish Valuation Office, Dublin, 1855, which gives details of arable and pasture land of Ralahine. Ralahine was surveyed and mapped in 1839–40 by a Capt. Stotherd and Lieut. Boteler, Royal Engineers, for the Ordnance Survey and printed as sheet No. 51, County Clare, 21 October 1843, as part of the Six-inch Townlands Survey.

105 Evidence to the writer by Cormac Halpin, of Newmarket-on-Fergus, grandson of William Halpin.

106 The communities were two townlands in County Clare, Rynamona and Luough. (C. Arensberg and S. T. Kimball, *Family and Community in Ireland*, 1940; C. Arensberg, *The Irish Countryman*, 1939, referred to in R. Frankenberg, *Communities in Britain*, 1966.

107 R. Frankenberg, *Communities in Britain*, pp. 35–7.

5
Owenism during the 1830s

It is difficult to disentangle the strands of the Owenite contribution to the co-operative movement in the early 1830s from that of trade unionist and other more politically radical forms of agitation. Reformers with grand ideas of social and economic transformation used highly emotional terms and sought to gather as wide a support as possible but the language available to them was imprecise; hence there were no clear distinctions in the propaganda for (say) co-operation, union shops and trade clubs. One must also make allowances for the political immaturity of many of the working class appeals for solidarity, and indeed allow for some confusion over aims by the reformers themselves. The words 'co-operation' and 'co-operate' are, and were, loose in their connotation; it would be difficult, for instance, to analyse the real significance of an appeal in the January 1831 issue of the *Poor Man's Guardian*: 'First, therefore Co-operate, then claim your rights, and the foremost is Reform in parliament.'[1] If this message was inconsistent with later appeals, presumably co-operation in the context of the *Poor Man's Guardian* meant political action—in May 1831 the programme for reform was announced as a 'Declaration of Rights of Man' and acquirement of full value of labour.[2]

Henry Hetherington who, with Lovett, was an active member of the British Association for the Promotion of Co-operative Knowledge and proprietor of the *Poor Man's Guardian*, fulminated at the political immaturity of the Owenites.

> What have the 'genuine' Owenites in London done against these enormities, but paralyse the nobler efforts of others, by deprecating politics? Nero fiddled while Rome was burning and the benevolent Owenites are dancing jigs at two-shilling hops...[3]

From the 1830s the Owenite movement drew its supporters from a wide range of social backgrounds; this can be seen clearly when one assesses the contributions of leading Owenites, practically all of whom managed to combine their Owenism with other interests and capacities. To some extent there was bound to be this broad diffusion

Above The site of Orbiston House, now park land adjoining the golf course

Left Orbiston community pillars, now standing in the Sixth District Council park: the only relics remaining of the community house

Above Ralahine castle today

Below Farm buildings and cottages at Ralahine

when it is noted that the main period of Owenism spanned a whole generation from 1820 to 1845. There were some Owenites who remained wholehearted disciples throughout the period, and others who were sympathisers rather than adherents but who shared common interests in educational and social reform. There were yet others who toyed with Owenism, became disillusioned and sought other paths for reform, or who lost their early idealism altogether. This diapason was not peculiar to Owenism, it was a characteristic of most reform movements; but this approach to the Owenites helps to explain the impact of Owen and his followers. Owen was so eclectic that most reformers could subscribe to at least part of his creed.

The three leading Owenites from the 1830s were E. T. Craig, William Pare and John Finch. All gained some practical experience in organising a community experiment. Craig was an inveterate educationist who took many of his precepts from Owen but was never a doctrinaire follower of his. Pare was a successful business-man and railway statist, with deep interests in co-operative education. Finch, who managed an iron foundry, had some of Owen's crankiness and was a zealous disciple of the master, but he went further in upholding the all-embracing social virtues of teetotalism.[4] George Mudie had shed his Owenism by the 1830s; Alexander Campbell was becoming more occupied in anti-truck campaigning and Scottish trade unionism; G. J. Holyoake, after a short experience of lecturing, was moved towards secularism. There were many others on the fringe of Owenism, such as Rowland Detrosier and J. E. Smith, and there were also ex-Owenite converts to other causes, such as William Lovett. The rich sympathisers of the 1820s, such as A. J. Hamilton and William Thompson, also had their counterparts from the late 1830s during the last phase of Owenism.

The first anniversary meeting of the British Association for the Promotion of Co-operative Knowledge, in June 1830, was indifferently attended. There were 738 members of the Association, but two-thirds had not paid their subscriptions for the previous quarter; debts were £58, and assets £25.[5] The Association did not feel obliged to adopt all Owen's views, but co-operators were grateful to him for giving them a sense of purpose and identity. 'He it was who impressed upon our minds a conviction of our importance, who convinced us, the working men, that we were the pillars of the political edifice; that we sustained the whole superstructure of

society ...' Strict equality was the desideratum: 'Nothing short of
co-operation will secure the permanent happiness of the people at
large; a change that will demand from all equal labour in the
production and equal participation in the enjoyment of the produce ...'[6]

The fourth report of the committee and proceedings of the Association mentioned the missionaries who had been appointed

> for the purpose of visiting, and to explain the best methods of keeping
> accounts in Co-operative Stores; the best modes of arranging usual business
> attached to the management of societies, and to explain the true principles
> of co-operation ... This sub-committee has made several visits to different
> societies, and has affected considerable improvements among them.

An indication of the growth of local co-operation during the period
May 1829 to June 1830 is given below in table 1 for societies in
Manchester and Salford, showing mainly low general weekly sub-
scriptions but wide variations of weekly takings per head.[7] (None
of the societies was reported as manufacturing, but the Owenian
Society expected to do so in the near future.)

Friendly societies in Manchester and Salford, 1829–30

	Date established	Members	Weekly subns.	Capital	Weekly takings	
First Chorlton Row	3 May 1829	18	1s 1d	£100	£20	Dividends after 4 years
Economical	22 August 1829	30	3d	£57	£25	Division
Temperance	26 October 1829	40	3d	£42	£14	Non-dividing
Independent Hope	26 February 1829	45	3s 0d	£70	£60	,,
Perseverance	12 April 1830	56	4d	£24	£11	,,
Amicable	1 May 1830	24	4d	£10	£7	,,
Friendly	10 April 1830	27	4d	£18	£6	,,
Benevolent	22 April 1830	124	4d	£45	£46	,,
Good Intent	8 May 1830	48	3d	£10	£7	,,
Fortitude	1 June 1830	15	3d	£2	£1	,,
Owenian	15 June 1830	26	4d	–	–	,,

In July 1830 the wholesale purchasing agency associated with the First Liverpool Co-operative Society reported on the scale of its operations:

> It may be interesting to our brother co-operators to hear, that the Purchasing Establishment works most satisfactorily, and is supported with much spirit by the co-operative societies of the neighbouring counties ... Enquiries have been received from and answers sent to the societies at Halifax, Carlisle, Huddersfield, Blackburn, Bentham, Leicester and Holywell.[8]

Purchases from Liverpool of over £250 had been made during the previous month from seven societies as far afield as Kendal and Coventry, to whom a commission of 2 per cent had been charged. Several members of the Liverpool society made shoes for fellow co-operators. The Chester society also, it was reported, 'has lately commenced the shoemaking business ... £20 were expended in stock ... partial or constant work to six members.' The Huddersfield society advertised that it manufactured 'broad and narrow cloths of every description and quality, kerseymeres, waistcoat pieces, stuffs for pantaloons and gowns ...'[9]

An appeal was issued by Exeter co-operators, probably in 1830, for subscriptions to employ redundant workers on the land. An incipient community could be set up with funds from 5,000 county subscribers each contributing 1s weekly—'it will be a matter of no difficulty, after the first fortnight, to commence building the first community and manufactory; and one community and manufactory may be regularly commenced each six months following...'[10] There would be an estimated 50,000 contributors and 2,000 members for each community, with subscription offices to be opened in each county town.

A number of the community projects in the early 1830s were urban in conception. One such model was for an area of thirty-three acres, with an inner quadrangle 'nearly three times as large as Russell Square',[11] and would include a diagonal line to coincide with a meridian to ensure equal distribution of natural light and be convenient for astronomy.

A London society—the First Community Society—instituted a system of probation for new members:

> On the proposal of Mr —— to be admitted a member of this community, an examination was strictly entered into as to his qualifications, when it was decided that Mr ——, not having a sufficient knowledge of the prin-

ciples of co-operation, is not considered at present eligible; but that he may
attend our meetings to gain that information, so that at a future period he
may again present himself to be admitted.[12]

The aspiration for self-education by the working class co-operators
was becoming even more insistent. Already by 1830 the mechanics'
institute movement was receiving strong criticism from workers
seeking means for self-improvement. One 'oppressed workman'
complained that the institutes could never cater for more than a
small proportion, as 'none of these seminaries commence teaching
at a later period than a quarter past 8 in the evening, and will any
man in his right senses affirm that it is possible for the workers in
public factories to get forward in time . . . when even very few of
their works stop exactly at 8 o'clock . . . ?'[13] But members of the
Bolton Mechanics' Institute found time to attend lectures on co-
operation in 1830, at which, to protect themselves against redundancy, they were urged: 'Get capital and buy your own machines . . .
All the essential points of co-operation, union, trading, friendship,
education and improvement, may be obtained in a town where the
members are scattered, as effectively as in a community.'[14]

A circular letter from Manchester co-operators, including E. T.
Craig, was distributed on 5 May 1831, appealing to societies to send
delegates to a meeting in Salford with the objects of forming a
'General Union Company of Co-operative Societies' for purchasing
goods for co-operative stores, material for manufacturing, and subsequently to form a community.[15] This first Co-operative Congress[16]
duly met in Manchester on 26 and 27 May 1831 as a result of the
invitations of the recently constituted Manchester Association for the
Spread of the Principles of Co-operation. An address was issued to
societies from the Congress:

> Let it ever be remembered that Trading Fund Associations are only step-
> ping stones to Communities of Mutual Co-operation . . . Co-operation seeks
> to put the Working Classes in that situation where they shall enjoy the
> whole produce of their labour, instead of the small part called 'wages'.
> This can be done only by the establishment of Communities . . .

Dates of formation of societies were given in the Congress papers:
three societies before 1829, seventeen during 1829, fifteen in 1830,
eleven in 1831 and twelve in 1832 (seven societies did not give starting dates). Birkacre (near Chorley) advised that it had funds of
£4,000 and employed 150 members; twenty-nine societies each had
funds of over £100, including Kendal with £453 and Loughborough

with £400. Nevertheless, the gross funds notified from the societies (£6,500) were insufficient to meet the initial expenses of even a small community experiment. In all, sixty-five societies were listed as represented at the congress, including the Rochdale Friendly Society, formed in October 1830 with fifty-two members and ten families employed in manufacturing flannel. Salford First Society ran a school for 200 children, Hulme had a Sunday school, and Bolton an evening school. Although most societies had under 100 members, a wide range of manufactures was reported: shoes, stockings, tin ware, brushes, razors, files, cutlery, beaver hats and many types of cloth and garments.

A resolution was moved by Owen to set up a North-west United Co-operative Company to be based on Liverpool and to commence operations on 1 August 1831. The community ideal was also ventilated.

> This Congress consider it highly desirable that a Community, on the Principles of MUTUAL CO-OPERATION, UNITED POSSESSIONS, AND EQUALITY OF EXERTIONS AND OF MEANS ENJOYMENTS should be established in England as speedily as possible, in order to show the practicability of the co-operative scheme; and further ... that such a Community may be formed by the means recently suggested by the First Birmingham Co-operative Society ...

The Birmingham society had supported the plans laid down by William Thompson, but the Birmingham co-operators wanted the incipient community to be established in England, with each of the 200 co-operative societies throughout the kingdom electing a resident member and supplying him with £30 capital.

John Scott Vandeleur attended the first Co-operative Congress as a delegate from 'Ralahine Co-operative Society', which claimed to 'deal in or manufacture' provisions, flax growing and linen manufacturing. Presumably, Vandeleur felt justified in claiming that his nascent plans for an agricultural association at Ralahine could be classed as a co-operative society in advance of any constitution—at the third Co-operative Congress, which was attended by another Ralahine delegate, W. Maloney, it was stated that Ralahine co-operative had been set up in April 1831, seven months before the rules were approved.

Francis Place believed that shortly before the dissolution of the British Association for the Promotion of Co-operative Knowledge a splinter group, which included Henry Hetherington, met in April 1831 and formed the Metropolitan Trades Union, the title of which was afterwards changed to National Union of the Working Classes and as such was joined by William Lovett, James Watson and John Cleave—all original members of the Association.[17] It appears that the Association had been approached by a group of carpenters who were looking for assistance in furthering their plans for reform. These radical ideas of the workers' right to the whole produce of labour spread rapidly in the atmosphere of disappointment felt by the working classes after the passing of the reform Bill. At least one of the sources of Chartism can thus be traced to the National Union of the Working Classes and to its Owenite affiliates—it was possible, and remained possible, for Owenites to subscribe to political radicalism because Owenism never required unilateral allegiance from its followers.

The second Co-operative Congress met in Birmingham on 4–6 October 1831. Fewer delegates attended than at the first congress. Birkacre Calico Printers' Society had opened a dyeing works and gave a more realistic figure of £1,000 for its capital, although it still claimed a large membership of 1,500 (3,000 at the first congress) and promised £300 weekly purchases from the Liverpool Co-operative Company. Orrell, near Wigan, reported that all its thirty-seven members were employed by the Society, but no details of the type of work are given. Two delegates had walked the whole distance from Glasgow to attend the Birmingham congress.[18]

Robert Owen played down the proposed wholesale warehouse at Liverpool, despite the fact that he had moved the resolution at the first congress. At the Birmingham congress he thought that the 'only good the Societies could effect in this matter was to communicate to each other a knowledge of the best markets for different articles'. The principal theme was now to be education, and 'to make arrangements for obtaining the best of everything in the best manner'. As far as wholesaling was concerned, he thought co-operative societies were incapable of competing with the large manufacturers and capitalists.[19] He then announced that the 'chief end of community is to make the members better calculated for their different positions in Society'.[20]

Land plans still proliferated, notwithstanding the consolidating resolutions passed at the first Co-operative Congress. An incorporated national company was proposed with a capital of £3 million to be raised in Exchequer bills to provide employment for the Irish.[21] Labourers would be sent on to the land and, when all were located, ten hours' labour of an average workman in one trade would be counted the same value as in any other trade, 'except where the work is very sore, when such a reduction in the hours will be made as may be agreed on by competent judges . . .'[22]

By 1832 the first flush of co-operative storekeeping was weakening:

> Three or four years ago there were (we believed) sixteen trading societies in this town [Manchester]; but owing to repeated failures in consequence of the bad management of unsuitable storekeepers, and the general apathy evinced by members themselves . . . all that remains are the mere fragments of four, and these, with the exception of one of them, will shortly be scattered to the wind. The smoke of the trading societies has so long hung in clouds before the public eye in Manchester, that for a length of time it has scarcely been possible to get even a glimpse of the beauties of the science of the social system.[23]

Several months later, co-operation in Manchester apparently reached its nadir when it was reported:

> There are now no trading societies in Manchester, the Co-operatives in this town, being of the opinion that men and women must first acquire benevolent feelings, and a desire for moral improvement, or they will never cordially unite or continue long together; and they are quite convinced that ignorance alone is the great barrier . . . They have therefore cast aside the drudgery of the shop system, and turned their attention to the culture of the mind.[24]

Co-operative storekeeping in Manchester had not been successful, claimed James Rigby in October 1833, because co-operative stores were in back streets and initially they had operated on a cash-only basis. Subsequently, credit was allowed to the extent of each member's subscription:

> This, however, proved eventually the dissolution of our association; and after two years, when we came to balance our affairs, we found that we had not gained 6*d* . . . Hence we came to the conclusion, that our money would have been better in the bank, or spent on education; for in that case we should have had wealth and knowledge where now we have nothing.[25]

But there were exceptions to the general collapse of co-operative storekeeping. Portsmouth Co-operative Society reported in June 1833 that it had begun with weekly subscriptions of 6*d*: 'It has now a mill, bakehouse, brewery, piggery; and employs two carts to carry the different provisions to members' houses.'[26] There is also an interesting observation that the First Western Co-operative Union

Society, in Poland Street, London, was operating a dividend on purchases system as early as 1832: 'That every member of the Union shall receive a percentage upon his or her dealings, to be paid quarterly.'[27]

A visitor to Birkacre in 1832 still found the print works there very active—'millwrights, smiths, masons, carpenters, labourers, block and machine makers, printers, cutters, drawers, colour makers, engravers, madder dyers, and crofters, all at work in their different departments . . .' Some of the workers were converting a large house, formerly occupied by a manufacturer, into apartments. The printers were engaged on silk patterns and had already laid out £2,000 on industrial premises. They paid £600 annual rent and had factory room for 400 workers: 'There is no Mastership, no rivalling one another, all is Peace and Brotherhood. They have their Agent in the market and have more orders than they can supply—all their patterns are entirely new . . .'[28]

A third congress was held in London in April 1832 at which John Finch enunciated a nine-point creed for the co-operative system. Even at this date there was a looseness of distinction between co-operative societies and trade unions:

> There have been Societies formed in various parts of the kingdom, called Trade Unions, or Co-operative Societies, the object of which is to unite their members in the attainment of knowledge and also to obtain possession of capital.[29]

Birkacre and Ralahine were lauded at the third congress as the most successful of the co-operative ventures. It was reported that Birkacre had lately taken over an estate and was employing 300 of its members. Enthusiasm for co-operative manufacturing was whipped up by the delegate from Huddersfield.

> Mr Hurst here exhibited to the meeting several specimens of handkerchiefs, flannels, gown prints, Britannia-metal tea-pots, and some beautifully finished knives, etc. manufactured by various co-operative societies in the North of England. 'I have now upon my back, a co-operative shirt, and here's a co-operative coat, and here's a co-operative waistcoat.' (Loud laughter.)

The North-west of England United Co-operative Company reported on its progress since December 1831: thirty-one societies had dealt with the wholesale agency and sales had amounted to £1,830. Despite a deficit of £26, the company hoped to reduce its commission to one per cent on purchases.

In August 1832 further progress at Birkacre was reported—the estate there comprised 54 acres, out of which 14 acres were occupied by reservoirs. The premises had been taken over from the end of September 1831, but the figures now given in August 1832 relating to the previous year did not correspond with those given at the first Co-operative Congress: '300 members; fund, £400; sums subscribed, £500. Manufactures at Birkacre included calicoes, muslins, silks, palmareens, valences, terenetts, battistes, bombazines, woollens, etc.'[30]

By the fourth congress, which met at the King's Arms, Castle Street, Liverpool, in October 1832, the number of delegates had dwindled to twenty-nine. Many of the societies were losing members—Birmingham First Society had merely twenty-five, and London First Society only thirty-six. Pare and Lovett were secretaries of these two societies. Todmorden was the largest reported society, with 250 members, of whom it claimed to employ 150. A newcomer reported to congress was the Social Missionary Society, with 180 members.

Co-operators during the early 1830s were commonly disparaged as 'levellers'. It was retorted on their behalf: 'It is true; but then, they level by raising themselves, not by sinking others.'[31] Labour was at a discount, therefore the remedy was not to combine to raise wages but to go out of the market and become capitalists. During 1832 the earlier sporadic proposals for some form of labour exchange system for co-operative goods now received the blessing of Owen through one of his creations, the Association for Removing Ignorance and Poverty by Education and Employment, which listed among its aims the reception of goods 'to be exchanged on the equitable principles of *labour*, for *equal value of labour* through the medium of Labour Notes'.[32] Labour exchanges were therefore to become the vehicle for implementing a labour theory of value. A labour-based medium of exchange would enable purchasing power to keep in line with production, as a deficiency of demand was a consequence of an inadequate circulating medium. Associated with the exchanges were to be equitable banks of exchange to act as intermediaries between a labour note circulation and that of currency of the realm. Owen pointed out that the new system had been first announced in his 'Report to the County of Lanark'. It was no answer, however, to assert that labour notes would pass as money when the dire needs of co-operators were for provisions rather than manufactured goods: as one critic put it, provisions 'have to be *purchased*, not exchanged'.[33] On the other hand, it was claimed that London shopkeepers were taking labour notes at par.[34] Despite the above telling criticism, the proposed labour exchange banks aimed at eradicating shopkeepers, who, it was thought, would not be able to counteract the pressure by setting up shop elsewhere. 'Labour Banks will follow you, depend on it, wherever you go, not like a dog, to protect, but like a lion, to destroy.'[35] The banks would then use their profits for education and purchase land for settlement.

The labour exchange was therefore a 'halfway house between shop and Utopia'.[36] Its operators were producers rather than consumers. They wanted total reform through changes in production, marketing and currency, and they were not strictly communitarians. There was no implicit need to abandon old society in order to support the labour exchange experiments.

The First Western Co-operative Union added a labour bank to its shop. In the summer of 1832 an exchange was opened in Gray's Inn Road, London,[37] organised by shopkeepers with a later influx of artisans. In March 1833 the London United Trades' Association was formed to co-ordinate the supply of co-operative producers' goods. The labour exchange at Gray's Inn Road removed to the Surrey Institution, Blackfriars Road, and phoenix-like, the Gray's Inn Road premises were taken over by the National Land and Equitable Labour Exchange Company from January 1833.[38] By July 1833 there was another, grander body, the National Equitable Labour Exchange Association, launched as a fusion of consumers, producers, and co-operative missionaries with ideas of social regeneration and community.

At Birmingham there were more practical proposals for integrating a labour exchange with suppliers of raw materials and foodstuffs from as far afield as south-west Ireland. Plans for the Birmingham labour exchange were laid at a meeting in November 1832. It was decided to open an exchange as soon as £2,000 was deposited.[39] Robert Owen was duly appointed governor of the exchange on its opening in July 1833.[40]

The sixth Co-operative Congress, which met in Huddersfield in April 1833, was preoccupied with plans to launch the Grand National Consolidated Trades' Union and with talk on the progress of labour exchanges—Owen reported that the Birmingham exchange had 400 depositors and 500 shareholders.[41] By the end of 1833 a profit of £200 on exchange transactions at Birmingham was reported to a quarterly meeting.[42] Charlotte Street labour exchange in London set up a school with 100 scholars on its nominal roll in October 1833 and charged half their fees in labour notes, but the school had to leave the bazaar premises because of the disturbance it caused to exchange transactions. The school equipment was certainly rudimentary; a piece of chalk was used 'with which we gave lessons on the floor'.[43] An early example of the appropriation of the term 'Rational' by co-operators appeared in a reference in November 1833 to another London society formed in Westminster to establish a 'Rational' School.[44]

Labour exchanges were also a means of bringing trade unions into the co-operative movement: William Pare urged Birmingham trade unionists to plan provisions stores and provide employment for workers locked-out at Derby. Pare applauded the idea of a general union, but he also looked forward to workers' self-employment: 'Let the Trades' Unions of England send over their surplus commodities worked up at their Trades' Manufactures to Ireland' and acquire provisions in return.[45] Owen went a stage further and proposed a Masters' Union which would enable masters and men to elect 'a union of friendly communication between them'.[46]

Some trade unions did produce and market their own goods through the labour exchanges, but most trade unionists looked more keenly towards the Grand National Consolidated Trades' Union than to the co-operative or labour exchange movement—despite such calls to brotherhood as appeared in *The Pioneer*: 'The Potters' Union; the Clothiers' Union; the Builders' Union; the Co-operative Unions . . . what are they but so many divisions of a moral army?'[47] The National Equitable Labour Exchange, on its part, offered to accept goods from the trade unionists of Derby, Worcester and Yeovil.[48] The language of *The Pioneer* became even more inflammatory during the Derby lock-out: 'Brothers! Make ready, now, for active warfare! The masters are in league with one another . . . Derby has fallen.'[49] Syndicalist sentiment in *The Pioneer* did not aspire to communities, nor to Robert Owen, although 'it is well known that Mr Owen has identified himself with the *extreme* left, both in theology and politics'.[50]

Already by October 1833 Owen was calling the labour exchanges a mere 'drop in the bucket' in contrast to the total reforming and self-improving capacity of the working classes. He now wanted a

National Moral Union of the Productive Classes with branches for communities, education and social improvement: 'The Exchange is but a bagatelle' compared to community experiments.[51] Owen launched his Society of National Regeneration in November 1833 from an office in Manchester.[52] The tenor of his appeal for fraternity was reciprocated in an address subscribed to Owen by Ebenezer Elliott, the 'Chartist rhymer', representing Sheffield Owenites in 1834: 'You came among us as rich man among the poor, and did not call us rabble. This is a phenomenon new to us. There was no sneer on your lips, no covert scorn in your tone.'[53] The Society for Promoting National Regeneration published its own journal, the *Herald of the Rights of Industry*, in Manchester during 1834.

The labour exchange movement finally collapsed in the aftermath of the downfall of the Grand National Consolidated Trades' Union. No further issues of labour notes were made after 31 May 1834.[54] Working within a capitalist system, the labour exchange experiments had paradoxically to accept a currency system of exchange and valuation: converting labour time into labour value and notes would not obviate eventual reconversion into monetary exchange value, except in a closed system, to which patently the labour exchange could never aspire. Labour exchanges would have fitted more readily into a system of established co-operative communities rather than acting as a precursor to community.

The Grand National Consolidated Trades' Union changed its name to 'British and Foreign Consolidated Association of Industry, Humanity and Knowledge' and in an official document pointed out that the interests of employers and workers were really the same, as masters had gradually risen out of the mass of workmen.[55] Robert Owen was to be self-styled 'Grand Master of the Order'.[56] 'The movement collapsed, dragging down with it in the dust the labour exchanges, co-operative societies, the movement for the eight-hour day, syndicalism, and even a great part of the Owenite Utopias and tenets of salvation.'[57] This interpretation must be tempered, as far as the Owenite and co-operative movement is concerned, for in 1834 the *New Moral World* replaced *The Crisis*, and this new journal was to have an unprecedentedly long life for a working class periodical and was to act as a medium for the communitarian debate during the late 1830s which led to the foundation of Queenwood, the purest example of an Owenite community. It should also be conceded that the first, enthusiastic, phase of co-operative storekeeping during the

period 1829–32 was already fading by 1834. After 1834 many working class supporters deserted the Owenite hierarchy and moved towards Chartism. Perhaps this explains why the bulk of Chartists
accepted Owenite social criticism but rejected Owenite dogma.

Some co-operators became too impatient to await the establishment of a community. 'On 8 April 1834 Manchester and Salford
Community Company sent off twenty-three members to Cincin-
natti to purchase land for community on an Owenian plan.'[58] The
procedure for transforming society was announced in the first issue
of the *New Moral World*.[59] In the following issue it was declaimed:

> The time for man's regeneration is come! The hour of his deliverance
> from sin and misery is at hand! Behold the coming of that new life, when
> the world shall be so changed that every man shall sit under his own vine
> and his own fig tree, and there shall be none to make him afraid.[60]

The preliminary government would be the 'First Lodge of the
Order of the New Moral World' and the steering body was now
being called 'The Association of All Classes of All Nations to form
a New Moral World'.[61] The object was no less than 'to form an
entirely new state of society through the reorganisation of production and distribution, for re-organising character and providing
beneficial government for all'. The means were to be propaganda,
the mutual supply of necessaries without competition and, 'as soon
as practicable, to found establishments to beneficially employ, well
educate, and render happy all the members of the Association'.[62]
The government of the Association was 'to be paternal and one
of unity'. There would be a 'Social Father of the New Moral
World', a senior council (aged over 35), and a junior council (25–35
years). The Social Father was to be elected by the councils.

An example of one of the wilder contemporary fantasies for social
regeneration was a proposal submitted to Owen for a 'Floating Co-
operative Community' to be established on an old man-of-war
moored in the Thames and using the tides for mechanical power[63]:
'Here then is habitation—Let the inhabitants be men, women and
children.' As a further illustration of the many calculations being
made for a model community, there was a plan outlined in the
New Moral World of 2 May 1835 which was based on 1,000 acres
for 500 members with an estimated annual surplus of £5,000,
initial building expenses of £15,000, and loans of £21,000 at a total
yearly charge of £3,000.

The succession of Owenite bodies—the Association of All Classes

of All Nations (1835), the Community Friendly Society (1836), the
National Community Friendly Society (1837), the Universal Community Society of Rational Religionists (1839), the Home Colonisation Society (1840)—all show in their titles the bias towards
community plans. The members of the Community Friendly Society
were not as numerous as those of the parent society—the Association
of All Classes of All Nations—but they paid larger and separate
sums as weekly subscriptions. 'In one case a penny per week was
found sufficient to carry forward the general work.'[64] Only members
of the Community Society could be elected into the community.

The Association of All Classes of All Nations had been established
on 1 May 1835. Its close allegiance to Owen was emphasised in the
New Moral World:

> Let it be remembered that the great object of this Association is, to carry
> into practical operation the System of Society propounded by *Robert Owen*
> —not the views which this or that individual may have formed of that
> System—but Robert Owen's own views of it, and under his immediate
> direction . . .[65]

The *Laws and Regulations* of the Association were later bound in
Manchester together with the *Social Bible* and *Social Hymns*[66]: the
volume was dedicated to Robert Owen, 'The Great Propounder and
Able Advocate'. A creed for the Association was given which stated
that its objects were:

> to effect an entire change in the Character and Condition of Mankind, and
> thus form a New Moral World through religion of charity and an equit-
> able system of united property, which property is to be created by the
> members of the Association, without infringing upon the rights of any
> private property now in existence.[67]

In the new moral world the problem of property would be extin-
guished—'the continuance of private property will be seen to be an
evil of enormous magnitude, and will be, in consequence, eagerly
relinquished by all . . .'[68] The president, or 'parent', was to have
the title of 'Father of the New Moral World'. There would be three
classes of progression for members: candidates for admission had
to qualify 'by studying the first number of the *New Moral World*,
and after three months' probation and having passed their examination before the Senior Council, will sign declaration of their adherence . . .' A labour currency had passed out of fashion: prices
within the new moral world were to be equitable, and 'until better
arrangements can be made the purchase and sale . . . shall be with

the regular currency of the country or by mutual exchanges . . .'[69] As soon as there were sufficient members a community would be set up, 'and establish an entirely new state of society, without priests, lawyers, military, buyers or sellers, or money changers; to be composed of one superior, intelligent, industrious class . . .'[70] Members were to subscribe according to their means but at a level of not less than 3*d* weekly for those who wished to enter communities. Charity towards all was to be the credo of membership of the new moral world:

> We have been requested to state, what is to be the religion of the Millennium. We reply: It will be the increasing practice of promoting the happiness of every man, woman and child, to the greatest extent in our power, without regard to their class, sect, party, country or colour.[71]

A Social Institution was opened in Great George Street, Salford, in January 1836, and in February the Association of All Classes of All Nations removed its London headquarters to Burton Street Rooms from Charlotte Street Institution.[72] The first of a new series of Owenite congresses was held at Burton Street Rooms from 2 to 16 May 1836 and plans were laid for the next congress to meet in Manchester in the following May.

The Community Friendly Society, set up in London in 1836, traced its origin to 'friends originally part of an Association called the "Moral Union" and who later met on 13 March 1834 and formed a Society called the "Social Land Community".'[73] Obstacles to entering the community were to be overcome with utopian simplicity: 'I tell you that if 1,000 individuals, taken in families and without any selection—except as regards their moral habits—were to walk out of Birmingham or Coventry at Lady-day . . . they would, by Michaelmas, be as thoroughly an agricultural population as if they had been native to the employment.'[75]

Interesting provisions for social security were included in the rules of the Community Friendly Society[75]: a relief fund for sickness and funeral benefit on the basis of a weekly contribution of 4*d* on an average wage of 16*s,* and allowances at the rate of 8*s* weekly, an employment fund with somewhat smaller allowances, and a community fund. The relief allowances would not become payable until six months of subscriptions had been received: benefit would then be 'until death, or until elected into any establishment of the Society'. Unemployment allowance would be paid only if it could be shown that the unemployment was 'not caused by any strike or combination or any misconduct'. Owen was strong on industrial discipline; he had little time for the irresponsible activities of trade clubs. Weekly subscriptions to the community fund were 6*d* for males and 3*d* for females. Directors could use the fund for the purchase of food and household goods:

> and a dividend of one-third of the Profits shall be made to each Member according to the amount of Purchases made by such Member during that time. The remaining two-thirds shall be added to the Community Fund ...No Dividend shall be made to any member unless his or her Purchases for the time amount to or exceed One Pound.[76]

When in community there would be no need for subscriptions:

> No property or produce of Labour of any kind whatsoever in any Establishment shall be allowed or considered to belong to any individual Resident, except wearing apparel and articles of personal adornment or use; but all property and produce of Labour...shall belong to the Society...[77]

There is no evidence that any actual contributions or allowances were made; the friendly society provisions merely added folios to the Owenite paper commonwealth. But the London Community Friendly Society did at least operate a shop in John Street on two evenings each week, and reported a sum of £177 in its community fund by March 1837. From the evidence given in this report, co-operative activities had almost ceased in London, apart from those of the Community Society. The inactivity was ascribed to general disillusionment among the working classes, and it was felt 'that some time must elapse before sufficient confidence will be restored as to induce them once more to turn to *Co-operation* as the only means of rescuing themselves from their numerous grievances'.[78]

By mid-1837 a 'national' Community Friendly Society with Robert Owen as president was inaugurated.[79] James Braby and John Finch were two of its trustees, William Clegg was treasurer and G. A. Fleming secretary; all these officials were later to become involved in the Queenwood community. At an early meeting of the new Society it was recommended that its funds should be transferred from savings banks to the Commissioners of National Debt, presumably as a show of patriotism. The National Community Society formed two branches in London, at City Road and Great Queen Street.[80]

A member wishing to enter the community would have to contribute £50 to supplement membership subscriptions of 1*s* weekly

Above Farm buildings on the Queenwood estate

Below Harmony Hall

Above The masters' cottages at Queenwood, now a private house
Below The chapel (right) and laundry room, now farm cottages

before admission. A fund was to be accumulated at a minimum rate of £2,500 yearly for each batch of fifty community residents.[81] Once in community, 'new wealth' would be created sufficient to enable all members eventually to enter the community. Outside contributions augmenting the value of community production would provide for successive intakes of residents on a draft system.

A second Congress of the Association of All Classes of All Nations was held at the Social Institution, Great George Street, Salford, from 1 May to 25 May 1837.[82] Representatives from sixteen towns attended and appointed G. A. Fleming as editor and secretary of the *New Moral World*, publication of which was to be transferred from London to Manchester, along with the combined office for the Association and the National Community Friendly Society: 'Manchester is the most likely seat of experiments, and London the centre of promulgation'.[83] The Association of All Classes of All Nations aimed to create a network of branches throughout the country as a basis for the dissemination of propaganda concerning community projects and for the collection of subscriptions towards establishing a community. Branch societies, each with its own charter, were opened during 1837 at Birmingham, Blackburn, Bradford, Bristol, Dewsbury, Huddersfield, Leigh, Leeds, Liverpool, Paisley and Stockport. Many of these local societies took rented accommodation for their meetings, but there were instances of local hostility which took the form of restricting and denying the use of premises to the Owenites.

The second traceable use of the title 'hall of science' appeared in *The Union* of 31 December 1831 when it referred to proposals for the erection of a building to be called the Manchester Mechanics' Hall of Science.[84] Subsequently, the institution was renamed the New Mechanics' Institute and came under the presidency of Rowland Detrosier. It was argued that the new institute would not supplant the existing mechanics' institute in Manchester because the latter was only fitfully attended by workers, who had little leisure 'and still less inclination to study the mere abstract principle of an employment, the labour in which is daily depreciated in value, and nearly half the produce of which is taken out of their pockets by direct and indirect taxation'. By February 1832 600 shares at £1 each had been taken up for the new mechanics' institute.[85] The halls of science were coming to be thought of as complementary to the mechanics' institutes because they would graft moral education on to technical knowledge as a prerequisite for converting old society and entering the new.

To return to the central body of the Owenites, the central board of the AACAN reported in 1837 that there were fifteen branches in all, with a total membership of 1,500, whereas at the time of the 1836 congress there were only three branches—London, Manchester and Stockport.[86] Some branches continued to meet with local opposition, and others planned to enlarge their premises: Huddersfield issued a prospectus for the erection of a large hall in December 1837. Halifax claimed that it was deprived of its assembly room because of 'religious persecution' in February 1838.[87] The minutes of the proceedings of at least one of these branch societies are extant and give details of a meeting of 'Friends to the Rational System of Society founded by Robert Owen' held at Liverpool on 15 October 1837 which resolved to form itself into a branch of the Association. John Finch was elected president and a member was instructed 'to procure twelve copies of the *Social Bible*, three dozen of the *New Moral World* and £1 of tracts on Socialism from Manchester'.[88] By 1837 there was an implied acceptance of the term 'socialist' to denote 'Owenite': 'Not a Socialist can fairly lay claim to the name who does not unite in association, and in funds for community.'[89] A large room behind the York Hotel, Tarlton Street, Liverpool, was acquired at £2 monthly rental, and thirty bench seats, candlesticks, snuffers and a piece of canvas 'as a cushion' were procured. John Finch and two other members were to be 'Elders of this Branch' with a duty to examine candidates and power to refuse to admit those who drank. Meetings were held weekly 'for instruction in the principles of the rational system of society'. A group of 'Social Friends' at Everton, Liverpool, who wished to apply for a charter from the Association in November 1837 included a bookkeeper, an engineer, a joiner, a grocer, a gas-fitter, tailor, painter, hairdresser, printer and a labourer. Early in 1838 a Liverpool District board was formed and the board members made themselves available for lecturing assignments as far afield as Glasgow. The *New Moral World* thought it would be possible for local branches to subscribe to regional premises large enough to accommodate members from several branches.[90] It was anticipated that suitable halls of assembly would be erected in every large town and would confer the advantage of property ownership as a preliminary to superseding the existing arrangements of society. The Liverpool proposals raised a fundamental issue. Would the Owenite movement grow more successfully by concentrating its resources on the provision of assembly premises at the branches, or would funds be better used in concentrating all efforts on the establishment of communities? The alternatives were not, however, mutually exclusive because effective activity at branch level could lead to a higher level of subscriptions to central community funds. Indeed, enthusiasm for community could be fostered only at branch meetings in the long gaps between annual congresses.

The Manchester board was written to by the Liverpool Owenites in October 1838 to provide a replacement official for John Finch, who was giving a course of lectures at Chester. Liverpool branch formed a joint stock company in order to build a new assembly hall in Lord Nelson Street. The prospectus for this Liverpool hall of science included the following specifications:

> On the roof of the building will be a leaded platform 19 ft × 72 ft, on which will be an observatory for astronomical purposes, and this platform commands a beautiful view of the town, the river and the docks.

There was to be an upper-storey lecture hall, including 'an organ and organ gallery' and seating for 1,500.[91] By December 1839 the Hall of Science Building Society included 148 subscribers who had taken up 680 shares at a nominal value of £6 10s, with £2 10s payable on issue. It was intended to open the hall at Easter 1840.

Although Liverpool preceded Manchester with plans for a hall of science, the first hall to be opened was at Sheffield, in March 1839.[92] The Manchester Owenites opened their hall at Campfield in June 1840, at an estimated cost of £6,000 for a building which included school and committee rooms, coffee lounges and 'a gallery promenade'. Halls were acquired in other towns to emulate the example of Manchester, and many of them housed Owenite day and Sunday schools. For those meeting places which did not achieve the status of halls of science the title 'social institution' was used. Rochdale opened a new social institution in April 1838, and Charles Howarth wrote to Owen in December 1839 that in the intervening period they had struggled to gain the support of public opinion— 'We have also succeeded in getting a few of middle classes to join us and if you can come we are confident many of the middle and higher classes would attend to hear you . . .'[93]

In seeking a stage-development analysis for Owenism in the period after the first flush of co-operative storekeeping (1829–31), one must interpose the halls of science phase between the labour exchanges (1832–34), and the culmination and *dénouement* of Owenism at Queenwood in the 1840s. Increasingly there was to be argument whether the halls of science were amply justified in terms of cost, but in retrospect the activities at the halls of science must be treated as an important aspect of working class education, perhaps too much overlooked by historians[94] and overshadowed by the officially sponsored mechanics' institutes. The secretary of the Central Board wrote to Owen, 'The building of these "Halls" will bust our "community fund" in the beginning, though they will doubtless prove geese which will lay golden eggs.'[95] There was also discussion whether there should be a central fund for the building of halls of science so that all premises would belong to the movement at large and be vested in trustees on the same lines as Methodist chapels, which virtually belonged to the Methodist Conference.[96] In the last resort, the halls of science foundered as centres of Owenite propaganda. Some became associated with the growing secularist movement during the 1840s; the Sheffield Hall of Science admitted its loss of impetus when it was reported in 1842 that the associated Rational School had failed, largely because Holyoake had 'grown tired of it'.[97] There was apparently only one fully-fledged hall of science in London (at City Road) until as late as 1842, when Lambeth Hall of Science was opened, although there had been plans to build an institution at John Street as early as 1839.[98] The Society for the Diffusion of Useful Knowledge reported, 'The number of members of Socialist institutions in London is much smaller than of members of Mechanics' Institutions, but the attendance . . . is much greater.'[99]

In all, £22,000 was raised to build halls of science up to mid-1840.[100] The sum is impressive but not overwhelming when one considers that the Owenites could claim sixty-two branch societies and that 'perhaps 50,000 persons who are representatives of families regularly attend the Sunday lectures and there are many others who dare not appear'. It should also be noted that the Central Board, even as late as 1841, gave precedence to halls of science over the establishment of communities.[101] The halls of science phase did at least provide a forum for the development of Owenite thought and activities without any compulsive disruption of the livelihood of its supporters.

The third congress of the Association of All Classes of All Nations and the first of the National Community Friendly Society met in Manchester in May 1838 and discussed the subject of community experiments. A committee of the Community Society was appointed 'to wait upon such capitalists as may be deemed favourable to our views'. William Pare reported that a map had been marked with branch locations and possible branch development; the country was to be divided into six districts, excluding Ireland, which could not afford a missionary—the Central Board 'might annex the Isle of Man, or even all Ireland, to Liverpool'.[102] Each district missionary should be paid 30s. weekly. Pare also moved a proposition that the Central Board and the *New Moral World* should remove to Birmingham which was:

> the centre of the kingdom, from which railways were constructed, or constructing, in all directions . . . Next, it contained within a small circle, a quarter million inhabitants, and was surrounded by a great number of manufacturing towns in the Midland counties, where branches were likely to be sooner or later established . . .[103]

G. A. Fleming explained that the circulation of the *New Moral World* had increased during the period since the Central Board removed from London to Manchester.

Congress appointed Clegg, Finch and Joseph Smith to enquire after a suitable estate for a community, and the Central Board took to task those members 'who have supported trade unions benefit societies and building societies with heavier subscriptions and for more trivial objects . . . and yet they expect less time and more money will accomplish the vast objects of community'.[104]

Robert Owen again showed his hand at the third congress concerning the suitability of the poorer elements of the working classes for the community. The congress delegate from Blackburn mentioned the 'number of ardent friends to the cause of Socialism, who were too poor, however, to contribute even to the contingent fund. Could they be admitted as members?' Owen responded that it was the earnest endeavour of the Association to improve the conditions of such people 'but to effect this, funds were needed; and the operations of the Society could not be clogged by these parties in the meantime'.[105]

To help raise capital, Alexander Campbell suggested an issue of 'social exchequer bills'. William Pare argued that the public would not invest until the Society could point to a community in successful operation. Owen wanted a capital of not less than £1 million; his plan was 'establishing not one but several communities completed, so that parties intended to inhabit them shall have nothing to do but enter upon them'.[106] Owen thought the first community 'should be within a circle of thirty miles from London—not nearer than twelve, not further than thirty'.[107]

The six missionary districts based on Birmingham, Glasgow, Leeds, Liverpool, Manchester and London were put under the control of the social missionaries Alexander Campbell, F. Hollick, J. Rigby, C. F. Green, Lloyd Jones and R. Buchanan. Each branch within a district was to organise class groups of up to fifteen members. Subscriptions were to be charged at 1s a week for males, 6d for females. The directors of the Community Society included Owen, Pare, Clegg and Finch, as trustees, G. A. Fleming as secretary and editor of the *New Moral World*, and four other directors. The reports and papers of the third congress included a statistical table giving a *résumé* of the growth and extent of the organised Owenite movement, from which it is apparent that only one-third of the 1,734 members in the thirty-three branches of the Association of All Classes were subscribers to the National Community Society.[108]

Yet another congress was held on 22 October 1838 at Birmingham. The sub-committee appointed at the congress in May to investigate the possibilities of suitable estates for community reported in September that an estate of 1,000 acres in Norfolk was on the market, but the members of the visiting committee found the area damp and unhealthy and 'subject to exhalations'. Subsequently a deputation visited James Hill's estate of 700 acres at Wretton, some seventeen miles from King's Lynn, which Hill agreed to sell for £11,500; £1,000 was deposited by the Owenites and the date for completion of the contract was specified as 20 November 1839.[109]

There was mounting controversy from early 1839 concerning the nature of the labour supply suitable for a community experiment. Hired labour was thought incompatible, as it would not lead to a unity of labour and rewards. A resolution of the dilemma would be to engage outside labour only during the initial stages of community development, as it was argued that members could easily acquire proficiency in agricultural pursuits:

> The Socialists must first become agricultural labourers, or agricultural labourers must become Socialists, to carry on a successful community of

united interests on land; for in a community as proposed by our Social Father, very few tradesmen will be required (as such) except in erecting the buildings; and after they are completed, most of them will be required to lend a hand to cultivate the soil.[110]

A year later the matter was still being ventilated. 'My only fear,' said F. Hollick in August 1839, 'has been with respect to the quantity of agricultural skill among the social body. I never expected to meet with a person who was a good farmer, a good Socialist, and a man of general knowledge and strong mind, at the same time.'[111] A Coventry member suggested shoemaking and watchmaking as suitable activities for the community—six watchmakers could complete twenty-four timepieces in a month at a cost of £61 and a saleable value of £100.[112]

By the time of the fourth congress in Birmingham 1839 the number of branches listed was fifty-five, of which thirty-eight had been formed since January 1838. A spread of activities into north-east and south-east England was becoming noticeable and was diminishing the earlier concentration along the Manchester–Birmingham–London axis: new branch centres included Doncaster, Newcastle-on-Tyne, Darlington, Dundee, Chatham, Brighton and Reading. It was claimed that the branches could accommodate upwards of 25,000, and that lectures were being held in seventy-seven places. Delegates explained some of the difficulties facing the branches. Bath had not been able to increase its members 'from want of talented lecturers, and the place being a focus of Chartist agitation, the members had agreed, for the present, to suspend their meetings'; R. Buchanan, from Leigh, 'regretted that the Chartist agitation had drawn away the attention of many of the members'.[113] The two organising bodies were formally united into one parent society—the Universal Community Society of Rational Religionists.

Returns from twenty-six branches were submitted, showing 285 male candidates for the community, 151 wives and 457 children—a total of 893 persons—and it was estimated that members could take £6,836 collectively into the community. It was not thought necessary to give details of the occupations of members, 'as it is very diversified'. Owen pontificated to the thirty-four congress delegates that 'they must now take their stand as men of business, he would advise them to make use of as few words as possible, in order that they might the more speedily transact their business'. 'Rational religion', he explained, 'was simply that each member should do all in his power to promote the happiness of all, without distinction of class, sect, country or colour...'[114] Owen warned them of the dangers of over-precipitation: to construct and perfect a model community was to achieve something unique:

> or, perhaps, except by myself, ever been conceived in the imagination; it is to put together a curiously and nicely constructed machine for performing all the business of human life, in such a manner that all shall have a good physical, mental, moral and practical character formed for them...

It was apparent that he was still thinking of community as an agent of amelioration more in psychological and ethical than in economic terms. James Rigby wanted some evidence of members' solidarity in support of the principles of the Society, and warned Owen that a lack of asseveration had weakened all previous co-operative bodies. Owen replied in obscurantist fashion—'he had erred in supposing they were more advanced than he found them to be. If all could not agree, he must wait another year ... all that was required now was to show that they had feelings of charity for all.'[115]

The estates sub-committee reported on its visit to a landed property in the south of England, but did not mention that the estate in question was at Tytherley in Hampshire, owned by Isaac Lyon Goldsmid, a London bullion merchant who had been an acquaintance of Owen since the activities of the British and Foreign Philanthropic Society in 1823. Owen had first inspected the Goldsmid estate in Hampshire in 1835, ostensibly

> to ascertain if he [Goldsmid] could better the condition of the labourers who were employed by the farmers on his property. He found...that it was the most easy and natural thing imaginable to enable them...to maintain their families in comparative comfort, by merely letting them half an acre of land per family, to cultivate by the spade, at a higher rent than any farmer by the plough system could afford to give.[116]

Further details were given by the estates sub-committee, which reported that the Tytherley soil was of medium quality and the land was free of tithes. In all, about 700 acres were available, 200 of which were extraparochial. The members inspecting the Hampshire property included C. F. Green, who had visited Shaker communities in the United States, Robert Owen and James Braby. A deputation from the Colonisation Society (made up of former members of the Society of Rational Religionists) waited on congress and elaborated on their plans to emigrate to America to found a community, but congress was 'not in a position to assist, as the

Society was about to commence practical operations in England'.

Heaton Aldam, an agriculturist who had farmed at Whaley Bridge in Derbyshire for ten years, received a deputation at the Birmingham congress and subsequently visited Queenwood farm, the home farm of the Tytherley estate, in company with a Mr Drake, a neighbouring tenant farmer of Goldsmid's. Aldam's report was hardly encouraging. 'I found it to be *dry chalk* land, badly farmed, and in a very poor state and condition, it is capable however of very great improvement, and will pay well for it—the improvement to be effected by the introduction of *bone manure*.' Aldam, with some prescience, considered the estate 'highly suitable for an educational establishment' and noted that 'the produce of the land is turnips, wheat, barley, seeds, sainfoin and vetches'.[117] But there were some drastic disadvantages to the Tytherley site as a prospective socialist community—it was too far from the main branches of the Society of Rational Religionists, it was not suitable for manufacturing activities, there were no adequate running water and no nearby coal deposits, nor was the nature of the soil appropriate for spade cultivation. Aldam was not, however, a firm exponent of spade cultivation. He had written previously to the *New Moral World*:

> I am sure that the human frame, once accustomed to the delightful plough, calls not for the toilsome spade ... Ploughing was upright and healthy ... Socialism would not much ameliorate the condition of mankind by curving their spines to mother earth.

Owen prevaricated over the decision to embark on a single community project; he wanted two estates, one an agricultural and educational community, the other to be a combined manufacturing and agricultural settlement. It was thought that many middle class sympathisers would be willing to join such a community as board-residents. John Finch emphasised that the Society included many engineers and manufacturing workers, and 'doubted whether either of the proposed estates were suitable for several of their best members'. The congress delegates also disagreed over the qualities of leadership and sources of talent. Owen asserted the need for men with a superior education: 'The middle classes are, by position, the business classes of the world.' He was later to crystallise his views even more severely in terms of middle class leadership:

> Now, the middle class is the *only* efficient *directing* class in Society, and will, of necessity, remain so, until our system shall create a *new* class of very superior *directors* as well as *operators;* a class very superior to any

men or women who have ever yet lived ... The working class never did
direct any permanent successful operations.[118]

William Pare reminded delegates that in order to stock the proposed
estates the Society would have to seek men of capital. G. A. Fleming
drew attention to the growing schism between community-firsters
and those other parties who wanted an intensified campaign for
building halls of science; he was of the opinion that the principles of
community had to be made known universally as a prerequisite for
success, and the only way to do this was by having adequate centres
for meetings.

As a forewarning of future inadequacies in financial control,
William Pare complained at the state of the books at the previous
congress in 1838. 'Though the accounts were not very clear when
the books came from Manchester, on examination, everything was
found to be satisfactory. Mr Fleming had never professed to be a
book-keeper ... Since October, they had engaged a book-keeper at
25 shillings per week.'

A discussion took place at the 1839 congress over the appointment of
a governor for the proposed community. Owen stated his earnest desire to visit members of his family in America during the ensuing
autumn in order to arrange his affairs in case of his death. It was
resolved that Owen's visit to America (after an absence of ten years)
would enable him to devote his attention to the proposed communities
in England on his expected return to England about April 1840

> and being satisfied of the practicability of his advising with the executive,
> while absent, on the important business connected with such establish-
> ments ... do hereby express their cordial consent to the temporary absence
> of the President, as not necessarily interfering with, or retarding the
> arrangements requisite for proceeding with practical operations with the
> least possible delay.[119]

Despite Owen's coincidental decision to renew acquaintance in
America with certain members of his family precisely at the time of
inception of the first model community, and after he had preached
social salvation for almost a quarter of a century, the delegates at
the fourth congress felt they could not proceed without Owen as
titular head, even if he evaded their expectation of his active leadership. A resolution was passed 'that Mr Owen is hereby appointed
the Governor of the first Community and of any other community
to be begun previous to the assembling of the next Congress.'[120]

Owenite propaganda was becoming most effective by 1839. Upwards of half a million copies of a variety of publications were being distributed annually. Supporting petitions to the House of Commons from twenty-one towns had been submitted—'an inexpensive mode of directing the attention of the superior classes'.[121] An article in the *London and Westminster Review* in April assessed this impact— 'those who habitually watch the progress of opinion are aware that Owenism, in one form or another, is at present, the actual creed of a great portion of the working classes'. Advertisements appeared in *The Times* and *Weekly Dispatch* to recruit talented lecturers for the movement. Liverpool branch formed a Rational School Society in July 1839: 'no hope remains of escaping from the frightful evils inseparable from ignorance and superstition unless the people unite, and determine to educate themselves'.[122] In the school, 'all will be trained in the same manner, and to the same extent without any distinction except what is rendered necessary from the peculiar natural organisation of each child'.

John Finch wrote to Owen in apocalyptic language in June 1839:

> My dear Sir, the time for the emancipation of the world is now fully come, the little stone cut out of the mountain without hands will itself become a great mountain ... There is no other name under the heavens given among whereby they can be saved ... Owen is chosen Governor of the first Community, he shall choose as his Deputy John.[123]

But Finch went on to give some constructive advice that the community should be in one of the manufacturing districts, as many members were in engineering trades, and the community should manufacture machines and steam engines 'because these are the most profitable trades we can follow ...'

Robert Owen was presented at court to the young Queen Victoria during the summer of 1839 and *The Times* correspondent commented:

> The presentation of Robert Owen at Court by Lord Melbourne is one of the most humiliating events which have recently occurred. It might have indeed, been hoped that we should at least be spared the sin and shame of such a national degradation.[124]

A report of the occasion in a Parisian journal was more percipient, if less resentful. 'Upon the whole, it still remains a matter of doubt whether Robert Owen was presented to Queen Victoria, or Queen Victoria to Robert Owen.'[125]

A draft lease for the Tytherley estate was drawn up and forwarded to W. H. Ashurst, an eminent City solicitor, colleague of Rowland

Hill and legal adviser to Robert Owen, for his comments and advice. Ashurst wrote a detailed reply to Owen on the terms of the lease, which, he advised, had been carefully worded to satisfy Goldsmid's interests. Clauses had been appended to the lease to prevent any multiplication of poor law settlements which could add to the parochial rates if the experiment should fail. The covenants were not unreasonable but they would not protect ratepayers against settlement to be obtained by birth. Ashurst added that the 'Landlord objects to your buying down the rent below £200 . . . an indisposition on his part to vacate during his lifetime his position as landlord of the property.' (Goldsmid's solicitor had been written to suggesting that the remaining £200 should be paid by lessees after forty years' tenure, but Goldsmid would not concede, even though this would not interfere with his object of remaining in the position of landlord.) Nor did Goldsmid wish to part with his shooting rights, except over the portion of Crown land. Ashurst pointed out the inconvenience of always having a rental of £200 and having the important buildings on a leasehold site, a leasehold fast running out, and subject to a clause of forfeiture 'if any timber is cut contrary to the stipulations', or any land used for buildings contrary to the covenants.[126] The landlord's reserved right of shooting also implied that game must not be disturbed:

> Now suppose a community established; consider the walks and other uses the community may necessarily make and require for the comfort of men and women instead of harbouring hares and partridges, and then consider the inconvenience of this power in a litigious landlord, without the power of tenants to buy.

There were other hazardous possibilities: with some prescience Ashurst warned, 'Suppose the Bishop and Clergy of the diocese wish to crush you, they would buy the head lease, enforce all the covenants rigidly, and if they could not work a forfeiture, would work a pretty considerable lot of inconvenience and annoyance.'

Despite the admonitions of Ashurst, the Central Board proceeded with the legal negotiations to lease the Goldsmid estate, the majority of its members unaware of the slender rights of proprietorship that could be claimed over what were intended to be the first socialist acres in Britain. In August, and again in early September 1839, the Central Board wrote to Owen, who was in Scotland, and pleaded with him to return to England to speed up the arrangements for setting up the long-awaited community experiment.[127] Some weeks later, at a Central Board meeting in Birmingham on 26–27 September 1831, it was announced that Owen had given notice of withdrawal from the office of governor of the forthcoming community, on the grounds that Tytherley would be merely "a preliminary working community adapted to the views and habits of the better-conditioned of the working classes' rather than 'a community according to his ideas of a community, calculated for the general population of a country'. Owen would, however, recommend Finch, Green and Aldam as suitable persons to direct operations, and as a concession, he would retain nominal office as governor until the next annual congress, to avoid the expense of having to convene a special congress.[128]

Owen was nearer the truth when he warned that the members were too impatient to wait for the necessary growth of community funds. He did not, however, leave much time for any policy reorganisation, as his resignation of the governorship was received but four days before the date of legal possession of Tytherley, 1 October 1839. The Owenites agreed to purchase farm stock, implements and grain, and to hand over £1,000 for timber and as a security to Goldsmid. Farm stock included 280 sheep, six horses and twenty tons of hay. Hence it was thought there was plenty of food available until the first socialist harvest, provided intending residents 'can be satisfied with good mutton, bread and potatoes'.[129] The lease was for ninety-nine years of Queenwood farm and the adjoining land at an annual rental of £350. 1 October was restyled in the Owenite calendar '1st day: 1st month, year 1, New Era.'

William Galpin, the Dorchester banker who was later to contribute so generously to the community funds, made an early comment: 'The important step of the first Community is one which must materially decide the progress of Socialism for the present generation.'[130] He also foresaw the danger of hostile public opinion and recommended a Normal School for Socialism to help counteract criticism.

Notes

1 *Poor Man's Guardian*, 8 January 1831, p. 2.
2 *Ibid.*, 27 May, 1831, pp. 3–4.
3 *Ibid.*, No. 31, 14 January 1832, p. 246. For Owen and trade unionism, see G. D. H. Cole, *Attempts at General Union, 1818–34*, reprinted from *International Review for Social History*, 1939, and *Socialist Thought: the Fore-*

runners, 1789–1850, 1955, pp. 120–131.

4 See his series of twelve letters published in pamphlet form as *The Millenium: the Wisdom of Jesus and the Foolery of Sectarianism*, 1837; also *Society as it ought to be, or, Social Diseases and Social Remedies, Part I, by a Liverpool Merchant*, 1847.

5 *British Co-operator*, No. 5, August 1830.

6 'Address of the British Association for the Promotion of Co-operative Knowledge to Labourers, Mechanics and Artisans of the United Kingdom', *Poor Man's Guardian*, 31 December, 1830, pp. 4–6. (Address signed 'William Lovett, Secretary'.)

7 *British Co-operator*, No. 6, September 1830. E. T. Craig was the first president of the Owenian Society: 'The society was the first to establish an educational agency, by means of a news and reading room, lectures, library, and discussions. All the unstamped newspapers were taken and laid upon the table of the newsroom in Edward Street, Hanover Street... This newsroom of the unstamped was a novelty at that time in Manchester.' (*Co-operative News*, 17 October 1874, p. 194.)

8 Letter from Charles Fry, purchasing agent, First Liverpool Co-operative Society, *Chester Co-operative Chronicle*, No. 3, 24 July 1830.

9 The Chester society commenced on 26 May 1830 with a capital of £26, and stocked flour, soap and candles. By 22 September 1830 subscriptions had grown to £83, and trade to £646, with gross profits over four months of £88 (*Chester Co-operative Chronicle*, No. 3, 24 July 1830, and No. 6, 1 October 1830.)

10 *The Address of Working Classes of Devonshire to their fellow Labourers throughout Great Britain and Ireland*, a broadsheet printed in Exeter, annotated on the flyleaf, 'The Owenite Address, perhaps written by Owen himself. Extremely rare, if not unique. The date would seem to be about 1830.' Goldsmiths' library.

11 *Description of an Architectural Model for a Community upon a Principle of United Interests as advocated by Robert Owen, from a design by Stedman Whitwell*, 1830, p. 5.

12 Extract from minute book, First Community Society of London, 65 Old Street, 18 June 1830, reported in *British Co-operator*, No. 5, August 1830.

13 *Herald to the Trades' Advocate and Co-operative Journal*, No. 4, 16 October 1830, p. 57.

14 Rev. F. Baker, *Lectures on co-operation, 19 April and 3 May 1830*, reprinted from the *Bolton Chronicle*.

15 Co-operative Congresses, *Reports and Papers*, 1831–2, Goldsmiths' library.

16 There is obscurity over the adoption by the co-operators of the term 'congress'. Holyoake maintained that it was an American term 'introduced by William Pare, and had not been in popular use in England'. (G. J. Holyoake, *Sixty Years of an Agitator's Life*, 1906, Part I, p. 134.)

17 B.M., Place MSS 27791, f. 246, and 27822, f. 19, quoted in R. F. Wearmouth, *Some Working Class Movements of the Nineteenth Century*, 1948, pp. 52–3. See also Graham Wallas, *Life of Francis Place*, 1898, p. 271.

18 *Report of Proceedings of the Second Co-operative Congress, October 1831*, p. 3. Perhaps the first sales of 'co-operative' milk were at Birmingham, by an

unemployed co-operator for whom members of the Birmingham Co-operative Society subscribed 6*d* each and purchased milk cans, yoke and pony; the Society paid him 15*s* weekly, 'all out of profits, arising from the sale of *Co-operative milk*.' (*Lancashire Co-operator*, No. 5, 6 August 1831.)

19 *Report of Proceedings of the Second Co-operative Congress, October 1831*, p. 4.
20 *Ibid.*, p. 11.
21 *Lancashire and Yorkshire Co-operator*, No. 6, 12 November 1831.
22 *Ibid.*, No. 8, 10 December 1831.
23 *Ibid.*, September 1832.
24 *The Crisis*, 2 February 1833, p. 31.
25 *Ibid.*, 19 October 1833, pp. 58–9. The *New Moral World*, VIII, 1 (new series), No. 1, 4 July 1840, also ascribed the malaise in co-operation to store-keeping, which 'converted members into money-seeking, money-loving, higgling shopkeepers...'
26 *The Crisis*, II, No. 25, 29 June 1833, p. 195.
27 *Poor Man's Guardian*, No. 43, 7 April 1832, p. 341.
28 Letter from Carson, of Haigh, near Wigan, 1 March 1832, Robert Owen correspondence, No. 522.
29 *Report of Proceedings of the Third Co-operative Congress, April 1832*.
30 *The Crisis*, No. 34, 27 October 1832, p. 135. The subsequent history of Birkacre is not known; there are no further reports on its activities after 1832.
31 W. Hawkes Smith, *On Co-operation*, 1832, a 'reprint from article in *Monthly Repository*, July 1832, as a Review of the Report of the third Co-operative Congress; and other works', p. 8.
32 *The Crisis*, No. 15, 30 June 1832, p. 59.
33 Letter from 'A Disciple of the Rational System of Society', *Poor Man's Guardian*, No. 68, 29 September 1832, p. 551.
34 *The Crisis*, No. 34, 27 October 1832, p. 134.
35 *Ibid.*, No. 29, 22 September 1832.
36 W. H. Oliver, 'The labour phase of the co-operative movement', *Oxford Economic Papers*, No. 3, October 1958.
37 Deposits at Gray's Inn exchange at the end of sixteen weeks: 445,000 hours, valued at £11,000; total exchange or sales, £9,400. (Reported in the *Birmingham Labour Exchange Gazette*, No. 1, 16 January 1833, p. 4.
38 *The Crisis*, II, No. 2, 19 January 1833.
39 *Birmingham Labour Exchange Gazette*, Nos. 1–5, 16 January 1833–9 February 1833, *passim*.
40 *The Crisis*, No. 30, 3 August 1833, p. 238.
41 *Ibid.*, No. 17, 4 May 1833, p. 130.
42 *Ibid.*, No. 18, 28 December 1833, p. 144.
43 *Ibid.*, No. 19, 4 January 1834, p. 150.
44 *Ibid.*, No. 12, 16 November 1833, p. 93, and No. 20, 11 January 1834, p. 155.
45 *The Pioneer*, 28 December 1833, p. 140.
46 *Ibid.*, No. 19, 11 January 1834, pp. 149–50.
47 *Ibid.*, No. 8, 26 October 1833, p. 60.
48 *Ibid.*, No. 25, 22 February 1834, p. 222.
49 *Ibid.*, No. 40, 7 June 1834, p. 392.

50 *Ibid.*, No. 40, 7 June 1834, p. 394.

51 Robert Owen, in *The Crisis*, October 1833, p. 62.

52 *Ibid.*, 7 December 1833, p. 117.

53 'Memorial to Robert Owen from the Sheffield Regeneration Society', *The Times*, 24 January 1834, quoted in G. J. Holyoake, *Life and Last Days of Robert Owen*, 1871, p. 19.

54 *The Crisis*, No. 8, 31 May 1834, p. 64. Robert Owen took over the *Crisis* from February 1834 until it ceased publication in August 1834.

55 *The Pioneer*, 11 January 1834, pp. 149–50.

56 *The Crisis*, No. 20, 23 August 1834, p. 152.

57 M. Beer, *History of Socialism*, p. 346.

58 Letter from J.H.W., Manchester, 21 April 1834, in *The Crisis*, No. 5, 10 May 1834, p. 40.

59 *New Moral World*, No. 1, 1 November 1834, p. 6. The sequence given was: First by the union of governments; second by the union of the landed aristocracy; third by the union of monied aristocracy; fourth by the union of both; fifth by the union of masters and men in manufacturing and farming; sixth by the union of operatives and peasants; seventh 'by an association formed of most rational from among all the preceding classes'. This progression into the new moral world was followed by an advertisement for the first festival of the 'Friendly Association of All Nations', to be held on 3 November 1834.

60 *New Moral World*, No. 2, 8 November 1834, p. 9.

61 *Ibid.*, No. 5, 29 November, 1834, p. 38.

62 *Ibid.*, No. 19, 7 March 1835, pp. 145–7.

63 *Ibid.*, No. 4, 22 November 1834, pp. 31–2.

64 Lloyd Jones, *Life, Times and Labours of Robert Owen*, 1890, II, p. 135.

65 *New Moral World*, 17 October 1835, p. 402.

66 Rousing verses and choruses were appended in the hymnal:

> We're like a hive of busy bees,
> Who wait an opportunity
> To place ourselves and all mankind
> In a bless'd community.

> Before we heard of Owen's plan
> Of serving one another
> We tried to outwit every one
> And all kind feelings smother.

See E. Yeo, 'Robert Owen and radical culture,' in *Robert Owen: Prophet of the Poor*, ed. S. Pollard and J. Salt, 1971, pp. 84–114.

67 *Laws and Regulations of the Association All Classes of All Nations*, 1835, p. xliii.

68 *Manual of the Association of All Classes of All Nations, No. 2*, 1836.

69 *Laws*, p. liii.

70 *Ibid.*, p. liv.

71 *New Moral World*, No. 57, 28 November 1835, p. 33.

72 *Ibid.*, No. 68, 13 February 1836, p. 121.

73 *Rules of the Community Friendly Society established for the mutual relief and maintenance of the members and for the purpose of promoting the well-*

being of themselves and families upon the principle of Co-operation, 1836, p. 9, Howell collection.

74 Letter from W.H.S., of Birmingham, 14 December 1836, *New Moral World*, No. 114, 31 December 1836.

75 *Rules of the Community Friendly Society*, pp. 17–19.

76 *Ibid.*, p. 21.

77 *Ibid.*, p. 25. The rules were agreed at a meeting at 94 John Street, Tottenham Court Road, London, on 3 February 1836. The signatories included Henry Rose, as secretary, and William Cameron, as chairman.

78 'Report of the Community Friendly Society,' 2 March 1837, letter No. 884, Robert Owen correspondence.

79 *New Moral World*, No. 152, 23 September 1837, p. 389.

80 *Proceedings of the Third Congress, May 1838*, p. 13.

81 *New Moral World*, No. 138, 17 June 1837, p. 274.

82 Reported in the *New Moral World*, No. 137, 10 June 1837.

83 *Ibid.*, No. 136, 3 June 1837, p. 352.

84 *The Union*, 31 December 1831, pp. 91–3. The term 'hall of science' was first mooted in the *Co-operative Magazine* of October 1829, which reported a lecture delivered in New York by Frances Wright: 'Turn your churches into halls of science, and devote your leisure day to the study of your own bodies, the analysis of your own minds, and the examination of the fair material world which extends around you.' (*Co-operative Magazine*, October 1829, p. 227.)

85 *Poor Man's Advocate*, No. 6, 25 February 1832.

86 *New Moral World*, No. 164, 16 December 1837, p. 57.

87 *Ibid.*, No. 173, 17 February 1838, p. 134.

88 'Minutes of proceedings of a meeting of friends to the rational system of society founded by Robert Owen, commencing at Liverpool 15 October 1837', Howell collection.

89 *New Moral World*, No. 118, 28 January 1837, p. 105.

90 *Ibid.*, No. 191, 23 June 1838, p. 277.

91 Letter from the Liverpool Hall of Science, 6 December 1839, Robert Owen correspondence, letter No. 1210.

92 *New Moral World*, vi, No. 20, 9 March 1839, p. 312.

93 Letter from Charles Howarth, 9 December 1839, Robert Owen correspondence, letter No. 1203.

94 But see A. Black, 'Owenite education, 1839–51, with special reference to the Manchester Hall of Science', University of Manchester, Department of Education thesis, 1953; also 'The Owenites and the halls of science', *Co-operative Review*, February 1953, pp. 42–4.

95 Letter from Henry Travis, 18 August 1839, Robert Owen correspondence, letter No. 1142.

96 *New Moral World*, vi, No. 19, 2 March 1839, p. 304.

97 *Report of the Seventh Congress, 1842*. Sheffield Hall of Science was registered for the solemnisation of marriages.

98 Letter from C. F. Green in the *New Moral World*, vi, No. 47, 14 September 1839, p. 746.

99 Quoted in *ibid.*, x, No. 33, 12 February 1842, p. 258.

100 Quoted in *ibid.*, VIII, No. 1, 4 July 1840, p. 2.
101 *Ibid.*, 10 July 1841, p. 12.
102 *Proceedings of the Third Congress, May 1838*, pp. 18–19.
103 *Ibid.*, pp. 24–5.
104 *New Moral World*, No. 196, 28 July 1838, p. 317.
105 *Proceedings of the Third Congress, May 1838*, p. 36.
106 *Ibid.*, p. 50.
107 *Ibid.*, pp. 56–63.
108 Of the thirty-three branches of the AACAN in May 1838, one was founded in 1835, two were founded in 1836, thirteen in 1837, and seventeen in 1838 (to May). Manchester branch (Great George Street), the founder branch, had 500 paying members, of whom 147 subscribed to the National Community Society. A1 London branch (Great Queen Street), with 160 members, was the second largest branch. (The National Community Society had 658 members.) All A1 branch members subscribed to the community fund.
109 *New Moral World*, V, No. 1, 27 October 1838.
110 *Ibid.*, V, No. 12, 12 January 1839, pp. 182–3.
111 *Ibid.*, VI, No. 45, 31 August, 1839, p. 717.
112 *Ibid.*, VI, No. 44, 24 August 1839, p. 695.
113 *Proceedings of the Fourth Congress, May 1839*, p. 25.
114 *Ibid.* (Bloomfield Assembly Room, Great Charles Street, Birmingham).
115 *Ibid.*, pp. 60–2.
116 *New Moral World*, No. 48, 26 September 1835, p. 381.
117 Letter from Heaton Aldam, Whaley Hall, 8 June 1839, to G. A. Fleming at the Central Board, Robert Owen correspondence, letter No. 1107.
118 *New Moral World*, VI, No. 38, 11 July 1839, p. 595.
119 *Proceedings of the Fourth Congress, May 1839*, p. 147.
120 *Ibid.*, pp. 147–8.
121 *Ibid.*, p. 10.
122 Rules enclosed in a letter from John Finch, 31 July 1839, Robert Owen correspondence, letter No. 1135.
123 Letter of John Finch, Liverpool, 8 June 1839, addressed to 'Honoured Father', from 'Your Affectionate Son in Truth and Love', Robert Owen correspondence, letter No. 1108.
124 *The Times*, 11 July 1839.
125 Quoted in *The Co-operator and Anti-Vaccinator*, No. 318, 2 September 1871 (previously *The Manchester Co-operator*).
126 Letter to the director of the National Community Friendly Society, Birmingham, from W. H. Ashurst, 6 July 1839, Robert Owen correspondence, letter No. 1126.
127 Letters of Henry Travis to Robert Owen, 29 August and 5 September 1839, Robert Owen correspondence, letter No. 1151.
128 *New Moral World*, VI, No. 50, 5 October 1839, p. 799; also letter of Robert Owen to the Central Board, 27 September 1839, Robert Owen correspondence, letter No. 1166.
129 *New Moral World*, No. 50, 5 October 1839, pp. 797–8.
130 *Ibid.*, No. 55, 9 November 1839, pp. 870–1.

6

Queenwood, 1839–45

Queenwood was the only community to be officially sponsored by the Owenite movement. Both Orbiston and Ralahine received more attention from contemporary observers and historians, despite the fact that Queenwood survived much longer than either of the communities in Scotland and Ireland. Queenwood now seems improbable, a co-operative fable. But it did exist for six years and one can still tread the ground today and see remnants in a Hampshire copse of the sawn-off lamp standards and the granary cellars of Harmony Hall, the first status building of the co-operative movement.

One of the preoccupations of the Central Board of the Owenites immediately before launching the Queenwood experiment was the publication of the constitution and rules of the Universal Community Society of Rational Religionists, into which both the Association of All Classes of All Nations and the National Community Friendly Society had been fused. Members were to have an equal right of settlement in all future communities, although the first residents to be selected were to be useful producers, irrespective of their financial contributions. Subsequently, all members would be placed on the land, 'and any incumbrances, such as purchase money for the land etc., be speedily paid off'. Any individual sponsored by a branch society for residence in the community was subject to approval by the Central Board. Once in residence, there was to be uniformity of dress and furniture 'consistent with utility'. The ruling on property ownership was emphatic in its communalism: 'The whole land and other property of each and every community . . . and the energies of the members and their families located thereon, shall be held for ever as COMMON PROPERTY, applicable to the objects of the whole society . . .' The governor of the first and any succeeding community was to be given 'full power to direct, manage and control all the operations', until such time as members acquired sufficient knowledge to carry their own responsibilities.

East Tytherley, the parish in which the community was to be

sited, was, until the fourteenth century, a manor in possession of the Crown. In 1335 Edward III granted it to Queen Philippa (hence 'Queenwood') and the manor later passed to Chief Justice Henry Rolle in 1654, in whose family possession it remained until 1801, when Baron Rolle sold it to William Steele Wakeford of Andover for £56,000. The estate then passed into the hands of Francis Bailey in 1822.[1] Isaac Lyon Goldsmid,[2] the other party interested in the purchase, was precluded from acquiring the status of landowner— presumably Goldsmid anticipated Jewish emancipation, as he negotiated the land conveyance in the sole name of Bailey and in 1833, after the passing of the emancipation Act, the property was divided so that Goldsmid acquired Queenwood. Hearing of Owen's success in teaching children, Goldsmid spent some time with Owen to learn something of his methods for use with his own family. Goldsmid and his wife then 'trained and educated a family of eight, as nearly according to the system of New Lanark as a conscientious adherence to the Jewish religion would admit'.[3] East Tytherley manor house was not occupied by the Goldsmids after 1830: it was tenanted until 1854 by General Yates, uncle of Sir Robert Peel. In 1849 Bailey sold his moiety to Sir William Fothergill Cooke, one of the inventors of the electric telegraph, who in turn sold the property to F. G. Dalgety in 1866.[4]

The lease for the intended community included Queenwood farm, of 301 acres, situated astride the Romsey to Broughton road, and comprising thirty-three fields and 26 acres of woodland and 'parts' of East and West Buckholt amounting to 205 acres, with an agreement to use brickfields subject to royalties payable to Goldsmid of 2s 6d per 1,000 bricks.[5] The Buckholts, although in East Tytherley parish, were extraparochial Crown land and free from parish liabilities. A number of other adjacent properties were later acquired during the life of the community—Little Bentley farm in the parish of Mottisfont was taken over during the spring of 1842 on a fourteen-year lease at a rental of £180; Great Bentley was bought by Goldsmid and leased to the community in 1841 for ninety-nine years, but the lease was not executed until 1843, at a rental of £253; Rosehill, the only freehold property of the community, was purchased in 1842 at an auction for £2,900 and let to Thomas Marchant on a ten-year lease at 3 per cent of the purchase price.[6]

The lease for Tytherley was ninety-nine years for 534 acres at an annual rental of £376 (15s per acre). Further deposits, each of

£1,500, would become due in 1846, 1853 and 1860, and the rental would be brought down £50 at each of these dates. Thus for three reductions of £50 the lessees would need to pay £4,500, which at a notional interest rate of 5 per cent would earn £225. With the original £1,000 deposit, the total repayment over the first twenty-two years for 500 acres would be upwards of £15,000, which, expressed at thirty years' purchase, would make the value of Tytherley equivalent to £1 per acre—and this real rent would continue to the end of the ninety-nine-year lease, when the land and buildings would revert to the landlord; subsequently the trustees would in effect have to pay £275 in perpetuity for nothing. It was obvious that Goldsmid had made a better bargain than the Owenites. 'No wonder Sir Isaac Lyon Goldsmid, to accomplish his purpose, became a Socialist of Branch A1 London and paid £5 of his 2 shillings weekly subscriptions in advance.'[7] The trustees, Finch, Clegg and Green, had no power under the terms of the lease to allow any resident to engage an apprentice on terms by which he could acquire a settlement under the poor laws. There were also covenants against building without Goldsmid's permission.

The trustees took possession of the estate on 1 October 1839. With negligible resources at their disposal, the first residents arriving at Tytherley during October had to face considerable problems of estate management. It was hardly reassuring to them that Owen had resigned as governor on the grounds that the community was ill-conceived and premature. It is difficult to explain his dramatic turning away from his followers. After severing his connections with New Lanark in 1824 and retiring from business life, Owen seemed incapable of meeting and dealing with crucial issues. Time after time he evaded taking responsibility as decisive leader when the Owenite movement needed a firm hand in a crisis. All the qualities of good management which he demonstrated at New Lanark were somehow inverted, and he could never keep his plans within the bounds of available finance. When faced with intolerable situations which he had largely perpetrated by imbuing his followers with grandiose images of community life, Owen could always excuse himself from final responsibility and action by pointing out that his disciples had not followed his precepts. In the last resort he could claim that only he could visualise the new society, and on these almost logical positivist terms no one could prove him wrong.

Hence the responsibilities of governing Queenwood rested on John

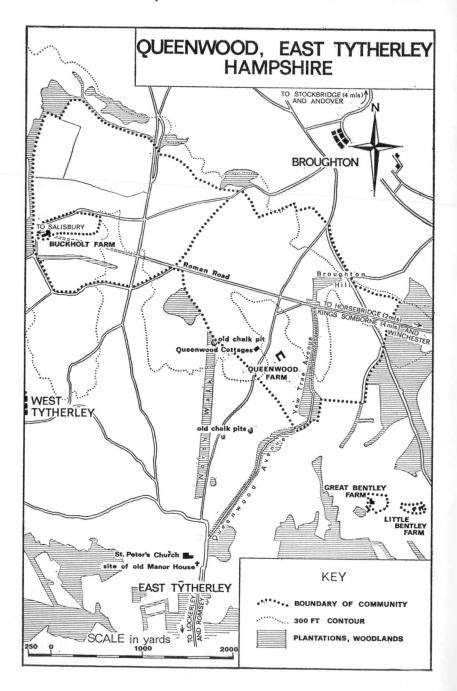

QUEENWOOD, EAST TYTHERLEY
HAMPSHIRE

TO STOCKBRIDGE (4 mls)
AND ANDOVER

N

BROUGHTON

TO SALISBURY

BUCKHOLT FARM

Roman Road

Broughton
Hill

TO HORSEBRIDGE (2 mls)
KINGS SOMBORNE (4 mls) AND
WINCHESTER

old chalk pit
Queenwood Cottages

QUEENWOOD
FARM

Yew Tree Avenue

WEST
TYTHERLEY

Northern Walk

old chalk pits

Queenwood Avenue

GREAT BENTLEY
FARM

LITTLE
BENTLEY
FARM

St. Peter's Church
site of old Manor House

EAST TYTHERLEY

TO LOCKERLEY
AND ROMSEY

SCALE in yards

250 0   1000   2000

KEY

•••••••• BOUNDARY OF COMMUNITY

·········· 300 FT CONTOUR

▨▨▨ PLANTATIONS, WOODLANDS

Finch and his two nominal assistants, who were to act as managers of the community under the general control of the Central Board. Finch was soon appointed acting-governor, with Aldam as director of agricultural operations. The new Owenite calendar was not sufficient to solve pressing problems of farm management; the handful of colonists, who were sponsored mainly from the branches in the industrial north, had scant experience of farm labouring, nor were they satisfied with the dilapidated farm buildings which had at first to serve as their accommodation.

An early editorial in the *New Moral World* discussed matters of community finance and argued against plans for a joint stock company; capital should be drawn from the members only, and if the experiment was successful 'capital will flow in, perhaps faster than it can be properly used . . . until then [there was] no hope of appealing to general public'.[8] John Finch suggested that branches should collect bones in depots to be called 'bone houses' and then charter a ship to transport them from Liverpool to Southampton. He argued that bones would be in their raw state and would be cheaper than the inferior alternative of bone dust—bones cost £6 to £7 per ton, and the expense of collection and carriage of the 150 tons needed for Tytherley would be around £3 per ton—hence there would be a saving of between £400 and £500 over the purchase of local bone meal.[9] Heaton Aldam later argued that the expense of carting bones to Tytherley was prohibitive; it would be better for branches to sell bones locally and send the proceeds to Tytherley; manure could then be purchased at Romsey.[10]

Along with woodash, urine, soot, rags and wool, bones had been used as a fertiliser since medieval times. Walter Blith, in the seventeenth century, esteemed them highly as a soil improver: 'Marrow bones, or fish bones, horn or shavings of horn . . . have a wonderful virtue in them.'[11] By the eighteenth century farmers around Sheffield had tested the value of bone meal, the discovery being attributed to the refuse heaps of scrap bones not required for bone-handled cutlery.[12]

Lord Ernle held that farmers at the time of the accession of Queen Victoria were aware of many fertilising agents (soot, salt, shoddy, hoofs, horns and bones) and such substances as marl clay, lime and chalk to counteract deficiencies of particular soils. But the early Victorian farmer knew little or nothing about nitrates, potash, sulphates or Peruvian guano. The first cargo of guano was consigned to a Liverpool merchant in 1835, but in 1841 it was so little known that only 1,700 tons were imported: six years later the figure was 220,000 tons. Bones were being imported extensively before this period of dramatic increase in the demand for guano—the value of imports rose from £14,000 in 1823 to over £25,000 in 1837. Originally the bones were broken down into small pieces by hammering but it was discovered that their effectiveness as a fertiliser was vastly increased by grinding them to a coarse meal. By the early 1840s bone-crushers were being powered by steam.[13] John Finch would in all probability have been aware of the importation of guano into Liverpool and one can surmise that, having discussed the subject of fertilisers with Heaton Aldam, he naturally thought of shipping bones from Liverpool to Southampton. By the mid-nineteenth century many enterprising farmers added guano and phosphates in some form either as crushed bones or as a super-phosphate, which was produced by treating bones with sulphuric acid. The experiments of the soil chemists confirmed the value of these practices by the best farmers.

The members of the Central Board looked to Owen for guidance over the affairs at Tytherley, but Owen was hardly forthcoming: Henry Travis informed him in December that they wanted to 'go ahead' immediately with a school, 'and we much want your advice on the subject'.[14] Finch also wanted to see Owen to discuss the former's proposed laws for Tytherley and discuss the erection of industrial buildings there.[15]

A letter was published in December from Owen, who had lately been to New Lanark, where he had met the builder and the architect of the New Lanark mill extensions, Mr Haddow and Mr Whitwell—'the only three persons [the third being Owen] in existence who have anything like accurate knowledge of what is required in practice to constitute a community such as I have always had in contemplation'.[16]

The recruitment of additional residents for Tytherley was surprisingly difficult considering the long years of enthusiastic expectation of community life: a meeting of Bradford branch for nominating a member for residence was convened, 'but not an individual could be found so circumstanced as to allow him to be put in nomination'.[17]

Owen was not present at a meeting of Finch, Green, Fleming, Hobson, Bewley and Travis which was called to select residents for

Tytherley. It was decided to arrange a draft of members, but 'of law-making we did nothing—there we sat—and it was purgatory from 2 till 9'.[18] The point of dispute was over the disposition of the expected surplus production which would accrue at Tytherley. The original laws had made the community liable to pay over any surplus to the Central Board to enable further communities to be established. Finch and Green insisted, however, 'that the community when established shall be the property of its inhabitants when they have paid back to the Society all the money it has cost'— otherwise the residents would remain 'bondmen' for ever, and that would destroy initiative.

Oldham branch reported in November that it had a town grocery and provision shop in Yorkshire Street which was run by the branch members. There was a letter from James Lowe of Salford announcing that four members were going to Tytherley by the 6 a.m. train accompanied by others from Bolton. The party included Charles Hill (carpenter), George Crompton (as ploughman), James Gillow (as agricultural labourer), J. Flitcroft (bricklayer)—'they are all fine active young men of the most reputable character'.[19] An editorial announced a need for joiners.[20] Other new members arriving at Tytherley at the end of 1839 included one Clarkson (labourer) and Hill (sawyer), both from Bradford, and a Mr and Mrs McMillan from Greenwich. On 4 December a foundation stone was laid for a building which was to act as dormitory for eighteen residents until the erection of a permanent community block, when the sleeping quarters would become a workshop.[21]

By the end of November wheat was being sown, three plough-men had been hired and many local agricultural workers were asking for jobs at the prevailing wage of 9s per week. Finch calculated that the capital cost of the community on the basis of 500 residents would be £14,000, and if each male resident could bring £50 with him the whole capital outlay could be repaid within seven years, provided the residents worked nine hours daily. He asked new members to bring tools, bedding and a stock of clothes; all articles brought into community would be valued and treated as subscriptions. A railway itinerary was given for those travelling to Tytherley: Liverpool to Birmingham, 17s, Birmingham to London, 20s, London to Basingstoke, 6s, and then by coach to Wallop, 7s. Advice was given on the use of local building materials—cottages could be constructed of chalk, which could be reduced to mortar and then mixed with straw; chalk was used by the locals because bricks were expensive.[22]

The expenditure on Tytherley up to 31 December 1839 was £3,378. There were 3,310 paying members, but only 783 were contributing to community funds (198, London A1; 97, Salford; 71, Birmingham; 53, Leeds; all other branches had fewer than fifty subscribers each). Community subscriptions amounted to £1,171 (£500, London; £209, Liverpool; £52, Leeds). Salford was the branch with the largest subscribed membership (440), followed by London A1 with 302.[23]

Even before the advent of the Tytherley community, the Owenites came under attack in the learned journals. The *Quarterly Review* was particularly venomous: Owenism was a great and spreading sect professing atheism, the irresponsibility of man, appetite and self-indulgence, community of goods and the abolition of marriage. These doctrines were 'not only incompatible with *our* political constitution, moral obligations and religious duties, but, we will boldly assert, wholly irreconcilable with any system whatsoever of human society'.[24] By early 1840 the invective against the Owenites was even more virulent. 'Every foul sink of doctrine which has been opened of late years in this country, all run together into this grand cloaca of Owenism. The present is a sewer avowedly drained off from the lucubrations of the Benthamites.'[25] The *Quarterly Review* feared the effectiveness of Owenite propaganda—350 towns were being regularly visited, and it was estimated that upwards of 100,000 attended Owenite lectures. A foreign observer considered the Owenites numbered as many as 500,000 by 1840.[26]

By 1840 the term 'socialist' was becoming synonymous with 'Owenite', but there was still confusion between the terms 'socialism' and 'communism'. A correspondent could write to the *New Moral World* in 1838 maintaining that he was a socialist, but not an Owenite: 'By Socialism, I understand, simply and only, a system of equality of general property in which the lands, houses, implements, food are ... shared in common.' Hence Methodists could be socialists and keep their doctrine, whereas Owenism was 'Socialism mixed up with exclusiveness; and that the exclusiveness of no religion'.[27] But by 1840 the distinction, if any, between socialism and Owenism was lost. W. L. Sargant, writing over twenty years later on Orbiston, and explaining the demise of that community, said: 'All hopes were founded on a system of socialism, not on that of communism: that is, on the adoption of the greatest possible amount of co-operation short of community of property.'[28]

The Hampshire community soon drew opprobrium from the clergy. The presentation of Robert Owen to the young Queen was thought to be reprehensible, and the Tories lost no time in making political capital out of Lord Melbourne's indiscretion. In Birmingham citizens were encouraged to sign a petition pleading for a proscribing of socialist activities as a menace to established society, religious belief and morality. The enclave of socialists in Hampshire was referred to during a debate in the House of Lords on 24 January 1840, when the Bishop of Exeter presented a petition signed by 4,000 citizens of Birmingham praying that socialism be put down. Further petitions from Cheltenham, Dudley and Worcester[29] were presented by the Bishop of Exeter on 30 January, and he drew the attention of Lord Normanby, the Home Secretary, to the incongruity of an avowed socialist holding office under the Crown as superintendent registrar of Birmingham. The bishop queried whether William Pare, the person concerned, was still acting as registrar. Lord Normanby replied that Pare acted as vice-president of the Rational Society from May 1838 to May 1839, but he had resigned that position and had ceased to be an officer or have any connection with the Society from June 1839. The bishop pressed his charges. In a speech on 4 February he warned that the aim of socialism 'was by the diffusion of its doctrines to destroy the existing laws and institutions of this country'. A Birmingham clergyman had said:

> Socialism is not much increasing; but infidelity is, through the socialist missionaries, the bitterest enemies of revelation and all established institutions. Their publications are fifty or sixty in number; no fewer than half-a-million were dispersed in May last, and the circulation of them is greatly increasing.[30]

The Bishop of Exeter then gave an account of the opening of the Huddersfield hall of science in November 1839, when G. A. Fleming contended he would prove God was either a fool or a liar. The petition from Birmingham referred to a lecture at the local social institution at which the socialists had claimed to have the support of men in civic office in the town. Lord Normanby thought it unwise to proscribe socialism, but he noted 'the instances of the foundation of communities and other facts relating to the subject' which had come to light in various parts of the country. Where these

activities had not come to the notice of the government it was the
bounden duty of local justices and others to notify the authorities
of anything they might think worthy of representation. Lord Normanby pointed out that William Pare had been recommended by
two-thirds of the ninety poor law guardians in Birmingham when
he was appointed registrar. Lord Melbourne felt that if the Lords
addressed the Queen on the need for an inquiry into the activities
of the socialists, undue publicity would be given to the sect. 'He
[Lord Melbourne] had been charged with giving a great impulse
to the system by introducing Mr Owen at court, but their Lordships
were now going to introduce him a second time, and in a way that
would give him and his sect a much greater and stronger encouragement.' Indeed, the socialists themselves would welcome such an
inquiry, argued Lord Melbourne. The Archbishop of Canterbury
then referred the activities of the socialists—'The missionaries sent
forth by the socialists were, he understood, for the most part active
and intelligent, and very often educated persons . . .' These socialists
denied the truth of future rewards and punishments and they played
on human passion—a community of woman had been advocated.

The Home Secretary did, however, accede to the demands of the
bishops that Pare be dismissed, and notice of a motion appeared in
the votes of the House of Lords: 'That a humble address be presented to Her Majesty praying that Her Majesty will be graciously
pleased to give directions that the appointment of Mr Pare the
Registrar of Births and Marriages in the town of Birmingham, be
forthwith cancelled.'

William Pare on his part submitted a personal petition to the
House of Lords, remonstrating against the accusations laid against
him. He denied having used the same rooms for both his socialist
activities and his duties as registrar, or of having placed a socialist
sign and inscription over the door. He admitted holding office for
two years in a 'Society of socialists' and having acted as vice-president for one year, but he had resigned that position in May 1839.
The offending lectures referred to in the debate, asserted Pare,
were in fact given by a surgeon dentist of Birmingham on the
subjects of free will and philosophical necessity, but public lectures
were also held in the rooms, which the Birmingham socialists frequently hired out to other bodies and for other functions. On one
occasion Pare had been invited to chair a discussion between a Mr
Murphy and a Reverend Mr Foye on the subject of 'The Personality

of the Deity' but the audience had been warned that no expressions of approbation or disapprobation would be allowed lest the decorum of the meeting should be disturbed. In the course of the debate in question Mr Murphy had expressly stated that the socialists were not connected with or answerable for his personal doctrines or arguments. Pare added that John Brindley, a schoolmaster and well known as a lecturer antagonistic to phrenology and socialism, had challenged Murphy to a second public discussion on the same subject with Pare again as chairman, and on the conclusion of that debate Pare had stated his opinion that such discussions had better be discontinued, as they would lead to useless speculations and angry disputations. Pare concluded his petition by stating that members of the National Community Friendly Sociey held various religious opinions; Pare himself was no longer a member of any socialist society and was not responsible for the different religious opinions published or privately entertained by individual socialists.

The petition was of no avail, and Pare was compelled to resign from his post as registrar, not because of the truth of the Bishop of Exeter's assertions but on the general grounds that an avowed socialist should not hold an office of profit under the Crown. Thenceforth Pare used personal initials and oblique references to hide his identity in his involvement with Queenwood community and the Rational Society. This anonymity was not really necessary after 1842, when he left Birmingham for good and gave up his public commitments in the borough. Many leading citizens, including G. F. Muntz, G. Edmonds, the clerk of the peace, the town clerk and councillors, attended Pare's farewell dinner. George Edmonds said he had known Pare since childhood; they had both attended the same church for many years and 'if Mr Pare had come to erroneous opinions on religious matters, there could be no doubt he had adopted them from conscientious convictions'. Another speaker acclaimed Pare as the most active reformer in Birmingham after Thomas Attwood.

In the bewildering range of his public activities, Pare found no difficulty in reconciling his interest in political and civic reform with his dedication to co-operation. Unlike Robert Owen, he was sympathetic to the Chartists; perhaps they could be won over to the co-operative cause. Pare never thought in terms of rival movements; he could support any genuine claim for social improvement, whatever the agency. Robert Owen, during the last thirty years of his life, was virtually unemployed and something of a liability to his disciples. Pare, on the other hand, could pursue a successful career as a railway statist and later as a manufacturer without one whit losing his business sense or his enthusiasm for co-operation. Nor is there any evidence of him ever falling foul of his fellow co-operators. He was blessed with an equable disposition rarely found among zealous reformers. John Finch, Isaac Ironside, E. T. Craig and G. J. Holyoake were all rather prickly characters and tended to crankiness. Rank-and-file co-operators, as well as their leaders, held Pare in high regard, and Holyoake thought of him as the true successor to Owen. Always even-tempered without becoming a bore, Pare's enthusiastic claims were always for co-operation, never for himself. In any period of difficulty for the co-operative movement he offered his services freely and often with considerable financial sacrifice. This ready availability and unstinted support from a successful businessman was unique during the pre-Rochdale era. The other Owenites included many who were self-educated, but few who had achieved any success in the capitalist world. John Finch was a flourishing iron merchant, but his bonnet buzzed with too many bees. Co-operation had to wait until the third quarter of the nineteenth century to gain the support of reformers with the qualities of William Pare. His counterparts were J. M. Ludlow and Vansittart Neale; perhaps we can also see something of Pare in the communitarian visions and land settlement experiments of Thomas Hughes. Before leaving Birmingham, Pare had visited the Hampshire community, but he could hardly have expected that he would be called upon in 1842 as the only person who could resolve the utter confusion and impending bankruptcy of the colony.

Having become the subject of a debate in the House of Lords, the Owenites were hounded particularly by John Brindley, the clergyman from Chester. The Home Secretary felt obliged to take notice of information[31] submitted to him on the activities of the Owenite meetings at the Tytherley community and throughout the country. Lord Normanby acknowledged in a letter of 8 February 1840 to the Bishop of Exeter, 'Five cases transmitted with reference to the address recently voted to Her Majesty respecting the proceedings of the Socialists . . . The informant in each case appears to be John Brindley . . .'[33]

Tytherley was first brought under official scrutiny when the Duke of Wellington (a Hampshire landlord) wrote to William Steele Tomkins as J.P. for the district on 1 February 1840:

> A petition to the House of Lords had been communicated to me to which your name is signed, stating that a Socialist Institution has been established in the neighbourhood of Broughton ... As J.P. it is your duty to take notice of the proceedings, more particularly as this association has announced and published that it has objects inconsistent with the doctrines of the Christian religion, with the duty of Christians, with morality; with the very existence of Society. Notice any breach of law. Draw the attention of the influential classes of the people in your neighbourhood to the danger and mischief ... induce them to refrain from giving their attendance upon its meetings, and to persuade their servants and dependents to follow their example.[33]

Further details of activities at Tytherley were submitted to the Home Secretary from a Broughton clergyman. The Home Office replied:

> I acknowledge letter of the 20th enclosing a written paper said to be the substance of a lecture delivered at East Tytherley on Sunday 18 January by a person named Finch (governor of Queenwood Community) and to have been written down as the lecture was heard by a poor man residing in the Parish of Broughton and which was attested by yourself—Lord Normanby requests to know whether the person ... can prove as a witness that those very words or any entire passages were spoken by Finch ... and whether you yourself can give any evidence on that subject. If the person ... can prove not merely the *substance* of the lecture but entire passages, Lord Normanby desires that he may go before Mr Tomkins the Magistrate and give him information as to the words which he heard ...
>
> Lord Normanby directs me to inform you, with reference to that part of your letter in which you state that you have been informed, that persons after attending the lectures leave Queenwood on a Sunday in a tumultuous manner, and that a public house in the Village of Broughton is filled by some of the party who return home afterwards in a state of intoxication and that thirty-nine men and women have been counted in one group, who have stopped near the house of a farmer, shouting and crying 'Queenwood Socialists for ever'—such illegal proceedings ought to be put down by the magistrates in the neighbourhood.[34]

The local justice of the peace at Broughton was written to on the same date:

> I am in receipt of 21st enclosing two Reports of Lectures on February 2nd and 9th with No. 69 of the *New Moral World* and I am to request you to inform his Lordship whether the Reporter will be able to prove as a witness the correctness of these reports and the language therein attributed to the person named Finch.

...His Lordship desires any legal proof of the blasphemous language used by Finch on Sunday 26 January...Lord Normanby only awaits for further information before he submits the case to the Law Officers of the Crown for their opinion...[35]

More widespread attacks on socialism by pamphleteers continued throughout 1840. Scurrilous personal accusations were levied and dark insinuations made of general depravity: the editor of the *New Moral World* was charged with seducing his wife's sister.[36] If there were no checks on conduct, said one critic, we would all become depraved.[37] Perhaps the most antagonistic and protracted attacks on socialism were to be found in the issues of *The Anti-Socialist Gazette and Christian Advocate* published from October 1841 to December 1842 and edited by Brindley. The Owenites responded with a battery of propaganda—pamphlets,[38] published debates, tracts, lectures, meetings and missionary activities. Socialist plans were to be carried out in strict compliance with the laws of the State; taxes would be paid to the State as required. 'The Socialists take no part in the agitation for political changes, as they are convinced that permanent prosperity and happiness can be gradually secured for every human being under any form of government which recognises the principle of toleration.'[39] The property of members would be made common 'only so far as they voluntarily place the same at the disposal of the Society'. Lloyd Jones affirmed that the Owenites 'were not of the poorest—were indeed, as a rule, the most provident . . .'[40]

John Finch had arrived at Tytherley on 1 January 1840, when he 'found nearly all the members here that were in the first draft: six children, three women, eighteen men. The main inconvenience was having some members in lodgings at Broughton.'[41] The *New Moral World* described the activities of the colonists. In February 1840 they were engaged in digging, gardening, manuring and ploughing, excavating clay for bricks, and attending evening classes in dancing, drawing, grammar, geography, elocution, agriculture and music. A mathematics class met daily from 5.00 to 6.30 a.m. Presents for Queenwood poured in from sympathisers from all over the country; narcissus bulbs, trees and seeds were sent from the 'Inmates of Community Cottage, Vauxhall Road, Birmingham'. A Mr Spindle and his wife went to Tytherley as ploughman and dairywoman: 'We took the opportunity of sending some more trees; and I added two hives of bees, and a tombstone under which I hope to rest.'[42]

Tytherley residents did not cut themselves off from their Hampshire neighbours:

> Last Sunday morning I and one or two more of our friends went over to our parish church in which we had a pew belonging to our farm ... Mr Phillips, our worthy pastor ... appeared pleased with his new guests, and he preached us a good social sermon.[43]

A 'community cart' was on its way to Tytherley from Sheffield in May 1840 with the words 'Queenwood Community' painted on its side.[44] But it was reported that insufficient care was taken over nominating members for the community from the branches. Too many had arrived before accommodation was available and without any immediate prospect of employment.

The London branches wanted to send ordinary members as representatives to the forthcoming Co-operative Congress rather than missionaries, as this would lead to self-election and would emulate the Methodist conferences, which were 'annual gatherings of reverends and doctors'; nor should stationed lecturers be restricted to teaching at a single branch—'the consequence of which may tend to that narrow and sectarian system which we as Rational Religionists ought with vigilance to endeavour to prevent'.[45]

At the May 1840 congress, which met at Leeds, a member of the Central Board stated that residents at Tytherley had been drafted there primarily to put the farms in order, but the majority of members had wanted more rapid community settlement because it was thought this would encourage more contributions. These expectations had been thwarted through diversion of funds to the building of halls of science. Owen argued that the Central Board should not draft any who could not earn their maintenance. They would find it cheaper to hire labour than to use that of members who were willing but unskilled.[46] He further suggested the completion of community arrangements before any further admission of residents. 'As, however, with their present limited means, they could not do this, they must exercise the strictest vigilance in all they did.'

C. F. Green, as a member of the supervising council for Tytherley, reported that the management of the community had devolved almost entirely on Finch and Aldam.[47] Green had visited Tytherley frequently and had recently spent five weeks there with his family, but he had to report unrest among the residents—some of whom were unaware of their position *vis-à-vis* the governor. Finch had ordered a strict embargo on alcoholic drink, and this had caused annoyance.

The cost of providing a dining hall and sleeping apartments at Tytherley was given in an auditor's report to Congress as £352. There were other expenses for fitting up a blacksmith's shop and enlarging stables, also £5 for 'fitting up a shop at Broughton'. G. A. Fleming reminded Congress delegates of the history of the Society: 'They began without a shilling. They rented a small office in a somewhat incommodious situation, and the desk and few chairs with which it was furnished were obtained upon credit.'[48]

Doctrinal matters were brought to the attention of Congress delegates, and an address containing an official declaration of the Principles of the Universal Community Society was adopted. Home colonies were advocated 'to accommodate eight distinct classes in the present generation; or one class, superior to any existing class, in the next generation'.[49] Branch A1 in London had adopted a system of examination for membership. A series of specimen questions was listed:

> How do you distinguish the feelings from the convictions? . . . Why is it necessary, in the state of transition between the present state of society and that proposed by the Socialists, to make man responsible for his actions in violation of principles which declare him to be irresponsible?[50]

The Owenite creed included the 'Five Fundamental Facts': character is formed by environment, feelings are independent of will, feelings create motive to action called the will, each individual is unique, an infant can become a very inferior or superior person, according to external circumstances. It is scarcely necessary to point out some of the inconsistencies and irrelevancies in the above statement, which purports to contain the basic tenets of Owenite belief. Following on the 'Five Fundamental Facts' were 'Twenty Laws of Human Nature'.[51]

Owen lectured delegates on his plan for a £600,000 community from whose towers 'would be reflected at night, by powerful apparatus, the new koniophostic light, which would brilliantly illuminate its whole square'.[52] According to Owen, the experiment at Tytherley would serve as a normal school 'in which the working classes would be properly fitted to carry out more enlarged and perfect arrangements'. Fleming brought Owen's listeners down to earth by agreeing with the splendid plans, 'but he believed they would all agree with him in thinking the plan was far too extensive for them to adopt at Tytherley . . .' Owen remained in the clouds; he disparaged the efforts of his followers but gave them no example of active leadership. All community plans and experiments were uninformed; in effect Owen had given up hope for the present generation. Some indication of his repudiation of personal involvement in previous phases of Owenite activity is given in a report in the *New Moral World* of a lecture he gave at Nottingham:

> 'Were you in any way connected with Orbiston?' Answer—'No.' 'Was Gray's Inn Labour Exchange of your contrivance?' Answer—'No.' 'Was New Harmony an attempt to carry out your principles?' Answer—'My principles have never been carried out.' 'He [Owen] then commenced his lecture, produced plans for the building of houses and every requisite for a Community, in which capitalists may invest their money, and realise more than 100 per cent.'[53]

As an indication of the political innocence of the Owenites, Congress was told that the Central Board had applied to 'The "Board of Commissioners for the issue of Exchequer Bills for Public Works" for a loan of £20,000, in aid of establishment in Hampshire which, however, was not acceded to'.

In the course of a debate on property rights, C. F. Green argued that communal property should belong to the residents rather than to the Society as a whole. Alexander Campbell argued that this would lead back 'to the old individual system'; he preferred a system which the residents could draw a ratable surplus which would be personally disposable.

C. F. Green replaced Finch as acting governor during the summer of 1840. Heaton Aldam resigned on the grounds that 'it was absurd to place a man at the head of any department, if he was not allowed to manage . . .' Hunt of A1 branch supported Aldam's views that manual labour could be hired cheaply, 'but the labour of a manager or director, was of a very different nature, and was comparatively scarce and valuable'.[54] The debate over the comparative merits of hired versus residents' labour was to continue throughout the life of the community. Some years after the collapse of the Hampshire community, a working class observer wrote that Queenwood was 'an attempt to convert skilled artisans, used to good wages, into agriculturalists upon bad land; and to satisfy them with agricultural labourers' fare, and no money wages'.[55]

Rigby and Fleming urged during the summer of 1840:

> that as one means of securing the success of the estate at Tytherley, neither the Governor nor the Central Board, singly, or conjointly, shall take any

steps for the erection of buildings, the establishment of trades, or occupations, or for any other purpose, *until* they have the pecuniary means for so doing in their possession.[56]

The selection of suitable trades for Tytherley was a subject of continuous discussion during 1840. A motion was carried that printing should be established, 'but that the Educational Establishment shall take preference of all industrial arrangements except agriculture unless special funds be subscribed for any other purpose'.[57] Watchmaking had been recommended by Coventry branch as early as August 1839 as a suitable activity for Tytherley, but since it was a highly skilled trade it was hardly an appropriate means of providing work for any unemployed members. Owen, however, thought watchmaking suitable, as the community would be wise to confine its operations to light trades requiring little capital; but the articles so produced must be of the highest quality, 'like that obtained by the Shakers and Rappites'. It would be fruitless, argued Owen (quite sensibly) to produce staple commodities until the community had acquired sufficient capital to install the best machines and to purchase raw materials in bulk.[58] In the event, watchmaking was undertaken at Queenwood, and an example of its workmanship is extant at the Robert Owen Museum at Newtown, Montgomeryshire, with the subscription 'This watch was made by the Queenwood Community and was the property of Dr John Watts of Manchester'. On the watch there is an inscription, 'Queenwood Community No. 2'.

When C. F. Green was appointed acting governor there were fifty-seven residents at Tytherley but there was an exodus during July and August 1840 as a result of stringent domestic economies. Weekly maintenance costs were brought down to 7s weekly, so that only twelve adults and seven children remained—Messrs Sprague, Crompton, Swindells, Hill, Flitcroft, H. Smith, Gillow, J. Smith, and four of their spouses. James Rigby of Leeds replaced Green as acting governor in October 1840.[59] John Finch wrote at this time from Liverpool that he was going to a fancy dress ball as a threefold character: 'King of Teetotallers, John the Baptist and Bishop of the New Moral World'.[60]

John Brindley, the anti-socialist cleric, gained access to letters written by Tytherley residents.[61] J. Armitage wrote to his brother and sister on 12 April 1840, 'It is more like a workhouse than anything else . . . I never will come to Sheffield again, I should be so laughed at.' Armitage did, however, return to Sheffield, whence he wrote on 9 August 1840 giving details of others who had left Tytherley, including a watchmaker, upholsterer, sawyer, joiner and several gardeners. The quality of the food at Tytherley was coarse: 'Mr Green sent the good bacon to London to be sold, we had to eat the bad.' Money was wasted—£10 was spent on tea urns and china-ware. Brindley also printed an extract from one of Armitage's correspondents:

> Sectarian Socialism is fairly exploded. Men cannot be made COMMUNITY ANIMALS ... The individual competitive strife without any association is only civilized barbarianism, while communityism is yet more mischievous and vicious delusion.[62]

Isaac Ironside called Brindley 'this parson's scavenger'.[63] Armitage had subscribed but 20s to the community fund, and his fellow members at Sheffield branch had paid the outstanding balance of £49. Ironside refuted the accusations concerning the poor quality of food—he had visited Tytherley in April 1840, when he found 'the bread was quite sweet, though brown, like all farmhouse bread'.

Socialism had spread its doctrine, but there was little financial support for the realisation of its plans. The funds spent during the first eighteen months at Queenwood were mainly collected during 1837–38 and early 1839. Just when funds were sorely needed there was apathy in the branches, brought about by depressed trade, which in turn affected community contributions; but the main cause of lack of funds was 'the want of some provision for an immediate benefit to members contributing these funds, and a definite period being fixed at which the member who has now completed his share could claim from the Directors all the benefits which the Society can confer upon residents in community'.[64] The Central Board permitted the withdrawal of two-thirds of each member's contribution to the community fund, which

> will give to the Community Fund the character of a Savings Bank, and to some extent also that of a benefit, sick and burial fund, for all those members who are now subscribing to such institutions, but who may be also desirous of securing, through one series of payments, the advantage of a residence in community.[65]

Petitions to the House of Commons from several towns for an inquiry into socialism were submitted during March 1841, including one from 'inhabitants of Rochdale, members of the Universal Society of Rational Religionists, commonly called Socialists', with 299 signatories.[66]

By the sixth congress, which met in Manchester during May 1841, support from many branches was weakening. Lectures on the advantages of community and verbal reports of Queenwood were all that the local members could aspire to; something more tangible was required to maintain the enthusiasm of the thousands of supporters who had hardly any chance of getting to Queenwood.[67]

Rigby, the acting governor, reported on affairs at Queenwood, where he 'found much discontent and disorder existed. No party was to blame for anything which had been done: it all arose from a desire to carry out their objects quicker, than practical measures, to ensure success, could be put into operation'. He had investigated and found many debts—the community 'owed for bone dust; they owed the landlord for timber; there was an account for the poor rates; and another for bricks and slates; there was the china account and one due to Mr Smith'.[68] Nevertheless, better relationships prevailed between the community and the parish—Rigby had been invited to become a nominee for the local board of guardians. He immediately wrote to London and was advised to accept, but because he did not fulfil the minimum residence qualification of twelve months he had to withdraw. However, the local churchwardens proposed he should take the chair, 'and he actually sat as chairman of the meeting in the parish church of Tytherley. At that meeting they raised the clerk's salary 10s a year.[69]

G. A. Fleming wanted clarification of Owen's position in connection with the newly formed Home Colonisation Society and whether it and Congress could go their separate ways. William Galpin explained to Congress that he had been called to a meeting of the Central Board during the previous August to consider differences between Owen and his colleagues on the Central Board. After several days of discussion, Owen

> declared that he went forth alone to the world for the prosecution of larger plans than the Central Board contemplated. He (Mr Galpin), together with Mr Travis and several other gentlemen in London, formed the provisional Committee of an association, called the Home Colonisation Society.[70]

Lloyd Jones later commented *à propos* the infusion of the Home Colonisation Society:

> Practically, the Home Colonisation Society superseded the old society, by

causing such alteration to be made in its constitution as reduced it to a subordinate position, in which it became a follower and helper with little or no power of initiation in anything that required the spending of money, or that involved the safety of what was, or what might be, invested.[71]

The Tytherley residents demanded a fuller say in the management of the community and in the election of the officials and governor, but Owen and the Central Board would not concede it because they felt they would be endangering the interests of the large loan holders of the Home Colonisation Society: 'The first step was to stop the Society, acting through its branches, from sending residents at will.'[72]

The officials at the time of the sixth congress were W. Galpin and J. Finch, vice-presidents; Henry Travis, general secretary. The members of the Central Board were Hunt, Braby, Newall, Hurlstone, Corss (all of London), Hobson (Leeds), T. Brown (Manchester), W. Russell (Glasgow) and C. Brown (Bristol). Whittaker and Ironside were the official auditors. Robert Owen was still nominal governor of Queenwood, with James Rigby acting governor. The six Central Board lecturers—Connard, Simpkins, Farn, Knight, Watts, Clarke—had their paid appointments terminated at the end of three months. The seven social missionaries included Lloyd Jones, John Ellis, Alexander Campbell, Charles Southwell, W. Spiers, R. Buchanan, Joseph Smith; and the five 'stationed lecturers' were J. N. Bailey, H. Jeffery, F. Hollick, T. S. Mackintosh, G. J. Holyoake.[73]

Finch and Fleming were instructed to make arrangements for 'accommodation . . . for such persons as are willing to pay for their support at Queenwood, they conforming to the rules of the establishment for such parties'. Owen answered a query from Finch as to the extent of the liability of subscribers to the effect that 'according to the Act of Parliament they were only answerable for the amount of their subscriptions'. The secretary then mentioned the letters patent Act of 1837, which allowed limited liability. Owen then acceded that it would be desirable to acquire such letters patent and a suitable motion was passed.

The methods of keeping accounts were shown to be perfunctory in a report to the sixth congress.[74] From October 1839 to mid-April 1840 £6,580 had been spent on Tytherley, of which £6,081 had been advanced by the Community Society. There were fifteen adult and five child residents maintained at an average weekly cost of 7s 1d per head, including one shilling pocket money. It was quite apparent from the account that the farming activities could not be made fully self-supporting. Methods of book-keeping needed much improvement. The reporter recommended:

> I submit that a set of books should be opened by someone perfectly competent to the task, upon the system of double entry, in which the bookkeeper should be thoroughly instructed; and that there be the most complete analysis of receipts and expenditure, so as to enable the officers of the Society... to have the fullest opportunities of ascertaining the progress, or otherwise, which is being made in the several departments of industry, and, consequently, the utility of persevering in a certain line of conduct, or altering it to meet circumstances as they arise.[75]

A balance sheet was submitted as at 4 April 1841. A fictitious asset of £2,000 for 'increased value of Farm say £100 p.a.', calculated 'at ordinary rate of estimating the result of manure and labour expended on a farm', was not sufficient, however, to balance liabilities, which exceeded assets by £533. Nor was there any allowance for depreciation of assets.

The delegates at the sixth congress issued several addresses, including one in the nature of an appeal to the annual congress of the Journeymen Steam Engine and Machine-makers' Society: 'Capital alone is now required by us. Lend us, then, such sums as you can conveniently spare... It is the safest and best investment of your funds that can be made.'[76] But the Journeymen Steam Engine Makers were not forthcoming.[77]

A foundation stone was laid on 30 August 1841 at Tytherley by Robert Owen for a building which was to be named Harmony Hall and which was to take up such a disproportionate share of the declining contributions to the Society's funds. Within the foundation stone was a cavity encasing a copper box safeguarding a selection of Owenite publications for the benefit of posterity.[78] Accommodation in the building was designed on a lavish scale and the facilities would include piped water, private bedrooms, classrooms, library, lecture rooms, offices, dining room. Owen acclaimed:

> I have named our new Establishment 'Economy' and the new Parish 'Harmony'. The Crown land is not in Tytherley or Broughton parish; and it must form a Parish by itself. It will be then 'Economy in the Parish of Harmony, Hants'.[79]

The denomination 'Economy' was soon dropped and the building and community was generally referred to as 'Harmony Hall'.

Anti-socialist propaganda continued unabated during 1841. A cautionary tale was told of 'Sudden death of a Young Woman on her way to hear the Socialists'.[80] A Mary and Fanny Light of Red-lynch intended to walk nine or ten miles to hear a Sunday lecture at Queenwood but within a mile and a half of the community Mary Light said ' "How giddy I feel," and she instantly fell to the ground, breathed only twice, and was taken up a corpse.' Previously she had been in good health, 'but in an evil hour on the Friday evening, she agreed . . . that, as they had heard much talk about the Socialists, they would go on Sunday to hear, that they might judge for themselves'. The coroner's verdict was 'Died by visitation of God'.

A prospectus was issued in January 1842 for floating a new Home Colonisation Company with a capital of £1 million in £50 shares 'to establish colonies in Great Britain and Ireland'.[81] During the same month a baby born in community was named by Owen 'Primo Communist Flitcroft, or the first born in Community': 'It is a lovely child and all are fond of it.'[82]

Owen and Hansom, the architect of Harmony Hall, arrived at Queenwood in February to prepare for the installation of heating and ventilating apparatus.[83] The layout of the hall consisted of three ranges of apartments: the ground floor included library and dining rooms, with sleeping apartments for single persons on the second storey above the library; the central block contained offices and store rooms; the third section contained schoolrooms and baths. A Miss C. Hagen, a member of a Quaker family from Derby, was appointed by Owen to superintend the children in the community.

William Pare visited the community in March in order to inspect the accounts.[84] Depreciation appeared for the first time as an item in the balance sheet ended March 1842, but only for the general fund. The community fund showed a debit balance of £2,171; loans from the Home Colonisation Society amounted to £9,100, subscriptions to £4,921 and general loans to £2,674.

In April 1842 a list of branches with halls of science included Liverpool, Manchester, Sheffield, Stockport, Macclesfield, Huddersfield, Halifax, Glasgow, Worcester and Bristol, and there were social institutions at A1 London, Lambeth, Finsbury, Hyde, Failsworth, Leicester, Darlington, Bradford, Birmingham and Paisley.[85] There was total accommodation for 21,000, and although few premises were as yet owned by the Society, thirteen branches were registered as places of worship, nine had day schools and twelve had Sunday schools. But John Finch had to report that lectures were discontinued at the Liverpool Hall of Science because of arrears of rent to the building society, which had decided to dispose of the premises. The trade depression was affecting other branches apart from Liverpool. Hyde reported factory stoppages and the closure of its Owenite school:

> Vehicles are passing through the streets continually, conveying goods, or boxes of provisions to Liverpool. The people are going to America by sixty or more per week... Some of our best members are gone, others are going, and others in despair because they have not the means to go.[86]

Owen's twenty-seventh address to disciples in April 1842 emulated the Chartists by announcing a nine-point 'Charter of the Rational System for the transition state from pandemonium to the paradise'.[87] The programme of reform would include graduated property tax, the abolition of all other taxes, full employment, 'sound practical national education', full liberty, the 'adoption of home-made national money, based on nationally secured property and the credit of the nation', home colonisation, judicious laws of divorce, and a change-over from inferior circumstances. An address from the seventh congress was submitted to the Chartists:

> You frighten the educated and wealthy by asking for the means of unlimited power before you have the knowledge how to use it... what would be of real service would be a wise education and permanent employment.

The trade unions were also appealed to: 'Why cannot you use funds to employ?' Steady habits of industriousness would be achieved if the trade unions would see the advantage to be derived from settling workers on the land.

The seventh congress had met at Harmony Hall and was attended by twenty-four delegates, who were warned by Owen that 'They must abandon, at once, all the vulgar notions of aristocracy and democracy.' Owen was looking forward to uniting the Home Colonisation Society with the Rational Society (from the 1842 congress the title of the Rational Religionists was foreshortened thus). A manifesto was issued to the 'Government and Peoples of the Nations most advanced towards civilisation, first year of the Millenium, May, 1842, old style' and signed by Robert Owen, 'Governor of the First Normal School to form Rational Communities'.[88] The manifesto was appended 'Harmony' and from then onwards the community was referred to as Harmony Hall, despite a reiteration from Owen that the title should be 'Harmony'. 'I suggest that entire establishment be denominated 'Harmony'—as it would be wrong to continue with Queenwood, which was merely name of home farm.'[89] The local Press maintained a conspiracy of silence over Harmony Hall.[90] As late as 1842 the *Hampshire Chronicle* misreported by quoting from the *Standard* newspaper: 'Mr Owen has taken his leave for ever of Rose Hall, [*sic*] Hants., for America.'[91] There was also a report of Hansom lecturing at the Reading Mechanics' Institute, but no mention of him being the architect of Harmony Hall.[92] But a Southampton minister of religion, the Rev. James Crabb, published a tract because he was 'alarmed at increase of Owenite Socialism in this town and neighbourhood'.[93] There was no mention of Harmony Hall, which was referred to obliquely as the 'Social Colony'. Southampton mechanics and artisans, 'yes, and even amongst those who are highly respectable in life', were warned against being deluded by plausible offers of residence at Harmony Hall.

Brindley had paid three visits to Tytherley by July 1842—'that manifestation of melancholy folly, the Socialist community in Hampshire'. He found that the local villagers abhorred socialism, but 'amongst the youth of both sexes, however, it made its ravages', and socialist workmen engaged on building operations for Harmony Hall had lodged with villagers, 'so that scarcely a house has been without its infidel inmate'.[94]

Having set up the Home Colonisation Society to achieve some measure of independence from the Central Board, Owen's wide appeal for funds was answered by a mere handful of personal friends, including Bate and Galpin. Other potential loan subscribers may have been deterred by the insecurity of capital in a situation where a £1 shareholder had as much say at congress as a large investor. The £15,000 of loans from the Home Colonisation Society were put at the personal disposal of Owen, with a proviso that he should not over-spend these resources. Building operations on Harmony Hall, however, had to be brought to a halt when Owen could locate no new source of loans. William Pare, as auditor, stated that £18,000 had been expended to 31 March 1842.[95] By August a special congress had to be convened to determine the future of Harmony Hall, as 'It had however very recently become known that the Governor of Harmony had been proceeding with practical operations faster than the means of the society would warrant...'[96] There were outstanding tradesmen's accounts of over £2,000, apart from the Home Colonisation Society loans.

Owen had previously resigned as governor in July 1842, 'solely that new energies may be given to some of your friends possessing many valuable qualities to direct in some of your departments, but who are unequal in other respects to the task which is now to be performed'. Congress, on seeking a replacement governor, would 'have to do that which its President has always had to do, work a perfect system with imperfect agents, and make the necessary allowances for the difficulties of their situation'.[97] Owen added a rider that he had not met with a single person with the right qualities to direct so difficult a task. He did, however, accept full personal responsibility for extending the scale of operations by incorporating the Great and Little Bentley properties and thus exhausting the Society's funds. He attempted to justify his actions by pointing out that the properties concerned were in the market and the general economic distress impelled him to pursue arrangements to provide extra employment. Unfortunately, when measures were almost completed to receive extra residents, 'the funds in hand were expended'. Owen then concluded his report as late governor: 'Who, with such objects in view, and in sight of the very means to commence these great and glorious measures for the benefit of the present generation and of all future generations, could stop in the progress of these proceedings?' In such fashion did Owen explain the damaging consequences of his governorship of Harmony Hall and agree to vacate his kingdom and offices as president of the Rational Society and editor of the *New Moral World*.

Several delegates at the special congress were prepared to excuse Owen's irresponsibility over money.[98] Alexander Campbell exclaimed that 'All he had failed in was a paltry matter of finance'. Another delegate thought that one might just as well have expected that Napoleon at the height of his military career would be stopped by a failure in the supply of ammunition. Hunt commented that he felt convinced that 'nothing short of an inexhaustible treasury could keep pace with the expenditure of the Governor... There is one thing, however, and only one thing, which capital can never be brought to do, and that is to commit suicide', and this was precisely what it would do if capitalists supported home colonies, for the ultimate object in establishing these colonies is not only the emancipation of labour from the thraldom of capital but the ushering into existence a new order of capitalists in the persons of the capitalists themselves, who would be the more formidable because in their persons labour and capital would be united...All this the capitalists are fully sensible of, and they would advance their money to retard rather than hasten what to them would be a calamity.

Work on Harmony Hall was therefore suspended from July 1842, and severe retrenchment was ordered to enable the community to survive. The Central Board was to remove from London to Harmony Hall.[99] An advertisement was published for a principal for the community school, but it was stated the emoluments would be 'very moderate'. A committee was detailed to prepare a frugal dietary table, and each resident was to decide what he could dispense with without interfering with health and comfort: 'The majority already abstain from animal food...'[100] Compelling debts were resolved after interviews with creditors, and temporary financial accommodation was secured. In this impasse in the fortunes of the Society a new leader was sought to replace Owen. The position was virtually untenable, and drastic economies would merely postpone the nemesis. There was only one possible choice for a new director of the community: a man of balanced views, businesslike capacities, and of sufficient courage—William Pare. He was not eager to take over the task, but once having made the decision, he removed his growing family to Harmony and sold £500 worth of railway shares, which he forthwith contributed to the funds of the Society. John Finch was once more made nominal governor and president of the Society, but he would accede to this only upon the understanding that affairs should be administered by Pare, 'an old and well-tried friend to the cause...who was so situated as not to be able to accept any office from the Society at present...'

Plans were laid to raise another £5,000 to pay off pressing tradesmen's claims, to continue farming operations, and establish a school. The confidence of the colonists was regained; there was a fresh influx of residents throughout the autumn of 1842, and the immediate debts were gradually cleared, but at the cost of further economies in the standard of living of the colonists, which was reduced almost to a workhouse level of diet. Dissension became rife, and Pare found it difficult to reconcile the warring factions: in the words of the *New Moral World*, 'each member thought himself as much the Governor as was the Governor'. Despite the privations of the colonists, the building operations, which had been interrupted during the summer of 1842, were renewed without any reduction in quality of workmanship or materials. The building so far had cost £15,000, and included such refinements as a miniature railway for transporting meals from the kitchen. Part of the accommodation at Harmony Hall was designed for use as a boarding school, which had attracted thirty-five fee-paying pupils by May 1843 at £25 a year including board and clothing; the other pupils attending were children of the residents.

G. J. Holyoake visited Harmony Hall in 1842, as did Alexander Somerville. Both were impressed with the kitchen:

> I can say nothing adequately descriptive of the fittings of the kitchen... the London architect who superintended the erection of the whole, said that there were very few kitchens so completely and extensively fitted up as it in London.[101]

Somerville found brickmakers and lime burners and nine plough teams at work, with a reservoir being built to conserve liquid manure. He was favourably impressed, and pondered that the gentry

> would do well to show the working population, that good farming is not necessarily an adjunct of Socialism; else, perhaps, the working population will think the doctrines of those who pay best, employ most, and produce the greatest abundance of crops, are the best doctrines...[102]

G. A. Fleming repeated the justification of Owenite plans and explained away their innocuity in the pages of a new working class journal:

> Their general adoption seems to offer the only speedy and effectual method of warding off a violent revolution and rendering these classes contented or comfortable, while at the same time it will effect this result without, in any degree, trenching upon the existing rights and privileges of any class of the community.[103]

He went on to speculate that the Rational Society

> seems originally to have been established on the ruins of the 'Co-operative Societies' which were so rife in this country from 1829–34 ... We believe that there are still a few of them in existence, but, with the exception of one at Huddersfield, their condition is anything but satisfactory.

The co-operative society at Huddersfield had a large grocery store, 'and profits which are periodically divided... employment in various kinds of manufactured goods is given to the members of the Society, which are afterwards sold, and the profits added to the common stock.'[104]

Partly to discourage members of the Rational Society from subscribing to friendly societies ('many of our friends are members and subscribe their incomes to the various societies of Odd Fellows, Druids, Foresters, etc. and which are chiefly held in public houses . . .'),[105] and partly as an insurance against the vicissitudes of the old immoral world in which most members were fated to remain, a Rational Sick and Burial Society was formed at Manchester Hall of Science in February 1842, after a query from Leeds whether the sick and burial provisions of the original Owenite Society were still in existence. The Manchester branch invited delegates from other branches in July 1842 and drew up a code of laws. By 30 November there were ten branches with 300 members enrolled, and by the end of 1843 the Manchester Rational Sick Society was reporting applications for membership 'from Odd Fellows etc.'.[106] The friendly societies had too much show and surplices. 'In most of them the contributions, though apparently moderate, are so increased by fines and other indirect expenses, as to render the cost too great for the present depressed condition of the working men',[107] whereas the Rational Sick Society had no processions and no feasts. On the other hand, the friendly societies demonstrated that the working classes were prepared, and able, to contribute large capital sums when sufficiently motivated—Alexander Campbell gave an instance of the extent of friendly society funds:

> One of the sections of Oddfellows during one quarter had not less than 12,000 tramp tickets out, at an average cost of 1s. 6d. daily, thus making the expense of supporting tramps £900 per day, for that one section only.[108]

Engels thought in 1842 that the English working class movement fell into two sections:

> The Chartists are theoretically the more backward, the less developed, but they are genuine proletarians all over . . . The Socialists are more far-seeing, propose practical remedies against distress, but, proceeding originally from the bourgeoisie, are for this reason unable to amalgamate completely with the working class.[109]

But in retrospect Engels contradicted his earlier observation of the social origins of the Owenites.

> In order to find people who dared to use their own intellectual faculties with regard to religious matters, you had to go amongst the uneducated,

the great unwashed, as they were called, the working people, especially Owenite socialists.[110]

An example of the personal background and social convictions of an unnamed Owenite from Stockport was given in a letter received by Isaac Ironside in February 1843:

> I cannot pay any subscription to the Community Fund, nor to the Branch, though I am the oldest member ... I should be glad of any situation as book-keeper, warehouseman, overlooker of power looms, either in England or abroad. I was nine months in France in 1830 ... Nearly seventeen years ago, I attended Detrosier's chapel, when (though short of 16) I got the Protestant faith shifted from me ... Later took up reading Carlile, then Short Time Question; heard Owen at the National Regeneration Society and I and several other reformers open Branch No. 3 on 28 May 1837. Then aged 25 and elected President and had paid three years into a building club and built five single houses and was weaving on six looms and wife on four looms. Doing well. But in preaching Socialism had become notorious and have worked out of town for past year. Lost job. Hoping to sell some of my houses.[111]

Walker, the ironfounder, of Sheffield, asked Isaac Ironside in 1843 for his opinion on Harmony Hall. Ironside advised him to write to General Yates (uncle of Robert Peel), who owned a neighbouring estate:

> Mr Walker did so, and read him the General's reply, which was, that the members were a very model and orderly set of people, and an example to the neighbourhood; that they employed the poor people in the works with which they were proceeding, and they had reduced the poor-rates very considerably.[112]

John Finch resigned as president of the Rational Society and governor of Harmony Hall in April 1843, 'with the earnest hope that the only individual capable of filling this important situation at the present interesting crisis, may be unanimously re-elected'. Finch pointed out that all the pressing commitments had been met and looked forward to seeing the experiment self-supporting by the end of 1843. He therefore felt free to journey to America to proclaim tidings of social redemption.

Robert Owen renewed his homilies to the residents of Harmony Hall during the summer of 1843 in the form of letters, exhorting them to greater individual production, and to press ahead with completing the school premises. The residents made an oblique retort in an address to the Rational Society, emphasising that their relationships were harmonious and they were imbued with the principles of the social system; moreover, they intimated, 'we feel it our duty to acknowledge the confidence we have in our present Governor, as a man of business habits, and also of kindly feeling, for which we highly esteem him . . .'

Owen was guilty of deviousness at the 1843 congress, when he was pressed over his attitude towards increased democracy. John Buxton questioned Owen on the matter and Owen diverted the veiled accusation by saying, 'It is uncertain who the President may be.' Buxton snapped back:

> Not at all; you declared to the deputation, of which I was a member, that no other individual was capable of taking the Presidency of this Society . . . and it was solely for this reason that I, and those who thought with me, agreed to relinquish, for the present, the elective form of government with respect to the appointment of the Central Board.[113]

J. Smith, another delegate, complained that 'many in the branches had not confidence in the operations of Mr Owen now . . . He (Mr Owen) had been used to carry on such extensive operations, that he could not work on a small scale; he could not keep within the means placed at his disposal'.[114] Notwithstanding the criticisms, Owen was then elected president and governor in place of John Finch, but Pare continued to run the affairs of Harmony Hall as deputy governor. A statistical return to the 1843 congress included data from twenty-seven branches only; many branches reported shrinking membership. A1 branch subscriptions to the community fund, for instance, had fallen from 105 to 69 between May 1842 and May 1843. Lambeth branch had sent a party of twenty-five emigrants to the United States with a fund of £2,000. Lloyd Jones thought that the apathy in the branches dated from the time of dismissal of social missionaries: at worst, branches had 'split up into phrenological committees, festival committees and dancing committees'.[115]

William Pare reported to congress that the Harmony Hall residents numbered thirty adults and fifteen children at the time he had taken over as governor in July 1842. By May 1843 there were forty-five members and twenty-five children; sixteen members were employed in the house department, twelve in the gardens and farm, four were farm tradesmen and eight were builders. In all, 720 acres were in cultivation at Queenwood, Buckholt and Little Bentley farms. There had been a small experiment with spade cultivation to show how far horsepower could be eliminated, but it was yet too early to see the results. Dr Oestreicher, a German, had been recently appointed principal of the school, which had sixty-one pupils in attendance, of whom thirty-five were fee-paying. It was hoped soon to bring the school within the reach of all the members in the branches of the Rational Society. A portion of the pupils' timetable included industrial pursuits 'suited to age, capacity and interest'. A small steam engine was being erected for pumping water for Harmony Hall, and it was recommended that the trades of printing and of manufacturing agricultural implements were suitable for the community. Pare was realistic in his assessment that hired labour was more productive on the farms than that of the colonists. The cost of accommodating the residents had been further reduced to 5s 7d per head per week, of which 4s 7d was for food. A congress delegate who had been in the community since 1839 complained that he was still having to wear the same suit of clothes. There is evidence that the inmates had some uniformity of apparel, as an advertisement in the *New Moral World* invited tenders for supplying clothing for Harmony Hall—'olive broad cloth, woollen velveteens, Orleans cloth for women's dresses etc.'.[116]

To make the community viable, it was planned to increase the establishment to 300 colonists, and to provide an industrial school for 1,000 so that school fees could be reduced to £12 or £13 a year and thus make it possible to accept children from the working classes. Harmony Hall was not deemed suitable for an industrial college, but it was to be regarded as an indispensable preliminary to such an establishment; it had been designed as a normal school for instructing those destined to manage future communities.

The pilot, however, was not to be dropped, and it was affirmed that 'the general superintendence of the operation at Harmony has been again confided to the long-tried friend who has conducted them since last Special Congress'. William Pare was not eager to continue in office, but he agreed to remain, on the expressed wishes of Congress and of Owen. The task facing Pare was unenviable. Harmony Hall was draining all sources of funds; £11,667 had been remitted in cash during the year ending March 1843, and the community could show only £214 as surplus proceeds from the labours of the forty-three residents and hired labourers on more than 700 cultivated acres of the estate, which had been extended by incorporating Rosehill and Little Bentley farm. The situation was deteriorating rapidly. After four years of endeavour, the *per capita* cost of settling a member in the community was in the region of £700, and that with a standard of living, if not of physical accommodation, much below that of the old immoral world—at least for those colonists who were skilled artisans and perforce were reduced to the level of agricultural labourers. It says much for their loyalty and idealism that Harmony Hall survived as long as it did. Despite these drastic economies, the Central Board recommended the occupation of Great Bentley farm and that Rosehill should not only be a boarding house with superior accommodation for paying guests[117] but should also continue to accommodate the Central Board until sufficient funds were available to remove the office to London. Owen took up permanent residence at Rosehill.

Another muck-raking attack on Harmony Hall by an ex-resident was published in 1843. R. J. Reid, A.M., the author, had been a teacher in the Aberdeen area and had met Owen in Scotland in December 1842.[118] Reid had asked if he could visit Queenwood; the request was granted on condition that Reid should apply to the Central Board 'for something to do during my stay'. He had now seen 'the loathsome reptile Owenism' and was completely disillusioned. He was also severely critical of the regimen at Harmony Hall and instanced that a subsoil plough had been acquired from Smith of Deanston, but the plough was 'rusting and rotting in the farm yard, the Socialists, silly fellows, hardly knowing what a subsoil plough is, or how to use it'.[119] Nor were the members honest— a slate for stolen articles was kept hanging in the dining room: 'If my gun be not forthcoming I'll publish the theft in the *New Moral World* and if that be not enough in the leading London newspapers.'[120] There was peculation of subscriptions: a poor widow had claimed the contributions of her late husband as shown on his community card, but the Central Board had notified her that the sums had been paid into a sinking fund.[121]

Lloyd Jones gave a different version of Reid's association with the community.[122] Reid had applied at the end of 1842 for a post as accountant and offered to become a 'working bee'. He was tried out as a book-keeper, said Lloyd Jones, and was found to be unsuitable but he had stayed on at Harmony at communal expense, which had given him an opportunity of hunting through the residents' correspondence before finally being asked to leave.

Almost to coincide with the anniversary of the special congress called in August 1842 to rescue Harmony Hall from Owen's extravagant expenditure, Owen addressed his followers on 3 August 1843 on the significance of Harmony Hall and his future plans for the community. 'It is intended that these eight inscriptions should contain knowledge, on the outside of this building, of more real value to the human race than is now to be found within all the universities of the world.' The next stage in the development of the community would be an appeal, for an additional £25,000 for the 'educational and industrial college at Harmony'.[123] Great Bentley farm, of 297 acres, was taken over in October 1843.[124]

A 'tradesman of the Midland Counties' spent some days at Harmony Hall and described the living quarters.[125] Each section of the Hall had a separate staircase

> and when once upstairs, there is no possibility of communicating with persons on any other section without going down again. This precaution shows how thoroughly the Founder of the System understands human nature—it likewise shows that virtue is the end and sin of his system.

There were water taps and waste pipes installed in each of the bedrooms and the garden wall had a cavity section, with flues for hot air.

A teaching timetable is extant for October 1843.[126] The school hours were from 7 a.m. to 5 p.m., Monday to Saturday. The class lists included J. Galpin, R. Galpin, J. Rigby, C. Allsop, T. Allsop, Caroline Pare, Emma Pare and Charlotte Galpin, and the regimen comprised geography, geometry, drawing, gardening, French, arithmetic, natural history, dictation with music, history, letters, and a weekly evening lecture. However, the organisation of the school left much to be desired; Frederick Bate, who had contributed his considerable fortune to the Home Colonisation Society, wrote to Pare in April 1843 and instanced:

> Mr Atkinson's invitation to live at Harmony I cannot accept; it would drive me mad to witness the rudeness, the utmost rudeness and disorder prevailing in the schools and be at the same time told that all is excellence and beauty...

Bate had at this time the unenviable task of acting as treasurer to the Society. He ended his letter: 'I have not waited upon any of the creditors, for I have not sufficient nerve to see them without money...'

A Stockport member pondered the difficulty of supporting Harmony Hall when the halls of science were a drain on funds: 'Are we to stay in the town with the building, an infatuated sect of religionists! . . . Are we going to settle down with some kind of sectarianism?'[127] Manchester branch community fund contributions dropped sharply from 1843, and Liverpool sold its hall of science to the Oddfellows for £4,600. Rochdale branch was also a victim of the general malaise. 'Our good friends at Rochdale were in a much worse position. They were inclined to abandon their meeting place, dispose of the furniture and dissolve as a branch.'[128]

The anti-corn law agitation and the ten hour movement were at their height during 1844, and the vice-president of the Rational Society conceded 'it is doubtful to what degree any exertion of ours could arrest the popular torrent in either of these directions and turn it towards communities. Both of the parties named have an immediate object in view . . . Both have large funds and influential classes at their back . . .'[129] A more effective policy for the Rational Society would be to train for a future missionary campaign when the corn law agitation subsided, and to make Queenwood self-supporting:

> Let it be always remembered by every professed friend of the Rational System of Society, that failure at Harmony would not only entail severe loss and suffering on the best supporters of the cause but be felt as a heavy blow and great discouragement . . . it would put back the index hand on the dial of progress at least half a century in this country, and would inevitably scatter beyond the possibility of recall the members and friends of the Society, whose fate, as an association, is now indissolubly linked with that of the Harmony establishment.[130]

Stringency became even more necessary during 1844. During the year ending 30 March 1844 barely £385 had been subscribed to the community fund, but over the same period £3,016 had been expended at Harmony Hall. Pare reported to congress that twenty-nine members and their children had been admitted to the Community since the previous congress in 1843. These admittances did not, however, lead to any increase in the number of colonists, as there was a steady exodus back to the old immoral world. The nominal roll stood at seventy-five by May 1844 (forty-seven members and twenty-eight children), a considerable falling-off from the figure of November 1843. Pare pointed out tartly that more could be achieved if members were more willing to carry out directions. He had to admit that the experiments in spade cultivation were not decisively favourable; to accomplish sufficient deepening of the subsoil by the spade would require more capital than by any other method.

Congress was eager to bring in more residents to Harmony Hall, But Pare raised a lone protest against the shallow economics of the proposal. He would prefer to see a larger balance in the bank before acting on the recommendation. The hired labourers were generally more efficient as farm workers than the residents and, however much the costs of accommodation were pruned, it was still cheaper to pay a wage of, say 9s to an outsider than to recruit male residents and have the responsibility of maintaining their families. Moreover, claimed Pare, it was good public relations to employ local labour, for he believed that this had forestalled any expression of bad feeling in the locality towards Harmony Hall. Certainly there had been no evidence of open antagonism to the community over the five years since its inception. Pare took the members to task for not being amenable to discipline over timekeeping; he had instructed them to write on a slate the duties performed during the day, but it was not being done. Alexander Campbell thought that the labour of each member should be valued by the governor, but Pare thought this would lead to acrimony.

Pare was once again reappointed acting governor by the 1844 congress. Owen addressed the delegates regarding the decision. 'He [Owen] could not accept office in connection with the Society unless he could have full authority, without reference to previous resolutions of congress.' (There had been growing criticism from working class members of the superior arrangements of Owen's high table at Rosehill.) Owen was refused *carte blanche*, and congress agreed 'that the resignation of Mr Owen, as President of the Society, be accepted'. David Vines was elected president on 27 May, but did not attend congress until the following day, when he stated that he would not hold office unless Owen was president and that further- more he could not accept the presidency as long as Owen was alive. John Buxton, the delegate from Manchester, commented, 'It was too bad to try to force Mr Owen upon them in such a way.' The resignation of Vines from his short-lived tenure as governor was then accepted, but 'at this stage of the proceedings, considerable excitement prevailed and it was thought advisable to adjourn for a time'.[131] On the resumption of the meeting of congress, Buxton proposed John Finch for president, but no seconder was forthcom- ing. Eventually Buxton was himself proposed and elected as president and governor, receiving nine votes in favour and five against. The estrangement which had been growing between Owen with his middle class sympathisers from the Home Colonisation Society, and the working class members from the branches of the Rational Society, was now an open schism. Owen refused to lead the Society except on his own terms, and he withdrew from Harmony Hall, taking with him his supporters, David Vines, Lloyd Jones, Frederick Bate and Alexander Campbell. Pare also refused to continue in office as acting governor under Buxton. In the standard biography of Robert Owen by Frank Podmore there is no mention of the fact that Pare acted as governor of Queenwood for a longer and more crucial period than did Owen himself, or indeed of any of the succession of governors between 1839 and 1842—including Finch, C. F. Green, and Rigby. This omission of Pare from the fullest published account of Harmony Hall has undoubtedly diminished the importance accorded to his role in the history of Owenism.

Appended to the 1844 congress reports were accounts showing liabilities of £30,000, for which subscriptions had been raised of £5,500, general loans of £8,600, and Home Colonisation loans of £13,400. A table of cost of food per head gave a figure of 4s 11d per head as the weekly bill during April 1844. It was abundantly clear that Harmony Hall was fast approaching bankruptcy; £2,000 was due for rent arrears and other bills; also outstanding were the current rent and taxes for the year, which amounted to over £1,100. Income from school fees, boarders and visitors had been £1,300 during the year, but the outgoings under these headings far exceeded income.

A 'ways and means' account for the forthcoming year included as income school fees at £1,500, 'shares, etc.' at £3,500—which could hardly be treated as an item of income—and £1,534 for expected sale of wheat. On the expenditure side of the account 'rent due' was £538, current rent £809, tithes £160, poor rate £120, window tax £47, insurance £31, and cost of food £2,000. There was little hope that the branches would, or could, subscribe a sufficient sum to clear these debts, and the new Central Board, 'composed of working men entirely', could not expect much support from those personal friends of Owen who had previously come to his aid under the auspices of the Home Colonisation Society. Vines echoed the view of Owen that government by working men would be impossible: 'Now what idea can a working man have of government? ... he is a creature of circumstances and how can he acquire ideas of governing as a working man? If they did, they would cease to be working men.' Buxton put on a brave front in an address at Manchester in July 1844: 'With property estimated at upwards of £30,000, and trades-men's liabilities not amounting to one twentieth of that sum, we have no fear of insolvency.' He looked forward to a co-operative store being set up in the community and being able to dispense with hired labour—fifteen agricultural workers had been discharged since congress. Buxton reported that the principal of the Harmony Hall school would not agree to his salary of £200 being cancelled, and he had therefore been asked to withdraw, and was to be replaced by a branch member of the Rational Society, who would give his services without payment. In August 1844 Owen announced his departure for America and told the 600 sitting down to his farewell breakfast, 'One difficulty to be removed at Harmony was the strong desire for democracy.'[132] Stringency followed stringency during the remaining months of 1844 and early 1845. Parsimony found pinch-penny opportunities in such concoctions as 'community mocha', a synthetic coffee made from wheat grain. The 'pater' of Ham Com-mon Concordium visited Harmony Hall and noted that the com-munity was providing its own tea and coffee, 'and if the latter has not the exquisite flavour of the Arabian bean, yet I can assure my readers that, to an individual devoted to the success of this place, a cup of Community Mocha is a pleasant beverage'.[133] Meals became more sparing than ever, and the inmates developed vege-tarian tastes, not necessarily by conviction. Nevertheless, the library at Harmony Hall had nearly 1,400 volumes and 'the whole expense of it has been borne by the members having agreed to refrain from drawing any of the weekly allowance money for some time to come'.[134]

Doubts were increasingly expressed during 1845, not only concern-ing Harmony Hall but also about the socialist solution generally:

> A co-operative colony of socialists, wanting the means for developing their peculiar views, would only establish the truth of combination for produc-ing wealth, and this has been already done in a very superior manner by a colony of the most ridiculous fanatics ... The great desideratum would still be wanting—the means of proving the superiority of Socialism over all other systems.[135]

Buxton gave a forthright and penetrating address to the Society on 8 March 1845, tracing the ten years of the Owenite movement: some had argued that Owenites should, like the White Quakers, have withdrawn from society and have ignored public opinion initially, using any surplus wealth from community pursuits to send forth missionaries. It had been asserted that the Owenite lecturers were men of 'one idea' culled from the *New Moral World*: 'This is an error: few working men read so much, and none studied more, according to their means, than did the pioneers of Socialism.'[138] Buxton analysed the Owenites into three classes: those who joined the movement as a social diversion, those who aimed at subversion of all institutions, and those whose sights were kept on the object of community.

Pare pleaded for the repayment of his loan, still outstanding after two years, 'to enable me to make a new home for myself and family, having broken up my old one to serve the Society'. In a letter of February 1845 he repeated his plea, and felt obliged to remove one of his daughters from the school at Harmony Hall. He reminded the Central Board that he had raised the £500 by selling his railway shares. He also referred to his tenure as acting governor from 1842 to 1844, and pointed out there was no active Central Board between the 1842 special congress and the congress of the following year. During the interim period the only authority had been Finch, who had assembled the heads of departments within the community but had not kept any minutes or records. Pare thought that Owen had felt forced to retire in 1844 on account of jealousies raised by working class members.

Reports from the branches were as discouraging as the affairs at Harmony Hall. John Finch wrote from Liverpool on 9 April 1845, 'We have a neat little meeting room at a small rent, and no paid lecturer, for the purpose of enabling us to do more for Harmony.'

The cost of accommodation at Harmony Hall was estimated at £13 3*s* per head per year in 1845, based on an amortisation rate of 6 per cent on premises valued at £14,800 and the use of £2,500 furniture depreciating at 15 per cent annually. Hence the sum of £13 3*s* was really a notional rent. In addition, there was board and clothing and the members' weekly personal pocket allowance of one shilling. The annual cost of residence was therefore £37 9*s* 6*d* per head. Quite obviously, the productive capacity of the residents could not cover their upkeep, let alone provide a surplus: £126 allowance money was owing to members; only two of the original residents remained in May 1845, including Swindells, who claimed

£13 allowance money owing.[137] An assessment of potential income from the farming activities of the community in May 1845 observed that money had been lost through insufficient capital improvements, manuring, livestock, and seed. Total rent and taxes due was £1,002 and interest payments £800.[138]

By March 1845 there were debit balances of 6s 10d in the general fund of the Rational Society and £145 in the community fund. Over the entire period of subscriptions to the community, the Central Board, A1 branch and Salford had between them contributed £5,116 out of a total of £8,892.[139] By the time of the 1845 congress, loans had amounted to £24,496, of which £14,348 came from the Home Colonisation Society. In all, there were loans from 359 individuals and thirty-nine societies. Total income from farming activities between 1839 and 1844 had amounted to barely £4,900.

The congress of May 1845, attended by only twelve delegates, was confronted with pressing claims and could offer no solution to the impending insolvency. The inevitable dismemberment came during the following months, with the colonists leaving Harmony Hall one by one. There was much less recrimination than might have been expected: the collapse of the new moral world was not made a source of bitterness, but rather of continuing aspiration. The promised land had eluded the colonists through their lack of organisation, but it would come to future generations. Some of the innate honesty and incomprehension of this band of idealists is seen in a postscript by a member: 'There were receipts for sums amounting to £14,000 advanced by the Home Colonisation Society entered in a 6d pocket-book—and many of them in pencil.'[140]

Goldsmid was pressing for payment of arrears of rent and local tradesmen for settlement of their bills. Congress delegates 'had now discovered that mere changes in policy will not place the affairs of Harmony upon a sure and solid basis: something more was required to be done, or it was clear the Society could not long retain possession of the property.' The estimated value of the property was £25,676, with liabilities £39,915, leaving a deficit of £14,239. A committee of congress was formed to seek a purchaser or tenant for Harmony Hall. A number of claims from ex-residents were submitted to the Central Board—a George Hornsby claimed £71, including allowance money, wages, tools, 'compensation for breaking up house at request of Mr Owen', clothes and 'value of two clocks'.[141]

Conditions at Harmony Hall were precarious: 'We wait as quietly as we can till we know what the Society wills.' An excursion to Stonehenge by forty residents was 'accompanied by a pony and cart with provisions, viz. bread and ham and mocha'.[142] In a report of 22 June the governor was stacking hay and earthing up potatoes; his wife was working in the laundry. The first death in five years of the Community occurred during these last days.

Robert Owen was reported back in England on 13 June, and announced that 'he should be able to do as much good in one year in America as he could do in England in ten'.[143]

Pare estimated that £10,000 would save the situation, and that Harmony Hall could be successful as an agricultural college. The congressional committee decided to advertise Harmony Hall for sale in *The Times* and *New Moral World*, but were in some doubt as to the extent of the individual liability of members and officers of the Society. Ashurst advised that the officers were liable for tradesmen's debts, and as for the liability of members, 'if the question is ever legally agitated, it will end in the Court of Chancery, and from the nature of the case, the number of the parties, and the many changes which have taken place in the law of the Society, a beneficial result could never be worked out for any party'.[144]

A special congress was convened in London on 14 July 1845 attended by twelve delegates, including Campbell, Ironside, Lloyd Jones. A letter from George Smith from Salford was read stating that most members had wanted a working men's community and,

> no mere Agricultural plan with a huge CLUB HOUSE of rich people to devour the produce, and just have enough of workers there (as Russian serfs) to do the drudgery... There is no use in Owen telling us we have 'no experience' in the matter, and further insult us by writing us down as so many asses who can't understand—what he says, are the plainest truths in nature.

Owen returned to America on 20 July.[145]

It was noted that, of the three trustees for the community, John Finch was in America, Clegg was in Todmorden, and C. F. Green had never paid any attention to the affairs of the trust for some years. There also remained some doubt whether these trustees had any legal power, as the trust deed had not been executed. To remedy the situation a resolution was passed that G. Bracher, J. Buxton and F. Bate should be appointed assignees in their place. Pare agreed to act if Bracher declined the office, and in due course Pare thus became an assignee.

Congress adjourned on 23 July and decided to call together creditors for the assigning of claims. In August Ironside and Galpin took over the Bentley estate from the assignees. The *New Moral World* journal was sold to James Hill. Many branches dissolved—London A1, at a meeting on 24 August, 'having stated . . . their inability to carry on the Institution' disposed of their institution, which was described as a 'General Literary and Scientific Institution, John Street'. The social institution at Charlotte Street[146] passed into the hands of Charles Southwell and became known as the Paragon Coffee House. Another general meeting was called at John Street to convert the Owenite Rational Society into a National Land and Building Association.[147] Invitations were sent out with little avail to branch members of the Rational Society to join the new body, which would endeavour to secure Harmony Hall as an industrial school.

The rump of the Owenites published from 30 August 1845 the first issue of *The Moral World* as a replacement for the lost *New Moral World*. The legal position of the affairs of the Rational Society was explained—shareholders and subscribers were liable for full debts contracted with non-shareholders. The sum due to tradesmen, external loan-holders and landlord was about £7,000.

> As long as any of the shareholders have not equally borne their quota of this loss, their individual property is liable to make it up to those who have paid more than their share. We need not point out how plentiful a crop of equity suits there may rise from such seed.[148]

By September it was reported from Harmony Hall, 'The Hall is now nearly empty, the principal residents being those who are required by official connexion with the experiment in its present position.'[149] In November, the prospects were even dimmer:

> The building is only suitable for public purposes; to an individual it would be a burden, and worth no more than its value as old materials. For a County Agricultural College, or a County Asylum, or similar public object, its capabilities are great and peculiar.[150]

G. A. Fleming had written to Owen on 5 October from Avenue Cottage, Queenwood, in which he mentioned that Ashurst and Allsop had guaranteed *The Moral World* for its first eight weeks (the periodical ran to eleven issues, from 30 August to 8 November 1845). As for the community:

> the hall is now entirely cleared and shut up. Next Sunday I believe Messrs Clegg, Finch, Green and the assignees are to have a final consultative meeting...Pare has finally retired from the assignees. Mr Bracher takes his place...Mrs Fleming has been very poorly. My three girls are with Mrs Bugden at Ham Common. John is apprenticed to the printer of the *Moral World* in London—the other two boys are with us here at the Cottage. Rigby is with Pare on the railway.[151]

Harmony Hall was to be auctioned in London on 5 December 1845, but the sale was withheld on the instruction of trustees Finch and Clegg, who maintained that the assignees had no authority to dispose of the property without first having called a meeting of creditors. The estate was described as comprising 534 acres of Queenwood and Buckholt farms, including building 'partly in the Elizabethan style' which would be suitable for an agricultural college for Hampshire. Apart from Harmony Hall, there were detached buildings and a farmhouse with total living accommodation on the estate for 150 persons. Pare wrote to Owen on 14 December 1845 concerning the postponement of the sale of Queenwood, which was 'simply on account of the legal difficulties in the way of winding up. I almost fear the affairs may now get into Chancery ... The ultimate winding up rests with the lessees, Messrs. Clegg, Finch and Green.'[152] The winding up of Harmony Hall made little progress and Pare again wrote to Owen in March 1846, 'I have serious doubts whether or not in the end the lawyers will not swallow all.' Every source of income was cut off; Galpin and Ironside had agreed to purchase the Little Bentley stock and crops, but the money could not be received because the lease could not be assigned without Pare's signature as the attorney of Owen—Ashurst, the solicitor, refused to allow this until his own claims against the Society were paid. Sir Isaac Lyon Goldsmid would have nothing sold from the community farms unless he received half the receipts. Pare added, 'I really think you are doing more good in America than circumstances would permit you to do here just now.' Public opinion was, however, progressing rapidly, 'and will I think progress faster without our direct aid than with it'. Bate, one of the chief contributors to the Home Colonisation Society, died in May 1846, in extreme poverty.

The settlement of affairs remained protracted. As late as May

1846 Buxton wrote to the Central Board, 'About three weeks ago Messrs Finch, Pare, Bracher and myself met, and after a long conversation, not of the most agreeable character, we decided to put the business in train for settlement.' The trustees deemed themselves to be liable for the affairs of the community and, being anxious to protect their interests, they were prepared to deal perfunctorily with Buxton, who was upholding himself as the staunch representative of all those working class members of the Society who had contributed to the community fund. It was agreed to make a list of creditors, but in the interval Finch possessed himself of the key of Harmony Hall and entered with Davis, the farm superintendent, through a window, as the secretary's office was locked and the key kept by Buxton. Davis tried to eject Buxton, who had his thumb dislocated in a scuffle on the stairs. On 8 June Buxton was sufficiently recovered to write that Pare had also been at Harmony Hall for two days and had told him to leave the estate. All the other residents had dispersed. So ended the socialist experiment, apart from Buxton's resistance to eviction.

The obvious weakness at Harmony Hall was financial, but the deeper malaise lay in the confused aim of the experiment—its implicit purpose was to demonstrate that labour, irrespective of whether it was manual, skilled, or managerial, could become so united and rewards be so distributed as to prevent excessive wealth and poverty from remaining a prevailing characteristic of an economic system. Successful operation of a farm, school, or boarding establishment *per se* would not have justified this aim.

Notes

1 *Hampshire Field Club Papers*, 1920, Winchester Public Library. See also leases of 1801 and 1822, and deeds of partition, Bailey and Goldsmid, 1833, 134/5, 136/7, 144/6, Hampshire Record Office.

2 Palmerston had written to Goldsmid in 1838, 'I shall not fail to assure Lord Melbourne how zealously your influence in Hampshire was exerted in favour of myself and my colleague during our south Hampshire contest'. Letter of Palmerston, 28 June 1838, letters written to Sir Isaac Lyon Goldsmid concerning the foundation and early history of the University of London, Mocatta papers, University College, London. These letters concern financial, charitable, agricultural and Jewish affairs. The correspondents include David Ricardo, T. R. Malthus, James Mill, Disraeli, Daniel O'Connell, Brougham, Faraday, Samuel Gurney, the Duke of Kent, Birkbeck, Elizabeth Fry, Robert Owen, and particularly Lord Holland.

3 Robert Owen, *Life of Robert Owen, written by himself*, 1857, 1, p. 150.

4 Sir Isaac Lyon Goldsmid (created baronet in 1841, died 1859) passed his moiety to his heir, Sir Francis, and then in succession to Sir Julian Goldsmid, who sold it to F. G. Dalgety in 1879, in whose family the property had remained to the present day.

5 Schedules of lease at 19 September 1839, Goldsmid, Finch and others. (Schedules of lease at Hampshire County Record Office.)

6 *New Moral World*, XIII, No. 39, 22 March 1845, p. 309.

7 R. J. Reid, *Exposure of Socialism*, 1843, p. 23. The sum of £275, payable annually in perpetuity, was a notional figure derived from foregone interest at 5 per cent on the total £5,500 deposited during the leasehold.

8 *New Moral World*, VI, No. 55, 9 November 1839, p. 871.

9 *Ibid.*, p. 873. See also p. 184 below.

10 *Ibid.*, VII, No. 26, 4 April 1840, p.1218.

11 Walter Blith, *The English Improver, or, a New Survey of Husbandry*, 1649, p. 118.

12 In a York edition of John Evelyn's *Terra* of 1778 it is mentioned, 'At Sheffield it has now become a trade to grind bones for the use of the farmer.' (Quoted in Lord Ernle, *English Farming, Past and Present*, 1961, p. 218.) John Evelyn's *Terra; a Philosophical Discourse of Earth, relating to the Culture and Improvement of it for Vegetation* was first published in 1675. See also *The Observer*, 18 November 1822: 'WAR AND COMMERCE.—It is estimated that more than a million bushels of human and inhuman bones were imported last year from the continent of Europe into the port of Hull. The neighbourhood of Leipsic, Austerlitz, Waterloo, and of all the places where, during the late bloody war, the principal battles were fought, have been swept alike of the bones of the hero and of the horse which he rode. Thus collected from every quarter, they have been shipped to the port of Hull, and thence forwarded to the Yorkshire bone grinders, who have erected steam engines and powerful machinery, for the purpose of reducing them to a granulary state. In this condition they are ... sold to the farmers to manure their lands.

13 J. Allen Ransome, *The Implements of Agriculture*, 1843, includes steam-driven bone crushers in a list of agricultural implements in use in 1843. See C. S. Orwin and E. H. Whetham, *History of British Agriculture, 1846–1914*, 1964, p. 7.

14 Letter of Henry Travis, 6 December 1839, Robert Owen correspondence, letter No. 1194.

15 Letter of John Finch, 5 December 1839, *ibid.*, No. 1198.

16 *New Moral World*, VI, No. 61, 21 December 1839, p. 976.

17 *Ibid.*, 26 October 1839, p. 844.

18 Letter from Henry Travis, 16 November 1839, Robert Owen correspondence, No. 1187.

19 *New Moral World*, VI, No. 58, 30 November 1839, p. 926.

20 *Ibid.*, No. 59, 7 December 1839, pp. 937–8.

21 *Ibid.*, No. 61, 21 December 1839, p. 969.

22 *Ibid.*, VI, No. 56, 16 November 1839, p. 890.

23 *Report of Community Fund, July–December 1839*.

24 *Quarterly Review*, CXXIX, 1839, p. 305.

25 *Ibid.*, CXXX, March 1840, p. 496.

26 Flora Tristan, *Promenades dans Londres*, second edition, 1840, p. 383.
27 Letter of Thomas Steward from Elland, 10 August 1838, in the *New Moral World*, 20 October 1838.
28 W. L. Sargant, *Robert Owen and his Social Philosophy*, 1860, p. 289.
29 From January to March 1840 twenty-six petitions with 4,394 signatures were submitted to the House of Commons against socialism, and in the same period twenty petitions were received, signed by 4,198, in favour of socialism. (*Reports and Papers of the fifth Co-operative Congress, May 1840.*)
30 *The Times*, 5 February 1840.
31 The Home Office did not see socialism as a revolutionary force. 'The bare fact of men calling themselves Socialists holding a meeting, cannot be construed into a breach of the Peace.' (Letter to the Rev. W. H. Bellairs, Edgeley, Stockport, 19 May 1840, Public Record Office, H.O. 41/30: Socialists.)
32 *Ibid.*, H.O. 41/30, letter from Lord Normanby to the bishop of Exeter, 8 February 1840.
33 Newspaper cuttings of Sir George Cooper. (File at Hampshire County Record Office.)
34 Home Office letter to the Rev. D. Tucker, Broughton, Hampshire, 24 February 1840.
35 Home Office letter to Steele Tomkins, Broughton, Hants., 24 February 1840.
36 Rev. J. Mather, 'Socialism exposed', in *Lectures against Socialism, delivered under the direction of London City Mission*, 1840, p. 23.
37 D. Brown, *A Complete Refutation of Principles of Socialism or Owenism*, 1840. See also J. Barker, *Abominations of Socialism*, Newcastle, 1840, and *The Overthrow of Infidel Socialism*, Oldham, n.d., in the Howell collection, Bishopsgate Institute.
38 C. J. Haslam, *Who are the Infidels ... Socialists or Christians?* 1840; 'Junius', *Six Letters on the Theory and Practice of Socialism*, 1840.
39 *Statement submitted to the Marquis of Normanby relative to the Universal Community Society of Rational Religionists by Branch A1*, February 1840, p. 14.
40 Lloyd Jones, *Life, Times and Labours of Robert Owen*, 1890, II, p. 147.
41 *New Moral World*, VII, No. 66, 25 January 1840, pp. 1048-9.
42 *Ibid.*, VII, No. 73, 14 March 1840, p. 1172.
43 *Ibid.*, VII, No. 80, 2 May 1840, p. 1276.
44 *Ibid.*, p. 1286.
45 *London Social Reformer*, I, No. 2, 9 May 1840, pp. 28-9.
46 'Supplement to the report of the fifth congress, May 1840,' *New Moral World*, VII, No. 87, 20 June 1840, p. 1331.
47 'Supplement to Congress report, May 1840,' *New Moral World*, VII, No. 84, 30 May 1840. C. F. Green had first heard of Owenism in 1832. He had visited America and found competition more severe in New York than in England. For a time he had lived with the Wyandot Indians and later visited the Shaker community of New Lebanon.
48 'Supplement to the reports and papers of the fifth Congress,' *New Moral World*, VII, No. 85, 6 June 1840, p. 1291.
49 *Declaration of Principles of the Universal Community Society*, 1840, p. 6.

50 'System of examination for candidates for membership,' 1840, Robert Owen correspondence, letter No. 1249.

51 Robert Owen, *Outline of a Rational System of Society*, 1840, Social Tract No. 7.

52 'Supplement to the report of the fifth Congress, May 1840,' *New Moral World*, VII, No. 86, 20 June 1840, pp. 1332–3.

53 *New Moral World*, VIII, No. 3, 18 July 1840, p. 36.

54 *Ibid.*, VIII, No. 2, 11 July 1840, p. 27.

55 John Watts, *Co-operative Societies Productive and Distributive: Past, Present and Future*, 1861, p. 64.

56 *New Moral World*, VIII, No. 4, 25 July 1840, p. 59.

57 *Ibid.*, VIII, No. 1, 4 July 1840, p. 11.

58 'Supplement to the report of the fifth congress,' *New Moral World*, 20 June 1840, p. 1349.

59 *New Moral World*, VIII, No. 14, 3 October 1840, p. 213.

60 *Ibid.*, VIII, No. 17, 24 October, 1840, p. 270.

61 J. Brindley, *A Voice from Tytherley, being a faithful account of the Hampshire Heaven . . .*, 1840, Hampshire County Record Office.

62 *Ibid.*, quoting letter from Samuel Phillips to Armitage, 3 August 1840.

63 *Brindley and his Lying Braggadocio*, 19 September 1840, Robert Owen correspondence, letter No. 1290, also printed as broadsheet to the 'Public of Sheffield' by I. Ironside, Workhouse 1, Croft, Sheffield.

64 *New Moral World*, IX, No. 12, 12 March 1841, p. 178.

65 *Ibid.*, IX, No. 15, 10 April 1841, p. 234.

66 *Ibid.*, IX, No. 16, 17 April 1841, p. 250.

67 Reported in the *New Moral World*, IX, No. 21, 22 May 1841.

68 Report to James Rigby. in *Reports and Papers of the Sixth Congress, May 1841*, p. 333.

69 *Ibid.*, pp. 334–5.

70 *Report of the Sixth Congress, May 1841*, p. 353.

71 Lloyd Jones, *Life, Times and Labours of Robert Owen*, II, pp. 145–7.

72 *Ibid.*, p. 145.

73 *Report of the Sixth Congress, May 1841*, pp. 366–7.

74 'Sixth Congress, report from Tytherley,' *New Moral World*, IX, No. 24, 12 June 1841, p. 363.

75 *Ibid.*, p. 364.

76 *Report of the Sixth Congress, May 1841*, p. 370.

77 *New Moral World*, X, No. 2, 10 July 1841, p. 12.

78 *Ibid.*, No. 11, 11 September, 1841, p. 85.

79 *Ibid.*, No. 12, 18 September 1841, p. 95.

80 *Anti-Socialist Gazette*, No. 3, 1 December 1841, p. 44.

81 *New Moral World*, X, No. 28, 8 January 1842, p. 219.

82 *Ibid.*, X, No. 29, 15 January 1842, p. 231.

83 *Ibid.*, X, No. 35, 26 February, 1842, p. 279.

84 *Ibid.*, X, No. 38, 19 March 1842, p. 298.

85 *Ibid.*, X, No. 43, 23 April 1842, p. 346.

86 *Ibid.*, X, No. 41, 9 April 1842, p. 328.

87 *Ibid.*, X, No. 43, 23 April 1842, p. 337.

88 'Reports and papers of the seventh Congress, May 1842,' *New Moral World* x, No. 49, 4 June 1842, p. 394.

89 *Ibid.*, p. 395.

90 See, for instance, *The Hampshire Chronicle*, which during November 1839 included long accounts of Chartist riots in south Wales but no mention of Tytherley.

91 *Hampshire Chronicle*, 22 August 1842, in which there is a further reference to Owen's departure 'from governorship of N. Harmony [*sic*] at Tytherley'.

92 *Ibid.*, 16 May 1842.

93 J. Crabb, *Consider the End, or, Owenite Socialism Exposed*, 1842, Hampshire County Record Office.

94 *The Antidote*, No. 1, July 1842, p. 5.

95 'Address of Congress to members of the Rational Society,' 6 August 1842, *New Moral World*, xi, No. 7, 13 August 1842, pp. 57–8.

96 'Proceedings of special Congress, August 1842,' *New Moral World*, xi, No. 6, 6 August 1842, p. 41.

97 *Ibid.*, p. 43.

98 'Proceedings of special Congress, 1842,' *New Moral World*, xi, No. 7, 13 August 1842, pp. 51–2.

99 *New Moral World*, xi, No. 8, 20 August 1842, p. 64.

100 *Ibid.*, No. 16, 15 October 1842, p. 128.

101 'A journey to Harmony Hall,' letter No. 20, reprinted from the *Morning Chronicle*, 13 December 1842, in *The Whistler at the Plough*, p. 112.

102 *The Patriot*, 27 December 1842.

103 *The Union: a Monthly Record of Moral, Social and Educational Progress*, ed. G. A. Fleming, No. 5, August 1842, p. 160.

104 *Ibid.*, No. 9, December 1842, p. 362.

105 'Report of Congress, May 1843', *New Moral World,* xi, No. 50, 10 June 1843, p. 227.

106 *New Moral World*, xii, No. 31, 27 January 1844, p. 247.

107 *Ibid.*, 27 January 1844, p. 247.

108 'Reports and papers of the seventh Congress, May 1842,' *New Moral World*, No. 49, 4 June 1842, p. 390.

109 F. Engels, *The Condition of the Working Class in England in 1844*, (1892 edition), p. 238.

110 F. Engels, *Socialism, Utopian and Scientific*, trans. E. Aveling, 1892, pp. xiii–xiv.

111 *New Moral World*, xi, No. 32, 4 February 1843, p. 259.

112 *Ibid.*, xi, No. 47, 20 May 1843, p. 381.

113 'Report of Congress, May 1843,' *New Moral World*, xi, No. 50, 10 June 1843, p. 417.

114 *Ibid.*, p. 406.

115 *Ibid.*, p. 410.

116 *New Moral World*, xii, No. 21, 18 November 1843, p. 168.

117 Board residence charges were advertised at 5s per day; £1 10s per week, £52 10s yearly. (*New Moral World*, xii, No. 39, 23 March 1844.)

118 R. J. Reid, *Exposure of Socialism*, 1843.

119 *Ibid.*, p. 24.
120 *Ibid.*, p. 37.
121 *Ibid.*, p. 35.
122 *New Moral World*, xii, No. 13, 23 September 1843, pp. 99–100.
123 *Ibid.*, xii, No. 7, 12 August 1843, p. 52.
124 *Ibid.*, xii, No. 19, 4 November 1843, p. 149.
125 *Ibid.*, xii, No. 23, 2 December 1843, p. 177.
126 Robert Owen correspondence, letter No. 1319.
127 Letter from 'A Socialist,' 19 January 1844, *New Moral World*, xii, No. 32, 3 February 1844, p. 256.
128 *New Moral World*, xiii, No. 6, 3 August 1844, p. 44.
129 *Ibid.*, xii, No. 44, 27 April 1844, p. 349.
130 *Ibid.*, xii, No. 43, 20 April 1844, pp. 340–1.
131 *Ibid.*, xii, No. 50, 8 June 1844, p. 402.
132 *Full Account of a Farewell Festival given to Robert Owen on his Departure for America*, 1844. The farewell breakfast was held at London A1 branch.
133 *New Moral World*, xiii, No. 24, 6 December 1844, p. 189.
134 *Ibid.*, xiii, No. 23, 30 November 1844, pp. 181–2.
135 *The Movement*, No. 58, 22 January 1845, pp. 30–31, letter from 'W.C.'.
136 *New Moral World*, xiii, No. 38, 15 March 1845, pp. 300–1.
137 *Ibid.*, xiii, No. 48, 24 May 1845, p. 391.
138 *Ibid.*, xiii, No. 45, 3 May 1845, p. 364.
139 *Ibid.*, xiii, No. 47, 17 May 1845, p. 376.
140 *Ibid.*, xiii, No. 57, 26 July 1845, p. 465.
141 *Ibid.*, xiii, No. 52, 21 June 1845, p. 424.
142 *Ibid.*, xiii, No. 52, 21 June 1845, p. 426.
143 *Ibid.*, xiii, No. 56, 19 July 1845, p. 459.
144 *Ibid.*, xiii, No. 54, 5 July 1845, p. 441.
145 Other Owenites had departed for America—the Colony of Equality at Spring, Wisconsin, was started with twenty-one members in September 1843. See letter to John Street, Social Institution, from T. Hunt, in the *New Moral World*, xiii, No. 58, 2 August 1845, pp. 471–2.
146 *New Moral World*, xiii, No. 62, 30 August 1845, p. 507.
147 *Ibid.*, xiii, No. 64, 13 September 1845, p. 521.
148 *The Moral World*, No. 3, 13 September 1845, p. 18.
149 *New Moral World*, xiii, No. 4, 20 September 1845, p. 28.
150 *The Moral World*, No. 10, 1 November 1845, p. 76.
151 Robert Owen correspondence, letter No. 1392.
152 *Ibid.*, letter No. 1398.

7
Aftermath and conclusions

The Owenite movement soon disintegrated after the collapse of Queenwood, but the settlement of bankruptcy claims on the community remained extremely protracted.

John Buxton wrote in January 1846 that the *Herald of Progress* was 'the organ of the Rational Society and the only paper in England advocating Mr Owen's views'.[1] But by June 1846 *The Reasoner and Herald of Progress* stated, 'the Rational Society is broken up, that no object remains before it . . .'.[2] It had been decided that all members who were prepared to pay 1s (which was the annual subscription) would be recognised as having paid up all their arrears. The Owenite social missionaries had dispersed—Hollick was in America, Mackintosh was lecturing on his electrical theory, Watts was in business in Manchester, Buchanan and Fleming were employed by the London Press, Ellis was teaching, Southwell was lecturing at his own coffee house.[3]

Buxton issued a notice convening a meeting to discuss the affairs at Harmony Hall on 29 June 1846, to be followed by a special congress on 30 June. He subscribed the notice: 'John Buxton, President of Rational Society, Governor of Harmony and one of the Assignees of the Rational Society's Property'.[4] The situation at Harmony Hall descended into pathos when Buxton reported that Edward Finch had brought six men on 9 June and ejected him: 'I am now writing in the open air.'[5] Finch also evicted Mrs Buxton: 'She was dragged into the road with one child in her arms, and four others clinging to her screaming.' The ever-commiserative Galpin provided blankets, which were spread over oak planks by the roadside, and there the Buxton family spent the night, 'I pacing the road in front of them.'[6]

In March 1847 Harmony Hall was leased for twenty-one years at £600 yearly to George Edmondson,[7] a Quaker schoolmaster from Tulketh Hall, Lancashire, with power to purchase the original lease.[8] Edmondson had formerly been in the service of the Emperor of Russia. He renamed Harmony Hall Queenwood College and within a year had spent more than £1,000 on improvements. John Finch wrote to Owen on 2 July:

> should be very happy to see you here next week but am afraid, as Mr Edmondson is coming in a few days, and the whole premises are in confusion ... we could not find accommodation suitable for you, besides which Marchant has let Rose Hill to Mr Cook, who lives there...[9]

Queenwood College was soon to gather together, either as staff or students, perhaps the most impressive list of future scientists and savants in any scholastic establishment during the nineteenth century. Henry Fawcett entered the college as one of its first pupils on opening day, 3 August 1847.[10] In the same month John Tyndall joined the staff, and was later joined by Edward Frankland, Thomas Hirst[11] and Dr H. Debus. John Tyndall[12] conducted investigations on diagmetic polarity at Queenwood on his return from the University of Marburg in 1851. Frankland was also engaged in research at Queenwood on the 'isolation of alcohol radicles'.[13] Tyndall and Frankland rose at 4.00 a.m. to exchange lesson notes. An early prospectus of Queenwood College included 'railway surveying and levelling', bridge and road building, chemistry 'applied to agriculture, engineering (analysis of fluids, metals, building materials)', so that the pupils could be fitted for the present age, which was 'distinguished by its character of utility'—witness the many recent social reforms, sanitary measures and application of chemistry and mechanics to agriculture: 'Sciences form a kind of gymnasium for the intellect.'[14]

The early success of Queenwood College was not matched by any marked progress in settling the legal claims and responsibilities of the Owenites. Finch reported in March 1848 that tradesmen's debts:

> have mostly been compounded and everything has been done to prevent litigation and waste of the property. All they would have to do would be to make some arrangement with Mr Edmondson to settle with the lessees to relieve them from their responsibilities; when these things were done the lessees would most gladly resign their situation of risk responsibility and anxiety without profit...[15]

But the original Owenite trustees refrained from issuing any accounts of receipts from the new lessees of the Queenwood estate, and it became obvious, at least to Pare, that Chancery proceedings

would have to be undertaken to enforce a statement of affairs to be
presented to the surviving members of the Rational Society.

Affairs at Harmony Hall were still no nearer a solution, and at
a specially convened meeting of the Central Board of the Rational
Society on 2 July 1851 it was resolved to present a petition to Parliament to enquire into the Society and so to hasten an equitable
settlement of affairs. The petition was to be presented by Roebuck
and copies were to be sent to the *Reasoner*, the *Leader* and the
Sheffield Free Press—papers still giving some mention of Owenite
views after the demise of the *New Moral World*. Copies were also
despatched to Sir Isaac Lyon Goldsmid, Messrs Finch, Green,
Clegg, Bracher, Edmondson, Ashurst, Atkinson & Co., Buxton,
Owen, 'and the promoters of Christian Socialism'. The moribund
branches of the Rational Society were requested to prepare their own
petitions. In the petition of the Central Board, reference was made
to the 1845 balance sheet of the Society, which showed that £37,794
had been subscribed but that the property was valued at only
£25,676, leaving a deficit of £14,239, after deducting tradesmen's
debts of £2,121; that John Finch forbade the sale of the estate; that
the congress held in April 1846 had instructed Robert Owen and
William Pare to confer with the lessees and assignees in order to
reach a speedy settlement of affairs... that in May 1846 Finch
broke into Harmony Hall and took away papers and on June 9
ejected Buxton... that a subsequent meeting was held at Rosehill,
where William Pare proposed and had accepted certain resolutions
on behalf of Finch. The estate had since been in the possession of
Finch and Edmondson.

Nothing further is heard of any parliamentary inquiry. The many
poor members of the Rational Society had to await another decade
before their claims were adjudicated.

In 1856 John Finch assigned his interests in 'leasehold premises
at East Tytherley' to his son Edward Finch for the sum of £10, 'to
release Edward Finch his heirs and executors by these presents'.[16]
But it was left to William Pare to file a Bill in the Rolls Court
against Clegg, Green and Finch, making the trustees, and one of
each of the classes of members, parties to the suit for the settlement
of debts.[17] The case was heard on 30 April, 1 May and 23 May 1861.
Pare referred to the loan of £500 he had made to the Rational
Society in May 1842, which was pronounced valid by the court.
Evidence was given of the assignment of all the property at Har-

mony Hall to Buxton, Bate and Bracher in 1845, and reference was made to the special congress held in June 1846 which resolved that the appointment of assignees was not legal and that the property remained in the rightful possession of the trustees to the original lease of September 1839. The trustees had subsequently resisted the sale of the leasehold, and their present defence against a claim that the rights of the parties should be declared and that the trustees should account for their receipts was to seek to prove that Pare was not in reality a creditor; moreover the Society itself was illegal. The Master of the Rolls, however, laid down 'there is quite sufficient to show that it was a *bona fide* friendly society'. The trustees then asserted that the Rational Society had been formed to propagate natural religion and to end all moral restraint and to destroy private property. Lord Romilly admitted that the Society was based on irrational principles and 'seeks to realise a visionary and unattainable object', but it had not been founded for irreligious and immoral doctrines. The court held the defendants liable to show account and for an inquiry to be made as to the identity of the creditors and their priorities.[18] A decree of Chancery was made on 11 July 1863 for the sale of the leasehold estate, and the proceeds of £3,900 were paid into the Bank of England on 24 December 1863, subject to the lease of 1847 between the trustees and George Edmondson. In so litigious a manner did Harmony Hall flicker out.

The Queenwood leasehold passed to Benson and Foster, sugar refiners in Manchester, and they in turn leased the property to Richard Davis in 1872 for a further twenty-one years at a rental of £383.[19] In 1896 Harmony Hall ceased to function as a college and became a centre for teaching poultry farming and electrical engineering. The entire building was destroyed by fire on 10 June 1902.[20] Captain Dalgety, who had recently renovated the building, sent his fire engine to the scene, but it was of little use owing to water shortage, and soon 'the whole building of about eighty rooms became a complete ruin, and but little salvage was taken from it'.[21] Charles Willmore,[22] the retired principal of the college, perished in the fire. It was reported that the premises were insured for £8,000. At the present day it is still possible to discern remnants of Harmony Hall—there are a disused lodge, two sawn-off lamp standards in the original driveway, and the foundation stone with its cavity for archives as described by Robert Owen. The original dairy, laundry room and chapel still stand, and the reservoir can be seen in the woods behind Queenwood cottages.

Many Owenites turned their attentions to emigration as an alternative when hopes faded of any successful outcome at Queenwood. A Co-operative Emigration Society at Sheffield in 1845 advertised its advantages to members whose funds were limited. Wise after the events of 1825 to 1845, the Society laid down that there would be no community of property in its emigration scheme.

There were also more severely paternalistic community proposals, such as those of John Minter Morgan, the Owenite sympathiser who founded a 'Self-supporting Village Society' in 1846 to promote the religious, moral and social improvement of the working classes by forming settlements of upwards of 300 families each on the land on a basis of combining agricultural with manufacturing employment. Morgan defended his support of spade husbandry by referring to the extraordinary increments in produce obtained from small holdings at Chat Moss in Lancashire. But it must be inferred from his *Christian Commonwealth*, published in 1850, that no such communities were established, for Morgan was still arguing over the objections raised to his original prospectus.

With the decline of Owenism, the halls of science and the associated rational schools merged into the secularist movement. Irrespective of the weight of the contribution of these local Owenite schools, it would be difficult to agree with G. D. H. Cole, at least as far as Britain was concerned that 'The schools were always the best conducted part of the various Owenite communities in this country and America.'[23] An example of the successful metamorphosis of an Owenite hall of science occurred at Manchester, where the building at Campfield became the Manchester Free Library from 1851: 'It is indeed the spacious *winter park*, in which they [the working classes] can find at once amusement, solace, occupation and instruction.'[24] Leon Faucher's observations in 1844 were pertinent and comprehensive. The hall was

> an immense building in Camp Field, raised exclusively by the savings of the mechanics and artisans, at a cost of £7,000, and which contains a lecture hall—the finest and most spacious in the town. It is tenanted by the disciples of Mr Owen. In addition to Sunday lectures upon the doctrines of Socialism, they possess a day and Sunday school and increase the number of their adherents by oratorios and festivals—by rural excursions and by providing cheap and innocent recreation for the working classes. Their speculative doctrines aim at the destruction of all belief in revealed religion, and the establishment of community of

property; and they are vigorously opposed by the evangelical portion of the religious public. It is, at the same time admitted, that they have done much to refine the habits of the working classes. They are mostly advocates of temperance societies, and never allow fermented liquors to be drunk at any of their festivals. They were among the first to introduce tea-parties at a low rate of admission; and the popularity they have obtained by these endeavours to improve the habits of their fellow townsmen, is one great cause of their success in the propagation of their system. The large sums of money they raise, prove that they belong to the wealthier portion of the working classes.[25]

A number of leading Owenites could mix business careers with co-operative ideals, and were not personally affected by the social evils they wished to remedy. W. H. Ashurst, the City solicitor, spent about £600 on keeping alive a co-operative journal, *The Spirit of the Age*, in 1849, and he also lent £50 to Holyoake to attend lectures at London University. Thomas Allsop, a member of the Stock Exchange and the owner of a large business in Regent Street, was also an Owenite sympathiser. Thomas Dixon Galpin, the son of William Galpin, married Emma Pare in 1851, and with Petter and Jeffrey founded the publishing firm of Cassell and Co., many of whose members were reputed to be ex-Owenites.[26] Others were made bankrupt or virtually ruined as a result of their support of Owenism—A. J. Hamilton, Frederick Bate, William Galpin—but the collapse of Owenism in 1845 did not damage the business capacities of Finch, Pare and G. A. Fleming, who, although disillusioned, returned to profitable pursuits in the iron trade and in journalism. Ironside went into local politics, Craig into lecturing and education, James Rigby went to act as Robert Owen's nursemaid.[27] However, neither Pare nor Finch showed any marked inclination towards the practice of Owenism in their industrial relations as employers.

Soon after Owen's death in 1858 there was a crop of adverse journal articles and biographies: a writer in the *Westminster Review* in 1860 argued that, provided community of property ideas were eliminated, there was a place for corporate activity (he instanced the success of Rochdale co-operation),

but were it acted upon by a nation and enforced by a Government, the consequences would be the utter destruction of individuality, the reduction of all intelligence to the same dead conventional level, the extinction of all personal liberty, and the production of a stagnant or retrograde civilization, such as exists in China...[28]

As for Robert Owen, 'his biography is more interesting than his works ... But even here we feel that he lived too long: too long for himself, too long for his friends, and far too long for his biographer.'[29]

II

This foregoing study of the three leading Owenite communities has had a two-fold purpose: first, to relate the experience of the experiments to Owenite thought in general; second, in so doing, to provide a more comprehensive appreciation of the place of Owenism in nineteenth-century social history.

Although the specific aims varied between the communities and over the life of any one community, the common purpose was to create a system of harmonious human relationships and a thoroughgoing reform of social and economic institutions, including property, within a framework of agriculture and manufacturing industry. If one measures success in terms of achievement of stated objects, then the communities must be regarded largely as failures. An investigation of their experience also serves to help evaluate Owen's effectiveness. Whilst at New Lanark, Owen had listed the priorities for the new social arrangements, which needed for their fulfilment a system of controls made available within a community—'What are the best arrangements under which these men and their families can be well and economically *lodged, fed, clothed, trained, educated, employed, and governed?*'[30] The community was therefore Owen's controlled laboratory wherein he could experiment and justify his assertions on the merits of education, equality, social welfare provisions and the economy of high wages. Individualism would wither away and exploitation would be avoided; harmonious relationships between individuals and between communities would grow with the removal of the impositions caused by competition, and a relaxation of the restrictions of family life would go hand in hand with economies in communal domestic arrangements and services.

But Owen and the Owenites had no satisfactory answer to the problem of production in a community setting, nor were they consistent in their views on equality of reward or property. Perhaps the most intransigent problem of all was that of devising an efficient form of democratic government: the Owenite experiments, although short-lived, provided some evidence that without a resolution of this problem the model community would degenerate into patriarchy or anarchy. Owen hoped that community experience would enable members to adjust easily from a competitive to a co-operative society.

There was scant sign of any convincing proof of the validity of Owen's main hypotheses for successful community organisation. At Queenwood, the most Owenite of the experiments, we have seen the inadequacy of its educational provisions,[31] its production problems, and its precarious living standards, which were often at bare subsistence level.

All three communities demonstrated that the main economic obstacle, which was never satisfactorily overcome, was the heavy capital charge of acquiring legal title to large tracts of land within an industrialising economy. Once the communities were established it was difficult to select suitable lines of production not requiring large-scale equipment and yet having a readily marketable output. Strong social cohesion could have been achieved if it had been possible to incorporate a sufficiently wide range of craft skills to enable communal self-sufficiency to be possible, but the communities never accomplished this norm. (The Spa Fields experiment did at least provide an example of an urban attempt at social living, but with no control or infringement of the members' trades or crafts.)

Apart from Spa Fields, all the communities were planned on a pronounced agricultural basis. Their pictorial propaganda depicted sylvan scenes of contentment but with a background impression of the good living made available by the new technology. In concept these communities were perhaps more an antithesis to the squalor of the nineteenth century town than examples of romantic pastoralism: they could not have publicised their emotional message without an unprecedented growth of towns having taken place.

Despite their importance, the communities have been largely ignored in the literature on Owen and the co-operative movement, and what little there is available is generally unsatisfactory on a number of grounds. Holyoake, in his *History of Co-operation*, wrote disparagingly of the experiments as 'The lost communities'. Craig's book on Ralahine was read widely, but as a timely study of agricultural improvement when the subject of Irish land reform was in the air. In Podmore's standard biography of Owen little attention is paid to the communities, and he explains in the preface that the 3,000 Owen letters had come to light only at a late stage in the production of the book. Hence Podmore's fullest account of a community—Queenwood[32]—had to rely almost entirely on refer-

ences in the *New Moral World,* with the result that insufficient
emphasis is given to the importance of William Pare either at
Queenwood or in the Owenite movement. Alex Cullen's *Adventures
in Socialism* is the sole definitive account of Orbiston, but Cullen
was an architect, not a social historian, and although he used
original source-material he provides insufficient documentation and
references. Moreover, less than half of the book is concerned with
Orbiston.

Biographies of Owen published since the 1920s rely on secondary
sources for their sketches of the communities. Hence the need for
revision of the so-called histories of the communities: nothing original has been added since Cullen, and the general impression remains
today almost what it was nearly a century ago when Holyoake was
writing and showing more interest in the growth of retail co-operation than in the Owenite phase. Because Holyoake's journalistic
accounts are notoriously unreliable the gap in the early history of
co-operative experiments is even more glaring.

Paradoxically, the conclusion drawn from the present study en-
dorses the generally held impression of Owen being more closely
identified with New Lanark than with any subsequent communities.
All that he did after New Lanark can be explained in terms of his
experience there. This, of course, is the particularly British view of
Owen; in America his activities were more purely communitarian
and his contribution is seen largely in those terms.

The varying social and political responses and reactions to industrial change were bound to remain unco-ordinated because a collective policy was not possible in the circumstances prevailing in
the early nineteenth century. The experiences of the working class
in evaluating the cornucopia of doctrines and social remedies did,
however, help to make its leaders more articulate and sometimes
more discriminating, and, viewed with hindsight, were a necessary
stage towards political enfranchisement and maturity. Many of the
aims and policies followed by the early trade unionists and Owenites were, for instance, in conflict. Trade unions wanted immediate
economic gains through wage bargaining: Owenism wanted social
transformation in which bargaining would be irrelevant. Yet there
were times and points of fusion—Doherty saw the opportunity of
using the popularity of Owen's appeal as a means of bringing organised workers into a mass movement. On the other hand, although
Owen was drawn willingly into the working class movement, more

particularly during the early 1830s, he was never wholly convinced
that the workers on their own initiative could achieve any worthwhile goals. Certainly he helped to infuse enthusiasm into a number
of trade union campaigns, but the actual involvement of and relationships between Owenites and members of the Grand National Consolidated Trades Union are difficult, indeed impossible to untangle
at all, at this interval. G. D. H. Cole has said, 'How fully the Trade
Unions were ever converted to Owenism it is impossible to say.'[33]
To what extent, for instance, the potters' union became involved in
the GNCTU is far from clear, nor is there any reason to believe
that Owen increased the membership of the potters' union: Owen
'wielded great power over the Union leaders, but it is equally true
that he had none over the potters in the mass'.[34] Simpson, the
secretary of the union, felt impelled to write to Owen on 20 October
1833, 'There is great hue and cry against you; all the religious world,
so called, are opposed to you.' A co-operative pottery works was put
into operation in June 1834, but it had failed by the end of the year.
The evidence is that the experiment was kept separate from the
union's other activities and that it was launched to provide jobs
for unemployed potters, although Owen maintained that the venture
was a first step towards dispensing with master employers.[35] The
GNCTU was an illusory means of bringing together divergent and
discordant groups of trade unionists, political radicals and Owenite
co-operators, and there is hardly any justification in believing that
a trade union seeking membership on a national basis would use
that power to apply the principles of co-operation throughout
industry. The working class perhaps made more use of Owen than
he did of them, and there is little doubt that the co-operative commonwealth as formulated by Owen would have brought the working class under a paternalistic or autocratic regime.[36] It might very
well be that the working class movement saw these implications and
used Owen to further its own ends, in so far as it could articulate
them, rather than follow him: an immediate change-over to a
co-operative system was really the most radical of all the movements
from below—too radical even for root-and-branch reformers. Nevertheless, the syndicalist elements of Owenism continued to simmer in
the minds of some trade unionists long after the debacle of the
GNCTU: as late as 1845 some members of the National Association
for the Employment of Labour subscribed to syndicalist ideas; the
potters were told that the Association would use its funds to

'gradually extend [its] sphere of action until the working classes eventually [became] ... their own employers'.[37]

There were further problems arising from Britain becoming the first industrial society. Because there were no precedents, radical social commentators had to rely on prediction, which they often identified with truth, and truth with conformity to their particularist reform measure, be it free trade, temperance, mesmerism, secularism, spiritualism. Radical reformers also tended to subscribe to pseudo-scientific pursuits (e.g. phrenology).[38] Impressed by the revelations of physical science, they convinced themselves that social enquiry and experiment could adduce counterpart certainties. Owen, and to a lesser extent his followers, mistook statistical minutiae for ends, not means of control. The Owenite socialists, like most of the early Victorians, had a passionate faith in statistics, but a very weak sense of statistical proof. The Owenites had all the faults of amateurishness typical of their period: 'vagueness, carelessness in observation and recording, lack of definition, unintelligent categorisation, and an absolute disregard for possible alternative explanations'.[31] Early Victorian culture was resolutely amateur and it was socially optimistic. For social ills there were social remedies which could be assimilated and applied once knowledge was acquired.

The dogmas of the political economists which were taken up so enthusiastically by the middle classes during the 1830s and 1840s were disseminated in the form of cautionary tales for working class readers. The moral was middle class apologist; but the popularisers could hardly justify an economic system with so much ugliness and degradation. The strength of the Owenite socialists over the writers of economic tracts such as Harriet Martineau and Charles Knight was in their humanity.[40] During the second half of the nineteenth century there developed two cultures quite apart from the earlier 'two nations'—the informed generalist laymen and the specialist professional—and in this world there was no place for universal social remedies such as Owenism.

In the mass, the working classes from the late 1830s on preferred Chartism to Owen's industrial radicalism. Chartism was certainly more successful than Owenism in collecting support funds but essentially it looked backwards to a pre-industrial society. Feargus O'Connor would take labour out of the industrial market in order to raise the wage rates of those who remained, and he used this argument to show that the Chartist land colonies would bring benefit to all; Owenism approached the problem more directly in terms of standard of living, which it believed would be improved within a system of communities.

The insecurity felt by the working classes during the first half of the nineteenth century did not arise so much from the employers' control of capital as from the workers' own lack of land: 'The real danger from the new wealthy class was that they might buy up land.'[41] Both Chartist and Owenite land hunger grew out of this sense of being denied a just standard of living as a worker within the industrial system.

Werner Sombart argued that the attitude of resignation towards industrial capitalism shown by the English working classes from the 1850s created the institutions of modern co-operation and trade unionism, which became the backbone of all modern labour movements.[42] The gap in socialism in England between 1850 and 1880 could be explained in terms of national character—Sombart's impression was that the English in general lacked the power of speculative thought and systematisation: they restricted themselves to limited, attainable aims, and, given the general improvement in prosperity after 1850, it was in the practical interests of whatever political party was in power 'if not to help forward, at any rate not to hinder, the movement of the working classes to improve their material position . . .'[43]

Although social commentators during the later half of the nineteenth century acknowledged the permeation of socialist ideas into legislation, it was generally felt that communitarian experiments were not amenable to the British temperament. The utopian visions of communal harmony illuminated by Owenism did, however, inspire a constant stream of publications throughout the nineteenth century and beyond. Robert Pemberton, who was perhaps the last self-acknowledged convert to Owenism, wrote in utopian style his *Happy Colony* in 1854, about a classless society to be planted in New Zealand and financed through shilling subscriptions. James Silk Buckingham, among many other interests and activities, was moved to translate into town planning schemes some of Owen's ideas on model communities. As was the case with Owen, Buckingham thought of virgin sites and constructed theoretical solutions which did not make allowance for the dynamic nature of town development. Buckingham built on bourgeois values; he did not

criticise social institutions: his 'Victoria' was a model town association with limited liability shareholders.

The home colonies idea, which was sponsored by liberals during
the 1850s, survived simply as a method of alleviating urban unemployment.[44] But the broad issues of the land question remained
in continuous debate throughout the second half of the nineteenth
century, and not merely restricted to the problem of Ireland.
Reformist strands of land nationalisation schemes and single-tax
Henry Georgeism can be seen underlying the more basic fears of
the harmful consequences from a lessened dependence on the soil.

Steward Headlam's Guild of St Matthew, formed in 1877, was
primarily a religious body, but Thomas Davidson's Fellowship of
the New Life (1883–98) was a vaguely Ruskinian, vaguely Owenite
society[45] which had been anticipated by Ruskin's Guild of St George
in 1871. Poverty and 'illth' were regarded as the by-products of an
unsatisfactory but remediable industrial system.[46] The Fellowship
of the New Life had neo-Owenite ideas of community, but in one
such scheme the fellowship pointed out that it was planning, 'not
with a view to the formation of a small Earthly Paradise of select
persons', but merely to establish associated homes, simple co-operative industry and educational provisions.[47]

William Morris, in his utopia, *News from Nowhere* (1890),
thought along the same lines as Owen over the potential social
benefit of machinery. He described, in 'How the change came', that
the aim was to 'get the machinery of production and the management of property so altered that the 'lower classes' . . . might have
their slavery somewhat ameliorated' and use this machinery for
achieving a state of practical equality, 'because "the rich" would be
forced to pay so much for keeping "the poor" in a tolerable condition that the condition of riches would become no longer valuable
and would gradually die out'.[48] The poor were therefore the agents
for bringing in a state of equality. London would be transformed
into a collection of villages and the only monument to be preserved
from the nineteenth century society was the Houses of Parliament,
which were to act as a storage depot for dung.

An old Owenite sympathiser wrote in 1880:

> No one suspects of Socialism the promoters of public baths and wash-
> houses, improved dwellings for the working classes, reformatory and in-
> dustrial schools . . . the Rational Society has long ceased to exist. Yet in
> practice and without the name, Socialism flourishes more widely and

strong than ever ... its fundamental tenet, 'man is the creator of circumstance', may be recognised in all the legislation of the last quarter of a
century.[49]

This prognosis from 1880 spoke in the same Owenite language as
did a verdict published thirty years earlier, when it was argued that
Owenism had acted indirectly in sponsoring:

> the establishment of co-operative stores ... public baths and wash-houses,
> model lodging houses, ragged schools ... These things arose out of the
> conviction that was gradually forced upon the public mind of the duty
> and necessity of raising the humbler classes from the ignorance and
> material wretchedness to which attention was so loudly called by Mr
> Owen and his disciples.[50]

An American commentator forty years after the disruption of the
last Owenite experiment saw three characteristics of early socialism:
it was non-violent, it refused State help, and it had enthusiasm for
co-operation as the basis of economic organisation.[51] But even before
the decline of Owenism the term 'socialist' was given a much wider
connotation than 'co-operation'. W. Hawkes Smith had written in
1843:

> Co-operation may serve a provident society, a joint stock manufacturing,
> a farming concern ... Socialism refuses to be confined within the range
> of any individual object ... It is the universal workman, the school-
> master, the preacher, the economical director, and house steward—it is
> production and distribution—it is education, natural philosophy, logic
> and ethics, health, wealth and contentment.[52]

At least one social reformer as late as 1900 was still applying
Owenite remedies: A. R. Wallace, the Natural Scientist,[53] saw
communities, each with 5,000 residents, as the solution to problems
of unemployment:

> Numerous self-supporting co-operative labour colonies being thus estab-
> lished all over the country, their connection by tramways where required
> ... [which would compel capitalists to offer higher wages]. The whole
> of surplus profits would then be distributed among the various classes
> of workers, manual and intellectual, and labour would, for the first
> time, receive its full and just rewards.[54]

Even his ideas on vocational education in a system of communities
were distinctly reminiscent of Ralahine:

> Every child taught to help in the simple agricultural processes ... and
> besides this each person would learn at least two trades or occupations,
> more or less contrasted; one being light and sedentary; the other more
> active and laborious.[55]

The Owenite community experiments were unique because of their very comprehensiveness. They were not concerned only with improving productive capacity and industrial relations, with applying ethical standards to business in the way that many of the industrial entrepreneurs, including Owen, had built into their mill villages, but more importantly they were also involved in matters of social relationships and behaviour, property rights and government. Their attempts to provide communal standards of living comparable to those of skilled artisans in capitalistic enterprise were bound to fail on many counts—not least through inattention to matters of financial control to ensure the most efficient allocation and use of resources. Primarily the communities collapsed through inadequate knowledge of social behaviour and from a confusion over social purpose which, taken together, led to disillusionment on the part of community residents and their financial supporters. Subscription for community was the first investment without 'strings' in working class enterprise.

Perhaps the community idea as a solution for social atomism and deprivation was also bound to fail because of incompatibilities between its ethos and its structure. Any community experiment must assume some organisational pattern to accommodate the decision-making process, and it must deal with the problems of personal status and participation of its members. Where communities have been successful there has been a *consensus ad idem* which sometimes takes the form of sectarian fanaticism in the eyes of outsiders. A leader of messianic proportions is not needed, except perhaps in the incipient stages of community formation. But nineteenth-century community ideology could not achieve its ultimate purpose through the successful launching of merely a prototype settlement. To have mass appeal, 'community' meant a spreading network of communities and peaceful abdication from the established power structure of society through emulation. Granted that communities were to be thus proliferated, then a charismatic leader would no longer be required—indeed, a Robert Owen would become an increasing liability. This is no more than saying that the sum is greater than the parts and the role of a community founder or leader is more important than his personal contribution. It is even more important that some provision should be made for corporate succession.

Owen viewed the family as a divisive influence because of its insularity and introspection. The family therefore reduced the

effectiveness of his ambitions for the communal education of children. It also restrained improvement in the status of women. The
lightening of domestic drudgery through mechanical aids and the
adoption of communal catering to enable fuller personal development and participation of wives and mothers were salient factors in
Owen's plans for communal living. At the same time he aimed to
loosen the child–parent bonds which tended to perpetuate the
ingrained attitudes of the old society—attitudes which he regarded
as the major obstacle to social conversion.

How far did the experience of the leading community experiments provide any evidence of waning solidarity of the family as
an institution? In the eyes of the Establishment gross immorality
was the besetting sin of the Owenites, and it was feared that their
closed communities would provide a prurient opportunity for every
kind of depravity. The invective reached a crescendo during the time
of the debate on Owenism in the House of Lords in 1840, when
Queenwood was widely vilified in sermons and broadsheets. With
the earlier communities there had been negligible public criticism
and moral indignation as neither Orbiston nor Ralahine survived
long enough for any disruption to take place in family relationships.
Indeed, the evidence at Orbiston shows that the majority of the
residents preferred their private apartments to the alternative of
communal messing, despite higher unit living costs. At Ralahine
there is no indication that the Irish peasant households suffered
any infringement of authority except over the creation of an infants'
dormitory and some provision of schooling. As regards Queenwood,
the residents adhered to all the trappings of their previous domestic
background. Although there was an attempt to change the calendar,
husband and wife admissions to the community continued to be
introduced as Mr and Mrs, and residents used these familial titles
throughout their stay, so that children kept their surnames, even
children born in community. If the family was to be destroyed,
then at least a new personal prefix denoting identification to the
community rather than one's family would have been a fitting
symbol for the new systemites to show to the outside world. The
Queenwood residents fully ventilated their opinions and grievances
in the copious reporting of communal activities in the *New Moral
World*, but although there were sporadic quarrelling, accusations of
theft, laziness, inefficiency and injustice, there were no publicised
comments on immorality or indications of licence. The total impres-

sion is more one of sobriety and social conformity than shared wives, creches or dismemberment of the family group. Nor did the communities survive long enough educationally to exert much influence on the young, quite apart from the insufficient allocation of resources for schooling. We must conclude that the attack on the family which was so crucial to Owen's ideology had little influence on the community experiments.

The Owenite experiments provided a first secular alternative to the milieu of industrial society. The ranks of the Owenites included world-makers but possibly some escapists who were attracted to the communities because such settlements were a protective framework within which an individual could at least survive and then begin to adapt to communal patterns. Early Victorian industrialism could not provide any other alternative for what the twentieth century calls the social drop-out. All the lessons which were dinned into nineteenth-century working class consciousness warned of the dangers of social withdrawal—the abyss of destitution, with clearly drawn Hogarthian paths of descent, awaited cranks, misfits and drunkards. The status of the aspiring artisan was hard-won and precarious. Some of those who entered Queenwood were contracting out of relatively substantial positions in the social hierarchy of the industrial classes. Presumably they must have felt convinced that the prospects of sylvan communal bliss, albeit at a different and possibly lower level of subsistence to what they had attained as industrial workers, were justifiable as a fuller way of life. The young twentieth-century drop-out, as an individualised social denial, can, however, more readily survive on the fringe of society than could his nineteenth-century equivalent.

Perhaps the contemporary anthropologist who takes on a new way of life when he explores a 'primitive' culture also has something of the motivation and attitude we have noticed in the Owenite withdrawal. As with the Owenites, he maintains a foot in both worlds and it is hardly surprising that his learned conclusions generally point out the wholesome ecology of primitive culture and implicitly savour of personal intellectual dissatisfaction with the values of his parent society.

The two decades of communitarianism at least gave the working classes an opportunity for continuous association, in contrast to sporadic agitation and outbursts of political radicalism. The early co-operators became disillusioned over working-class solidarity, but they were not alone in their doubts that the masses would only 'come out' at peaks of excitement: Owen, Doherty, Lovett, all expressed concern over the workers' lack of cohesion and weak organising ability; hence the emphasis on self-improvement and education for the new society which became the common factor in the ideology of the early co-operative movement after the collapse of Orbiston.

Engels, as a contemporary observer, discounted the Owenites' contribution, but made some interesting comments on their social origins:

> They are recruited in part from the working class, of which they have enlisted but a very small fraction, representing, however, its most educated and solid elements ... They acknowledge no historical development and wish to place this nation in a state of Communism at once, overnight, not by the unavoidable march of its political development up to the point at which this transition becomes both possible and necessary.[56]

But in terms of community development Ralahine learned nothing from Orbiston, and Queenwood nothing from either of its predecessors. No reformer was directly involved in more than one of the three communities studied. Abram Combe and A. J. Hamilton were founder managers at Orbiston; E. T. Craig supervised Ralahine (with brief visits from John Finch and William Pare); Owen, Finch, Pare, James Rigby and John Buxton were all associated with Queenwood. Lloyd Jones and G. J. Holyoake[57] described what they saw at Queenwood, but as visitors, not as residents. Each of the communities studied was largely unique, and yet all three suffered from an amalgam of blind fate and internal dissension rather than from adverse outside pressures or hostility from the Establishment. If the communities had been successful, would they have been tolerated? All three failed, but perhaps the final question is not whether they would have survived had fate treated them more kindly, but how protracted would have been their eventual demise? They were certainly out of context in early nineteenth-century Britain.

Owenism ceased to be a part of the working class movement after the collapse of Queenwood, although individual Owenites continued to appeal for the infusion of idealism into the growing co-operative movement; but the co-operators were not particularly interested in maintaining unemployed members or setting up communities. The movement shed both its rationalism and its idealism and became the working man's counterpart to the Nonconformist conscience of the later nineteenth century. It moved sharply away from William

Pare's instruction that 'nothing in the way of profit of trade shall ever be divided . . . as Community of Property in Lands and Goods is the great object of this Society'.[58]

The co-operative movement after Rochdale was extremely success-ful if measured in growth of membership and value of transactions compared with the co-operative experiments before 1844. The 'new model' Rochdale principles of conducting business were consistent with other forms and institutions of working class self-help also growing in the same period. But it is unfair to contrast the points of efficiency of post-1844 co-operation with the weaknesses of the early co-operators, whose ideas were in a different sphere from shop-keeping. Moreover, part of the success of co-operation after 1844 was that it did not have to meet any strong organised opposition until the advent of the multiple grocery chains much later in the century. Many of these new outlets followed the precedent of retail co-operation in striving towards efficiency through the co-ordination of wholesaling and retailing and the standardisation of services but at the same time providing a comprehensive range of pure products at fair prices to be sold on a strictly cash basis. The emphasis after 1844 was therefore on self-help rather than neighbour or community; economic independence rather than co-operation. By the 1860s the community idea had almost disappeared. New members swamped the original idealists and there was a continued flow of support for the hard-headed Rochdale realists. In a recent paper on co-operation it is stated, 'To reform the world they had to come to grips with ordinary men and women. No movement can be successful until it takes people as they are and not as one would like them to be.'[59]

By the last quarter of the nineteenth century the British co-operative movement had become respectable, and evidence of this is shown by the representatives of the Establishment who delivered inaugural addresses at annual Co-operative Congresses—Sir Thomas Brassey (1874), Professor Hodgson, LL.D. (1877), the Bishop of Durham (1880), the Earl of Derby (1881), Lord Reay (1882). In 1890 Lord Rosebery could state that the capital of the co-operative movement was as large as the national debt had been in the reign of Queen Anne, and the ranks of the co-operators half as many again as the grand army Napoleon had led into Russia. In one sense co-operation had turned full circle in again counting on support similar to that expressed by those aristocratic sympathisers of Robert Owen's schemes during the immediate post-Napoleonic war years. From the early 1820s there had been years of constant difficulty and estrangement: it was not until co-operation dropped most of its social idealism that it could again come to rely on encouragement from those above, as a worthwhile exercise in working class self-help. Consumer co-operation is world-bettering rather than world-making, and the latter was a more distinctive feature of the pre-Rochdale period. One should not, however, exaggerate the proportion of dedicated community idealists among the early co-operators. Co-operative societies, before and after Rochdale, included many members who were more interested in co-operation as a savings and thrift institution to ensure the provision of staple dependable commodities at fair prices than as a transitory means for achieving mutual or wider social improvement.[60]

Socialism emerged again during the 1880s and 1890s and relied on winning militant support, but its theories of exploitation and class struggle failed to stir the British working class to collective action. Rather, it was trade unionism which was much more widely and impressively commented upon and written about than either socialism or co-operation, and it was trade unionism which was presented as the institution which would lead the nation into fuller community.[61]

Another important element of working class collectivism merits notice. The friendly society movement had an unbroken record of growth throughout the nineteenth century, and its membership far exceeded the combined number of registered co-operators and trade unionists.[62] This continuing need for community and mutuality in the face of social atomism and the hazards of adversity in the nineteenth-century town can also be witnessed in the opportunity offered for commercial exploitation of working class aspirations for respectability provided by the rapid growth of industrial life assurance during the last quarter of the century. The community instinct was also the force behind the expansion of working men's clubs and temperance societies—and perhaps still has some significance today in the spread of bingo halls.

Several generations later, Charles Gide wrote on the experience of the Owenite communities:

> A hundred unsuccessful experiments prove nothing against the one that succeeds. If they have failed it is merely because circumstances have not been favourable, and the only conclusion to be drawn is that it is not easy to combine these favourable conditions.

Somewhat apocalyptically he warned:

> It is by no means improbable that some day there may be one that will
> live on permanently. I do not even consider it unlikely that either this
> century or next these communitarian associations—or integral co-opera-
> tive societies, if you like,—may occupy as large a place in the world as
> the religious communities did in the Middle Ages.[63]

In terms of general economic and social history, communitarianism and its permeation help to explain the interval between the
1840s and 1880s—why Britain never accepted the revolutionary
alternative.

There is a constant search for community in the present-day
planning of new towns; there is also a danger that an established
sense of community, destroyed by the disturbance of 'improvement'
schemes, cannot easily be re-created. Community development is an
important influence in social cohesion in any type of settlement or
society, be it urban or rural, mature or under-developed. The techno-
structure of a community has to be planned but once incorporated it
becomes to some extent a limiting factor as far as the residents are
concerned—for surely the most important lesson from the Owenite experience for present-day planners is that people must be given some
freedom to develop their communities as they see fit, otherwise their
inchoate settlements atrophy or disrupt. This was the basic weakness of the Owenites' experiments, allied to their lack of experience
and inadequate capital. A recent essayist, distinguishing between the
Owenite co-operators and later Rochdale principles, has written,
'The community idea was the disposable superstructure upon a
sound doctrine of mutual self-help.'[64] It should not be inferred from
this statement that community and self-help are mutually exclusive.
The processes of community development should wherever possible
be built on a foundation of self-help.[65] On this score Ralahine was
the most effective of the Owenite socialist communities and Queenwood the least successful. At Queenwood Owen behaved in the
grand manner and bankrupted not only his circle of friends but also
many working men's aspirations: Owen was not really interested
in community development, nor was he, at heart, capable of co-
operation.

Quite apart from an appraisal of the Owenites and an analysis of
the effectiveness of their communitarian experiments, the character
of Robert Owen, which impinged so dramatically on the thought
and action of his followers, has required some reinterpretation:

Owen made theatrical appearances, but not always with a due sense of timing. His influence was immense almost in spite of his actions. Nevertheless his name should remain indissolubly linked, as he would have wished, with New Lanark rather than with any of the community experiments. His abiding weakness as a reformer was inconsistency and indecisiveness. His community plans varied wildly in their catchment, size, estimate of capital requirements, and analysis of class structure. A lesser weakness was his inability to develop schemes beyond the blueprint stage: with Owen a declaration of intent was sufficient, there was no need to provide for the organisational aftermath. And yet however much one attempts to reduce Owen's stature by pointing to the illogicalities and polemics in his writings one must concede the importance of the implicit truths portrayed therein. Owen had an intense social awareness, and on this score the economic consequences of his reform measures could afford to show inconsistency. The priority was to change society and economic institutions would then adjust to the new pattern of society.[66]

Robert Owen's unique contribution was not his grand co-operative solution to combat the evils of the new industrialism, rather it was to be found in his optimism, in his raising of hopes of betterment—that low wages, squalor and misery could be eradicated without bloody revolution or the destruction of Britain's industrial leadership. Owenism provided the industrial orders with a first secular creed for achieving the social good without rancour and with its optimistic expectations of early harmonious amelioration. Before we disparage his contribution, the gullibility of his listeners, and the weakness of their reasoning, we should remember that as impressive a mind as that of David Ricardo could voice second thoughts on the effects of machinery on the working class:

> I have been of the opinion that...an application of machinery to any branch of production as should have the effect of saving labour was a general good...[and that] the class of labourers...was...benefited by the use of machinery, as they would have the means of buying more commodities with the same money wages, and I thought that no reduction in wages would take place because the capitalist would have the power of demanding and employing the same quantity of labour as before, although he might be under the necessity of employing it in the production of a new, or, at any rate, of a different commodity...These were my opinions, and they continued unaltered, as for the landlord and the

capitalist; but I am convinced that the substitution of machinery for human labour is often very injurious to the interests of the class of labourers ... the opinion entertained by the labouring class, that the employment of machinery is frequently detrimental to their interests, is not founded on prejudice and error, but is conformable to the correct principles of political economy.[67]

Owenism was not backward-looking. It accepted the new technology and machine power and sought to control their use and benefit on a more equitable basis. On neither count, therefore, can Owenism be classed as other than progressive. But from another point of view Owenism did not enunciate anything new—equality and benevolence are old ideas, but they needed re-emphasising in the period of maturing industrialism.

Perhaps the most lasting and important contribution of Owen and Owenism is, in fact, the one most difficult to define or assess—that Owenism raised a protest of moral indignation and a plea that society should have a purpose—and that social reform should first of all take into consideration the nature of man. In effect, the role of the State was transformed by the social implications of industrialisation and urbanisation, and the history of the Owenite response to these two forces adds to our understanding of social change during the nineteenth century.

Thomas Hughes gave an inaugural address at the first of the modern Co-operative Congresses in 1869. He looked back to the early days of Owenism:

Some of us here will recollect how we used to be invited periodically to old Mr Minter Morgan's house to look at his model of a Church of England Self-supporting Village, which occupied the end of his dining room in Stratton Street. Well, it was nothing but a great picture which used to be illuminated from behind ... Old Mr Morgan has been dead these fifteen years, and the model village transparency has, no doubt, been long since rolled up, and has found its way to some old marine store shop. We too, have all got older, and (let us hope) wiser ... At the same time, we co-operators can never consent to give up hope of seeing English associations settling in clusters on English soil of their own.

The Owenite communities were defeated by the strength of ingrained attitudes older than industrial society. In seeking harmony and ultimate perfection they did not realise, as did Emerson, that a little wickedness is good to make muscle.

Notes

1 Letter from J. Buxton, 13 January 1846, Queenwood farm, to Miss F. Steer, Robert Owen correspondence, letter No. 1401.

2 *The Reasoner and Herald of Progress*, No. 1, 3 June 1846, p. 9.

3 *Ibid.*, No. 1, 3 June 1846, pp. 11–12.

4 *Ibid.*, p. 48.

5 *Ibid.*, p. 40.

6 *Ibid.*, p. 39.

7 'George Edmondson, 1798–1863', *Dictionary of National Biography*.

8 *Spirit of the Age*, 1 July 1848. The journal also referred to activities of the Leeds Redemption Society, which had acquired land in south Wales: 'We are now at the head of all Communist Movements in England.' (*Ibid.*, p. 14.) The Hollow Farm experiment in the Rivelin valley near Sheffield in 1848 was evidence of the continuity of Owen's ideas after the collapse of Queenwood, although it should be noted that Hollow Farm was also intended for pauper labour. (J. Salt, 'Isaac Ironside and education in the Sheffield region in first half of the nineteenth century', M.A. thesis, University of Sheffield, 1960.

9 Letter from John Finch, 2 July 1846, Robert Owen correspondence, letter No. 1471.

10 D. Thompson, 'Queenwood College', *Annals of Science*, 1955. See also L. Stephen, *Life of Henry Fawcett*, 1886, pp. 8–9.

11 Thomas Hirst (1830–92) succeeded Tyndall at Queenwood as lecturer in Mathematics. In 1865 Hirst became Professor of Physics at University College, London.

12 A. S. Eve and C. H. Creasey, *Life of John Tyndall*, 1945, pp. 17–37, *passim*.

13 'Sir Edward Frankland, 1825–99', *Dictionary of National Biography*. Frankland later claimed that Queenwood was the first English school to introduce the laboratory teaching of science.

14 Newspaper cuttings of Sir George Cooper, Hampshire County Record Office. See also the *London Society Advertiser*, 1862, p. 9.

15 Letter of John Finch, 7 March 1848, Robert Owen correspondence, letter No. 1582.

16 Assignment of interest in leasehold premises at East Tytherley, 19 November 1856, Hampshire County Record Office. Information about John Finch is given in R. B. Rose, 'John Finch, 1784–1857, Liverpool disciple of Robert Owen', *Transactions of the Historic Society of Lancashire and Cheshire*, cix, 1957.

17 Pare *v.* Clegg, *English Law Reports*, liv, Rolls Court, 1905, pp. 756–62.

18 Creditors who received dividends included William Pare, Thomas Galpin, Henry Travis, George Bracher, John Buxton, J. C. Farn, Isaac Ironside and George Simpson. (G. J. Holyoake, *History of Co-operation*, pp. 598–600.)

19 Decree, assignment and lease deposited at Hampshire County Record Office.

20 *Illustrated London News*, 21 June 1902, p. 917; *Hampshire Chronicle*, 14 June 1902.

21 *Salisbury and Winchester Journal*, 14 June 1902.
22 Charles Willmore, a progressive headmaster from Lindow Grove, Cheshire, took over Queenwood College from George Edmondson in 1864. John Hopkinson, a pupil of Willmore's, later became the first Professor of Electrical Engineering at King's College, University of London. (J. Grieg, *John Hopkinson, Electrical Engineer*, Science Museum monograph, 1970, p. 5.)
23 G. D. H. Cole, 'Robert Owen', in *Curiosities in Politics*, 1925, p. 13.
24 *Manchester Guardian*, 11 January 1851. The Manchester Hall of Science had enrolled as an institution under the Literary Societies Act of 1842, which exempted literary and scientific societies from the payment of local rates. (*New Moral World*, 25 November 1843, p. 173.)
25 L. Faucher, *Manchester in 1844: its Present Condition and Future Prospects*, trans. J. P. Culverwell, 1844, p. 25. See also E. Yeo, 'Robert Owen and radical culture', in *Robert Owen: Prophet of the Poor*, ed. Pollard and Salt, pp. 84–114.
26 S. Nowell-Smith, *The House of Cassell*, 1958, pp. 67–8, 75–7, and E. O. Greening, *Memories of Robert Owen and Co-operative Pioneers*, 1925.
27 Of other lesser Owenites, George Simpson, secretary at Harmony Hall, later became an accountant in Manchester and financial manager to Sir Joseph Whitworth. (*Co-operative News*, 24 July 1880, p. 489.) J. C. Farn, an Owenite social missionary, returned to his trade as ribbon weaver, and later became editor of the *Eccles Advertiser*. (*Co-operative News*, 29 October 1881.) His obituary notice claimed that he was a 'Liberal, Unitarian and Co-operator'. Dr Henry Travis was, apart from E. T. Craig, perhaps the last of the Owenite pamphleteers: see his *Co-operative System of Society*, 1871, and *English Socialism*, 1880. After Queenwood, Travis became physician to the Earl of Aylesbury. (*Co-operative News*, 16 February 1884.) J. E. Smith, another early socialist and editor of *The Crisis*, ended his days as editor of the *Family Herald*. (G. D. H. Cole, *Robert Owen*, p. 229.)
28 *Westminster Review*, October 1860, p. 383.
29 *Ibid.*, p. 385.
30 'Report to the County of Lanark', in *A New View of Society and other writings*, p. 260.
31 Two recent scholars have argued that Owen's educational principles 'could almost be summed up as Rousseauism applied to working class children'. (W. A. C. Stewart and W. P. McCann, *The Educational Innovators*, 1, *1750–1880*, 1967, p. 60.
32 In the 654 pages of text there is a chapter of forty-four pages on Queenwood, twenty-six pages on Orbiston, and no mention whatsoever of Ralahine.
33 G. D. H. Cole, *Life of Robert Owen*, 1963 edition, p. 127.
34 W. H. Warburton, *History of Trade Union Organisation in the North Staffordshire Potteries*, 1931, p. 70.
35 *Ibid.*, p. 77.
36 See V. A. C. Gatrell's introduction to *A New View of Society*, 1970, for a recent appraisal of Owen in relation to modern Conservatism: 'in temperament, in prejudice and in actual policy, Owen was a Tory' (p. 17). The idea of a society based on intrinsic rather than economic values was hostile to both liberalism and socialism.

37 W. H. Warburton, *History of Trade Union Organisation in the Potteries*, p. 70, and *Staffordshire Advertiser*, 8 May 1847.

38 Phrenology was typically a poor man's science, its rubrics easily acquired and readily practised. See R. G. Garnett, 'E. T. Craig, communitarian, educator, phrenologist', *Vocational Aspect*, xv, 1963.

39 R. K. Webb, *Harriet Martineau*, 1960, p. 244.

40 R. K. Webb, *Working Class Reader*, sees this rejection as an important schism between the middle and working classes: 'In the doctrine of political economy and their social implication lay probably the most clear-cut intellectual issue between the two classes.' (p. 100).

41 J. Macaskill, 'The treatment of land in English social and political theory', 1959, p. 125.

42 W. Sombart, *Socialism and the Socialist Movement*, 1909, p. 146.

43 *Ibid.*, p. 153.

44 J. Macaskill, 'The treatment of land', p. 203. Charles Kingsley supported communities and the maintenance of rural life: see his *Application by Associative Principles and Methods to Agriculture*, 1851.

45 F. G. Bettany, *Stewart Headlam*, 1926, referred to in H. Pelling, *History of the Labour Party, 1880–1900*, p. 34. For the Guild of St George, see W. H. G. Armytage, *Heavens Below*, 1961, pp. 289–304. Frank Podmore, the biographer of Owen, was a member of the Fellowship of the New Life and also a founder member of the Fabian Society.

46 Pelling, *History of the Labour Party*, p. 150.

47 *An Outline Scheme for the Establishment of Industrial, Educational, and Residential Settlement on Co-operative Principles in the Neighbourhood of London to be carried out by the Fellowship of the New Life* (n.d.), Library of Political and Economic Science, London School of Economics.

48 W. Morris, *News from Nowhere or An Epoch of Rest, being some Chapters from a Utopian Romance*, 1919 edition, p. 122.

49 T. Frost, *Forty Years' Recollections*, 1880, pp. 22–3.

50 'Social Utopias', *Chambers' Papers for the People*, 1851, p. 27.

51 E. R. A. Seligman, *Owen and the Christian Socialists*, reprinted from *Political Science Quarterly*, i, No. 2, 1886.

52 *The Movement*, No. 6, 1843, p. 42.

53 A. R. Wallace, 'Re-occupation of the land, the only immediate solution of the problem of the unemployed' in *Studies Scientific and Social*, 1900, Chapter XXVI, pp. 478–92.

54 *Ibid.*, pp. 491–2.

55 *Ibid.*, pp. 485–6.

56 F. Engels, *The Condition of the Working Class in England in 1844*, 1892 edition, p. 237.

57 Holyoake did not noticeably maintain his affiliations with Owenism after 1845. He became much more associated with the secular movement. (J. McCabe, *Life and Letters of G. J. Holyoake*, 1908, and E. Royle, 'G. J. Holyoake and the secularist movement in Britain, 1841–61', 1968.)

58 *Address at the Opening of the Birmingham Co-operative Society*, 'by a member', 17 November 1828, p. 32.

59 B. J. Youngjohns, 'Co-operation and the State 1814–1914', Co-operative College paper, 1954, p. 42.

60 This is argued in P. Hibberd, 'The Rochdale tradition in co-operative history: is it justified?' *Annals of Public and Co-operative Economy*, xxxix, 4, October–December 1968, pp. 531–57, with a rejoinder by P. Lambert, 'The Rochdale pioneers as originators', *ibid.*, pp. 559–61. Many co-operators must also have subscribed to other self-help institutions such as savings banks and building societies. There were more than a million depositors in savings banks by 1847, each with an average deposit of £30. (H. O. Horne, *History of Savings Banks*, 1947.)

61 S. and B. Webb, *Industrial Democracy*, 1897, and *History of Trade Unionism*, 1894.

62 The *known* membership of friendly societies in 1872 was 1,857,000 (the *actual* membership was estimated at 4 million), whereas trade union membership was 217,000 and that of co-operative societies 301,000. (P. H. J. H. Gosden, *Friendly Societies in England, 1815–75*, 1961, p. 7.

63 C. Gide, *Communist and Co-operative Colonies*, trans. E. F. Row, 1930, p. 216.

64 B. J. Youngjohns, *Co-operation and the State*, p. 36.

65 Self-help in its early stages was collectivist. Later, when it was sponsored by the middle classes they used it to safeguard individualism and tried to show that it was the antidote against collectivism. (J. F. C. Harrison, 'Adult education and self-help', *British Journal of Educational Studies*, vi, No. 1, 1957, p. 48.)

66 The last remaining link with Owenism is the present-day Rational Friendly Society, which can trace a continuous connection to the early 1840s. Between 1856 and 1883 the number of branches of the Rational Association Friendly Society increased from sixty-three to 502, but membership rose by merely 50 per cent to 35,000. By 1904 the Rational was the seventh largest of the UK friendly societies and had a membership of 100,000. The Rational Association Friendly Society and the Rational Association Friendly Collecting Society also maintain early Owenite associations by having their head office in Manchester. (*Rational Association Journal*, 1, No. 1, January 1891, and *Co-operative News*, 8 October 1904, p. 1236.)

67 D. Ricardo, *The Principles of Political Economy and Taxation*, Everyman edition, 1911, pp. 263, 264, 267.

Bibliography

General bibliographies of Owen and Owenism

A bibliography of Robert Owen, the socialist, 1771–1858, National Library of Wales, Aberystwyth (second edition 1925).
Goto Shigeru. Robert Owen, 1771–1858: a new bibliographical study, two vols., Osaka, 1932–34.
London Bibliography of the Social Sciences, London, 1931–37.
University of London, *Robert Owen, 1771–1858: catalogue of an exhibition of printed books held in the library of the University of London, October to December 1958*, London, 1959.

Manuscripts, repositories, papers, etc

Bishopsgate Institute, London:
1 George Howell papers, including pamphlets, society rules, etc, relating to early co-operation.
2 G. J. Holyoake collection: extracts from G. J. Holyoake's diaries, 1831–1845; also diary notebook, 1848–52 and notebook of lecture notes, 1838–39.

British Museum:
1 Francis Place add. MSS and newspaper cuttings.
2 Newspaper Library, Colindale.

Co-operative Union, Manchester:
1 Robert Owen correspondence: some 3,000 letters.
2 G. J. Holyoake letters and papers.

Family Welfare Association (Charity Organisation Society), London:
William Pare papers, pamphlets.

Goldsmiths' library, University of London:
1 William Pare papers, mainly press cuttings from the 1820s to the 1830s.
2 Ludlow collection: pamphlets and broadsheets.

Gourock Rope Co., New Lanark Mills:
Papers on New Lanark Mills, including wage books.

Motherwell Public Library:
Hamilton collection: papers on Robert Owen and the Orbiston community.

Robert Owen Museum, Newton, Montgomeryshire:
Artefacts and manuscripts.

University College, London:
Mocatta collection: letters of I. L. Goldsmid.

Contemporary works

The date of first edition is given if known. In cases where an edition other than first edition is used in this work the date of the edition consulted is given.

Contemporary journals and newspapers

The Advocate of the Working Classes, Edinburgh, 1826–27.
American Socialist, New York, 1877–78.
Anti-Socialist Gazette, Chester, 1841–42, continued as *The Antidote*, 1842.
The Associate, London, 1829–30, continued as *The Associate and Co-operative Mirror*, London, 1830.
The Bee, Liverpool, 1832–33.
Birmingham Co-operative Herald, 1829–30.
Birmingham Labour Exchange Gazette, 1833.
British Co-operator, London, 1830.
Carpenter's Monthly Political Magazine, London, 1831–32.
Chester Co-operative Chronicle, 1830.
Co-operative Magazine and Monthly Herald, vols. I–III, London, 1826–29, continued as the *London Co-operative Magazine*, vol. IV, London, 1830.
Co-operative News, London, f. 1871.
The Co-operator, Brighton, 1828–30.
The Co-operator, Manchester, 1860–71, continued as *The Co-operator and Anti-Vaccinator*, 1871.
The Crisis, or *The Change from Error and Misery to Truth and Happiness*, London, 1832–34.
The Economist: a Periodical explanatory of the New System of Society projected by Robert Owen Esq., and of a Plan of Association for Improving the Condition of the Working Classes, during their continuance at their present Employments, London, 1821–22.
Herald of Co-operation and Organ of the Redemption Society, 1847–48.
Herald of Progress, London, 1846.
Herald of the Rights of Industry, Manchester, 1834.
Herald to the Trades' Advocate and Co-operative Journal, Glasgow, 1830–31.
Lancashire Co-operator, Manchester, 1831.
Lancashire and Yorkshire Co-operator, Manchester, 1831.
Liverpool Mercury, 1838.
London Social Reformer, 1840.
The Magazine of Useful Knowledge and Co-operative Miscellany, London, 1830–31.
The Movement, 1843–45.
The Moral World: the Advocate of the Rational System of Society as Founded and Developed by Robert Owen, 1845.

The New Moral World, thirteen vols., 1834–46.
The New Moral World, developing the Principles of the Rational System of Society, London, vol. i, November 1834–October 1835; continued as *The New Moral World or Millenium*, London, vol. ii, October 1835–October 1836; continued as *The New Moral World and Manual of Science*, vol. iii, October 1836–October 1837, vol. iv, October 1837–October 1838; continued as *The New Moral World*, vol. v (new series), October 1838–July 1839; continued as *The New Moral World or Gazette of the Universal Community Society of Rational Religionists*, vol. vi (new series), July–December 1839, vii (new series), January–June 1840, viii (vol. i, third series), July–December 1840, ix (vol. ii, third series), January–June 1841, x (vol. iii, third series), July 1841–June 1842, xi (vol. iv, third series), July 1842–July 1843, xii (vol. v, third series), July 1843–June 1844, xiii (vol. vi, third series), June 1844–September 1845.
Robert Owen's Journal, London, 1850–52.
The Patriot, 1842.
The Pioneer, London, 1833–34.
Political Economist, London, 1823.
Poor Man's Advocate, 1832.
Poor Man's Guardian, 1831–35.
Promethean or Communitarian Apostle, 1842.
Rational Association Journal, Manchester, 1891.
The Reasoner, London, 1846.
Social Pioneer, Manchester, 1839.
Social Reformer, London, 1849.
Spirit of the Age, London, 1848–49.
Star in the East, Wisbech, 1836–40.
The Union, London, 1842–43.
The Union Pilot and Co-operative Intelligencer, Manchester, 1832.
United Trades Co-operative Journal, Manchester, 1830.
Voice of the People, Manchester, 1831.
Weekly Free Press, London, 1829–30.
Working Bee, Manea Fen, 1839–40.

Contemporary pamphlets and broadsheets

Address at the opening of the Birmingham Co-operative Society, 17 November 1828, 'by a member'.
Laws and regulations of the Association of All Classes of All Nations, 1835.
Manual of the Association of All Classes of All Nations, 1836.
Aiton, J., *Mr Owen's objections to Christianity and new view of society, refuted*, Edinburgh, 1824.
(Armagh), *Laws of the First Armagh Co-operative Society*, Armagh, 1830.
Bailey, J. N., *Preliminary discourse on the objects, pleasures and advantages of the science of society*, Leeds, 1841.
Baker, F., *First lecture on co-operation, 19 April 1830, reprinted from the Bolton Chronicle*, London 1830.
— *Second lecture . . . 3 May 1830*, London, 1830, as above.

Barker, J., *The overthrow of infidel socialism*, Oldham, n.d.
— *Abominations of socialism exposed*, Newcastle, 1840.
Barmby, J. Goodwyn, *The outline of communism, associality and communitarianism*, London, 1841.
Bower, S., *Competition in peril, or, The present position of the Owenites*, Leeds, 1837.
— *The peopling of Utopia*, Bradford, 1838.
— *A sequel to The peopling of Utopia*, Bradford, 1838.
Bowes, J., *The 'socialist beasts', or, An Exposure of the principles of Robert Owen*, Liverpool, 1840.
Bray, C., *An essay on the union of agriculture and manufactures and upon the organisation of industry*, London, 1844.
A bridge for the socialists, London, 1840.
Brindley, J., *The immoralities of socialism*, Birmingham, 1840.
— *A reply to Robert Owen's 'Fundamental principles of socialism'*, Birmingham, 1840.
— *A voice from Tytherley*, Macclesfield, 1840.
British and Foreign Philanthropic Society, *Proceedings of first General Meeting, held 1 June 1822*, London, 1822.
Brown, D., *A complete refutation of the principles of socialism and Owenism*, Glasgow, 1840.
A budget for the socialists, London, 1840.
(Carlisle), *Rules of Carlisle Co-operating Society*, 1829.
(Carlisle), *Rules of Co-operation Association*, 1830.
'Christianus', *Mr Owen's proposed villages for the poor shown to be highly favourable to Christianity*, London, 1819.
Co-operative Congress reports and papers:
   Society for the Promotion of Co-operative Knowledge, *Report of proceedings at second quarterly meeting, 8 October 1829*, London, 1829; continued as British Association for the Promotion of Co-operative Knowledge, *Report of third quarterly meeting of the Association for the Promotion of Co-operative Knowledge, January 1830*.
   Rules of the London Association for the Promotion of Co-operative Knowledge, London, 1829.
   Co-operative Congress: reports and papers, 1831–32.
   Report of proceedings of the second Co-operative Congress, held in Birmingham, October 1831.
   Report of proceedings of the third Co-operative Congress, held in London, April 1830.
   Report of proceedings of the fourth Co-operative Congress, held in Liverpool, October 1832.
   Rules of the Community Friendly Society, established for the mutual relief and maintenance of the members and for the purpose of promoting the well-being of themselves and families upon the principle of co-operation, 1836.
   Minutes of proceedings of the meeting of friends to the national system of society founded by Robert Owen, commencing at Liverpool, 15 October 1837.

National Community Friendly Society, *Rules, as revised by Congress*, London, 1838.

Report of Proceedings of the third Congress of the Association of All Classes of All Nations, and first Congress of the National Community Friendly Society, held in Manchester, May 1838.

Report of proceedings of the fourth Congress of the Association of All Classes of All Nations, May 1839.

Universal Community Society of Rational Religionists, *Constitution and laws*, London, 1839.

Address: Principles adopted at Congress, Leeds, 1840.

Full report of proceedings of the fifth Congress, Leeds, 1840.

Address to all classes, sects and parties...adopted...by the Congress held in Leeds, May 1840, London, 1840.

Report of proceedings of the sixth Congress of the Association of All Classes of All Nations, Birmingham, 1841.

Universal Community Society of Rational Religionists, *Address of the Congress...May 1842 to Chartists...and trade unions*, 1842.

Report of proceedings of the eighth Congress of the Rational Society, held in Harmony Hall, May 1843, London, 1843.

Rational Sick and Burial Association, *General laws*, Manchester, 1844.

Laws for the government of the Rational Sick and Burial Association, instituted January 1837, Manchester, 1845.

Report of the Co-operative Conference held at the hall of the Society for Promoting Working Men's Associations, 34 Castle Street, East Oxford Street, London, July 1852.

Report of the second Co-operative Conference, held at Manchester, August 1853.

Co-operative League, *Transactions*, Part II, 1852.

Co-operation: dialogue between a shoemaker and a tailor...by a member of the Metropolitan Trading Association, London, 1830.

A co-operator: remarks on the rational system, London, 1832.

Detrosier, R., *An address delivered at the New Mechanics' Institution, Manchester, 30 December 1829*, Manchester, 1829.

— *An address delivered to members of the New Mechanics' Institution, Manchester, on 25 March 1831, on the necessity of an extension of moral and political instruction among the working classes*, London and Manchester, 1831.

(Devonshire), *An Address to the working classes of Devonshire*, Exeter, 1830.

(Dublin), *Report of proceedings at the several public meetings held in Dublin*, Dublin, 1823.

Elements of socialism, Birmingham, 1840.

'Ethnicus', 'Why I am a socialist' in *A letter to a Christian friend*, Glasgow, 1840.

An exposure of Joseph Mather's pamphlet ('Socialism exposed') by a lover of practical Christianity, Bilston, 1839.

Finch, J., *Teetotalism*. Temperance Tract No. 4, Liverpool, 1836.

Finch, J., *The millenium: the wisdom of Jesus and the foolery of sectarianism*, Liverpool, 1837.
— *Moral code of the new moral world*, Liverpool, 1840.
— *Society as it is, and society as it ought to be ... by a Liverpool merchant*, Liverpool, 1847.
Fleming, G. A., *A vindication of the principles of the rational system of society*, Manchester, 1837.
— *The right application of science*, Leeds, 1839.
A full and complete exposure of the atrocious and horrible doctrines of the Owenites, London, 1840.
Hancock, E., *Robert Owen's community system*, London, 1837.
Hanson, J., *A statement of facts relative to the Birmingham town hall, with an appeal to the ratepayers and inhabitants of Birmingham*, Birmingham, 1834.
Haslam, C. J., *Who are the infidels: those who call themselves socialists, or followers of Robert Owen; or those who call themselves Christians or followers of Jesus Christ?*, third edition, Manchester, 1840.
Hawkes-Smith, W., 'On co-operation', *Monthly Repository*, July 1832.
— *The errors of the social system*, Birmingham, 1834.
Hobson, J., *Socialism as it is!*, Leeds, 1838.
Hollick, F., *What is Christianity? and have the persons calling themselves Christians any right to interfere with the free expression of opinions by other parties?*, Liverpool, 1840.
Holyoake, G. J., *Diaries*, especially 1849.
Hunt, T., *Chartism, trade unionism and socialism: a dialogue*, London, 1840.
Ironside, I., *Brindley and his lying braggadocio*, Sheffield, 1840.
'Junius', *Six letters on the theory and practice of socialism*, London, 1840.
(Lamberhead Green), *Rules at Lamberhead Green Trading Fund Society*, 1830.
(Liverpool), *Minutes of the Liverpool branch of the Association of All Classes of All Nations*, 1837.
(Liverpool), *Rules of the First Liverpool Co-operative Society*, n.d.
(London City Mission), *Lectures against socialism*, London, 1840.
(London Co-operative Society), *First Community of Mutual Co-operation, commenced April 1825*, 1825.
Macnab, H. G., *The new views of Robert Owen impartially examined*, London, 1819.
Marriott, J., *Community: a drama*, Manchester, 1838.
— *A catechism on circumstances, or, The foundation of a community*, London, 1840.
Mather, J., *Socialism exposed*, London, 1840.
McCormac, H., *On the best means of improving the moral and physical condition of the working classes*, London, 1830.
Miall, E., *Nonconformity*, 1842.
Morgan, J. M., *Remarks on the practicability of Mr Owen's plan ... to improve the condition of the lower classes, by 'Philanthropos'*, London, 1819.
— *An inquiry respecting private property and the authority and perpetuity of the apostolic institution of a community of goods*, 1827.

Morgan, J. M., *Letter to the Bishop of London*, London, 1830.
— *The reproof of Brutus*, London, 1830.
— *Letters to a clergyman on institutions for ameliorating the conditions of the people*, London, 1846.
Mudie, G., *Report of the committee appointed at a meeting of journeymen, chiefly printers, to take into consideration certain propositions . . . having for their object a system of social arrangements calculated to effect essential improvements in the condition of the working classes*, second edition, London, 1821.
Norton, H. H., *Community the only salvation for man*, 1838.
An outline scheme for the establishment of industrial, educational and residential settlements on co-operative principles in the neighbourhood of London, to be carried out by the Fellowship of New Life, n.d.
Owen, R., *An address to the inhabitants of New Lanark on opening the Institution for the Formation of Character, 4 January 1816*.
— *A new view of society, or, Essays on the formation of the human character preparatory to the development of a plan for gradually ameliorating the condition of mankind*, third edition, London, 1817.
— *A new view of society, extracted from the London daily papers of 30 July and 9, 11 August 1817*, London, 1817.
— *Letter to the public published in London newspapers, 10 September 1817: further development of the plan for the relief of the poor and the emancipation of mankind*.
— *New view of society, tracts relative to this subject*, 1818.
— *Address, City of London Tavern, 26 July 1819*.
— Report to the County of Lanark, 1820.
— *Outline of the rational system of society, founded on demonstrable facts, developing the constitution and laws of human nature; being the only effectual remedy for the evils experienced by the population of the world*, London, n.d.
— *The catechism of the new world*, Manchester, 1838.
— *Robert Owen's journal*, 1852.
— *Life of Robert Owen, written by himself*, 1, London, 1857. *A supplementary appendix to the first volume of the Life of Robert Owen*, 1A, London, 1858.
— *'A new view of society' and other writings*, ed. G. D. H. Cole, London, 1927.
Pare, W., *An address to the working classes of Liverpool on the formation of co-operative societies or working unions*, 1829.
— *The claims of capital and labour*, London, 1854.
— *Equitable commerce as practised in the equity villages of the United States*, London, 1856.
— *A plan for the suppression of the predatory classes*, London, 1862.
'Philopatrius', *Letter to Lord Melbourne, on his presenting Robert Owen, the founder of the immoral, blasphemous and atheistical system, misnamed 'Socialism', to the Queen*, London, 1839.
Practical Society, *Report of the Practical Society of Edinburgh*, Edinburgh, 1822.

(Preston), *Rules of the First Preston Co-operating Society*, 1829.
Rational Society, *A full account of the farewell festival given to Robert Owen on his departure for America*, London, 1844.
Remarks on the Owen plan to improve the condition of the working classes, 1819.
Remarks on the rational system as developed by Robert Owen, by a co-operator, London, 1832.
Rey, J., *Lettres sur le système de la co-opération mutuelle*, Paris, 1828.
Sargant, W. L., 'Robert Owen and his social philosophy', *Westminster and Foreign Quarterly Review*, October 1860.
Seligman, E. R. A., 'Robert Owen and the Christian socialists', *Political Science Quarterly*, I, 1886. reprinted in *Essays in economics*, 1925.
Smith, J. E., *Lecture on a Christian community*, London, 1833.
Social bible, Manchester, 1835.
Social hymns, for the use of the friends of the rational system of society, Manchester, 1835.
Social tracts, published by the National Community Friendly Society, n.d.
Somerville A., *Notes from the farming districts*, No. XVII, *A journey to Harmony Hall*, London, 1842.
— *The Whistler at the plough*, Manchester, 1852.
Southwell, C., *Socialism made easy, or, a plain exposition of Mr Owen's views*, London, 1840.
Spence, T., *On the mode of administering the landed estates of the nation as a joint stock company in parochial partnership by dividing the rent*, 1775. Paper read before the Newcastle Philosophical Society, 1775.
Statement submitted to the most noble the Marquis of Normanby relative to a universal community by the Society of Rational Religionists, by Branch A1, London, 1840.
Sturmer, F., *Socialism, its immoral tendency*, London, 1840.
Torrens, R., 'Mr Owen's plan for relieving the distress', *Edinburgh Review*, October 1819.
Travis, H., *Effectual reform in man and society*, London, 1875.
— *English socialism*, I and II, London, 1880.
A vindication of Mr Owen's plan for the relief of the distressed working classes, in reply to the misconceptions of a writer in No. 64 of the Edinburgh Review, London, 1820.
Watts, J., *Facts and fictions of political economy*, Manchester, 1842.
— *Co-operative societies, past, present and future*, Manchester, 1861.
Wayland, T., *National advancement and happiness considered in reference to the equalization of property, and the formation of communities*, London, 1832.
Whitwell, S., *Description of an architectural model for a community*, London, 1830.

Contemporary books
Adams, W. E., *Memoirs of a social atom*, London, 1903.
Booth, A. J., *Robert Owen, the founder of socialism in England*, London, 1869.

Booth, W., *In darkest England, and the way out*, London, 1890.

Bray, C., *Philosophy of necessity*, London, 1841.

Bray, J. F., *Labour's wrongs and labour's remedy*, Leeds, 1839.

Buckingham, J. S., *National evils and practical remedies*, London, 1849.

Campbell, A., *Letters and extracts from the writings of J. P. Greaves*, 1843.

Collet, S. D., *G. J. Holyoake and modern atheism*, London, 1855.

Colquhoun, P., *A treatise on the wealth, power and resources of the British empire in every quarter of the world*, London, 1814.

Edmonds, T. R., *Practical moral and political economy*, 1828.

Emerson, R. W., 'Power' in *Collected essays*, 1908 edition, London.

Engels, F., *The condition of the working class in England in 1844*, London, 1892.

— *Socialism, utopian and scientific*, London, 1892.

Frost, T., *Forty years: recollections, literary and political*, London, 1880.

George, H., *Progress and poverty*, New York, 1880.

Godwin, W., *An enquiry concerning political justice and its influence on general virtue and happiness*, London, 1793.

Gray, J., *A lecture on human happiness*, London, 1825.

— *A word of advice to the Orbistonians*, 1826.

— *The social system*, Edinburgh, 1831.

— *Lectures on the nature and use of money*, 1848.

Hazlitt, W., 'Robert Owen' in *Political essays, with sketches of public characters*, second edition, London, 1823.

Hennell, M., *An outline of the various social systems and communities which have been founded on the principle of co-operation*, London, 1844.

Hill, R. D. and F. D., *The Recorder of Birmingham: a memoir of Matthew Davenport Hill*, London, 1878.

Hodgskin, T., *Labour defended against the claims of capitalism*, 1825.

Holyoake, G. J., *Rationalism: a treatise for the times*, London, 1845.

— *Self-help by the people: a history of co-operation in Rochdale*, London, 1858.

— *Life and last days of Robert Owen of New Lanark*, London, 1859.

— *The history of co-operation in England*, two volumes, London, 1875–79; revised edition, London, 1906.

— *Self-help 100 years ago*, London, 1888.

— *Sixty years of an agitator's life*, two volumes, London, 1892.

— *Bygones worth remembering*, London, 1905.

Howard, E., *Tomorrow: a peaceful path to social reform*, London, 1898.

Hughes, T., and Neale, E. V., *A manual for co-operators*, London, 1881.

Jolly, W., *Education: Its principles and practice as developed by George Combe*, 1879.

Jones, B., *Co-operative production*, Oxford, 1894.

Jones, Lloyd, *The life, times and labours of Robert Owen*, London, 1889.

Kaufman, M., *Utopias, or schemes of social improvement from Sir Thomas More to Karl Marx*, London, 1879.

Kingsley, C., *Application by associative principles and methods for agriculture*, London, 1851.

Kirkup, T., *A history of socialism*, London and Edinburgh, 1892.

Linton, W. J., *James Watson*, Manchester, 1880.
Lovett, W., *Social and political morality*, London, 1853.
— *Life and struggles of William Lovett*, London, 1876.
Martineau, H., *Society in America*, two volumes, London, 1837.
— *Biographical sketches*, London, 1869.
Menger, A., *The right to the whole produce of labour*, with introduction by
    H. S. Foxwell, London, 1899.
Mill, J. S., *Principles of political economy*, 1883 edition, London.
Morgan, J. M., *The revolt of the bees*, London, 1828.
— *Hampden in the nineteenth century*, London, 1834.
— *The Christian commonwealth*, London, 1845.
— *The Church of England self-supporting villages for promoting the religious,
    moral and general improvement of the working classes, by forming estab-
    lishments of three hundred families on the land, and combining agricul-
    tural with manufacturing employment*, London, 1850.
Mudie, G., *The grammar of the English language truly made easy and
    amusing by the invention of 300 movable parts of speech*, 1840.
Owen, R. D., *Threading my way: twenty-seven years of autobiography*, Lon-
    don, 1874.
Packard, F. A., *Life of Robert Owen*, Philadelphia, Pa., 1866.
Sargant, W. L., *Social innovators and their schemes*, London, 1858.
Smith, W. A., *Shepherd Smith, the universalist*, London, 1892.
Thompson, W., *An inquiry into the principles of the distribution of wealth
    most conducive to human happiness as applied to the newly proposed
    system of voluntary equality of wealth*, London, 1824.
— *An appeal on one-half the human race, women, against the pretensions of
    the other half, men, to retain them in political and thence in civil and
    domestic slavery*, London, 1825.
— *Labour rewarded: the claims of labour and capital conciliated*, London,
    1827.
— *Practical directions for the speedy and economical establishment of com-
    munities on the principles of mutual co-operation, united possessions and
    equality of exertions and of the means of enjoyment*, London, 1830.
Tristan, F., *Promenades dans Londres*, Paris, 1840.
Wade, J., *History of the middle and working classes*, London, 1833.
Wallas, G., *Life of Francis Place*, London, 1898.
Webb, B., *The co-operative movement in Great Britain*, London, 1891.

Sources relating specifically to community experiments

ORBISTON

Articles of agreement of the Orbiston Company, 1825.
Campbell, A., *Trial and self-defence of A. Campbell*, Glasgow, 1835.
— (ed.), *Life and dying testimony of Abram Combe*, London, 1844.
— *New views of man and society*, 1844.
Combe, A., *Metaphorical sketches of the old and new systems*, Edinburgh,
    1823.

Combe, A., *An address to the conductors of the periodical press, upon the causes of religious and political disputes*, Edinburgh, 1823.

— *Observations on the old and new views and their effects on the conduct of individuals as manifested in the proceedings of the Edinburgh Christian Instructor and Mr Owen*, Edinburgh, 1823.

— *The religious creed of the new systems*, Edinburgh, 1824.

— *The sphere of joint stock companies, with an account of the establishment at Orbiston*, Edinburgh, 1825.

— *The new court*, No. 1. *The records of the new court, published by the First Society . . . for the Extinction of Disputes*, Edinburgh, 1825.

— *An account of Orbiston*, 1825.

Combe, G., *Education: its principles and practice*, ed. W. Joly, 1879.

(Price, A.), 'George Combe: a pioneer of scientific education', *Educational Review, University of Birmingham*, vol. 12, No. 3, June 1960.

Cullen, A., *Robert Owen and the Orbiston community: a paper read before the members of the United Y.M.C.A.s of Motherwell at Orbiston, 12 September 1896*, Hamilton, 1896.

— *Adventures in socialism: New Lanark establishment and Orbiston community*, London and Glasgow, 1910.

Gray, J., *A lecture on human happiness*, London, 1825.

— *A word of advice to the Orbistonians on the principles which ought to regulate their present proceedings*, 1826.

— *The social system*, Edinburgh, 1831.

Hamilton collection (Motherwell Public Library):

Inter alia: articles of agreement, Orbiston Company.

Abstract of valuation, Orbiston Company: report as to contents and estimated rents and value of lands and estate, 1828.

Memorial and abstract of the ranking and sale of Orbiston, 1830.

Deed of partition of Orbiston.

Diary of A. J. Hamilton.

The Political Thieves, A. J. Hamilton.

Lives and Death of A. J. Hamilton.

Letters of A. J. Hamilton, A. Combe, G. Combe, William Cobbett, W. Falla, Robert Owen, A. Paul.

Names of subscribers, Hamilton Subscription Library, 1824.

Hamilton, A. J., 'The soldier and the citizen of the world, with reflections on subjects of interest to the happiness of mankind', MS, n.d.

Hamilton, J., *Owenism rendered consistent with our civil and religious institutions*, 1825.

Henderson, G., and Waddell, J. J., *By Bothwell banks*, 1904.

Johnston, T., *History of the working classes in Scotland*, Glasgow, 1922.

Maxwell, W., *The history of co-operation in Scotland*, Glasgow, 1910.

McPherson, A., *Handbook of Hamilton and Bothwell*, 1862.

Orbiston Register (the register for the first society of adherents to divine revelation at Orbiston in Lanarkshire. N.B. With a circumstantial account of the rise and progress of the first British community founded on the important principles of co-operative self-directed labour).

Owen, R., 'Report to the County of Lanark' (with appendix by A. J. Hamilton giving a map of the area afterwards occupied by the Orbiston Community), 1821.

Pagan, J. H., *Antiquities of Bothwell*, Greenock, 1892.

Practical Society of Edinburgh, *Second report of the Economical Committee of the Practical Society, 13 February 1822*, Edinburgh, 1822.

Reed's Directory for the parish of Bothwell, 1888.

Scottish Notes and Queries, 1892.

Second statistical account for Scotland (Lanarkshire), 1845.

Third statistical account for Scotland (Lanarkshire), 1960.

Stother's Glasgow annual, 1911.

Wallace, J., *History of Bellshill*, 1955.

Newspapers

Bellshill Speaker.

Clydesdale Journal, 1821.

Dublin Morning Post, 1826.

Farmers' Magazine, 1820–21.

Glasgow Chronicle, 1823, 1832.

Glasgow Herald, 1826, 1828, 1831, 1911.

Glasgow Illustrated, 1904.

Glasgow Journal, 1832.

Glasgow Sentinel, 1821.

Herald to the Trades' Advocate and Co-operative Journal, 1830–31.

RALAHINE

Books and pamphlets (nineteenth-century)

'Agricola', *Considerations for landed proprietors*, Clare, 1831.

Barrow, J., *Tour round Ireland in 1835*, London, 1836.

Connery, J., *The Reformer*, Limerick, 1833.

Considerations addressed to the land proprietors of County Clare, Limerick, 1831.

Craig, E. T., *The Irish land and labour question illustrated in the history of Ralahine and co-operative farming*, London, 1882.

— *A remedy for the pacification of Ireland, illustrated by a sketch of Ralahine Agricultural and Co-operative Association, with suggestions on agricultural co-operation and regulations for co-operative farming*, London, n.d.

— *Work and Wages*, London, 1865.

— *The Organisation of co-operative farms.*

E. T. Craig, educationalist and social reformer, reprinted from the *Phrenological Magazine*, February 1883.

Dutton, H., *Statistical survey of Clare*, Dublin, 1808.

Fitzpatrick, W. J., *Life, times and contemporaries of Lord Cloncurry*, Dublin, 1855.

Frost, J., *The history and topography of the County of Clare*, Dublin, 1893.

Goupy, L., *Quaere et invenies*, Paris, 1853.

Hall, S. C., *Ireland: its scenery, character*, London, 1841–43.

Hancock, W. N., *On laissez-faire and the economic resources of Ireland*, Dublin, 1847.

— *Impediments to the prosperity of Ireland*, London, 1850.

Hines, G., *One of the old (co-operative) guard, being a sketch of life of E. T. Craig*, 1890.

Larkin, E. R., 'On the results of a scheme by Mr Vandeleur for improving the condition of labourers tried at Ralahine, Co. Clare', *Athenaeum*, 3 July 1847.

Lewis, Sir G. C., *On local disturbances in Ireland*, London, 1836.

Lewis, S., *A topographical dictionary of Ireland*, London, 1837.

Marsh, C. M., *Life of Arthur Vandeleur*, London, 1862.

O'Brien, R. B., *The Parliamentary history of the Irish land question from 1829 to 1869*, London, 1880.

O'Brien, W. S., *Plan for relief of the poor in Ireland*, London, 1830.

Owen, R., *Report of the proceedings of several meetings held in Dublin*, Dublin, 1823.

— *Letter to the nobility, gentry and clergy of Ireland*, Dublin, 1823.

— *Letter to the nobility, gentry, professions, bankers, merchants and master manufacturers of Ireland*, Dublin, 1823.

Pare, W., *The claims of capital and labour*, London, 1854.

— *Co-operative agriculture: a solution of the land question as exemplified in the history of the Ralahine Co-operative and Agricultural Association*, London, 1870.

Stubbs, C. W., *The land, the labourers: a record of facts and experiments in cottage farming and co-operative agriculture*, London, 1884.

Urwick, W., *Biographic sketches of James Digges la Touche*, Dublin, 1868.

Wallace, A. R., *Studies scientific and social*, London, 1900.

White, P., *History of Clare*, Dublin, 1893.

Books (twentieth-century)

A.E. (G. W. Russell), introduction to *An Irish commune*, Dublin, 1919.

Arensberg, C. M., *The Irish countryman: an anthropological study*, London, 1939.

Arensberg, C. M., and Kimball, S. T., *Family and community in Ireland*, London, 1940.

Connolly, J., *Labour in Irish history*, Dublin, 1910.

Digby, M., *Horace Plunkett*, Oxford, 1949.

Frankenburg, R., *Communities in Britain*, London, 1966.

McDowell, R. B., *Public opinion and government policy in Ireland, 1801–46*, London, 1952.

O'Brien, G., *Economic history of Ireland from the union to the famine*, London, 1921.

Pankhurst, R. K. P., *William Thompson, 1755–1833: Britain's pioneer socialist, feminist and co-operator*, London, 1954.

Plunkett, H., *Ireland in the new century*, London, 1904.

Ryan, W. P., *The Irish labour movement, from the twenties to our own day*, Dublin, 1919.
Vandeleur, J. O. E., 'Memoirs of the Vandeleur family', MS, n.d.

Articles in journals

Letter of E. T. Craig, *The Spectator*, July 1884.
Boyd, A., 'Robert Owen and the Ralahine experiment', *Irish Times*, 18 December 1958.
Clarke, D., 'The Dublin Society's statistical surveys', *Leabharlann,* xv, 1957.
Hogan, J. F., 'Early modern Socialists', ii, *Irish Ecclesiastical Record*, xxvi, 1909.
Kelly, R. J., 'A co-operative farm fifty years ago', *Month*, vii, 1884.
O'Donnell, G. J., 'The Ralahine experiment', MS, 1935.
Oppenheimer, F., 'Co-operative farm communities', *Bulletin of the University of Georgia*, xxxvi, 1936.
Ryan, D., 'William Thompson', *The Leader*, October 1954.
'Ralahine: the great experiment in co-operation', *The Plough*, February 1960.

Newspapers

American Socialist, December 1877–January 1878.
Clare Journal, 1831, 1833.
Dublin Evening Post, 1833.
Freeman's Journal, 1833.
Limerick Evening Herald, 1833.
Limerick Evening Post, 1833.
Liverpool Mercury, 1838 (series of letters on Ralahine by J. Finch).

Parliamentary papers and reports

Report of Select Committee on the Employment of the Poor in Ireland, 1823 (561), vi.
Report from Select Committee on the State of Ireland, 1825 (129), viii.
Report from Select Committee on the State of the Poor in Ireland, 1830 (589, 654, 655, 667), vii.
Report from Select Committee on Drunkenness, 1834 (559), viii.
Report of H.M. Commission of Inquiry into the Condition of the Poorer Classes in Ireland, 1835 (369), xxxii, 1837 (68), xxxi (second report); 1836 (43), xxx (third report).
Report from H.M. Commission of Inquiry into the State of the Law and Practice in respect to the Occupation of Land in Ireland (the Devon Commission), 1845 (605) xix, (606) xix, (616) xx, (657) xxi, (672, 673), xxii.

Manuscripts, repositories, papers, etc

Public Record Office, London:
Home Office, records relating to Ireland, H.O. 100.

Irish State Papers Office:

County Clare, number and nature of offences, 1833 (66), xxix, 413 (79), xxix, 405.

National Library of Ireland

Press cuttings relating to County Clare compiled by Theobald Fitz-Walter Butler, mss 3321–79.

Royal Irish Academy:

Halliday collection (pamphlets).

Irish Valuation Office:

Valuation lists of rateable property and perambulation book, Tomfinlough, 1855.
General valuation lists and field book, Ralahine, 1885.

Irish Public Record Office:

Will and schedule of assets, Mary Vandeleur, 1914.

Maps

Ordnance Survey, six-inch Townslands survey, sheet 51, 1843.
Oral evidence of Mr Cormac Halpin, Newmarket-on-Fergus.
Diary of William Halpin, 1886.

QUEENWOOD

Brindley, J., *A voice from Tytherley*, Macclesfield, 1840.
Colson, A. M., 'Revolt of Hampshire agricultural labourers', M.A. thesis, University of London, 1937.
Crabb, J., *Consider the end, or, Owenite socialism exposed*, Southampton, 1842.
Eve, A. S., and Creasey, C. H., *Life of John Tyndall*, London, 1945.
Frost, T., *Forty years' recollections*, London, 1880.
Gross, C. W. F., *Descriptive bibliography of G. J. Holyoake*, London, 1908.
Hampshire Field Club papers, 1920.
Holyoake, G. J., *A visit to Harmony Hall*, reprinted from *The Movement*, London, 1844.
— *History of Co-operation*, 1875–79.
— *Bygones worth remembering*, London, 1905.
Mudie, W., *Hampshire*, 1838.
Nowell-Smith, S., *The House of Cassell*, London, 1958.
Podmore, F., *Robert Owen, a biography*, London, 1906.
Reid, R. J., *Exposure of socialism: a refutation of a letter on Harmony Hall, by one who has whistled at the plough*, 1843.
'Social Utopias', Chambers' *Papers for the people*, No. 18 (Edinburgh, 1850–51).

Somerville, A., *Notes from the farming districts*, xvii, *A journey to Harmony Hall*, London, 1842.
— *Autobiography of a working man*, 1854.
Stephen, L., *Life of Henry Fawcett*, London, 1886.
Thompson, D., 'A mid-nineteenth century experiment in science teaching', *Annals of Science*, 1955.
Vancouver, C., *General Survey of the agriculture of Hampshire*, London, 1813.
Victoria County History of Hampshire, four volumes, 1900.
White's *Hampshire*, 1878.

Parliamentary papers and reports

Hansard Parliamentary debates, third series, Li 1840.
Report of Select Committee on Allotments (3), 1843, vii.
Census of the population of England and Wales, 1851.

Law report

Pare Clegg, *English law reports*, liv, Rolls Court (1905), 756–62.

Manuscripts, repositories, papers, etc

Public Record Office:

Home Office papers, 40/59, 41/30 (Socialism).
Home Office correspondence, 44 (Geo. iv and later), 1820–61.

Hampshire County Record Office:

Schedules of leases of Queenwood.
Newspaper cuttings of Sir George Cooper.
Post Office directory, 1848.
Parliamentary gazetteer, England and Wales, 1840, 43 v. 10.

Letters

Letters of I. L. Goldsmid in the Mocatta collection. University College, London, two volumes.

Newspapers

Co-operative News, 1902, 1904.
Hampshire Chronicle, 1839, 1942, 1902.
Illustrated London News, 1902.
The Moral World, 1846.
Morning Chronicle, 1842.
The Movement, 1843–45.
New Moral World, 1839–45.
Reasoner, 1846.
Reasoner and Herald of Progress, 1846.
Salisbury and Wiltshire Journal, 1902.
The Times, London, 1840.

Secondary sources

Books since 1900

Andrews, E. D., *The people called Shakers*, New York, 1963.

Armytage, W. H. G., *Heavens below: utopian experiments in England, 1560-1960*, London, 1961.

Ashworth, W., 'The genesis of modern town planning', Ph.D. thesis, University of London, 1950.

Balmforth, R., *Some social and political pioneers of the nineteenth century*, London, 1900.

Beales, H. L., *The early English socialists*, London, 1933.

Beer, M., *A history of British socialism*, London, 1919.

— *Social struggles, 1750-1860*, London, 1925.

Begbie, H., *Life of William Booth*, London, 1920.

Bestor, A. E., *Backwoods Utopias: the sectarian and Owenite phases of communitarian socialism in America, 1663-1829*, Philadelphia, Pa., 1950.

Bettany, F. G., *Stewart Headlam*, London, 1926.

Briggs, A., and Saville, J. (eds.), *Essays in labour history*, London, 1967.

Brinton, C. C., *English political thought in the nineteenth century*, London, 1949.

Brown, W. H., *A century of Liverpool co-operation*, Liverpool, 1930.

— *A century of London co-operation*, London, 1938.

— *Brighton's co-operative advance, 1828-1938*, Manchester, 1938.

Buber, M., *Paths in Utopia*, London, 1949.

Butt, J. (ed.), *Robert Owen, prince of cotton spinners*, Newton Abbot, 1971.

Clayton, J., *Robert Owen, pioneer of social reforms*, London, 1908.

Cole, G. D. H., *The life of Robert Owen*, London, 1925.

— *Chartist portraits*, London, 1941.

— *A century of co-operation*, Manchester, 1944.

— *Attempts at general union: a study in British trade union history, 1818-34*, London, 1953.

— *A history of socialist thought*, I, *The forerunners, 1789-1850*, London, 1953.

Cole, M., *Robert Owen of New Lanark*, London, 1953.

Davies, R. E., *The life of Robert Owen*, London, 1907.

Dent, J. J., *The co-operative ideals of Dr William King*, Manchester, 1921.

Dolleans, E., *Robert Owen*, Paris, 1905.

— *Individualisme et socialisme*, Paris, 1907.

Fay, C. R., *Co-operation at home and abroad*, 1908; fifth edition, 1948.

— *Life and Labour in the nineteenth century*, Cambridge, 1920.

Garnett, R. G., *A century of co-operative insurance*, London, 1968.

Gide, C., *Communist and co-operative colonies*, trans. E. F. Row, London, 1930.

Glasse, J., *Robert Owen and his life work*, London, 1900.

Gosden, P. H. J. H., *The friendly societies in England, 1815-75*, Manchester, 1961.

Gray, A., *The socialist tradition*, London, 1946.

Greening, E. O., *Memories of Robert Owen and the co-operative pioneers*, Manchester, 1925.

Halevy, E., *The growth of philosophic radicalism*, London, 1952.

— *Thomas Hodgskin*, Paris, 1903; trans. A. J. Taylor, London, 1956.

Hall, F., and Watkins, W. P., *Co-operation: a survey of the history, principles and organisation of the co-operative movement in Great Britain and Ireland*, Manchester, 1934.

Hampton, E. W., *Early co-operation in Birmingham*, Birmingham, 1928.

Harrison, J. F. C., *Learning and living: a study of the English adult education movement*, London, 1961.

Harvey, R. H., *Robert Owen, social idealist*, Berkeley and Los Angeles, Cal., 1949.

Hertzler, J. O., *History of utopian thought*, London, 1923.

Himes, N. E. (ed.), *Francis Place, political reformer: illustrations and proofs of the principle of population*, London, 1930.

Hutchins, B. L., *Robert Owen: social reformer*, London, 1912.

Infield, H. F., *Co-operative communities at work*, London, 1947.

Judges, A. V., *Pioneers of English education*, London, 1952.

Kropotkin, Prince, *Fields, factories and Workshops, or, Industry combined with agriculture and brain work with manual work*, 1912 edition, London.

Laidler, H. W., *Social–economic movements: an historical and comparative survey of socialism, communism, co-operation, utopianism*, London, 1948.

Littleton, A. C., *Accounting evolution to 1900*, New York, 1933.

Loucks, W. N., and Hoot, J. W., *Comparative economic systems*, New York, 1938.

Lowenthal, E., *The Ricardian socialists*, New York, 1911.

Marwick, W. H., *The life of Alexander Campbell*, Glasgow, 1964.

McAskill, J., 'The treatment of land in English social and political theory, 1840–85, B.Litt. thesis, University of Oxford, 1959.

McCabe, J., *Life and letters of George Jacob Holyoake*, London, 1908.

— *Robert Owen*, London, 1920.

Meakin, J. E. B., *Model factories and villages*, London, 1905.

Mercer, T. W., *Dr William King and 'The Co-operator'*, Manchester, 1922.

— *Towards a co-operative commonwealth*, Manchester, 1936.

Morris, D. C., 'The history of the labour movement in England, 1825–52: problems of leadership and articulation of demands', Ph.D. thesis, University of London, 1952.

Morton, A. L., *The English Utopia*, London, 1952.

— *The life and ideas of Robert Owen*, London, 1962.

Pelling, H. M., *The origins of the Labour Party, 1880–1900*, London, 1954.

Pankhurst, R. K. P., 'William Thompson, his life and writings', Ph.D. thesis, University of London, 1952.

— *William Thompson, 1775–1833: Britain's pioneer socialist, feminist and co-operator*, London, 1954.

Podmore, F., *Robert Owen: a biography*, London, 1906.

Pollard, S., and Salt, J. (eds.), *Robert Owen, prophet of the poor*, London, 1971.

Royle, E., 'G. J. Holyoake and the secularist movement in Britain, 1841-61', Ph.D. thesis, University of Cambridge, 1968.

Silver, H., 'Robert Owen and the concept of popular education', M.Ed. thesis, University of Hull, 1964.

— *The concept of popular education: a study of ideas and social movements in the early nineteenth century*, London, 1965.

Simon, B., *Studies in the history of education, 1780-1870*, London, 1960.

Smelser, N., *Social change in the industrial revolution*, London, 1959.

Sombart, W., *Socialism and the socialist movement in the nineteenth century*, sixth edition, London, 1909, with introduction by M. Epstein.

Thompson, E. P., *The making of the English working class*, Pelican Books edition, Harmondsworth, 1968.

Twigg, H. J., *An outline of the history of co-operative education*, Manchester, 1924.

Wearmouth, R. F., *Methodism and the working class movements of England, 1800-50*, London, 1937.

Webb, C., *Industrial co-operation*, Manchester, 1904.

Webb, R. K., *The British working class reader, 1790-1848*, London, 1955.

— *Harriet Martineau: a radical Victorian*, London, 1960.

Whyte, W. H., *The organization man*, Pelican Books edition, Harmondsworth, 1960.

Williams, R., *Culture and society, 1780-1950*, London, 1958.

Recent journal articles

Armytage, W. H. G., 'John Minter Morgan, 1782-1854, *Journal of Education*, LXXXVI, 1954.

— 'Pant Glas: a communitarian experiment in Merioneth', *Journal of the Merioneth Historical Society*, II, 1955.

— 'Technology and Utopia: J. A. Etzler in England', *Annals of Science*, XI, 1955.

— 'The journalistic activities of J. Goodwyn Barmby between 1840 and 1848', *Notes and Queries*, CCI, 1956.

— 'Ruskin as utopist', *Notes and Queries*, CCI, 1956.

— 'Manea Fen: an experiment in agrarian communitarianism, 1838-41', *Bulletin of the John Rylands Library*, XXXVIII, 1956.

— 'George Mudie, journalist and utopian', *Notes and Queries*, CCII, 1957.

— 'Liverpool, Gateway to Zion', *Pacific North West Quarterly*, XLVIII, 1957.

—'John Minter Morgan's schemes, 1841-45', *International Review of Social History*, III, 1958.

— 'The utopian tradition in English education', Vaughan Memorial Lecture, Doncaster, 1958.

Bestor, A. E., 'Evolution of the socialist vocabulary', *Journal of the History of Ideas*, June 1948.

Black, A., 'The Owenites and the halls of science', *Co-operative Review*, XXIX, February 1955.

— 'Owenite education, 1839-57, with particular reference to the Manchester Hall of Science', Dip.Ed. dissertation, University of Manchester, 1953.

Black, A. M., 'The Educational work of Robert Owen', Ph.D. thesis, University of St Andrews, 1949.

Briggs, A., 'Robert Owen in retrospect', *Co-operative College Paper*, 1959.

Garnett, R. G., 'E. T. Craig: communitarian, educator, phrenologist', *Vocational Aspect*, xv, summer 1963.

— 'Owen's descendant at New Lanark', *Co-operative Review*, December 1963.

— 'William Pare: a non-Rochdale pioneer', *Co-operative Review*, May 1964.

— 'A housing association for New Lanark', *Amateur Historian*, summer 1964.

— 'The Ideology of the early co-operative movement', University of Kent endowment lecture, University of Kent, 1966.

— 'Records of early co-operation', *Local Historian*, ix, No. 4, 1970.

Gorb, P., 'Robert Owen as a businessman', *Bulletin of the Business Historical Society*, xxv, 1957.

Harrison, J. F. C., 'The visions of the Leeds redemptionists: one of the last experiments in Owenite socialism', *Manchester Guardian*, 22 June 1955.

— 'Adult education and self-help', *British Journal of Educational Studies*, vi, No. 1, 1957.

— 'The steam engine of the new moral world: Owenism and education, 1817–29, *Journal of British Studies*, vi, No. 2, May 1967.

Howell, G., 'Voluntary and State socialism' (articles on Robert Owen), *Reynolds News*, 26 November–31 December 1905.

Infield, H. F., 'The sociological study of co-operation: an outline', *Co-operative College Paper*, 1956.

Mercer, T. W., 'A father of co-operation: the life and teaching of Dr William King', *Millgate Monthly*, June 1922.

Miliband, R., 'The politics of Robert Owen', *Journal of the History of Ideas*, xv, April 1954.

Muller, H., 'Dr William King and his place in the history of co-operation', *Yearbook of Co-operation*, 1913.

Musson, A. E., 'The ideology of early co-operation in Lancashire and Cheshire', *Transactions of the Lancashire and Cheshire Antiquarian Society*, lxviii, 1958.

Oliver, W. H., 'The labour exchange phase of the co-operative movement', *Oxford Economic Papers*, October 1958.

— 'Robert Owen and the English working class movements', *History Today*, November 1958.

Pollard, S., 'Dr William King of Ipswich: co-operative pioneer', *Co-operative College Paper*, 1959.

Rose, R. B., 'John Finch, 1784–1857: a Liverpool disciple of Robert Owen', *Transactions of the Historic Society of Lancashire and Cheshire*, v, 109, 1957.

Salt, J., 'Isaac Ironside and the Hollow Meadows farm experiments', *Yorkshire Bulletin of Economic and Social Research*, xii, 1960.

— 'Isaac Ironside: the Sheffield Owenite', *Co-operative Review*, July 1960.

— 'Isaac Ironside and education in the Sheffield region in the first half of the nineteenth century', M.A. thesis, University of Sheffield, 1960.

Youngjohns, B. J., 'Co-operation and the State, 1814–1914', *Co-operative College Paper*, 1954.

Index

*For titles of publications other than newspapers and
periodicals, please refer to the bibliography
The raised figures refer to a note on the page in question*

A. E. (George Russell), 128[99]
Agriculture
  and industry, 5, 9, 17, 65
  protection of, 10, 11
Ainslie, Archibald, 73, 89, 90
Aldam, Heaton, 155, 164[117], 169, 170, 179, 181
Alison, Sir Archibald, 7, 35[17]
Allen, William, 9, 35[23]
Allotments, House of Commons select committee report (1843), 37[61]
Allsop, Thomas, 219
American communities, 20, 22
American Socialist, 63[73], 121, 128[91]
Andrews, E. D., 38[78]
Antidote, 212[94]
Anti-Socialist Gazette and Christian Advocate, 178, 211[80]
Arensberg, C., 129[106]
Arkwright, Richard, 1, 3
Armytage, W. H. G., 38[77-8], 40[103], 60[4], 61[15], 239[45]
Ashurst, W. H., 157-8, 219
Association of All Classes of All Nations, 143, 144, 148
  branches, 145, 147, 148, 153, 164[108]
  laws, 145, 162[67], 162[69]
  manual, 162[68]
  removal of offices to Manchester, 147
  report (1838), 36[45]
  congresses, 145, 147, 151, 152, 153, 163[97], 164[98], 164[113], 164[119], 179, 184, 185, 188, 210[29], 210[46], 210[48], 211[52], 211[58], 211[68], 211[73]
Association for Promotion of Co-operative Knowledge, 55, 56, 63[95], 64[98]
Association for Removing Ignorance and Poverty, 139

Assurance, industrial life, growth of, 233
Athenaeum, 128[87]
Attwood, Thomas, 175

Babbage, Charles, 5, 34[2], 34[9]
Baker, the Reverend F., 160[4]
Bamford, Samuel, 8
Barker, Joseph, 210[37]
Barmby, John Goodwyn, 38[79]
Barrow, J., 125[28]
Bate, Frederick, 189, 198, 201, 205, 207, 219
Beer, Max, 38[76], 162[57]
Begbie, H., 40[107]
Bellers, John, 20
Bellshill Speaker, 99[120]
Bentley, Little and Great, farms, 166, 190, 196-8, 206, 207
Bestor, A. E., 13, 23, 36[37], 36[38], 38[82], 95[6]
Birkacre Calico Printers' Society, 134, 136, 138, 139, 161[30]
Birmingham Co-operative Herald, 63[79], 63[85]
Birmingham Co-operative Society, address at opening of, 52, 53, 63[80], 239[58]
Birmingham Equitable Labour Exchange, 140, 141
Birmingham Labour Exchange Gazette, 161[37], 161[39]
Black, A., 163[94]
Blith, Walter, 209[11]
Bolton Mechanics' Institute, 134
Bone-meal, plan for collection of, 169-70, 184, 209[12]
Booth, William, 40[107], 122, 128[96]
Bournville, 33
Braby, James, 146, 154, 185

Bracher, George, 205–6, 207, 208, 216
Bramwell, William, 40[107]
Brassey, Sir Thomas, 232
Braxfield House, residence of family of Robert Owen, 68
Bray, John Francis, 38[76]
Bright, John, 115
Brighton Co-operator, 51, 52, 63[72], 63[74]
Brighton co-operators, 92
Brindley, John, 175, 176, 178, 182, 189, 211[61]
British Association for the Promotion of Co-operative Knowledge, 130, 131, 132, 135, 154
British Co-operator, 64[97], 64[105], 64[108], 160[5], 160[7], 160[12]
British and Foreign Philanthropic Society, 45, 61[28], 61[30], 65, 66, 71, 102
Brougham, Henry, Lord, 36[43], 61[28], 208[2]
Brown, David, 210[37]
Brown, W. H., 63[88]
Buchanan, Robert, 152, 185
Buckholt, East and West, 166, 195, 207
Buckingham, James Silk, 128[92], 225–6
Butt, John, 36[48]
Buxton, John, 195, 200, 202, 205, 208, 214, 216, 231, 237[1], 237[18]

Campbell, Alexander, 131, 151, 152, 181, 185, 190, 193, 200, 201, 205
  and Orbiston, 79, 81, 83, 88, 90, 91, 93, 94, 98[88], 98[94]
Canterbury, Archbishop of, 41, 60[1], 174
Carlisle Co-operative Society, 55, 63[93]
Carlyle, Thomas, 28, 35[22]
Cassell & Co., publishers, 219, 238[26]
Catholic Emancipation Act, 124[7]
Chambers' Papers for the People, 40[100], 239[50]
Charlotte Street (London) Labour Exchange, 141
Chartism, and Owenism, 30, 136, 143, 153, 175, 188, 193–4, 224–5
Chartists, viii
Chester Co-operative Chronicle, 160[8], 160[9]
Chester Co-operative Society, 133, 160[9]

Children, House of Commons select committee report (1816), 1
Clare Journal, 125[30], 127[70], 127[79]
Cleave, John, 136
Clegg, William, 146, 151, 152, 167, 205, 207, 216
Cloncurry, Lord, 102, 120, 128[88]
Clydesdale Journal, 95[1]
Cobbett, William, 8, 9, 11, 35[20], 35[21]
Cole, G. D. H., 14, 35[22], 36[39], 38[76], 159[3], 218, 223, 238[23], 238[33]
Coleridge, S. T., 25
Colquhoun, Patrick, 21, 37[62]
Combe, Abram, 39[85], 65, 67, 68, 72, 73, 75, 77, 79, 82, 83, 91, 94, 95[8], 95[12], 96[28], 96[31], 98[78], 98[88], 99[103], 99[120], 231
  ability as an organiser, 93
  and Divine Revelation, 69, 76
  Edinburgh community experiment, 68
  health of, 79, 82, 87
  Old and New Systems, 68, 69
  parable of the cistern, 68
  views on New Lanark, 73
Combe, George, 87, 88, 89, 90, 98[87], 99[101]
Combe, William, 82, 83, 84, 85, 98[79]
Communionist, 38[79]
Communism, 25, 172–3, 231, 237[8]
  preface to *Manifesto* of Communist Party (1888), 38[81]
Communitarianism
  aspirations of, 30
  and competition, 26
  criticisms of, 30
  economic objects of, 27
  and equality, 26
  and the Establishment, 26, 30
  and industrialism, 28
  mystique of the land, 27, 28
  origin and use of term, 24, 25
  and politics, 31
  weaknesses of, 31
Community,
  ideas of, and early co-operation, 135
  present views on, 13, 234
  communities as social experiments, 29, 220
  previous studies of, 40[103]
  religious, 30
Community Friendly Society, 144, 145, 146, 163[78]
  rules, 162[73], 163[75]

Community Fund, report of (1839), 209[23]
Communities, Owenite,
  experience of, 220–2, 228
  accountability, 32, 156
  capital requirements, 59, 221
  contradictions and weaknesses, 31, **234**
  and democracy, 31
  division of labour, 48
  equality, 50
  external criticism of, 49
  external relationships, 31
  failure of, 40[108], 228, 231
  financial support, 32
  industrial pursuits, 153, 157
  internal organisation, 228
  labour supply, 152, 153
  leadership, 32, 155, 165, 228
  legal security of assets, 32
  and marketing, 17
  merits of, 32
  permeation of influence, 33
  and politics, 49, 50
  present day relevance, 234
  production, 17, 220, 221
  religion, 32
  return of candidates for, 153
  search for suitable site for incipient community, 152, 154
  social cohesion, 32, 231
  social idealism, 31, 224
Conacre, land tenure in Ireland, 101, 102, 104
Congress, Co-operative
  first (May 1831), 59, 134
  second (October, 1831), 37[64], 39[86], 136, 160[18], 161[19]
  third (April 1832), 138, 161[29], 163[80]
  fourth (October 1832), 139
  sixth (April, 1833), 140
"Congress", first use of term by co-operators, 160[16]
Connery, James, 127[73]
Connolly, James, 119, 127[81], 128[83]
Cooke, Sir William Fothergill, 166
Co-operation
  and early trade unionism, viii, 53, 131, 138, 141
  economic theory of, 49, 50
  and self-help, 52
  since Rochdale, 231–3
Co-operative Emigration Society, 218

Co-operative Knowledge, Association for Promotion of, 55, 56, 63[95], 64[98]
Co-operative Magazine and Monthly Herald, 46, 62[34], 62[58], 62[63], 63[70], 63[84], 97[44], 97[48], 97[55], 97[69], 97[72], 98[75], 98[80], 98[82], 98[83], 163[84]
Co-operative News, 64[110], 125[36], 125[45], 127[74], 128[97], 160[7], 238[27]
Co-operative Review, 163[94]
Co-operative societies
  and education, 134, 135, 136
  growth of early, 52, 54, 55, 56, 132, 134, 135
  manufacturing activities, 55, 56, 133, 135, 138
  peculation of funds, 40[106], 57
  reasons for failure of early retail societies, 55, 56, 133, 135, 138
  storekeeping, 57, 137, 142, 161[25]
  ventures, 58, 137
  views on credit trading, 51, 55
  wholesale trading, 57, 58, 133, 136, 138
Cork, prospectus of community at, 56
Corn laws, 199
Cottage system, 9
County Clare
  disturbances, 105, 106
  farm labourers' wages, 100, 104
  kinship patterns, 123
  Press cuttings, Theobald Fitz-Walter Butler, 128[86]
  Statistical survey (1808), 100
Crabb, James, 189, 212[93]
Craig, E. T., 52, 64[110], 100, 105, 108, 109, 110, 114, 115, 117, 124[22], 125[34], 125[43], 125[44], 131, 160[7], 176, 219, 239[38]
  first meeting with Vandeleur in Manchester, 106
  leaves Manchester for Ralahine, 106, 107
  draws up draft Constitution, 108
  and Ralahine, 121, 125[47], 126[49], 126[51], 126[56], 128[93], 221, 231
Crisis, 99[107], 126[52], 126[54], 127[65], 142, 161[24], 161[26], 161[30], 161[32], 161[34], 161[40], 162[51], 162[54], 162[56], 162[58]
Cullen, Alex., 95[5], 99[120], 222

Dale, David, 19
Dalgety, F. G., 166, 209[4]
Davidson, Thomas, 226

Debus, Dr. H., 215
Detrosier, Rowland, 131, 147
Digby, Margaret, 128[96]
Dividend on purchases, 51, 138, 146
Doherty, James, 53, 222, 231
Drunkenness, House of Commons select committee report (1834), 121, 128[92]
Dublin Evening Post, 127[76], 127[78]
Dublin Morning Post, 98[74]
Dutton, Henry, 124[1]

Ealing Grove School (London), 126[48]
Economist, 42, 43, 44, 60[2], 60[3], 61[8], 61[16], 96[19]
Eden, F. M., 11, 35[33]
Edinburgh, Practical Society of, 43, 45, 61[19], 67, 68, 92, 95[2]
Edinburgh Review, 35[22]
Edmonds, George, 175
Edmonds, T. R., 37[56]
Edmondson, George, 214–15, 216, 237[1], 238[22]
Edwards, Michael M., 34[3]
Elliott, Ebenezer, 142
Ellis, John, 185, 214
Emerson, Ralph Waldo, 28, 31, 40[104], 236
Emigration, 9, 195, 213[145], 218
Engels, Friedrick, ix, 25, 193–4, 212[109], 231, 239[56]
Equality, colony of, Wisconsin, 213[145]
Equitable Banks of Exchange, 139, 140
Equitable Labour Exchanges, 139, 140, 141, 142; *see also* Labour Exchanges, National Equitable Labour Exchange Co.
Ernle, Lord, 169
Evelyn, John, 209[12]
Exeter, Bishop of, 173, 175, 176, 210[32]
Exeter, co-operators, 50, 133
    Address of Working Classes of Devonshire, 160[10]

Fabian Society, 239[45]
Factory system, 5, 7
Falla, William, 17, 18, 36[53], 37[59]
Farn, J. C., 94, 237[18], 238[27]
Faucher, Leon, 218–19, 238[25]
Fawcett, Henry, 215, 237[10]
Fellowship of the New Life, 33, 226, 239[45]

Finch, John, 39[84], 54, 106, 108, 109, 115, 116, 125[39], 126[55], 126[60], 127[63], 128[87], 128[92], 131, 138, 146, 148, 149, 151, 152, 155, 157, 160[4], 167–9, 170, 176, 177, 178, 179, 181, 182, 185, 188, 191, 194, 195, 200, 201, 203, 207, 208, 215, 216, 219, 231, 237[9], 237[15]
Fitzpatrick, W. J., 128[88]
Fleming, George Alexander, 146, 147, 151, 152, 156, 164[177], 170, 173, 180, 181, 184, 185, 192, 206[214], 219
Flower, Richard, 68
Food adulteration, 115, 232
Foxwell, H. S., 48, 62[42]
Frankenberg, R., 129[106], 129[107]
Frankland, Sir Edward, 215, 237[13]
Freeman's Journal, 127[77]
Friendly societies, viii, 6, 11, 55, 63[78], 193, 233, 240[62]
Frost, J., 124[17]
Frost, T., 38[79], 239[49]

Galpin, Thomas Dixon, 219, 237[18]
Galpin, William, 184, 185, 189, 206, 207, 214, 219
Gaskell, Peter, 2, 5, 6, 34[5], 34[6]
Gatrell, V. A. C., 238[36]
George, Henry, 226
Gide, Charles, 233–4, 240[63]
Glasgow Herald, 90, 98[91], 99[113]
Godwin, William, 20, 21, 25, 37[69]
Goldsmid, Isaac Lyon, 37[59], 45, 61[28], 61[31], 154, 158, 166, 167, 207, 208[2], 209[4], 216
Gorb, P., 36[48]
Gosden, P. H. J. H., 35[34], 240[62]
Goupy, Louis, 128[89]
Graham, Sir James, 61[28]
Grand National Consolidated Trades Union, 140, 141, 142, 223
Gray, John, 38[76], 47, 78, 99[108], 99[111] criticisms of Orbiston, 92, 93, 97[58], 97[59]
Grays Inn Road, Equitable Labour Exchange, 140, 161[37], 181
Green, C. F., 152, 154, 163[98], 167, 170, 179, 181, 182, 201, 205, 207, 210[30], 216
Greening, E. O., 238[26]
Guild of St. George, 33, 226, 239[45]
Guild of St. Matthew, 226

Hall, Charles, 7, 35[18]
Halls of science, 147, 150, 163[84],
    163[94], 198–9, 218
  building operations, 149
  and community plans, 156
  costs and finance, 150
  and education, 150, 218
  list of, in 1842, 187
Halpin, Cormac, 129[105]
Halpin, William, 122, 129[105]
Ham Common Concordium (Surrey),
    38[79], 202, 207
Hamilton, Archibald J., 61[28], 65, 69,
    78, 83, 84, 91, 95[7], 96[13], 96[19],
    98[78], 98[79], 98[86], 98[90], 98[92], 99[101],
    99[104], 131, 219, 231
  agricultural interests, 69, 96[16]
  army career, 69, 96[13]
  attendance at Edinburgh Univer-
    sity, 72
  and cottage system, 70
  his explanation of failure at Orbis-
    ton, 87, 92
  family background, 69
  health, 87, 92
  meeting with Robert Owen, 70, 71
  offer of land to County of Lanark,
    70, 71
  and phrenology, 72
  relationships with Abram Combe,
    72
  his religious views, 96[25]
  his republicanism, 96[17]
  visit to Holkham, 72
Hamilton, General John, 65, 73, 95[3]
Hampshire Chronicle, 189, 212[90],
    237[20]
Hancock, Professor W. N., 120, 134[9]
Hansom, Joseph A., 187, 189
Harmony Hall
  naming of, 186, 187, 189
  building of, 186, 192
  layout, 187, 192
  suspension of building operations,
    189, 191, 198
  closure, 206
  sale, 205, 207
  as boarding school, 196, 198, 202
  legal settlement of affairs at, 207
  winding-up, 207
Harrison, J. F. C., 240[65]
Haslam, C. J., 210[38]
Hazlitt, William, 7, 35[16]
Headlam, Stewart, 226, 239[45]

Hennell, Mary, 40[100]
Herald of Progress, 214
Herald of the Rights of Industry, 142
Herald to the Trades' Advocate, 160[13]
Hetherington, Henry, 61[7], 130, 135
Hibernian Philanthropic Society, 67,
    102
Hill, James, 152, 206
Hill, R. and F. D., 63[77]
Hill, Rowland, 157–8
Hirst, Thomas, 215, 237[11]
Hodgskin, Thomas, 38[76]
Hogan, J. F., 124[15]
Holkham (Norfolk), visit of Robert
    Owen and A. J. Hamilton, 72
Hollick, Frederick, 152, 153, 185
Holloway, Mark, 39[98]
Holyoake, George Jacob, 22, 23, 37[75],
    131, 150, 160[16], 162[53], 176, 185,
    192, 219, 221, 222, 231, 237[18],
    239[57]
Home colonies, 9, 33, 180, 226
Home Colonisation Society, 144,
    184–5, 187, 188, 189, 190, 198,
    201, 204, 207
Home Office, correspondence con-
    cerning socialism, 174, 176–8,
    210[31], 210[34]
Horne, H. O., 240[60]
Howarth, Charles, 149, 163[93]
Huddersfield Co-operative Society,
    133, 192–3
Huddersfield Hall of Science, 173
Hughes, Thomas, 176, 236
Hume, James Deacon, 10, 11, 35[28],
    35[31]
Huttites, 25

Illustrated London News, 237[20]
Industrial Revolution, 1, 6
Industrial villages, 2, 33
Industrialisation, 1, 7, 8, 236
  remedies proposed for, 4, 5, 222
  social problems of, 4, 7, 230
Ireland
  Report of Select Committee on Em-
    ployment of Poor (1823), 102
  Report of Select Committee on Poor
    (1830), 124[10]
  Report of Devon Commission on
    Irish agriculture (1845), 101, 124[6]
Irish Agricultural Organisation
    Society, 121

Irish agriculture, wages and conditions, 102, 109
Irish land hunger and tenures, 100, 101
Ironside, Isaac, 176, 183, 185, 194, 205, 206, 211⁶³, 219, 237⁸, 237¹⁸

Jewish emancipation, 166, 208²
Judges, A. V., 36⁴²
'Junius', 210³⁸

Kelly, Richard, J., 128⁸⁵
Kimball, S. T., 129¹⁰⁶
King, Dr William (of Ipswich and Brighton), 51, 52, 57
King, William (of London), 63⁸³
Kingsley, Charles, 239⁴⁴
Knight, Charles, 224
Kropotkin, Prince, 128⁹⁷

Labour
    right to the whole product of, 26, 80, 136
    supply of, for community, 152, 153
    theory of value, interpretations of, 6, 48
Labour exchanges, 139, 140, 141, 142, 150
Labour notes, 139, 140
Laidler, H. W., 40¹⁰³
Lamberhead Green Trading Fund Society, 55, 63⁹⁴
Lancashire and Yorkshire Co-operator, 36⁵², 125⁴², 126⁵⁰, 161²¹
Land
    mystique of, to Owenites, 33, 53, 225
    nationalisation and common possession of, 8, 226
Larkin, the Reverend E. R., 128⁸⁷
Leader, 216
Letchworth (Herts.), 33
Letters Patent Act (1837), 185
Lewis, Sir George Cornewall, 102, 124¹¹
Limerick Chronicle, 128⁸⁶
Limerick Evening Herald, 127⁶⁹, 127⁷⁶
Limerick Evening Post, 127⁶⁸
Linton, W. J., 64¹⁰⁴
Littleton, A. C., 40¹⁰⁵
Liverpool First Co-operative Society, 54, 63⁸⁸, 63⁸⁹, 133, 160⁸

Liverpool Friends to the Rational System of Society, 148, 163⁸⁸
Liverpool Hall of Science, 149, 163⁹¹, 188, 199, 203
Liverpool Mercury, 125³⁹, 125⁴⁰, 125⁴¹, 126⁵⁵, 126⁵⁷, 126⁶⁰, 127⁶³, 128⁹⁰
Liverpool Rational School Society, 157
Lloyd Jones, 152, 162⁶⁴, 178, 184–5, 195, 197, 201, 205, 210⁴⁰, 211⁷¹, 231
London Community Friendly Society, 146
London Co-operative Society, 147, 139
London First Community Society, 133, 160¹²
London First Co-operative Manufacturing Society, 58
London First Co-operative Trading Association, 58
London First Western Co-operative Union Society, 137, 138, 140
London, halls of science, 150
London printers, Co-operative and Economical Society (Spa Fields), 42, 43, 44, 221
London Social Reformer, 210⁴⁵
London United Trades' Association, 140
Loucks, W. N., 40¹⁰³
Lovett, William, 58, 59, 60, 64¹¹², 64¹¹⁹, 130, 131, 136, 139, 160⁶, 231
Lowenthal, Esther, 38⁷⁶
Luddism, 6, 34¹²
Ludlow, J. M., 176

Macaskill, Joy, 37⁶¹, 239⁴¹, 239⁴⁴
Mackintosh, T. Simmons, 185
Maclure, William, 68
Magazine of Useful Knowledge and Co-operative Miscellany, 56
Malthus, T. R., 208²
Malthusianism, 11, 28
Manchester, Association for Spread of Principles of Co-operation, 134
Manchester, Co-operation, 132, 134, 137
Manchester Co-operator, 128⁸⁴
Manchester Guardian, 128⁸⁴
Manchester, hall of science, 149, 163⁹⁴, 193, 218, 238²⁴
Manchester New Mechanics' Institute, 147

Manchester, Owenian Society, 107
Manchester and Salford Dressers' and Dyers' Co-operative Society, 56
Manchester Unity of Oddfellows, 11
Manners, Lord John, 33
Marchant, Thomas, 166, 215
Marsh, C. M., 129[101]
Martineau, Harriet, 28, 39[97], 224, 239[39]
Mather, the Reverend J., 210[36]
Marx, Karl, ix
Maynooth (Ireland), 103
McCabe, J., 239[57]
McCann, W. P., 238[31]
McPherson, A., 99[119]
Meakin, Bridgett, 40[109]
Mechanics' Institutes movement, 134, 147, 150
Mechanisation, 5, 59
Melbourne, Lord, 173, 174, 208[2]
Menger, Anton, 38[76], 62[42]
Mercer, T. W., 63[69]
Métayage, system of land tenure, 111
Methodism, 172, 179
Metropolitan Trades Union, 135
Milk, Co-operative, first sale of, 160[18]
Mill, John Stuart, 40[106]
Millenarianism, 24, 25, 38[79]
and industrialism, 25
Millennium, 27
Molony, James, of Kiltanon, 104, 107, 122, 124[21]
Moral World, 206-7, 213[148], 213[150]
Moravian communities, 25, 38[80]
More, Sir Thomas, 29
Morgan, John Minter, 7, 33, 35[14], 40[101], 40[108], 61[28], 86, 218, 236
Mormonism, 24, 38[08]
Morris, William, 226, 239[48]
Motherwell
proposed community at, 45, 67, 71
estate of General John Hamilton, 67
sale to Orbiston community, 67
Movement, 213[135], 239[52]
Mudie, George, 39[92], 41, 42, 44, 45, 60[4], 61[25], 61[26], 93, 99[110], 131
Muntz, George Frederick, 175

National Association for the Employment of Labour, 223
National Bank of Scotland, 90
National Community Friendly Society, 144, 146, 164[108], 164[126]

National Equitable Labour Exchange Association, 140, 141
National Land and Building Association, 206
National Land and Equitable Labour Exchange Co., 140
National Union of the Working Classes, 136
Neale, Vansittart, 176
New Lanark, 2, 3, 16, 17, 18, 19, 68, 73, 103, 104, 170
New moral world, 144, 145, 162[59], 182
New Moral World, 98[85], 99[115], 125[66], 142, 143, 144, 147, 148, 151, 155, 161[25], 162[59], 162[65], 162[71], 163[74], 163[79], 163[81], 163[86], 163[89], 163[92], 163[96], 163[98], 164[109], 164[116], 164[118], 164[128], 172, 177, 180, 191, 196, 197, 205, 206, 209[6], 209[16], 209[19], 210[27], 210[41], 211[53], 211[56], 211[59], 211[61], 211[77], 211[81], 212[95], 212[99], 212[106], 212[111], 212[116], 213[122], 213[127], 213[133], 213[136]
Normanby, Lord, 173-4, 176, 177, 210[32], 210[39]
North-west United Co-operative Co., Liverpool, 135, 136, 138
Norton, H. H., 40[101]

O'Brien, George, 128[82]
O'Brien, R. Barry, 102, 124[4], 124[12]
O'Connell, Daniel, 120, 208[2]
O'Connor, Feargus, 120, 224-5
Oddfellows, Manchester Unity of, 11
Oliver, W. H., 38[78], 161[36]
Orbiston community
advertisements of work undertaken, 80, 81
and agriculture, 79, 83, 84
applicants, qualities sought of, 76
architecture and buildings, 75, 83, 99[120]
articles of agreement, 74, 96[30], 97[33]
building operations, 74, 83: progress report, 76, 77; suspension of, 79
children, 74, 77, 86
company of proprietors, 73
company of tenants, 73
demolition and disposal of buildings, 90, 91, 94
dispersal of residents, 85, 86, 87

Orbiston community—*contd.*
  disposal of musical instruments, 99[114]
  disruptive elements, 76
  domestic arrangements, 75, 77, 85, 229
  earnings and standards of living of residents, 79, 86
  equality of distribution, debate, 80, 81, 82, 83
  employment, 85, 86
  failure, explanations of, 87, 88, 91, 92, 93, 94, 172–3
  financial situation, 84
  food and catering costs, 77, 85, 86
  foundry, 79, 80, 98[93]
  importance of, 65
  labour valuation, 74
  and London co-operators, 77, 78, 83
  machinery department, 82
  Robert Owen, visits of, 68, 88, 98[94]
  possession by creditors, 89
  property rights in community, 82
  purchase price, 67, 73
  purchase of Orbiston by Mrs C. Douglas, 90, 99[102]
  religious toleration, 98[89]
  sale, offer of, 87, 90, 98[91]
  sale, judicial, 89
  shares in, 73, 76
  tenants: admission of, 74; decision to hand over community to, 77, 81
  theatre, 85, 86
  and William Thompson, 78
  trades, suitability of, 78
  trustees, 73, 90
  valuation, first legal, 88, 89, 98[95]
  re-valuation, 89
Orbiston memorial and abstract of sale, 90, 99[96]
Orbiston Register, 75, 77, 79, 87, 95, 97[45], 97[49], 97[64], 97[67], 97[70], 98[77]
Orwin, C. S., 209[13]
Owen, Robert
  origin and phases of his thought, 19, 20, 23
  his Plan and community ideas, 19, 20, 22, 39[86], 65, 146, 152, 180–1, 220–1, 222
  views on: balance between agriculture and industry, 9; character formation, 6, 10; class structure, 13, 14, 23, 222–3; competition, 6;

  economic factors, 1; education, 15, 36[43]; equality, 23; factory system, 3; family, 228–9, 230; home colonies and cottage system, 9; labour theory of value, 6, 13; mechanisation of production and labour, 3, 6, 13, 17, 18; money 23; politics, 14, 15, 39[86]; poor law, 5, 23; population, 18; poverty, 4; profits and profit motive, 3, 13, 16; property, 23; religion, 7, 15, 21; spade cultivation, 13, 17, 18; wages, 3; working class, 151, 156
  relationships: with Orbiston, 19, 76, 77, 93; with Queenwood, 23, 154, 181, 198, 200–1; with Ralahine, 116, 117; with Owenite followers and disciples, 41, 46, 47, 51, 54, 59, 60, 153; with established order, 4
  influence: on co-operative movements, 46, 136; as prophet and catalyst, 12
  life: American visits, 46, 68, 156, 202, 205, 207, 213[132]; attacks on, by Established Church, 14; business abilities, 16, 36[48], 62[33], 167; criticisms of, general, 65; and equitable labour exchanges, 46, 139, 140, 141, 142; experience at New Lanark, 19, 167, 222; and his family, 68; and William Godwin, 20, 21; and Ireland, visits to, 67, 102, 103, meetings at Dublin, 102, and Irish clergy, 102, 103, and J. S. Vandeleur, 103; middle class leadership and support, 14, 22, 23, 155, 156; paternalism, 16; rationalism, 15, 20; temperament, 14, 167, 234–5
Owen, Robert Dale, 21, 36[41], 37[71], 67
Owenism, ix, 24, 46
  as alternative to capitalist system, ix
  approaches to study of, vii
  attacks on, 172, 178, 187, 197
  not backward-looking, 11, 236
  and Chartism, *see* Chartism
  and classical economics, 10
  and closed economy, 10
  and co-operative movement, 46
  debate in House of Lords (1840) 173
  and education, 131

as an ideology, 13
literary campaign against, 172
missionary districts, 152
petitions, parliamentary, 173, 183,
216
and sectarianism, 172, 175
and socialism, 148, 172
stages of, 149, 150
support for, estimates of, 172
and trade unionism, 130, 222, 223
Owenite creed, 27, 38[83], 180
branches, 150, 152
halls of science and social institutions, 149, 150, 187, 218
hymns, 33
missionaries, 57
political immaturity of, 26, 178
propaganda, 150, 156–7, 172, 173,
178
schools, 150, 188
and socialism, common use of
terms, 24, 41, 148, 172
Owenites, latter-day, 227
business activities of leading Owenites, 131, 176, 219
relationships with Owen, 131

Packard, F. A., 36[49]
Pagan, J. H., 99[117]
Paine, Thomas, 25
Palmerston, Lord, 208[2]
Pankhurst, R. K. P., 62[41], 62[59]
Pare, Emma, 198, 219
Pare, William, 56, 57, 63[83], 105, 108,
109, 115, 116, 131, 151, 152, 156,
160[16], 176, 207, 231–2, 237[18]
and Birmingham Co-operative
Society, 53, 139
and Birmingham Labour Exchange,
117, 141
business interests, 131, 176, 219
character and effectiveness, 175
and Queenwood, 175, 187, 189, 191,
195, 196, 199, 200, 201, 203, 205,
206, 207, 208, 216, 222
visit to Ralahine, 117, 121, 125[27],
126[53], 126[57], 126[58], 127[62], 127[67],
127[68], 127[75], 231
as Registrar, Births and Marriages,
Birmingham, 173, 174–5
Pare *v.* Clegg (1861), 216–17, 237[17]
Patriot, 212[102]
Paul, Alexander, 81, 88, 98[92], 98[94]
as general secretary Orbiston, 83

as judicial factor legal sale of Orbis-
ton, 87, 89, 90
Peel, Sir Robert, 101, 166, 194
Pelling, Henry, 239[45]
Pemberton, Robert, 225
Philpotts, Henry (Bishop of Exeter),
173, 175, 176, 210[32]
Phrenology, 110, 175, 195, 224, 239[38]
Phrenological Magazine, 127[80]
Pioneer, 141, 161[45], 162[55]
Place, Francis, 135, 160[17]
Plunkett, Horace, 121, 128[96]; *see also*
Irish Agricultural Organisation
Society
Podmore, Frank, 12, 35[35], 56, 64[100],
95[5], 201, 221, 238[32]
Pollard, Sidney, 36[43], 36[48], 38[78], 40[101],
63[69], 162[66], 238[25]
Poor law, and industrialism, 11
Poor Man's Advocate, 163[85]
Poor Man's Guardian, 130, 159[1],
160[6], 161[27], 161[33]
Population, growth of, 1, 34[2], 34[6]
industrial, distribution of, 1
Port Sunlight (Ches.), 33
Portsmouth Co-operative Society, 137
Poverty, 5
Preston First Co-operative Society, 55,
63[91]
*Promethean or Communitarian
Apostle*, 38[79]
Property
rights of, 43
common, 28, 165

Quarterly Review, 172, 209[24]
Queenwood, 24, 33, 104, 142, 146,
150, 221, 229, 230, 231, 234
accommodation at, 179, 180, 185,
197, 203
accounts and expenses, 185, 186,
187, 201
acquisition of, 166
additions to community land, 195,
196, 198
bankruptcy, 201
capital costs, 171
debts, 190, 191
description of, 154, 155
distinctiveness of, early history of
estate, 165–6
expenditure, 172
exodus of residents, 182, 183, 199,
204, 208

Queenwood—*contd.*
  farming methods, 169, 172, 182, 187, 196, 199, 201, 204
  funds and subscriptions, 169, 171, 178, 186, 196
  government, 202
  Governors, 181, 182, 184, 185, 191, 194, 195, 200, 201, 203
  growing apathy and stringency, 202
  lease, terms of, 158, 166–7, 207
  liabilities, 185, 201, 204, 205, 206
  maintenance costs, 182, 186
  management of, 185
  neighbours of, 179, 184
  Robert Owen as Governor, 156, 159, 167, 190, 200, 203
  Robert Owen, views on, 195
  property rights of I. L. Goldsmid, 167
  property rights of residents, 171, 181
  recruitment of residents, 170–1
  residents, 195, 199
  school, 178, 182, 191, 192, 196
  selection of suitable trades for, 182, 196
  standard of living of residents, 191, 196, 197
  survey of, by Heaton Aldam, 155
  trustees, 205–6, 207, 208, 215
  wages, prevailing level of, 171
  wages, debate over hired or residents' labour, 179, 181, 196, 200
  weaknesses, 208
Queenwood College
  importance of in nineteenth-century education, 215, 237[10]
  and later history of Queenwood leasehold, 216, 217
  prospectus of, 215
  staff and pupils, 215

Ralahine, 59, 129[104], 135, 138, 221, 227, 229, 231, 234
Ralahine Castle, 100, 103, 123
Ralahine Agricultural and Manufacturing Co-operative Association, 109, 110
  aims, 115
  conditions of admittance, 110
  description of estate, 108
  dissolution of, 119
  distinctiveness of, 119, 123
  and Irish land history, 100, 119

later history of the estate, 122, 123
labour notes, 112, 114, 117, 120
livestock, 118
manufacturing and output, 114, 115
merits of, 119, 120
members, numbers of, 114
murder of land steward, 105
place in history of co-operative agriculture, 119
prices of foodstuffs, 109
regimen and domestic arrangements, 114, 115, 116, 126[57]
religion, 114
rent agreement, 110, 112, 115, 125[46], 125[47]
restrictions on members, 115
schooling, 114, 115
as source of agricultural produce for Owenite labour exchanges, 116
standard of diet, 126[60]
visit by John Finch, 108
visit by William Pare, 108, 114
wages, 110, 112, 126[56]
Ransome, J. Allen, 209[13]
Rappites, 182
Rational, first use of term, 141, 179
Rational Society, 188, 192, 206, 214, 215, 226
  congresses, 188, 189, 195, 201, 204, 205, 212[88], 212[96], 212[105], 212[108], 212[113]
Rational Friendly Society, 240[66]
Rational religion, definition of, 153–4
Rational Sick and Burial Society, 193
Rationalism, 25
Reasoner and Herald of Progress, 34[1], 216, 237[2]
Regeneration, Society for Promoting National, 10, 142
Reid, R. J., 197, 209[7], 212[118]
Rey, Joseph, 99[112]
Ricardo, David, 18, 21, 208[2], 235–6, 240[67]
Ricardian Socialism, 25
Rigby, James, 137, 152, 154, 181, 182, 184, 185, 201, 207, 211[68], 219, 231
Robertson, A. J., 36[48]
Rochdale Friendly Society, 135
Rochdale Owenites, 183, 199
Rochdale Pioneers, viii, 240[60]
Rochdale Social Institution, 149
Romilly, Lord, Master of Rolls Court, 217

Rose, R. B., 237[16]
Rosebery, Lord, 232
Rosehill (Queenwood), 166, 196, 197, 200, 215
Royle, E., 239[57]

Salford First Co-operative Society, 135
Salisbury and Winchester Journal, 238[21]
Salt, J., 36[40], 36[48], 38[78], 40[101], 162[66], 237[8], 238[25]
Saltaire (Yorks.), 33
Sargant, W. L., 36[40], 37[58], 172, 210[28]
Saville, J., 40[101]
Savings banks, 55, 240[60]
Scottish Union Insurance Co., 73, 89, 90
Secularism, 131, 150, 239[57]
Self-help, 4, 11, 232, 233, 234, 240[65]
Seligman, E. R. A., 239[51]
Shakers, 20, 24, 25, 32, 38[78], 38[80], 182, 210[47]
Sheddon, William, 79
Sheffield Free Press, 216
Sheffield Hall of Science, 149, 150, 163[97]
Sheffield Regeneration Society, 162[53]
Shotts foundry band, 99[114]
Sidmouth, Lord, 5
Sigerson, G., 124[8]
Silver, H., 36[43]
Smith, Joseph, 39[94], 151, 185
Smith, J. E., 40[101], 131, 238[27]
Smith, W. Anderson, 40[101]
Smith, W. Hawkes, 161[31], 227
Social bible, 144, 148
Social hymns, 144, 162[66]
Social Institutions, Owenite, 145, 149
Socialism, 202, 203, 210[31], 218, 225, 226–7, 233
   changing meaning of term, 38[82], 172
   early, 7, 25
   Owenite, 48, 148, 227
Social missionaries, 23, 151, 174, 185, 195
Social Missionary Society, 139
Society for Diffusion of Useful Knowledge, 150
Sombart, Werner, 225, 239[42]
Somerville, Alexander, 192, 212[101]
Southey, Robert, 7, 15, 35[15], 36[40]
Southcott, Joanna, 24, 38[77], 38[80]
Southwell, Charles, 185, 206, 214

Spade cultivation, 13, 17, 18, 19, 28, 36[53], 40[107], 44, 69, 155, 195, 199–200
Spa Fields, London Co-operative Community, 121, 128[94]; *see also* George Mudie
Spectator, 94
Spence, Thomas, 8, 20, 35[19], 37[68]
Spirit of the Age, 219, 237[8]
Star in the East, 126[48], 128[90]
Stewart, W. A. C., 238[31]
Strutt, Jedediah, textile mills, 1, 3
Stubbs, C. W., 127[81]
Syndicalism, 141, 142, 223–4

Teetotalism and temperance, 30, 131, 148, 179, 182, 219, 224
Terry Alts, agrarian violence in County Clare, 105, 106, 114, 125[28]
Thomis, M. I., 34[12]
Thompson, D., 237[10]
Thompson, E. P., 35[32], 38[77], 64[120]
Thompson, William, 26, 27, 39[88], 46, 47–50 *passim*, 52, 56, 57, 62[32], 62[44], 62[46], 64[101], 64[102], 64[103], 82, 93, 99[113], 116, 120, 131, 135
   relationship with Robert Owen, 59, 60
Todmorden Co-operative Society, 139
Torrens, Robert, 21, 37[55], 37[60]
Torrington, Viscount, 2, 34[3]
Trade unions
   and co-operative movement, viii, 53, 131, 138, 141, 188, 233
   Grand National Consolidated Trades Union, 140, 141, 142, 223
   Journeymen Steam Engine Makers, 186
   Metropolitan Trades Union, 135
   National Association for Employment of Labour, 223
   Potters Union, 223
Transcendentalism, 25, 38[83]
Travis, Henry, 163[95], 164[127], 170, 184, 185, 209[14], 209[18], 237[18], 238[27]
Tristan, Flora, 210[26]
Tyndall, John, 215, 237[11]
Tytherley, *see* Harmony Hall; Queenwood
Tytherley, East, manor of, 165–6

Union, 147, 163[84], 212[103]
United Trades' Co-operative Journal, 64[99]

Universal Communitarian Association, 38[79]
Universal Community Society of Rational Religionists, 144, 153, 180, 210[39], 210[49]
  Constitution and rules, 39[93], 39[95], 165
  examination of candidates, 180, 211[50]
  Statement to Marquis of Normanby, 39[87], 39[90], 210[39]
Urbanisation, social consequences of, 3, 4, 236
Ure, Andrew, 5, 34[8]
Urwick, Dr. W., 124[14], 124[16]
Utopianism, 14, 25

Vandeleur family, 103, 106, 118, 128[99], 129[103]
Vandeleur, Arthur, 122, 129[101]
Vandeleur, C. M., 120
Vandeleur, Emily (*née* Molony), 118, 122
Vandeleur, Giles, 103
Vandeleur, Colonel G. A. M., 129[101]
Vandeleur, Brigadier J. O. E., 129[101]
Vandeleur, John Scott, 100, 104, 105, 108, 109, 110, 111, 112, 114, 115, 124[20], 124[21], 135
  aims of, 116
  bankruptcy, 118, 119, 122
    estate improvements, 104, 106, 116
  lease to community, 111, 116, 119
  meeting with E. T. Craig, 106
  takes over Ralahine estate, 103
Vandeleur, Mary (*née* Molony), 122

Vandeleur, the Reverend W. E. G. O., 128[99]
Vegetarianism, 30
Victoria, Queen, Owen presented to, 157, 173
Villages of co-operation, 73, 74
Vines, David, 200, 201

Wallace, Alfred Russel, 122, 128[98], 227
Wallas, Graham, 160[17]
Wallscourt, Lord, 117, 120
Warburton, W. H., 238[34], 239[37]
Watson, James, 57, 136
Watson, William, 45
Watts, Dr John, 182, 211[55], 214
Wayland, T., 39[99]
Wearmouth, R. F., 160[17]
Webb, R. K., 239[39]
Webb, Sidney and Beatrice, 240[61]
Weekly Free Press, 63[83]
Wellington, Duke of, 96[13], 175–6
Welwyn Garden City (Herts.), 33
Westminster Review, 39[89], 219, 238[28]
White, P., 125[28], 128[86]
Whiteboys, agrarian outrages in County Clare, 105
Whitwell, Stedman, 160[11]
Willmore, Charles, 217, 238[22]
Women, Owenite views on status of, 32, 44, 229
Woolwich Arsenal, early co-operation at, 60[3]
Wright, Frances, 163[84]

Yeo, Eileen, 162[66], 238[25]
Youngjohns, B. J., 240[59], 240[64]